The Ocean Economy in 2030

OECD
BETTER POLICIES FOR BETTER LIVES

This work is published under the responsibility of the Secretary-General of the OECD. The opinions expressed and arguments employed herein do not necessarily reflect the official views of OECD member countries.

This document and any map included herein are without prejudice to the status of or sovereignty over any territory, to the delimitation of international frontiers and boundaries and to the name of any territory, city or area.

Please cite this publication as:
OECD (2016), *The Ocean Economy in 2030*, OECD Publishing, Paris.
http://dx.doi.org/10.1787/9789264251724-en

ISBN 978-92-64-25171-7 (print)
ISBN 978-92-64-25172-4 (PDF)

The statistical data for Israel are supplied by and under the responsibility of the relevant Israeli authorities. The use of such data by the OECD is without prejudice to the status of the Golan Heights, East Jerusalem and Israeli settlements in the West Bank under the terms of international law.

Photo credits: Cover © MareLife, designed by Arild Saeter

Corrigenda to OECD publications may be found on line at: *www.oecd.org/about/publishing/corrigenda.htm*.

Foreword

The ocean economy is essential to the future welfare and prosperity of humankind. It is a key source of food, energy, minerals, health, leisure and transport upon which hundreds of millions of people depend. However, the maritime industry landscape is poised to undergo a profound transition. Long considered the traditional domain of shipping, fishing and – since the 1960s – offshore oil and gas, new activities are emerging that are reshaping and diversifying maritime industries.

The new "ocean economy" is driven by a combination of population growth, rising incomes, dwindling natural resources, responses to climate change and pioneering technologies. While traditional maritime industries continue to innovate at a brisk rate, it is the emerging ocean industries that are attracting most of the attention. These industries include offshore wind, tidal and wave energy; oil and gas exploration and production in ultra-deep water and exceptionally harsh environments; offshore aquaculture; seabed mining; cruise tourism; maritime surveillance and marine biotechnology. The long-term potential for innovation, employment creation and economic growth offered by these sectors is impressive.

But economic activity in the ocean is also characterised by a complex variety of risks that need to be addressed. Foremost among them are those related to ocean health from over-exploitation of marine resources, pollution, rising sea temperatures and levels, ocean acidification and loss of biodiversity. Unsustainable use of the ocean and its resources threatens the very basis on which much of the world's welfare and prosperity depend. Realising the full potential of the ocean economy, therefore, will demand responsible, sustainable approaches to its economic development.

Surprisingly perhaps, given its primordial role, the ocean economy has only recently begun to garner attention and move up the international policy agenda.

Numerous international organisations are involved in efforts to address the challenges of sustainable use of the ocean. The OECD – while contributing at international policy level to specific aspects of ocean-related issues such as fisheries, shipbuilding, marine biodiversity and biotechnology – has to date not turned its attention to economic activities in the ocean more broadly. This report is the first such endeavour by the OECD to consider the ocean from an economic perspective, with a view to exploring what the Organisation's future contribution might be in supporting national and international efforts towards a more sustainable development of the ocean economy in the future.

The three-year project on which this report is based grew out of a horizon scanning and scoping exercise performed in 2011 by the OECD International Futures Programme (IFP), now part of the OECD's Directorate for Science, Technology and Innovation (DSTI). The scoping assignment was funded by a voluntary financial contribution from the Korean Maritime Institute. The scoping results were presented and discussed at a special symposium during the EXPO 2012 held in Yeosu, Korea, and fed into the 2012 Yeosu Declaration on the Living Ocean and Coast (see: http://eng.expo2012.kr/is/ps/unitybbs/bbs/selectBbsDetail.html?ispsBbsId=BBS001&ispsNttId=0000060031).

The "Future of the Ocean Economy" project aimed to explore the growth prospects for the ocean economy, and its capacity for employment creation and innovation. It was designed as a cross-sectoral, cross-disciplinary foresight exercise. Particular attention has been devoted to the emerging ocean-based industries in light of their particularly high potential in terms of growth, innovation and contribution to addressing global challenges such as energy security, environment, climate change and food security. Hence, the present report examines the risks and uncertainties surrounding the future development of ocean industries, the innovations required in science and technology to support their progress, the environmental impacts of the industries, their potential contribution to green growth as well as their negative externalities, and some of the implications for planning and regulation. Finally, and looking across the future ocean economy as a whole, it explores possible avenues for action that could boost its long-term development prospects while managing the use of the ocean itself in responsible, sustainable ways.

The project has been undertaken in extensive collaboration with several other parts of the OECD, notably the Environment Directorate; the Trade and Agriculture Directorate; the Economics Department; the Centre for Entrepreneurship, SMEs and Local Economic Development; the International Transport Forum; the International Energy Agency; as well as with shipbuilding and biotechnology experts within DSTI. In addition, the project team collaborated with more than 200 external experts (see Annex A).

The cross-sectoral approach to the ocean economy is based on a series of ten specialised in-depth workshops, mainly hosted and funded by governments and organisations participating in the project. Most workshops were sector-specific. These comprised offshore wind, ocean renewable energy; deep-water oil and gas exploration and production; offshore aquaculture; deep-sea mining; maritime safety and surveillance; maritime tourism; marine biotechnology; marine spatial planning; and scenario building for the ocean economy. Eight of the workshops generated working papers that are being released in conjunction with the current volume (for details see Annex B).

The project was supported by voluntary financial and in-kind contributions from a wide range of government departments and agencies, corporations, research institutions, foundations and international NGOs who constituted the Project Steering Group. These are listed in Annex A Their contributions are acknowledged with sincere thanks.

Barrie Stevens directed the project, chaired the meetings of the Project Advisory Group and was the principal author of this report. Torgeir Edvardsen was responsible for project management and co-chaired the workshops. Anita Gibson provided technical and logistical support to the project, the meetings of the advisory group and the workshops. Anna-Sophie Liebender led the economic modelling work on the ocean industries as well as the projections of the ocean economy, and contributed several chapters. JongJune Lee and Daniel Mittendorf provided important contributions to the modelling work. Monique Biady, Mary-Ann Pham, Hayley Ericksen and Andrew Pham provided valuable research support in the early stages of the project. Jennifer Allain prepared the report for publication.

Special thanks go to Petyo Bonev (École nationale supérieure des mines de Paris) for foundation work and guidance on the modelling; to Carl-Christian Schmidt (former Head of the Fisheries Policies Division in the OECD Directorate for Trade and Agriculture) for sustained support in the early stages of the project and detailed critical comments of the overall draft report; and Jan-Stefan Fritz (University of Bremen) for valuable commentary and drafting assistance with key chapters. Thanks go also to Andrew Wyckoff, Dirk Pilat and Dominique Guellec for their valuable comments on drafts of the report.

Chapters 1, 2, 4, 5, 7 and 9 of the report were written by Barrie Stevens; Anna-Sophie Liebender drafted Chapters 3, 6 and 8. Given the wide scope and multidisciplinary nature of the report, several layers of review were necessary. First, members of the Project Steering Group, assisted by colleagues in their respective organisations, read and commented on various drafts of all the chapters. Second, where appropriate expertise was available in-house, draft chapters were reviewed by OECD experts. Third, as an additional measure, drafts of several chapters were reviewed by experts of specialised institutes and agencies not represented on the Steering Group. These included, among others, Ifremer and the French Agency for Development (AFD). Chapter 3 on the ocean environment benefited in particular from comments by experts attached to UNESCO's Intergovernmental Oceanographic Commission (IOC) and by researchers at the University of Rostock, Germany.

The project team wishes to thank all of their colleagues at the OECD (see Annex A) who provided valuable help and guidance with the statistical and modelling work.

Table of contents

Acronyms and abbreviations 11

Executive summary 13

Chapter 1. **An overview of the ocean economy: Assessments and recommendations** 17

Introducing the ocean economy 18
The ocean economy in 2030 30
Recommendations: An agenda for international co-operation for a sustainable ocean economy 34
Annex 1.A1. Scope of the ocean-based industries 46
Annex 1.A2. Measuring the value of marine ecosystems 49
Notes 51
References 52

Part I. Global trends and macro-factors influencing the ocean economy 55

Chapter 2. **Global trends and uncertainties to 2030/2060** 57

World population: Still growing, urbanising and ageing 58
Climate-ocean interactions 60
The global economy: Slower growth, geographical shifts and the rise of the middle class 62
Energy: Continuing dominance of fossil fuels but a changing energy landscape 65
Metals and minerals: Continuing pressures on the supply side 67
Global food supplies: Continuing pressures and uncertainties 69
Technological developments 71
Geopolitical developments: A multipolar world in flux 73
Concluding remarks 75
References 75

Chapter 3. **Expected changes to the ocean environment: Impacts on the ocean economy** 79

Introduction 80
Sea temperatures and sea levels 80
Acidification 84
Ocean as regulator of concentration of oxygen 87
Ocean currents and circulation patterns 91
Ocean and the hydrological cycle 93
Unsustainable fishing 94
Pollution 97
Conclusion 100
Notes 101
References 102

Part II. Critical factors influencing the emerging ocean-based industries 117

***Chapter 4.* Science, technology and innovation in tomorrow's ocean economy 119**

Science: Knowledge for the ocean economy 121
Incremental technology development in the ocean economy....................122
Disruptive and step-change innovations combining multiple technologies....................126
Promoting innovation for a sustainable ocean economy....................132
Concluding remarks 140
Notes 140
Annex 4.A1. EU multi-use ocean platform projects 141
References....................143

***Chapter 5.* International maritime regulation and emerging ocean-based industries 147**

Protection of marine biodiversity....................148
Pollution (air and ocean) 152
Maritime safety 156
Concluding remarks 159
Notes 160
References....................160

***Chapter 6.* Measuring the global economic contribution of ocean-based industries.......................163**

The OECD *Ocean Economy Database* 164
Sources and data used 165
Concluding remarks 175
Notes 176
Annex 6.A1. Current value estimation....................177
References....................180

Part III. Perspectives on and projections of the future of the ocean economy...............185

***Chapter 7.* Growth prospects, challenges and uncertainties for selected ocean industries............187**

Sectors with prospects for modest business and employment growth 188
Sectors with prospects for high long-term growth of business and employment....................190
Sectors with significant long-term potential but not operating at commercial scale for some time to come....................195
Concluding observations....................199
References....................200

***Chapter 8.* Ocean industries to 2030 ....201**

Business-as-usual scenario....................204
Summary of the results....................204
Value added and employment in the ocean economy in 2030 205
Industry-specific value added and employment in 2030....................207
Ocean industries to 2030 in two alternative scenarios 212
Concluding observations....................213
Notes 214
Annex 8.A1. Methodology of the business-as-usual scenario 216
References....................218

***Chapter 9.* Towards integrated ocean management 221**

A changing geopolitical landscape and governance of the high seas 222
Governance in economic exclusion zones 224
Pathways to more effective ocean management 227
Concluding remarks 240
References 240

***Annex A* Acknowledgments 245**

***Annex B* Workshops 251**

Tables

Table 1.1. Established and emerging ocean-based industries 23
Table 1.2. Overview of estimates of industry-specific growth rates in value added and employment between 2010 and 2030 32
Table 1.A2.1. Marine and coastal ecosystem services 49
Table 5.1. Impact of legislation on the different phases of offshore renewable energy development 151
Table 6.A1.1. Selected estimates of value of ocean-based industries, by country, region and world 178
Table 8.1. Overview of estimates of industry-specific growth rates in value added and employment between 2010 and 2030 205
Table 9.1. Economic instruments for ocean management 229

Figures

Figure 1.1. The concept of the ocean economy 22
Figure 1.2. Value added of ocean-based industries in 2010 by industry 24
Figure 1.3. Employment in the ocean-based industries in 2010 by industry 25
Figure 1.4. Growth in global seaborne trade 1970-2035 26
Figure 1.5. Towards the autonomous ship of the future 29
Figure 1.6. Value added of the ocean economy in 2030 in the business-as-usual scenario 31
Figure 2.1. Total population scenario to 2050 (in hundred thousands) 59
Figure 2.2. Global GDP growth set to slow over next 50 years (annual average, constant 2005 PPP) 63
Figure 2.3. Global main dry bulk seaborne trade 1970-2035 69
Figure 2.4. Lower trophic fishing for more efficient protein production 71
Figure 3.1. Projected atmospheric greenhouse gas emission pathways 2000-2100 81
Figure 3.2. The world ocean currents of the thermohaline circulation system 91
Figure 3.3. Global trends in the state of world marine fish stocks, 1974-2011 (in percent) 96
Figure 4.1. Windows of opportunity oil spill response management decision-making system 131
Figure 4.2. Offshore wind potential interactions with other marine users 134
Figure 4.3. H2OCEAN multi-use platform process 138
Figure 5.1. Shift in fuel mix for all major ship types combined, 2010-30 (in percent) 154
Figure 6.1. Value added of the ocean-based industries in 2010 by industry 167
Figure 6.2. Employment in the ocean-based industries in 2010 by industry 167
Figure 6.3. Value added of shipbuilding and repair by region in 2010 169
Figure 6.4. Employment in shipbuilding and repair by region in 2010 169
Figure 6.5. Value added of marine equipment by region in 2010 170
Figure 6.6. Direct value added of global port throughput by region in 2009 170
Figure 6.7. Value added of marine and coastal tourism by region in 2010 171

Figure 6.8. Value added of industrial capture fisheries by region in 2010 172
Figure 6.9. Value added of industrial marine aquaculture by region in 2010 173
Figure 6.10. Value added of fish processing by region in 2010 173
Figure 6.11. Value added of offshore oil and gas by region in 2010 174
Figure 6.12. Value added of offshore wind production by region in 2010 175
Figure 7.1. Global fish production: Data and projections, 1984-2030 188
Figure 7.2. Seaborne trade projection, 1985-2040 (in million tonnes) 191
Figure 7.3. Past vessel completions (1995-2014) and future new building requirements (2015-35) 192
Figure 7.4. Projected growth in global cruise tourism to 2035 194
Figure 7.5. Depth ranges of possible future mining activities and jurisdictions in the deep sea 198
Figure 8.1. Value-added of the ocean economy in 2030 in the business-as-usual scenario 205
Figure 8.2. Overview of industry-specific value added 2010 and 2030 206
Figure 8.3. Comparison of the direct employment in the ocean economy in 2010 and 2030 206
Figure 8.4. Value-added of industrial capture fisheries in 2030 by region in the business-as-usual scenario 209
Figure 8.5. Value-added of marine aquaculture in 2030 by region in the business-as-usual scenario 210
Figure 8.6. Shares of value-added of offshore wind in 2030 212
Figure 8.7. Value added in the ocean economy under different scenarios 213

Boxes

Box 1.1. What makes the ocean economy different from a land-based economy? 19
Box 5.1. Gaps in international ocean regulation 149
Box 9.1. Potentially disruptive trends in satellite technology with implications for ocean management 238

Acronyms and abbreviations

ABNJ	Area beyond national jurisdiction
AIS	Automatic identification system
ANN	Artificial neural network
API	Application programme interface
Area	Areas beyond national jurisdiction
ASV	Autonomous and semi-autonomous surface vehicle
AUV	Autonomous underwater vehicle
BRIICS	Brazil, Russian Federation, India, Indonesia, China and South Africa
CBD	Convention on Biological Diversity
CCZ	Clarion Clipperton Zone
CO_2	Carbon dioxide
ECA	Emission control area
ECDIS	Electronic Chart Display and Information System
EEZ	Economic exclusion zone
EIA	Environmental impact assessment
EWEA	European Wind Energy Association
FPSO	Floating storage and offloading vessel
GDP	Gross domestic product
GHG	Greenhouse gas
GNSS	Global satellite navigation system
GOC	Global Ocean Commission
GOOS	Global Ocean Observing System
GVA	Gross value added
HVDC	High-voltage direct current
ICT	Information and communication technology
ICZM	Integrated coastal zone management
IEA	International Energy Agency
ILO	International Labour Organization
IMO	International Maritime Organization
IPCC	Intergovernmental Panel on Climate Change
ISA	International Seabed Authority

ISIC	International Standard Industrial Classification of All Economic Activities
ITF	International Transport Forum
IUCN	International Union for Conservation of Nature
IUU	Illegal, unreported and unregulated (fishing)
LNG	Liquefied natural gas
MFP	Multifactor productivity
MPA	Marine protected area
MRE	Marine renewable energy
MSP	Maritime or marine spatial planning
MSR	Marine scientific research
NGO	Non-governmental organisation
NOAA	National Oceanic and Atmospheric Administration
NSR	Northern Sea Route
OPEC	Organization of the Petroleum Exporting Countries
OSV	Offshore supply vessel
OTEC	Ocean thermal energy conservation
ppm	Parts per million
PSSA	Particularly sensitive sea area
RD&D	Research, design and development
REE	Rare earth elements
RFMO	Regional fisheries management organisation
ROV	Remotely operated underwater vehicle
S&T	Science and technology
SEA	Strategic environmental assessment
SIP	Strategy Implementation Plan
SME	Small and medium-sized enterprise
SMS	Seabed massive sulphide
SNA	System of National Accounts
TEEB	The Economics of Ecosystems and Biodiversity
UAV	Unmanned airborne vehicle
UNCLOS	United Nations Convention on the Law of the Sea
UNIDO	United Nations Industrial Development Organization
UNSNA	United Nationals Systems of National Accounts
VMS	Vessel monitoring system
VTS	Vessel Traffic Service
WHO	World Health Organization

Executive summary

For many, the ocean is the new economic frontier. It holds the promise of immense resource wealth and great potential for boosting economic growth, employment and innovation. And it is increasingly recognised as indispensable for addressing many of the global challenges facing the planet in the decades to come, from world food security and climate change to the provision of energy, natural resources and improved medical care. While the potential of the ocean to help meet these challenges is huge, it is already under stress from over-exploitation, pollution, declining biodiversity and climate change. Realising the full potential of the ocean will therefore demand responsible, sustainable approaches to its economic development.

The ocean economy encompasses ocean-based industries (such as shipping, fishing, offshore wind, marine biotechnology), but also the natural assets and ecosystem services that the ocean provides (fish, shipping lanes, CO_2 absorption and the like). As the two are inextricably inter-linked, this report addresses many aspects of ecosystem services and ecosystem-based management all the while focusing on the ocean-industry dimension.

The global ocean economy, measured in terms of the ocean-based industries' contribution to economic output and employment, is significant. Preliminary calculations on the basis of the OECD's *Ocean Economy Database* value the ocean economy's contribution in 2010 very conservatively at USD 1.5 trillion, or approximately 2.5% of world gross value added (GVA). Offshore oil and gas accounted for one-third of total value added of the ocean-based industries, followed by maritime and coastal tourism, maritime equipment and ports. Direct full-time employment in the ocean economy amounted to around 31 million jobs in 2010. The largest employers were industrial capture fisheries with over one-third of the total, and maritime and coastal tourism with almost one-quarter.

Economic activity in the ocean is expanding rapidly, driven primarily by developments in global population, economic growth, trade and rising income levels, climate and environment, and technology. However, an important constraint on the development of the ocean economy is the current deterioration of its health. As anthropogenic carbon emissions have risen over time, the ocean has absorbed much of the carbon, leading to ocean acidification. Also, sea temperatures and sea levels are rising and ocean currents shifting, resulting in biodiversity and habitat loss, changes in fish stock composition and migration patterns, and higher frequency of severe ocean weather events. The prospects for future ocean development are further aggravated by land-based pollution, in particular agricultural run-off, chemicals, and macro- and micro-plastic pollutants that feed into the ocean from rivers, as well as by overfishing and depleted fish stocks in many parts of the world.

Looking to 2030, many ocean-based industries have the potential to outperform the growth of the global economy as a whole, both in terms of value added and employment. The projections suggest that between 2010 and 2030 on a "business-as-usual" scenario basis, the ocean economy could more than double its contribution to global value added, reaching over USD 3 trillion. Particularly strong growth is expected in marine aquaculture, offshore wind, fish processing, and shipbuilding and repair. Ocean industries also have the potential to make an important contribution to employment growth. In 2030, they are anticipated to employ approximately 40 million full-time equivalent jobs in the business-as-usual scenario. The fastest growth in jobs is expected to occur in offshore wind energy, marine aquaculture, fish processing and port activities.

In the coming decades, scientific and technological advances are expected to play a crucial role both in addressing many of the ocean-related environmental challenges mentioned above and in the further development of ocean-based economic activities. Innovations in advanced materials, subsea engineering and technology, sensors and imaging, satellite technologies, computerisation and big data analytics, autonomous systems, biotechnology and nanotechnology – every sector of the ocean economy – stands to be affected by these technological advances.

In a context of such rapid change, regulation and governance will struggle to keep up. The world is increasingly multi-polar and, notwithstanding the recent COP21 breakthrough, has been experiencing growing difficulty in forging international consensus on global and regional issues key to the ocean environment and ocean industries. At least for the foreseeable future, regulation of ocean activities is expected to continue to be largely sector-driven, with efforts focusing on the integration of emerging ocean industries into existing and fragmented regulatory frameworks.

The future growth of ocean-based industries on a scale suggested by this report highlights the prospect of growing pressures on ocean resources and ocean space already under considerable stress, not least in economic exclusion zones (EEZs), where most of the activity takes place. The inability so far to deal with these pressures in an effective, timely way is attributed in large part to what is historically a sector-by-sector management of marine activities. Much as a response to growing pressures, recent years have seen a significant increase in the number of countries and regions putting in place strategic policy frameworks for better ocean management within their EEZs. However, many obstacles stand in the way of more effective integrated ocean management, which will need to be addressed in the near future.

In order to boost the long-term development prospects of emerging ocean industries and their contribution to growth and employment, while managing the ocean in responsible, sustainable ways, this report puts forward a number of recommendations to enhance the sustainable development of the ocean economy.

- ***Foster greater international co-operation in maritime science and technology as a means to stimulate innovation and strengthen the sustainable development of the ocean economy.*** This entails *inter alia*: undertaking comparative analyses and reviews of the role of government policy *vis-à-vis* maritime clusters around the world, notably in respect of their effectiveness in stimulating and supporting cross-industry technological innovations in the maritime domain; establishing international networks for the exchange of views and experience in establishing centres of excellence, innovation incubators and other innovation facilities in the field of cross-industry maritime technologies, and improving the sharing of technology and innovation among countries at different levels of development.
- ***Strengthen integrated ocean management.*** In particular, this should involve making greater use of economic analysis and economic tools in integrated ocean management, for example by establishing international platforms for the exchange of knowledge, experience and best practice, and by stepping up efforts to evaluate

the economic effectiveness of public investment in marine research and observation. It should also aim to promote innovation in governance structures, processes and stakeholder engagement to render integrated ocean management more effective, more efficient and more inclusive.

- ***Improve the statistical and methodological base at national and international level for measuring the scale and performance of ocean-based industries and their contribution to the overall economy.*** This could include, among other tasks, the further development of the OECD's *Ocean Economy Database*.
- ***Build more capacity for ocean industry foresight,*** including the assessment of future changes in ocean-based industries, and further development of the OECD's current capacity for modelling future trends in the ocean economy at a global scale.

Chapter 1.

An overview of the ocean economy: Assessments and recommendations

This chapter summarises the key findings of the report and offers a set of recommendations to strengthen international co-operation in the sustainable management and development of the ocean economy of the future. It puts forward a working definition of the ocean economy which encompasses not only the ocean-based industries but also the natural assets and ecosystem services that the ocean provides. Focusing on the ocean industries, the chapter outlines the findings of the OECD Ocean Economy Database *and briefly presents the estimates of the current value added and jobs provided by the ocean economy worldwide. Turning its attention to the future, the chapter describes the principal forces driving the ocean economy forward, and estimates value added and employment in the global ocean economy by 2030. The results suggest rapid growth of most ocean industries over the next couple of decades, putting increasing strain on the ocean environment and its resources and posing significant challenges to ocean management. The chapter ends by proposing a set of recommendations for governments, business and research which could significantly enhance sustainable ocean management.*

The ocean and its resources are increasingly recognised as being indispensable for addressing the multiple challenges that the planet faces in the decades to come. By mid-century, enough food, jobs, energy, raw materials and economic growth will be required to sustain a likely population level of between 9 and 10 billion people. The potential of the ocean to help meet those requirements is huge, but fully harnessing it will require substantial expansion of many ocean-based economic activities. That will prove challenging, because the ocean is already under stress from over-exploitation, pollution, declining biodiversity and climate change. Hence, realising the full potential of the ocean will demand responsible, sustainable approaches to its economic development.

Introducing the ocean economy

At the centre of attention in this report on the economic development of the ocean is the future evolution of established and emerging ocean-based industries and activities. Broadly speaking, established ocean activities encompass shipping, shipbuilding and marine equipment, capture fisheries and fish processing, maritime and coastal tourism, conventional offshore oil and gas exploration and production, dredging, and port facilities and handling. Emerging ocean-based industries and activities are characterised by the key role played by cutting-edge science and technology in their operations. They include: offshore wind, tidal and wave energy; offshore extraction of oil and gas in deep-sea and other extreme locations; seabed mining for metals and minerals; marine aquaculture; marine biotechnology; ocean monitoring, control and surveillance. Looking further to the future, there are fledgling or, as yet, "unborn" industries which could potentially join this category. Examples are carbon capture and storage (CCS) and the management of ocean scale protected areas.

There is no hard and fast distinction between established and emerging industries. Indeed, some degree of overlap does exist, not least where segments of established ocean industries manifest clear indications of rapid growth and quite dramatic rates of innovation. For example, shipping and port activities are moving increasingly to highly sophisticated levels of automation; coastal aquaculture is well established in some countries, but at industrial scale it is becoming a highly science- and technology-intensive activity and is looking to expand further offshore; ocean monitoring and surveillance are benefiting from massive advances in satellite technology, tracking and imaging; and the cruise industry is turning its attention to new destinations such as the Arctic and Antarctica. Nonetheless, the division into established and emerging industries offers a pragmatic and manageable approach for the project.

The landscape of traditional maritime industries will be undergoing significant change in the coming decades. This is partly driven by global economic growth and increasing demand. In the shipping sector, for example, container traffic looks set to continue to grow very fast, with volumes likely to triple by 2035 (OECD, 2015). Fisheries production worldwide is expected to expand by around a fifth over the next ten years, although the main driver of overall production will be aquaculture (OECD and FAO, 2015). Even if improvements have been made in recent years, there is little or no room for further expansion in wild fish catch in the absence of strict management plans to rebuild stock abundance to biologically sustainable productivity levels. And in tourism, ageing populations, rising incomes and relatively low transport costs will make coastal and ocean locations ever more attractive. Concurrently, developments in traditional maritime industries will also be shaped by climate change, as shifts in temperature, ocean acidity and rising sea levels affect movements of fish stocks open up new trading routes, affect sea port structures, and create new tourist destinations and attractions, whilst destroying others.

Emerging ocean-based industries offer vast opportunities for addressing many of the big economic, social and environmental challenges facing humankind in the years ahead. These emerging ocean industries are developing and applying a range of science and technological innovations to exploit the ocean's resources more safely and sustainably, or to make the oceans cleaner and safer and to protect the richness of their resources. The activities differ considerably in their stage of development: some are relatively advanced while others are still in their infancy. To bring them on stream on a scale that would allow them to contribute in a meaningful way to global prosperity, human development, natural resource management and green growth will require considerable research and development (R&D) effort, investment and coherent policy support.

Such efforts, however, need to be shaped and directed with a view to the future, which is why this project has its sights set on 2030 and beyond.

Economic activities in an ocean environment

Management of economic activities in the ocean needs to be put into the physical context in which it operates: a fluid, buoyant, three-dimensional environment that covers about two-thirds of the planet's surface. The obvious – and in some cases less obvious – differences between land and sea have important implications as to how human activities are managed in the two very different environments. Nonetheless, although these differences affect the context and outcomes of marine operations, many of the concepts and techniques deployed in marine planning and management tend to be borrowed from practices on land.

Box 1.1. What makes the ocean economy different from a land-based economy?

Difference #1: The sea is much larger than land

Implication: Natural marine processes, ecosystems and species are not confined to maritime legal boundaries. Different legal regimes apply to a single activity depending on where it takes place, even within the jurisdiction of a single coastal country (territorial waters, contiguous zone, economic exclusion zone), and is further compounded by the interests of other countries in areas beyond national jurisdiction (international waters).

Difference #2: Water is less transparent than air

Implication: Remote sensing technology is not able to penetrate deep below the sea's surface. This makes it much harder and much more expensive to know what's going on in the water column and the seabed. Marine research and monitoring costs are extremely high, which helps explain why we know much less about what goes on in the ocean than about what happens on land.

Difference #3: The sea is more three-dimensional than land

Implication: Marine life occurs from the sea surface down to the deepest ocean trench, while on land only comparatively few species (i.e. those with the ability to fly) can sustain themselves above the land surface. The same also applies, to a certain extent, to human activities. This renders two-dimensional maps less useful, and increases the complexity of marine spatial planning and management. It also makes it more difficult to study the marine environment, how it works, how it is affected by human activities (see difference #2), and how the ocean benefits the economy and human well-being.

Box 1.1. **What makes the ocean economy different from a land-based economy?** *(continued)*

Difference #4: The sea is fluid and interconnected

Implication: What happens in one place may affect what happens elsewhere, as pollutants and alien species are carried by ocean currents and/or vessels to much greater distances than on land.

Difference #5: Marine species can potentially travel much longer distances than terrestrial ones

Implication: This makes the management of human activities that use marine resources particularly difficult, as they are accessible to almost anyone.

Difference #6: Aggregations or clusters of animals in the water column can shift rapidly from one location to another

Implication: The mapping of these species and their movements is more difficult, and measures to protect or manage them need also to shift in time and space accordingly.

Difference #7: Nutrients and pollutants can be retained for several decades until they are returned by ocean circulation

Implication: There can be significant time lags between the periods when certain human activities take place and the time when their impacts occur, potentially placing significant burdens on future generations.

Difference #8: Lack of ownership and responsibility in the ocean are even less favourable to sustainable development than on land

Implication: Private utilisation of the ocean and its resources is usually dependent on licenses or concessions from public authorities. National authorities have the power to allow private activities in areas under the jurisdiction of the coastal state; the International Seabed Authority can license activities in the area, but in international waters, private activities have much fewer controls. Common property regimes are even scarcer than on land given the mobile nature of many marine resources, which makes the exclusion of non-authorised users extremely difficult.

Difference #9: Humans do not live in the ocean

Because the sea is not our natural environment, our presence is dependent on the use and development of technology. Our sparse presence in the sea also makes it much more difficult, and costly, to exercise adequate law enforcement.

Sources: Crowder and Norse (2008); Douvere et al. (2007); Douvere (2008); Ehler and Douvere (2007); Grilo (2015); Norse and Crowder (2005).

The ocean economy as a cluster of interconnected industries

Ocean industries are not developing in isolation, neither from one another nor from the ocean environment of which they are part. On the contrary, they interrelate and interact with other activities and their ocean surrounds in a myriad of different ways. But as long as maritime industries and the exploitation of marine resources are perceived as individual and separate activities, approaches to their development and their sustainable management risk remaining piecemeal and limited in their effectiveness.

Recent history has demonstrated time and again that once closely interconnected clusters of economic activities begin to be perceived as an economic system or "economy" rather than as a fragmented collection of individual sectors, they garner more attention and benefit from more coherent strategic approaches to their development.

Examples abound. With the advent and rapid expansion of information and communication technology (ICT) in the second half of the 20th century, the notion of the "information economy" became a household name. Also about that time, most governments around the world were developing separate plans for the construction and renewal of transport systems – rail, road, air, water, energy systems, ICT networks, water provision and treatment, etc. Not until it became increasingly clear that all these systems and networks are closely interconnected did one begin to see the emergence of more integrated "infrastructure" planning (OECD, 2007). More recently, the different segments of the space sector with their highly complex and steadily globalising value chains have come to see themselves as the "space economy", reaching from launchers, satellite construction and operations down to everyday applications in farming, transport, meteorology and global communications (OECD, 2011). Similarly, the different strands of the relatively young biotechnology sector – health and medicine, agriculture and food, industry – have come to be perceived more and more as a "bioeconomy" (OECD, 2009), to such an extent that there are now over 30 countries around the world with "bioeconomy" in their strategic goals (German Bioeconomy Council, 2015).

Differences in terminology

The terminology relating to the ocean economy is used differently around the world. Commonly used terms include: ocean industry, marine economy, marine industry, marine activity, maritime economy and maritime sector. "Ocean" is usually used in Ireland and the United States, whereas "marine" is widely used in Australia, Canada, France, New Zealand and the United Kingdom. "Maritime" is frequently used by the European Union, Norway and Spain. Often terminologies are also translated differently into English when they are taken from Japanese, Korean or Mandarin. The present report will endeavour to distinguish "maritime" and "marine" as follows: "maritime" will be understood as "being connected with the sea, especially in relation to seafaring, commercial or military activity", while "marine" will be understood as "of, found in, or produced by the sea, 'marine plants'; 'marine biology'".

While "industry" embodies only market-based activities in the private and public sectors, the term "economy" is better suited to capturing the notion of both market-based and non-market goods and services.

Definition and concept of the ocean economy

In addition to the differing terminology, there is still no universally accepted definition of the ocean economy. For example, for the European Commission (Ecorys, 2012), "the maritime economy consists of all the sectoral and cross-sectoral economic activities related to the oceans, seas and coasts. This includes the closest direct and indirect supporting activities necessary for the functioning of these economic sectors, which can be located anywhere, including in landlocked countries."

A similar definition is suggested by Park (2014) after conducting a meta study about existing different worldwide definitions and perceptions of the ocean economy: "The ocean economy are the economic activities that take place in the ocean, receive outputs from the ocean, and provide goods and services to the ocean. In other words, the ocean economy can be defined as the economic activities that directly or indirectly take place in the ocean, use the ocean's outputs, and put the goods and services into the ocean's activities."

The present report, however, considers that any definition of the ocean economy is incomplete unless it also encompasses non-quantifiable natural stocks and non-market goods and services. In other words, the ocean economy can be defined as the sum of the economic activities of ocean-based industries, and the assets, goods and services of marine ecosystems.

Figure 1.1 summarises this concept. Ocean-based industries can be divided into market flows and services and physical capital stock of the industries. Marine ecosystems represent natural capital and non-market flows and services. In many cases, marine ecosystems provide intermediate inputs to the ocean-based industries. An example is coral reefs. They provide shelter and habitat for fish nurseries and unique genetic resources, while at the same time providing recreational value for maritime tourism. Conversely, ocean industries can impact the health of marine ecosystems, e.g. through discharge if ship waste or pollution from oil spills.

Figure 1.1. **The concept of the ocean economy**

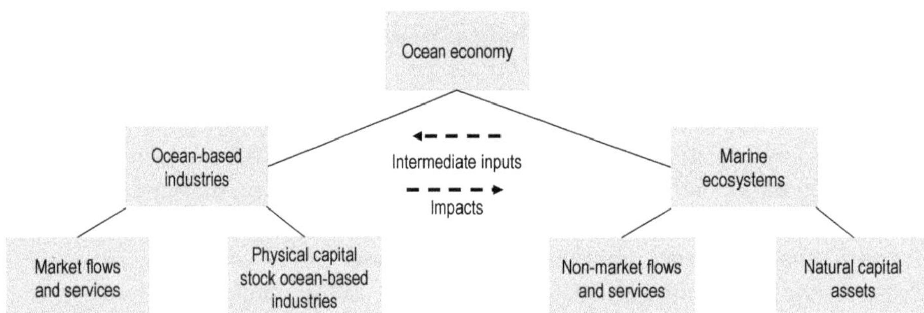

However, rigorous inclusion of the value of ecosystem assets and services in quantitative assessments, i.e. ecological accounting, is a new research field that only in recent years has begun to attract more significant interest (see further below).

Scope of the ocean economy

Ocean-based industries

It is conspicuous in studies of the ocean economy (see Chapter 6) that the sectoral scope of the ocean economy varies considerably by country. The number of categories chosen can range from 6, as in the case of the United States, to 33 in the case of Japan. Some industries may be excluded from the ocean economy in one country but not in another. Moreover, there are significant differences among countries in the delineation of the classifications and categories used. Internationally agreed definitions and statistical terminology for ocean-based activities do not yet exist (Park, 2014).

This report proposes the following scope (Table 1.1) for categorising established and emerging ocean-based activities, bearing in mind earlier remarks about overlapping definitions and the existence of highly dynamic emerging activities within traditional ocean industries. Explanations of each sector are offered in Annex 1.A1.

Table 1.1. **Established and emerging ocean-based industries**

Established	Emerging
Capture fisheries	Marine aquaculture
Seafood processing	Deep- and ultra-deep water oil and gas
Shipping	Offshore wind energy
Ports	Ocean renewable energy
Shipbuilding and repair	Marine and seabed mining
Offshore oil and gas (shallow water)	Maritime safety and surveillance
Marine manufacturing and construction	Marine biotechnology
Maritime and coastal tourism	High-tech marine products and services
Marine business services	Others
Marine R&D and education	
Dredging	

It should be noted, however, that due to lack of comprehensive and consistent data sets, not all of the above industries are covered in detail in this report (see Chapter 6).

Marine ecosystems

In addition to the market flows and services and the physical capital stock of ocean-based industries, the ocean economy also consists of marine ecosystems. Marine ecosystems encompass oceans, salt marshes and intertidal zones, estuaries and lagoons, mangroves and coral reefs, the water column including the deep sea, and the sea floor (Kaiser and Roumasset, 2002), all of which provide intermediary services relevant for ocean-based industries.

The interactions of society, economy and environment exercise an important influence on marine ecosystems through their dynamics and their broader biogeochemical cycle. This is because ecosystem services are dependent on one another and exhibit complex interactions that generate trade-offs in the delivery of one ecosystem service relative to the delivery of others. For the ocean economy, this is relevant because these interactions determine indirectly the viability of ocean-based industries. By way of illustration: coastal run-off and eutrophication, acidification through increasing greenhouse gas (GHG) emissions, and poor water quality through pollution lead to changes in fish migration patterns and even extinction of fish stocks. All are examples of how human activity indirectly intervenes in the functioning of marine ecosystems, thereby undermining the economic viability of the ocean economy.

Measuring the value of marine ecosystems is a difficult and complex exercise, but research efforts in the area have gathered considerable momentum in recent years. Estimates of the size of the benefits of marine ecosystem services suggest that these are considerable (for a review of a selection of such studies see Annex 1.A2), but much work remains to be done. Hence, as noted above, while many aspects of ecosystem services are taken into account here, the quantitative focus of this report is on ocean-based industries.

Ocean-based industries contribute roughly USD 1.5 trillion (2.5%) to global gross value added

The global ocean economy, measured in terms of the ocean-based industries' contribution to economic output and employment, is significant.

Calculations on the basis of the OECD's *Ocean Economy Database* value the ocean economy's output in 2010 (the base year for the calculations and subsequent scenarios to 2030) at USD 1.5 trillion in value added, or approximately 2.5% of world gross value added (GVA). To compare an industry's contribution to the economy across countries, the share of total GVA is preferred to the share of GDP. The System of National Accounts (SNA) recommends using GVA at basic prices for this purpose. The difference between total industry GVA and total GDP is taxes less subsidies on products, which varies across countries. This adjustment is made at the aggregate (total economy) level because, while time series of taxes less subsidies on products may be available by product, they are not generally available by industry. Furthermore, it should be noted that this study took the year 2010 and Revision 3 of the International Standard Industrial Classification of All Economic Activities (ISIC) as baselines in order to maximise the completeness, consistency and comparability of available data.

Offshore oil and gas accounted for about one-third of total value added of the ocean-based industries, followed by maritime and coastal tourism (26%), ports (13%) – measured as total value added of global port throughput – and maritime equipment (11%). The other industries accounted for shares of 5% or less (Figure 1.2). While the share of industrial capture fisheries is small (1%), it should be noted that inclusion of estimates of the value added generated by artisanal capture fisheries (mainly in Africa and Asia) would add further tens of billions of USD to the capture fisheries total (see Chapter 6 for detailed estimates).

Figure 1.2. **Value added of ocean-based industries in 2010 by industry**

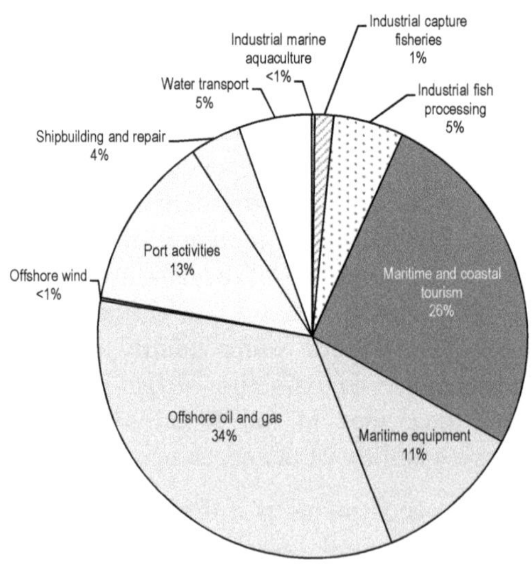

StatLink http://dx.doi.org/10.1787/888933334614

Note: Artisanal fisheries are not included in this overview.

Source: Authors' calculations based on OECD STAN, UNIDO INDSTAT, UNSD, World Bank (2013); IEA (2014); OECD (2014); and various industry reports.

The ocean-based industries contributed some 31 million direct full-time jobs in 2010, around 1% of the global work force (and about 1.5% of the global workforce actively employed). As Figure 1.3 indicates, the largest employers were industrial capture fisheries (36%) and maritime and coastal tourism (23%). The remaining industries accounted for shares of between less than 1% and 8%.

A number of qualifying remarks are in order here. First, the percentage share of total employment accounted for by capture fisheries would increase markedly if total jobs in artisanal fisheries were to be included, adding around 100 million fishers for capture fisheries and aquaculture (including inland activities) to the overall total. Second, in addition to industrial fish processing, there are millions of people (mainly women) involved in artisanal fish processing (see Chapter 6 for more details on capture fisheries, aquaculture and fish processing).

It is worth noting therefore at this juncture that the report's estimates for value added and employment in the ocean economy are extremely conservative. In addition to the qualifying remarks above, several important activities in the ocean economy (e.g. marine business and finance, ocean surveillance, marine biotechnology) are not captured due to lack of data.

Figure 1.3. **Employment in the ocean-based industries in 2010 by industry**

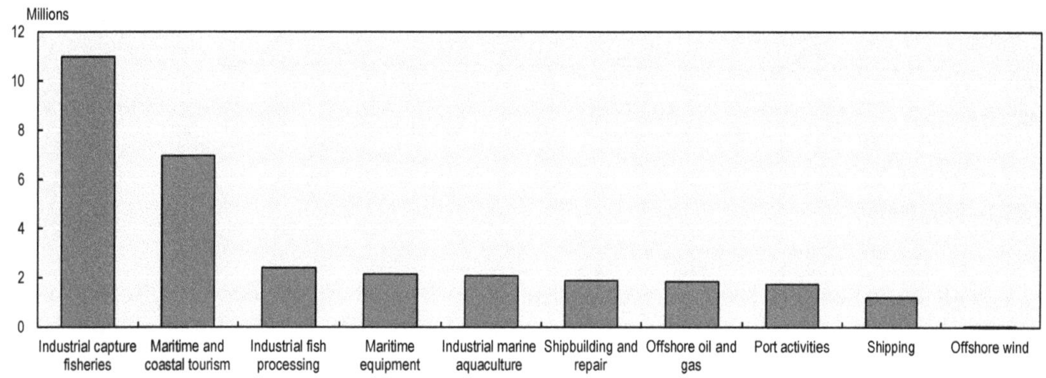

StatLink http://dx.doi.org/10.1787/888933334627

Note: Artisanal fisheries are not included in this overview.

Source: Authors' calculations based on OECD STAN, UNIDO INDSTAT, UNSD, World Bank (2013); IEA (2014); OECD (2014); and various industry reports.

Forces shaping the evolution of the ocean economy to 2030

The ocean economy of the next 20 years or so is being driven primarily by developments in global population, the economy, climate and environment, technology, and ocean regulation and management (see Chapter 2).

Population

Population growth, urbanisation and coastal development are at the heart of growth in the ocean economy. By 2050, an extra 2 billion people at least will need to be fed, raising demand for fish, molluscs and other marine foods from fisheries and aquaculture; as consumers they will stimulate sea-borne freight and passenger traffic, shipbuilding and marine equipment manufacturing, as well as exploration for offshore oil and gas reserves. Ageing populations will continue to target coastal locations for holidays, cruise tourism and retirement homes, and motivate the medical and pharmaceutical communities of the world to accelerate marine biotechnological research into new drugs and treatments.

Global economic growth and international trade

Along with population, the economy is one of the most dynamic drivers of developments in the maritime economy. Although the long-term prospects for global economic growth, and for the OECD area as a whole, remain modest, GDP per capita is expected to rise significantly over the next few decades. Global freight trade could more than triple by 2050. Since around 90% of international freight is carried by sea, the impetus to the shipping business and ports will be considerable.

Figure 1.4. **Growth in global seaborne trade 1970-2035**

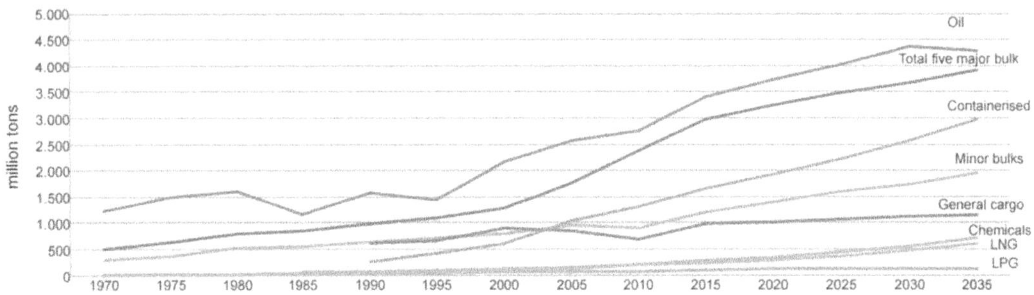

Source: SEA (2015).

With an expanding share of world production located in the People's Republic of China (hereafter "China"), India and Indonesia (almost 40% by 2030 and around 50% by 2050), and concomitant increases in incomes and wealth, especially in the burgeoning middle classes of the emerging economies and some of the rapidly developing countries, a gradual shift in trade patterns eastwards is inevitable. The consequences for ocean industries are huge. Careful consideration is already being given by shipping lines and shipbuilding companies to likely future changes in markets, routes, types of cargo and types of vessel that will be required. Higher incomes and upward consumption trends point to greater demand for marine tourism and especially cruise tourism. They also point to big shifts in dietary habits, which are expected to lift demand for fish and other marine products to new heights.

Food

In light of the expected increase in world population to 2050 and demand for food, the ocean clearly has an important part to play in supplementing the food supplies generated by agriculture. Indeed, in many parts of the world, marine produce will continue to be a prime source of protein and vitamins for millions of people, especially as the growing middle classes shift their spending to high-end protein products. However, the ocean's capacity to perform that role is increasingly undermined by overfishing and depleted stocks in many parts of the world as well as by the impacts of land-based pollution, not least the run-off of fertilisers and agricultural waste into coastal and estuary zones, which threatens marine life habitats, fish stocks, molluscs and so on. Growth in global capture fisheries is therefore expected to remain more or less flat over the next ten years or so. The increase in world demand for seafood will need to be absorbed by a significant expansion in aquaculture, especially in marine aquaculture. However, scaling up marine aquaculture will necessitate addressing a series of challenges ranging from the availability of additional sites and better management of the problems of disease and escapees, to dealing with the effects of climate change and reducing animal protein in feed based on wild fish catch.

Energy

Energy issues pervade the full range of maritime industries, both as energy users and energy suppliers. Market price levels and market volatility are crucial factors in the viability of offshore oil and gas exploration and production, as underlined by recent decisions to scale back, defer or abandon several offshore projects, since they are particularly capital intensive. Nonetheless, despite low oil prices, a good number of high-profile offshore projects have seen their development continue. In contrast to producers of hydrocarbons, consistently high oil and gas prices are an essential ingredient for the continuing progress of offshore wind and ocean renewables, as well as for the development of aquaculture-based algal biofuels. However, offshore wind is likely to continue to benefit from government subsidies in the years to come and, as capacity grows, from efforts to reduce production and running costs. Both factors should help offshore wind build more resilience to fluctuations in oil and gas markets. The global market for ocean energy systems (tidal, wave, ocean current, etc.), on the other hand, is not expected to scale up significantly in the medium term, but the longer term potential is enormous. Both offshore wind and ocean energy capacity should eventually benefit from the historic COP21 agreement and its support for renewable energy (see, for example, the recommendations submitted to the Paris COP21 by the Ocean and Climate Platform[1]).

Ocean environment

An important constraining factor on the development of the ocean economy could prove to be the expected further deterioration in the health of the ocean (see Chapter 3 for a detailed discussion). The ocean plays an important part in regulating the planet's climate, and is intricately linked with the Earth's land mass and atmosphere. Its ecosystem services include the regulation of atmospheric and marine carbon dioxide concentrations, the provision of oxygen, the hydrothermal convection cycle, the hydrological cycle, coastal protection and vital contributions from marine biodiversity. As anthropogenic carbon emissions have risen over time, the ocean has absorbed much of the carbon, leading to ocean acidification, rising sea temperatures and sea levels, shifts in ocean currents and so on. Concern about the future impact of climate change on the ocean's health is widespread and mounting. Indeed, following the Paris COP21 conference, the Intergovernmental Panel on Climate Change (IPCC) will be publishing a special report on the ocean, notably the effects of climate change on biodiversity, the functioning of marine ecosystems and the role of those ecosystems in helping regulate the planet's climate.

The implications for ocean ecosystems and marine diversity are considerable and are resulting in biodiversity and habitat loss, changes in fish stock composition and migration patterns, and higher frequency of severe ocean weather events. The consequences are being – and will continue to be – felt by fishing and aquaculture operations, the offshore oil and gas industry, vulnerable low-lying coastal communities, shipping companies, coastal and marine tourism, and marine bio-prospecting for medical and industrial purposes. The prospects for ocean health and ocean users are further aggravated by land-based pollution, in particular agricultural run-off, chemicals and macro- and

1. Available at: www.ocean-climate.org/?page_id=2876.

micro-plastic pollutants which feed into the ocean especially from rivers. In these matters, developing countries tend to be much harder hit than industrialised nations.

At the same time, however, changes in the ocean climate are set to create new business opportunities. This is illustrated, for example, by events in the Arctic, where the ice cap is expected to continue to melt in coming years, opening the Northern Sea Route (NSR) for commercially viable shipping. According to the latest modelling results (Bekkers, Francois and Rojas-Romagosa, 2015), a shortening of sailing times between north-east Asia and north-western Europe by around one-third compared to current use of the Southern Sea Route through the Suez would transform the NSR into one of the busiest shipping routes in the world, bring about a major shift in bilateral trade flows between Asia and Europe, and trigger a reorganisation of global supply chains both within Europe and between Europe and Asia. At the same time, receding ice cover would open the way for new economic opportunities ranging from oil and gas exploration to mining, fishing and tourism, introducing, however, further potential risks to the vulnerable Arctic environment.

Science, technology and innovation

In the coming decades, scientific and technological advances are expected to play a crucial role both in addressing many of the ocean-related environmental challenges mentioned above and in the further development of ocean-based economic activities. Innovations in advanced materials, subsea engineering and technology, sensors and imaging, satellite technologies, computerisation and big data analytics, autonomous systems, biotechnology and nanotechnology – every sector of the ocean economy stands to be affected by these technological advances. By way of illustration: commercial shipping appears to be on the verge of the introduction of autonomous ships and greater use of new fuels; oil and gas and seabed mining companies are all looking to robotics for their subsea operations; marine aquaculture is building on advances in biotechnology to improve fish health and welfare and reduce dependence on wild fish catches for feed; renewable ocean energies are making increasing use of advances in new materials and sensors; fisheries, maritime safety, ocean observation and environmental assessment will continue to benefit from the great strides that are being made in satellite technologies (communications, remote sensing, navigation); and cruise tourism is scaling up its on-board digital facilities for passengers and crew to unprecedented levels.

Some of these innovations are set to generate incremental benefits, others, however, are likely to prove more transformative and even disruptive, especially where they involve combinations of innovations from multiple technological domains.

Examples include: the near-term prospect of e-navigation being implemented in the shipping industry; the convergence of multiple technologies (biotechnology, satellite and sensor technologies, etc.) revolutionising the battle against offshore oil pollution; the great strides expected in seafloor mapping; the anticipated increasing use of multi-purpose offshore platforms; and the spread of ocean-scale undersea observatories (see Chapter 4 for more detail on these examples).

Figure 1.5. **Towards the autonomous ship of the future**

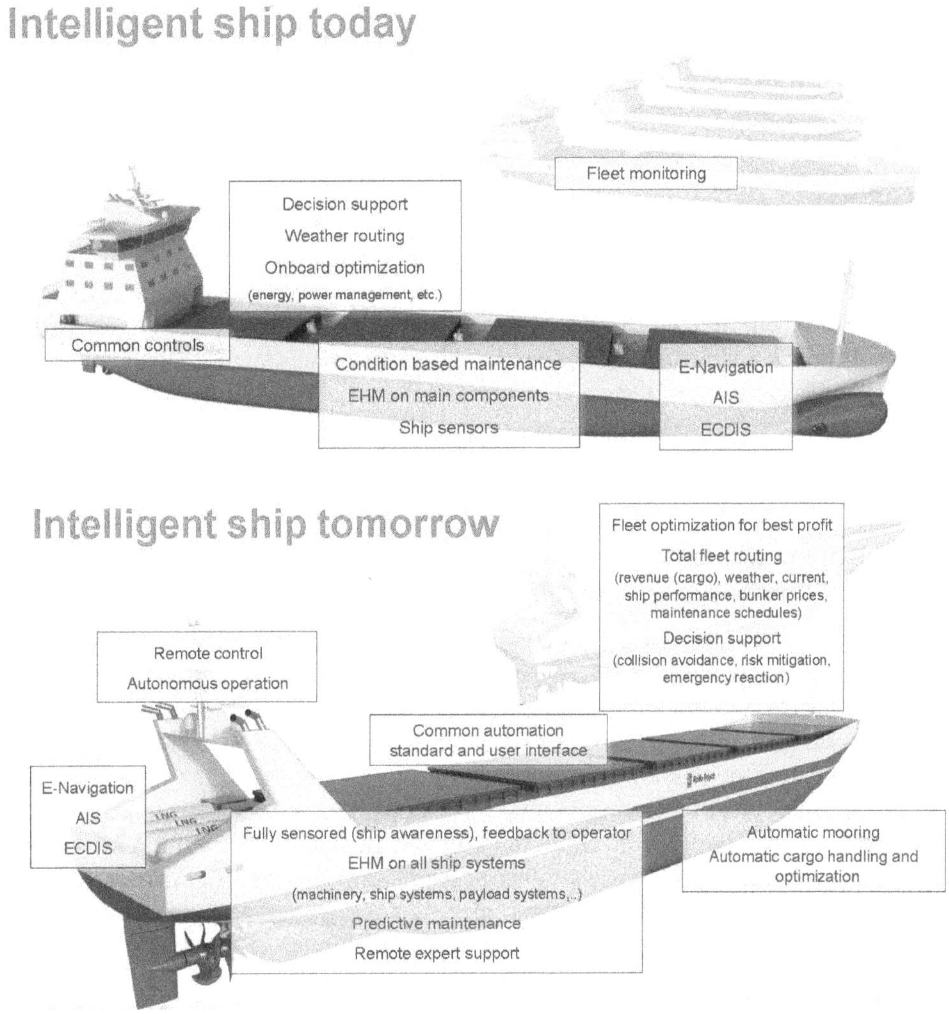

Source: Levander (2015).

International regulation and governance of the ocean economy

In a context of such rapid change as that outlined above, regulation and governance will struggle to keep up (see Chapter 5). The world is increasingly multi-polar in its power structure: there is the emergence of numerous countries and regions vying for economic power and the benefits that can be derived from projecting their growing economic power on to the geopolitical stage; new state players demonstrating their strength in particular crucial sectors – such as energy and other natural resources, space technologies, ICT – which allows them to assume a strategic importance in the global arena often far in excess of their size; and the appearance of new non-state actors such as city regions, urban clusters, international non-governmental organisations and foundations, which have seen their influence in the world grow as the high concentrations of knowledge, skills, financial clout and scale/network efficiencies raise their profile internationally. These developments are leading to a fragmentation of power and growing difficulty in forging international consensus on global and regional issues that are key to the ocean environment and ocean industries. Whether this involves climate change and

GHG emission levels or the governance of the high seas and area beyond national jurisdiction (ABNJ), the protection of marine biodiversity or international conventions on maritime safety, the path to international agreement appears increasingly complex and painstaking. At least for the foreseeable future, regulation of ocean activities is expected to continue to be largely sector-driven, with efforts focusing on the integration of emerging ocean industries into existing regulatory frameworks.

The ocean economy in 2030

Clearly the future of the ocean economy is being shaped by many different factors. These are reflected to varying degrees in a plethora of forecasts and projections on ocean industries produced in recent years by a wide range of international organisations, government agencies, industry associations and research establishments. Obtaining a coherent picture of the likely future of the ocean economy as a whole is very difficult, since all these studies use different methodologies, various time horizons and different assumptions (e.g. regarding global economic growth and trade). And since they are for the most part single-sector studies, the inter-linkages among the various ocean sectors cannot be captured.

Modelling the ocean economy's industries suggests that some of them have the potential to outperform average world economic growth

The "Future of the Ocean Economy" project endeavours to mitigate these shortcomings by projecting the development of the global ocean economy as a whole to 2030 on the basis of an enhanced ocean-industry database and a model based on broadly consistent assumptions and parameters. The projection is a business-as-usual scenario, or baseline scenario, which assumes a continuation of past trends, no major policy changes, no abrupt technological or environmental developments, and no major surprises. Value added and employment growth from the ocean-based industries continue to progress along the same trajectory to 2030 as in the past reference period. The model designed for this project requires country- and industry-specific employment and physical capital stock to be extrapolated under the assumption that past growth rates continue until 2030.

Global value added in the ocean economy "business-as-usual scenario" is estimated to grow to more than USD 3 trillion (in constant 2010 USD) by 2030 (Figure 1.6) and maintain its share of world total GVA (projected to reach about USD 120 billion by 2030) at around 2.5%. Maritime and coastal tourism, including the cruise industry, is expected to take the largest share (26%), followed by offshore oil and gas exploration and production with 21% and port activities with 16% (for further details see Chapter 8).

Again, these estimates are considered highly conservative. First, they do not yet include a good number of ocean-related sectors for which adequate data are presently not available. Second, they understate activity in certain sectors (such as shipping) for which numerous countries have had to be excluded due to lack of data. Third, the modest growth expected in some large industries (e.g. offshore oil and gas) masks comparatively high rates of growth expected in others (e.g. marine aquaculture, offshore wind, fish processing, port activities) and holds back overall average growth in the ocean economy as a whole (see Table 1.2).

These results suggest that many parts of the ocean economy have the potential to outperform the growth rate of the global economy as a whole. Indeed, such a conclusion is supported by a substantial number of sector-specific forecasts and projections conducted by a host of international organisations and agencies, industry associations and research institutes (see Chapter 7). They indicate strong growth in volume terms over the coming 15 years in shipping, shipbuilding and repair, port activity, marine supplies, marine aquaculture, offshore wind and marine tourism. They expect less strong growth in capture fisheries and offshore oil and gas. Ocean renewable energy, marine biotechnology and CCS are also considered to possess considerable potential, the scaling-up of which, however, is unlikely to happen before 2030.

Figure 1.6. **Value added of the ocean economy in 2030 in the business-as-usual scenario**

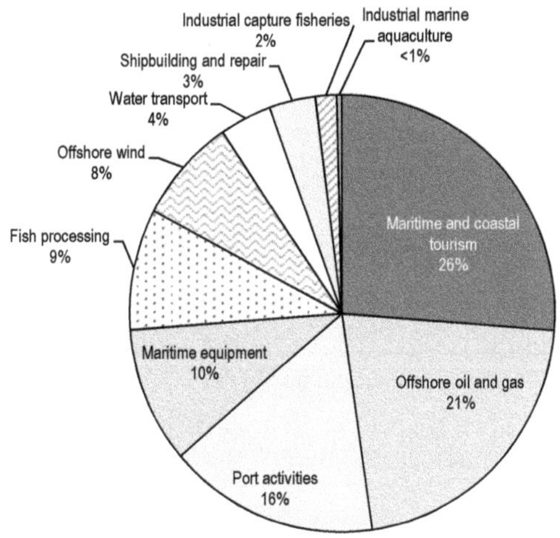

StatLink http://dx.doi.org/10.1787/888933334632

Note: Artisanal fisheries are not included in this overview.

Source: Authors' calculations based on OECD STAN, UNIDO INDSTAT, UNSD; Lloyd's Register (2014; 2013); World Bank (2013); IEA (2014).

Ocean industries also have the potential to make an important contribution to employment growth

In 2030, the ocean-based industries in the business-as-usual scenario are anticipated to employ over 40 million people, broadly unchanged over 2010 at more than 1% of the global workforce (of around 3.8 billion). A majority are expected to be working in the industrial capture fisheries sector and the maritime and coastal tourism industry. With the exception of capture fisheries, all the ocean industries selected here are likely to see their global employment levels grow at a faster rate than that of the global workforce as a whole. The majority of jobs in the ocean economy would be accounted for by maritime and coastal tourism and capture fisheries. The data for shipping cover high income, emerging and developing countries, but should be interpreted with caution since they only include direct full-time employment (see Chapter 8 for further details on employment).

The compound annual growth rate of the value added generated by the ocean-based industries combined between 2010 and 2030 is estimated at 3.5%, broadly similar to the growth rate of the total GVA of the global economy. At almost 30%, growth of employment in the ocean based-industries over the 20-year timeframe is expected to outpace that of the global workforce (around 19%). Table 1.2 presents a sector-by-sector comparison of the results of the projections to 2030 for the annual average growth rates of value added and employment for the ocean economy.

Table 1.2. **Overview of estimates of industry-specific growth rates in value added and employment between 2010 and 2030**

Industry	Compound annual growth rate for GVA between 2010 and 2030	Total change in GVA between 2010 and 2030	Total change in employment between 2010 and 2030
Industrial marine aquaculture	5.69%	303%	152%
Industrial capture fisheries	4.10%	223%	94%
Fish processing	6.26%	337%	206%
Maritime and coastal tourism	3.51%	199%	122%
Offshore oil and gas	1.17%	126%	126%
Offshore wind	24.52%	8 037%	1 257%
Port activities	4.58%	245%	245%
Shipbuilding and repair	2.93%	178%	124%
Maritime equipment	2.93%	178%	124%
Shipping	1.80%	143%	130%
Average of the total ocean-based industries	3.45%	197%	130%
Global economy between 2010 and 2030	3.64%	204%	120%[1]

1. Based on projections of the global workforce, extrapolated with the UN medium fertility rate.

Source: Authors' calculations based on OECD STAN, UNIDO INDSTAT, UNSD; Lloyd's Register (2014; 2013); World Bank (2013); IEA (2014); FAO (2015).

Alternative scenarios suggest that only relatively small differences in total value added would be expected compared to the business-as-usual scenario

Two alternative scenarios are offered – sustainable growth and unsustainable growth – which shape the future ocean economy in two different directions, one accelerating and the other slowing the future development of the ocean-based industries by 2030 (see Chapter 8). The main drivers for these alternative scenarios were defined in an internal workshop with the Project Steering Group in 2014. Drivers shaping the scenarios included economic growth, technological development, governmental regulations, and the state of the climate and ocean environment by 2030.

- The "sustainable scenario" assumes high economic growth and low environmental deterioration due to the development of resource-efficient and climate-friendly technologies combined with a supportive governmental framework that provides the right incentives to allow the ocean economy to thrive economically while meeting environmental standards.
- The "unsustainable scenario" assumes low economic growth and serious environmental deterioration. Coupled with faster than expected climate change and low rates of technological innovation, the ocean economy experiences a challenging outlook beyond 2030.

Value added in the business-as-usual ocean economy is USD 1.5 trillion in 2010 and USD 3 trillion in 2030. In the "sustainable" scenario, value added in 2030 is more than USD 3.2 trillion. Value added in 2030 in the "unsustainable" scenario is around USD 2.8 trillion. The difference between the two alternative scenarios would be expected to grow with time. Similarly, employment of the ocean economy in 2030 in the sustainable scenario is almost 43 million jobs, whereas that figure would be around 7 million smaller in the unsustainable scenario. Nevertheless, these are conservative estimates since not every ocean-based industry is included and only direct employment and direct value added are included.

An expanding ocean economy leads to growing pressures on marine resources and ocean space

The future growth of ocean-based industries on a scale suggested by this report highlights the prospect of growing pressures on ocean resources and ocean space already under considerable stress, not least in economic exclusion zones (EEZs), where most of the activity takes place. The inability so far to deal with these pressures in an effective, timely way is attributed in large part to what is historically a sector-by-sector management of marine activities (see Chapter 9).

Much as a response to those growing pressures, recent years have seen a significant increase in the number of countries and regions putting in place strategic policy frameworks for better ocean management within their EEZs, based for the most part on ecosystem approaches and making use of various spatial planning and management instruments such as integrated coastal zone management (ICZM), maritime or marine spatial planning (MSP), and marine protected areas (MPAs). Some of these countries have their strategic policy framework already in place, while others are at various stages of design and implementation. At the root of this overall policy shift is the growing recognition that management of the ocean needs to be based on an ecosystem approach. The interrelationship among uses and processes in the coast and ocean makes it imperative that ocean governance be integrated, precautionary and anticipatory.

Currently, some 50 countries have some form or other of spatial ocean management initiatives underway. Eight countries have government-approved marine plans that cover about 8% of the world's EEZs. By 2025, more than 25 countries will have government-approved plans that will cover about 25% of the area of the world's EEZs.

However, the scale and scope of each initiative differs considerably between countries. Moreover, in light of the expected rapid future expansion of ocean industry activity around the world and the increasingly crowded ocean space, time is of the essence in extending effective integrated management to as many coastal countries as possible. However, many obstacles stand in the way of more effective integrated ocean management, which will need to be addressed in the near future. They include for example: lack of scientific knowledge and data on ocean environment – compounded by complexity and uncertainty of the ocean environment; insufficient use of the scientific and technological tools to gather, process and analyse those data; lack of relevant socio-economic data; and the challenge of balancing the perceived interests of stakeholders, the distributional implications and equity considerations. Furthermore, the science has been slow to catch up with policy requirements with respect both to assessing and communicating trade-offs among human uses of the ocean, and to identifying strategies to mediate those trade-offs.

Integrated ocean management offers significant opportunities for addressing these challenges, but needs better tools to work with

Three routes in particular offer themselves as means for addressing the above-mentioned shortcomings and for enhancing the effectiveness and diffusion of integrated ocean management:

- greater use of economic analysis (e.g. cost-benefit analysis – identifying and quantifying types of cost, types of benefit, valuation techniques) and economic instruments (e.g. taxes, fees, tradable permits)

- better use of innovations in science and technology (e.g. advances in satellite applications, especially in combination with other technological innovations in such uses as drones, unmanned airborne vehicles (UAVs), sensors, mapping, imaging) especially for gathering more and better data quality
- innovation in governance and stakeholder engagement (co-ordination across government agencies, and wider but more effective and cost-efficient stakeholder consultation).

Economic analysis and instruments are part of the toolbox required to improve measurement and valuation of ecosystem services. They are useful especially in cases of competing claims for ocean space and the search for an appropriate balance between use of maritime space and protection of the ocean and coastal environment. However, lack of data on economic parameters (such as the non-market value of key ecosystem services) and environmental phenomena (such as the condition and interaction of specific marine animal habitats) together with the hitherto patchy implementation of spatial planning, have meant that economic instruments have so far been under-utilised in the ocean environment context.

Science, technology and data analytics are not being fully and effectively harnessed to the ocean management process. The data challenges facing effective marine spatial planning and ocean management are considerable. There is a great deal of uncertainty as to what is in the ocean; very little is known of the interactive effects of different uses and users in the ocean; and the ocean is a dynamic environment undergoing significant changes because of climate change. Large information gaps remain. Data on the marine resource is fragmented, difficult to locate, and biased towards the physical and ecological characteristics of the resource. This is due in part to the historical single sector approach to planning in the marine environment and the earlier emphasis on the biophysical rather than economic and social processes associated with the marine environment. When data are available, there is a diversity of data sources and data formats for policy makers, researchers and the public to disentangle.

Governance and stakeholder engagement are key to effective ocean management, i.e. co-ordination across government as well as the engagement of all relevant stakeholders – scientists, business, user industries and associations – in the process. However, given their long history of sector-based approaches, current governance structures are usually not well suited to handle these co-ordination and consultation tasks effectively across sectors, especially where resources are moveable and renewable (e.g. capture fisheries) and/or stationary and mostly non-renewable (e.g. oil and gas deposits). Different bureaucracies are usually in charge of handling the permitting for different uses and users, but they tend not to co-operate well, if at all. Moving from sector-by-sector management to integrated ocean management is a major institutional change.

The three routes to help improve ocean management are set out in more detail in Chapter 9.

Recommendations: An agenda for international co-operation for a sustainable ocean economy

What is required to boost the long-term development prospects of emerging ocean industries and their contribution to growth and employment, while managing the ocean in responsible, sustainable ways? This report emphasises the importance of taking a holistic view of the ocean economy, a perspective that is reflected both in the main findings and in the structure and thrust of the proposals below. Rather than taking a sector-by-sector approach, the recommendations cut across disciplines and sectors to try to provide a more integrated perspective on what might be done to achieve a desirable balance between economic development and environmental sustainability in the ocean context in the coming years.

The recommendations are broken into four groups:

1. Foster greater international co-operation in maritime science and technology as a means to stimulate innovation and strengthen the sustainable development of the ocean economy.
2. Strengthen integrated ocean management.
3. Improve the statistical and methodological base at national and international level for measuring the scale and performance of ocean-based industries and their contribution to the overall economy.
4. Build more capacity for ocean industry foresight.

1. Foster greater international co-operation in maritime science and technology as a means to stimulate innovation and strengthen the sustainable development of the ocean economy

Innovation in ocean-related science and technology will play a key role in the sustainable development of the ocean economy for two inter-connected reasons.

First, the ocean economy is a global stage on which myriads of businesses and indeed countries are competing vigorously with one another for markets. How those competitive forces will play out in the future depends to a very high degree on the ability of businesses to continually renew, adjust, upgrade and reinvent their products, production processes and services. Innovation holds the key to their survival and economic success.

Second, business-as-usual expansion of economic activities in the ocean is not an option for the future, as it would further jeopardise the ocean's health and resources, thereby undermining the very basis on which the ocean industries themselves depend. Innovation will be a critical ingredient in the search for solutions that enable business opportunities to be developed while minimising the impact on the ocean environment and marine resources. The scale and complexity of the challenges involved are such that international co-operation on technological innovation in the ocean industries will become increasingly indispensable.

The scope for a government role in promoting innovation across and among ocean industries could be considerable and is worthy of further exploration. Three pathways are traced below.

1. Better exploit potential technology and innovation synergies among ocean industries

Why is it important?

A high degree of potential interaction exists among ocean-based activities – offshore wind and ocean renewable energy with offshore oil and gas operations; marine aquaculture, tourism, marine research and marine biotechnology with offshore structures and platforms – as well as among the technologies deployed in those activities. Benefits could be reaped in the form, for example, of lower costs from shared common infrastructure, cross-fertilisation of technologies and innovative processes, reduced impact on the marine environment and more effective planning of the use of limited ocean space.

These tasks are often performed by maritime industry clusters, acting as agents of cross-sectoral technology transfer and stimulators of innovation synergies, not least among small and medium-sized enterprises (SMEs). However, looking around the world, many clusters only encompass a small part of all the maritime sub-industries; some are public, others private or mixed; some clusters have little interaction among sectors and cannot perform the tasks of co-ordination and cross-sectoral exchange; yet others have no remit to pursue cross-industry science and technology innovation initiatives. Moreover, many countries and regions around the world have no active maritime industry cluster at all. Government policy can help create, strengthen, sustain and expand maritime industry clusters. But there is no one-size-fits-all policy approach, and much depends on local and national circumstances.

Looking more to the future, recent years have seen the emergence of numerous initiatives (many still at the planning stage) around the world to create specific centres of excellence aimed at leveraging the potential synergies of technological innovations across maritime industries, often in liaison with maritime clusters. These initiatives include, for example, the Sealab Innovation Centre (Mediterranean), the San Diego Blue Tech Incubator (United States), the Ocean Space Centre (Norway) and the Ocean Technology Alliance (Canada). Many take the form of public-private partnerships, opening up opportunities for governments to promote innovation in the maritime sector in a variety of different ways.

What should be done?

- Comparative analyses and reviews of maritime clusters around the world are needed specifically with respect to their effectiveness in stimulating and supporting cross-industry technological innovations in the maritime domain. In particular, useful lessons could be drawn from examination of the role of central and regional governments in the clusters' innovation activities in terms of: the overall approach (e.g. "hands-on", "hands-off" or "enabling"); concrete measures such as financial support, incentives, de-risking; participation in the creation of requisite research infrastructures; or support for public/private and inter-firm co-operation and networks in order to promote a more efficient use of public and private resources and competences in innovation activity.
- Explore pathways for scaling up national maritime-cluster innovation schemes to international level, promoting network creation and collaboration among national clusters on specific maritime technology programmes around common sea basins and shared oceans; also, encourage alliances and bilateral agreements, not only with neighbouring clusters but also with more distant clusters where opportunities for co-operation are particularly rich.
- Initiate the creation of international networks for the exchange of views and experience with establishing centres of excellence, innovation incubators, etc. in the field of cross-industry maritime technologies, focusing in particular on key generic and enabling technologies.

2. Support efforts to accelerate more extensive mapping of the ocean floor

Why is it important?

A major impediment to our understanding and monitoring of environmental changes due to climate change, of the dynamics of marine ecosystems and of the ocean environment more generally, is a lack of knowledge of the ocean floor, particularly of the deep ocean. Recent advances in satellite altimeter technology and data management have made it possible to map the submarine topography of the planet's entire seafloor, but the resolution of this global data is low – 1.5 kilometres – and therefore short on detail. Mapping for much greater detail is a different matter. To date, only about 5% of the global ocean floor has been mapped in high resolution (usually by modern multi-beam sonar systems), and much of that is in national (EEZs) rather than in international waters. Biochemical, biological, habitat and deep-sea terrain mapping are much less developed and less widespread. Yet more detailed mapping is a critical tool in many respects: for detecting and observing at finer scales and at greater accuracies the undulations and composition of the seafloor; acquiring more detailed knowledge of entire marine ecosystems; protecting and tracking marine life; identifying natural resources, and regulating subsea resource exploration, extraction and equipment; siting offshore wind farms and marine aquaculture installations; preparing the terrain for hydrocarbon drilling operations and so on. Several major mapping initiatives are underway or planned, but mapping the remaining 95% is a Herculean task and would take many years to perform. The potential benefits of wider-scale mapping are huge, but prioritising the process is enormously challenging.

What should be done?

- Support international collaborative efforts led by international organisations (e.g. the International Hydrographic Organisation and the Intergovernmental Oceanographic Commission) and multilateral collaborations (e.g. the Atlantic Ocean Research Alliance) to map the ocean floor, notably in international waters and in the deep ocean, with a view to better understanding the physical and ecological consequences of climate change for marine biodiversity and key ocean services.
- Promote efforts to identify, explore and mitigate the barriers – economic, technical, legal, political – which hamper international co-operation in the sharing of existing seafloor mapping results among public institutions, research establishments and companies (e.g. oil and gas, offshore wind, seabed mining) active in ocean floor mapping, and explore the possibilities for pooling bathymetric and related data into data hubs accessible to the public.

3. Improve the sharing of technology and innovation among countries at different levels of development

Why is it important?

In all regions and at all levels of development, science, technology and innovation are prerequisites for sustainable long-term development. This applies no less to ocean industries, especially where they are a strategically important component of economic and social development. Particularly for developing countries with ocean-based activities, the creation, acquisition and adaptation of innovations in marine/maritime science and technology is a vital ingredient of efforts to tackle development challenges. Hence, advanced countries have an important responsibility to support developing countries, and in some cases also emerging economies, in the development of their scientific infrastructure and their policy capabilities in ocean-related activities. But in reality, the process can be a two-way street. Developed countries can benefit from the experience of emerging economies, for example, which may be less constrained by institutional and other "legacy" structures in building their science and innovation systems. Or from developing countries where century-old practices may embody useful knowledge for reshaping products and processes in modern business environments. The emphasis needs to be on capacity building and the creation of sustainable business opportunities in partnership with developing countries and the development of technologies that are appropriate to the sustainability challenges such countries face. Knowledge markets and networks can play an important role in the transfer of knowledge.

What should be done?

- Identify effective mechanisms and forums for the international sharing of good practices in the governance, design and implementation of innovation policy within the field of marine/maritime science and technology, among countries at different levels of development. Such mechanisms may include, for example, bilateral agreements, co-funding arrangements, collaborative projects, contract research and exchange of researchers. What is increasingly required, however, is also a better understanding of how knowledge markets and networks can facilitate access to the globalising knowledge market, supporting knowledge flows and transfers of intellectual property through such institutions as technology transfer offices, business incubators and multi-sector service provision centres.
- Promote collaboration among regional and national maritime industry clusters as a means of knowledge and best practice transfer. Where developing seafaring nations have no maritime clusters, governments should explore the potential advantages of helping create such clusters, in collaboration with industry and research, with a view to fostering innovation and technology exchange both within the country and with partner countries.

2. Strengthen integrated ocean management

As noted above, ocean activities are considered essential to meet future global challenges. However, pressures on the ocean environment – including over-fishing, pollution and habitat destruction – have continued to mount, not least as a consequence of growing ocean use. These pressures can be attributed partly to lack of knowledge and data on ocean processes and the impact of ocean industry activity, partly to a lack of effective management tools, and partly to what is historically a sector-by-sector based management of marine activities.

As stated above, recent years have seen a significant increase in the number of countries and regions putting in place strategic policy frameworks for better ocean management within their EEZs. However, given the acceleration expected in the use of the ocean and its resources over the coming years, it will be essential to step up both the effectiveness and the geographic spread of integrated ocean management around the world.

Three avenues could be pursued to achieve more effective and more widespread use of integrated ocean management: 1) make better use of economic analysis and economic instruments; 2) improve data collection, management and integration; 3) promote more innovation in governance structures, processes and stakeholder engagement.

1. Make better use of economic analysis and economic instruments in integrated ocean management

The ocean's natural assets and ecosystem services are an integral component of the ocean economy. Despite a growing body of research on identifying those assets and services as well as understanding and quantifying their contribution to the well-being and prosperity of humankind, our knowledge of the field remains quite poor. Similarly, while research into the complexities of the ocean environment and human activity therein has grown in recent years, prioritisation decisions on research investment have generally been guided by scientific interest without additional consideration of their potential economic utility, not least because cost-benefit analysis of investment in ocean observation and research is not well developed. Furthermore, management of activities in the ocean space has hitherto not made optimal use of economic instruments in its endeavours to achieve better outcomes and resolve potential conflicts among users of the ocean and its resources. On the contrary, management of the ocean environment has so far been dominated by the regulatory approach. Yet economists have long argued that market-based incentives, which apply monetary values, can in some cases be more efficient for environmental management than those based on "command-and-control" approaches (see Chapter 9).

Steps to address these issues are proposed below.

Improve measurement and valuation of the ocean's natural resources and ecosystem services

Why is it important?

Many ecosystem services are essential for human well-being, health, livelihoods and survival. Their degradation and the loss of biodiversity jeopardise their ability to maintain the flow of ecosystem services for present and future generations. Placing a value on ecosystem services in monetary units is key to communicating the importance of ecosystems and biodiversity to policy makers. Valuation can make for more efficient use of limited funds, and can offer guidance on user preferences and the relative value that current generations attach to ecosystem services. It can also help underpin decisions on the allocation of resources between competing uses. While substantial progress is being made towards circumscribing and valuing the role of ocean-based industries within the ocean economy, the route to valuing the ocean's natural resources and ecosystem services and measuring their economic contribution is proving infinitely more complex. In particular, assessments of ocean ecosystem services suffer from: limitations in data availability and reliability, a focus on specific regions and biomes, heterogeneity of conceptual models of values and differences in costing approaches.

What should be done?

- Work towards more comprehensive data collection and better accounting for the public goods and services provided by marine ecosystems as a tool for improving decision making and sustainable ecosystem management.
- Examine possibilities for improving methodologies to capture better the value of the ocean's natural assets and ecosystem services.
- In light of the growing body of knowledge on the interdependencies that exist within the ocean economy between ocean-based economic activities on the one hand and marine ecosystem assets and services on the other, explore how

alternative models of economic development might help attain a better balance between developing ocean use and preserving ocean health.

Evaluate the economic effectiveness of public investment in marine research and observation

Why is it important?

Fundamental scientific understanding of the ocean – its properties and behaviour, its health, role in climate change and influence on weather, etc. – is essential for understanding and managing ocean ecosystems. Equally, it is a vital pre-requisite for the sustainable operation of all ocean-based industries. Ocean observation therefore is a cornerstone of ocean science. A raft of infrastructures is required to perform modern ocean observation, including *inter alia*: ocean-going research vessels and autonomous systems collecting *in situ* data; satellite remote sensing, communications and global positioning; floating, submersible and fixed platforms and systems; modelling and computational infrastructure, as well as big data storage and management. At the international level, much is already being done via, for example, the work of UNESCO and the Intergovernmental Oceanographic Commission, the UN's Global Ocean Observation System (GOOS), the Census of Marine Life, as well as regional initiatives (e.g. Euro-Argo, the European Multidisciplinary Seafloor and water-column Observatory, and AtlantOS). Much of the investment in the research, data collection and infrastructure comes from public money. While numerous ocean observation initiatives have evaluated the effectiveness of their contribution to scientific fields of endeavour (such as ocean meteorology, measuring acidification, etc.), little effort has been undertaken to assess the economic value of the data produced. Yet, knowledge of that economic value could help generate much greater interest and financial participation in ocean research, and also help direct and, in some cases, prioritise research efforts.

What should be done?

- Initiate pilot projects, involving international collaboration of ocean research agencies, stakeholders and users, to explore the feasibility of assessing the economic value of ocean-related data. In a first phase, a selection of available and suitable data value chains could serve as case studies.

Strengthen the use of economic instruments and maritime and coastal spatial planning

Why is it important?

Economic instruments are designed to address the externalities associated with the use of natural resources by, for example, applying price-based instruments such as taxes, charges, user fees, individually transferable quotas, subsidies, payments for ecosystems and biodiversity offsets (e.g. habitat banking). Such economic tools are useful especially in cases of competing claims for ocean space and the search for an appropriate balance between use of maritime space and protection of the ocean and coastal environment. However, lack of data on economic and environmental parameters, coupled with high data-processing costs and the patchy implementation of spatial management to date, have meant that economic instruments have so far been underutilised in the ocean environment context. As a result, decision making and management have not been as effective and cost-efficient as they could be.

This is beginning to change, as non-market valuation methods (e.g. choice experiments, travel cost methods) have begun to generate increasingly robust values associated with ecosystem services. However, while there are numerous examples of their successful application, their use in the marine spatial context remains on the whole underdeveloped.

What should be done?

- Encourage the diffusion and implementation of economic tools in marine spatial planning by establishing international platforms for the exchange of knowledge, experience and best practice. In addition to marine economists, participants in such platforms should include marine environmental scientists and representatives of government agencies, regulators and users.
- Enhance integration of the temporal dimension into ocean management through the use of foresight techniques, thereby ensuring that planning and management benefit from advance knowledge of likely future changes both in the ocean environment and in ocean economic activities.

2. Improve data collection, management and integration

Why is it important?

In order to develop, assess and communicate ocean management processes, scientists and policy makers require data to develop and implement appropriate, effective and measurable indicators that assess performance in relation to stated goals and objectives. Effective implementation is highly dependent on scientific knowledge about the marine environment and the actual and potential impacts of human activities upon it. Considerable emphasis is therefore placed upon the need for data gathering, monitoring and evaluation to improve the knowledge of a poorly understood environment.

The last decade has seen an explosion in the amount of data generated across all aspects of life. The processing costs associated with data are declining, while cloud infrastructure increases, enabling open source technologies at scale. At the same time, advances in application programme interface (API), data-processing algorithms and machine learning ensure that data may be turned into actionable insights.

However, integrated ocean management faces huge data challenges. These range from lack of knowledge as to what is actually in the ocean or how different uses and users interact in the ocean, to the ocean dynamics of climate change and the fragmentation of data. The tools available for data collection and ocean monitoring have increased significantly over the last decade and include ship missions, landers and observatories, vehicles, autonomous underwater vehicles (AUV) and satellites. However, while these tools are the current state-of-the-art in marine monitoring, the relatively high costs of these platforms limit their spatial and temporal density. Accordingly, the benefits of data obtained – for example, from space-based technology – have never quite reached a "tipping point" where the value of their contribution makes them indispensable to marine monitoring. Hence, new cost-effective methods and technologies for collecting data are required that capture the uncertainty, complexity and change associated with the marine environment.

What should be done?

- Develop effective but flexible data-collection frameworks involving: regular and sustained engagement of experts in a broad range of natural and social sciences and user knowledge; the identification of the best scales for collecting and reporting data; a coherent framework for analysis; the development of user-friendly, open-source, efficient and transparent tools for data visualisation, integration and sharing; and a set of clear, reliable and measurable indicators for monitoring the effectiveness of ocean management in terms of achieving objectives set during the planning process.
- Develop a flexible, integrated data commons for the evaluation and monitoring processes. Such a data commons involves, for example, better data integration and sharing, easier access, geo-referenced data and virtually interconnected interoperable systems. Using the best-available data, measurable objectives of the plan should be linked to distinct indicators and targets at each step, which can be refined over time.
- Monitor the research, development and innovation landscape for upcoming technological developments that could be utilised in the preparation, implementation and evaluation of integrated ocean management schemes. Specifically in the marine/maritime field, a range of highly sophisticated technologies is currently in the pipeline which could lead to major improvements in data collection and management. These include, for example, high-performance sensors, underwater vehicles, rapid advances in imaging and mapping technologies, bio-based traceability tools and the growing use of low-cost customised micro-satellites. However, major changes in some of the leading-edge technologies are likely to occur outside marine-based science and technology. Hence, particular attention needs to be paid to inter-disciplinary research and development which will play an essential role in better integration of data-gathering technology in marine planning and monitoring.

3. Promote more innovation in governance structures, processes and stakeholder engagement to improve integrated ocean management

Why is it important?

Integrated ocean management is essentially a political process. It requires co-ordination across government as well as the engagement of all relevant stakeholders – scientists, business, user industries and associations – in the process. However, given their long history of sector-based approaches, current governance structures are usually not well suited to handle these co-ordination and consultation tasks effectively across sectors, especially where resources are moveable and renewable and/or stationary and mostly non-renewable. Different bureaucracies are usually in charge of handling the permitting for different uses and users, but they tend not to co-operate well, if at all. As noted above, moving from sector-by-sector management to integrated modes of ocean management constitutes a major institutional challenge.

There are broadly accepted elements in the ocean management process. In marine spatial planning (MSP), for example, guidance published by UNESCO in 2009 and recently updated shows a systematic process, beginning with preparatory steps, such as defining the objectives of a marine plan, analysing existing conditions, including the mapping of maritime activities, deciding on a preferred spatial scenario and approving the final plan. Stakeholder engagement is integrated into the overall process. Similarly, there exists an integrated coastal zone management (ICZM) protocol for the Mediterranean which is being adapted and applied to other sea basins.

But there is no single, recognised process for carrying out integrated ocean management or for co-ordinating across government or for engaging stakeholders. Practices vary from place to place, due to different geographies, marine pressures, legal requirements, planning cultures and so on.

Moreover, wider and deeper consultation with stakeholders cuts both ways: it can strengthen considerably the legitimacy of the planning, but it can also considerably lengthen the duration of the planning and permitting processes. Meanwhile, however, maritime space will rapidly become more crowded as the ocean economy continues to grow at a fast pace.

<u>What should be done?</u>

- Efforts to improve communication and co-operation across government departments and agencies involved in integrated ocean management should be stepped up. While not necessarily fully transferable, lessons can be drawn from successful structural and procedural reforms that governments have conducted around the world to expedite processes for MSPs, ICZMs and marine protected areas (MPAs). Also outside of the marine domain, governments have made significant progress in joined-up government approaches (e.g. in the management of major risks) and stronger strategic centre-of-government roles, thereby providing a rich pool of experience from which to draw.
- The effectiveness of stakeholder's participation in ecosystem-based ocean management needs to be supported by the best available scientific knowledge. This can be achieved through the organisation of open panels, peer reviewing of documents, and strong scientific guidance, able to incorporate and organise the needed scrutiny of contributions from research groups, non-governmental organisations (NGOs), private players and local communities.
- Innovative mechanisms should be developed to allow for speedier implementation of what is becoming an increasingly complex stakeholder consultation context. Again, international comparison of experience and good practice in such matters offers significant opportunities, as the timespans for widespread consultation appear to vary considerably from country to country and setting to setting. For large stakeholder communities, use of sophisticated media technologies, online consultation tools, social networks and local action plans offer promising avenues to be explored.
- Particular attention should be paid to the governance of the deep ocean, which offers significant opportunities for cross-disciplinary, multi-sectoral and multi-stakeholder stewardship both with and beyond national jurisdictions.

3. Improve the statistical and methodological base at national and international level for measuring the scale and performance of ocean-based industries and their contribution to the overall economy

Why is it important?

Putting a value on ocean-based industries raises public awareness of their importance, offering them higher visibility. It raises awareness among policy makers, rendering the industries more amenable to policy action; it enables progress in their development to be tracked over time; it also enables their contribution to the overall economy to be tracked in monetary and employment terms; and it lends weight to the perception of ocean-based industries as an increasingly interconnected set of activities whose defining common denominator is the ocean, its use and its resources. Moreover, as ocean-based activities and particularly the emerging ocean industries continue to grow, competition around the globe will intensify, making it essential for governments and businesses to be able to compare and position the national ocean economy at international level. However, official, internationally consistent and harmonised datasets for the world's ocean industries are not well developed and exist only for a limited number of industries. For emerging ocean industries, global statistical coverage is particularly poor.

What should be done?

- Encourage government agencies and services to step up efforts to improve national statistical data sets, particularly regarding emerging ocean-based industries, including through closer collaboration with non-official sources (maritime clusters, business associations, research institutions, NGOs) with a view to adjusting and incorporating new data into national statistical frameworks.
- Further develop the OECD's *Ocean Economy Database* by: 1) consolidating and updating relevant ocean-industry data in an internationally comparable framework; 2) improving data verification and calculation methods; 3) extending where feasible the range of ocean-related activities to include *inter alia* marine/maritime education and research, marine biotechnology, renewable ocean energy, marine business and financial services, maritime safety and surveillance; 4) mapping current and future demand for ocean-industry related skills; 5) refining the scenario methodologies; and 6) making the data available to stakeholders on a "one-stop-source" basis.
- Identify new and novel ocean-based activities of the future (e.g. management of ocean-scale marine protected areas; decommissioning of offshore oil and gas platforms).

4. Build more capacity for ocean industry foresight

Why is it important?

As an inter-connected ensemble of economic sectors operating at regional and global scale, it is essential for members of the ocean business community to be able to identify the long-term opportunities and risks facing their operations worldwide and to take their investment decisions accordingly. Equally, it is in the vital interests of governments of coastal states but also of many land-locked economies to understand the implications of an expanding ocean economy for the design and implementation of policy – policies that shape the competitiveness of their national maritime industries and which affect the health of oceans within their national jurisdiction and beyond. Other stakeholders in science, research and society more broadly have similar information requirements. Projections, scenarios, forecasts and future studies all can have their place in efforts to identify future issues, anticipate upcoming problems or opportunities, and support decision making.

What should be done?

- In light of the expanding economic use of the ocean, make greater and more regular use of foresight and other forward-looking techniques to help anticipate 10-20 years ahead the likely future development of ocean-based industries, assessing the likely impacts of their development on the ocean environment and paying attention not just to existing industries, but also to the emergence of new ocean-related activities.
- Conversely, continue to use foresight and other forward-looking techniques to assess the likely long-term impacts of future developments in the ocean environment – rising sea temperatures and sea levels, acidification, declining oxygen levels, shifts in currents and circulation patterns, loss of biomass and biodiversity, pollution especially from land sources, etc. – on ocean-based industries.
- Maintain and further refine the OECD's current capacity for modelling future trends in the ocean economy at global scale and ensure public accessibility of the results for governments, business and research.

Annex 1.A1.
Scope of the ocean-based industries

This report proposes the following scope for established and emerging ocean-based activities, bearing in mind earlier remarks about overlapping definitions. The following shows the complete list of definitions.

Established industries:

- "Capture fisheries": the economic activity related to catch production.
- "Seafood processing": processing and distribution of seafood and micro- and macro-algae. In other words, it is the economic activity related to the preparation and preservation of fish, crustaceans and molluscs; production of fishmeal for human consumption and animal feed; as well as processing of seaweed.
- "Offshore oil and gas in shallow water": exploration and extraction of crude petroleum and natural gas from shallow-water offshore sources, including the operation and maintenance of equipment as well as exploration services related to this activity.
- "Shipping": the transportation of freight and passengers through the ocean, cargo handling, renting and leasing of water transport equipment and other services incidental to shipping and water transport.
- "Ports": the operation and management of ports, such as storage, loading and unloading activities.
- "Shipbuilding and repair": the manufacturing, repair and maintenance of ships, boats, offshore platforms and offshore supply vessels. Offshore platforms are the facilities that explore and develop oil and gas in the ocean, such as floating storage and offloading vessels (FPSO), fixed platforms, spars, Tension Leg Platform and so on. Offshore supply vessels (OSVs), which are offshore support vessels, are special vessels to support offshore oil and gas exploration and production. The reason for including offshore platforms and OSVs in this sector is that some shipbuilders produce offshore platforms as well as ships.
- "Marine manufacturing and construction": the industry that provides goods to multiple sectors. It can be defined as the economic activity that includes the manufacturing of marine equipment and materials, such as machinery, valves, cables, sensors, ship materials, aquaculture supplies and so on. Marine construction denotes the economic activity that is related to construction in the ocean (seabed cables, pipelines, etc.) and marine-related engineering, such as port development and construction.

- "Maritime and coastal tourism, including cruise industry": all tangible and direct facilities of ocean-related tourism and leisure activities, such as marine sports, recreational fishing, aquariums, excursions to underwater cultural habitats, etc., restaurants, hotels and seaside accommodation and campgrounds located in a place near or adjoining the coast. In addition, new forms and destinations of maritime tourism, such as Antarctic and Arctic cruise shipping, are also included in this sector.
- "Marine business services": the economic activities related to services that support ocean industries. The sub-sectors under it are marine insurance and finance, marine consulting, rental, technical services, inspection and survey, labour supply services and others related to this activity.
- "Marine R&D and education": activities relating to research and development, education and training. Even though research and development and education are different from one other, they are integrated into one sector, because in general the same organisations, such as a universities and research institutes, perform these activities.
- "Coastal flood defences": construction and management activities designed to protect coastlines from increasing coastal erosion and flooding due to changing sea levels. Strictly speaking, this is not an activity conducted in the ocean or in support of ocean industries, and so is often excluded from definitions of the ocean economy.

Emerging industries:

- "Marine aquaculture": the farm production of seafood and micro- and macro-algae.
- "Ultra-deep and deep water oil and gas": the economic activity related to the exploration and extraction of crude petroleum and natural gas from offshore sources, and includes the operation and maintenance of equipment as well as exploration services related to this activity.
- "Offshore wind energy": the production of wind energy by generating electricity offshore. The construction of wind parks in marine waters is included in shipbuilding since offshore wind parks are produced by shipbuilders.
- "Ocean renewable energy": the production of ocean renewable energy, such as tidal energy, wave energy, osmotic energy and ocean thermal energy conservation (OTEC).
- "Marine and seabed mining": the production, extraction and processing of non-living resources in seabed or seawater. This includes minerals and metals from the seabed (in the deep sea), diamonds in estuary waters, marine aggregates (limestone, sand and gravel) and seawater dissolved minerals extraction.
- "Maritime safety and surveillance" describes the economic activity related to products and services in different maritime domains, ranging from pollution and fisheries control to search and rescue, customs and costal defence by government and public or private organisations.

- "Marine biotechnology": the economic activity related to "[t]he application of science and technology to living organisms from marine resources, as well as parts, products and models thereof, to alter living or non-living materials for the production of knowledge, goods and services".[1]
- "High-tech marine products and services": diverse areas such as advanced sensing and communications, data management and informatics, marine robotics and artificial intelligence, materials sciences and marine engineering. These technologies support activity in a number of marine sectors such as oil and gas, transport and shipping, fisheries and aquaculture, coastal tourism and safety, security and surveillance. They also underpin development in emerging sectors such as marine renewable energy, marine environmental monitoring and resource management.
- "Others" signifies economic activities not classified above but nonetheless in the course of development, e.g. seawater desalination for fresh water usage (agriculture irrigation, consumer and commercial use) and carbon capture storage.

1. The OECD general definition for biotechnology, which is available at www.oecd.org/health/biotech/statisticaldefinitionofbiotechnology.htm, has emerged as a global standard according to the workshop "The Long-Term Potential of Marine Biotechnology").

Annex 1.A2.
Measuring the value of marine ecosystems

Estimates of the size of the benefits of marine ecosystem services suggest that these are considerable. De Groot et al. (2012) provide global estimates of a number of ecosystems and services, including for open oceans, coral reefs, coastal systems, and coastal and inland wetlands. They find that the total value of ecosystem services ranges from USD 490/year[1] for the total bundle of ecosystem services that can potentially be provided by an "average" hectare of open oceans, to almost USD 350 000/year for the potential services provided by an "average" hectare of coral reefs. Even the global value of individual natural capital assets, such as corals, is estimated at nearly USD 797.4 billion (Cesar, Burke and Pet-Soede, 2003). In some tourist destinations, the value of coral reefs can be up to USD 1 million per hectare and year, as is the case for Hawaii (Cesar, Burke and Pet-Soede, 2003). Another example for estimating the value of ecosystem services comes from carbon sequestration. The Global Ocean Commission (GOC) estimates the global economic value of carbon sequestration associated with seas and oceans to range between USD 74 billion and USD 222 billion per year (GOC, 2014). These numbers make clear that the contribution of marine and coastal ecosystems to the overall value of the ocean economy is very large indeed.

Ecosystem services range from tangible to intangible services (e.g. food production versus aesthetic value), which are sometimes separated into "goods" and "services". As Table 1.A2.1 indicates, marine and coastal ecosystem services can be divided into four categories: supporting, regulating, provisioning and cultural (De Groot, Wilson and Boumans, 2002).

Table 1.A2.1. **Marine and coastal ecosystem services**

Ecosystem service	Definition	Marine and coastal examples
Supporting	Ecosystem functions that support and enable the maintenance and delivery of other services	Photosynthesis, nutrient cycling, soil, sediment, sand formation
Regulating	Natural regulation of ecosystem processes and natural cycles	Water regulation, natural hazard weather regulation, carbon sequestration, shoreline stabilisation
Provisioning	Raw materials, food and energy	Raw materials (e.g. seabed deposits, such as manganese nodules, cobalt crusts and solid massive sulphides, sand, pearls, diamonds), food production (e.g. fisheries and aquaculture), energy (e.g. offshore wind, ocean energy, offshore oil and gas) Genetic resources (source of unique biological materials, and processes of industrial interest)
Cultural	Benefits related with experiences of natural environments	Tourism, recreation, spiritual values, education, aesthetics

Source: Adapted from De Groot, Wilson and Boumans (2002).

Putting an economic value on the contribution of ocean-based industries is difficult enough; it is even more difficult to identify and value ecosystems and their provision of goods and services (Barbier et al. 2011; Polasky and Segerson, 2009). The values that are attributed to ecosystem services depend on the stakeholders that benefit from these services (Vermeulen and Korziell, 2002). These values include both use and non-use values.

Use values arise when ecosystem services are used in a direct manner, whether in an extractive way (e.g. for income or food) or in a non-extractive way (e.g. for observation or recreation). Non-use values, on the other hand, reflect a valuing of indirect services, notably for the supporting and regulating functions of ecosystems, such as maintaining water quality and community traditions (indirect use). Non-use values also include what are called "option value" and "existence value" – the former being the value of knowing now that we are maintaining the potential to provide ecosystem services in the future, while the latter reflects the value of the ecosystem services due to their mere existence, independently of anyone's current or future uses of these services.

Quantifying non-use values is particularly complicated. However, economists have developed a variety of methods to estimate the value of goods whose market is either imperfect or non-existent. These include revealed preference and stated preference methods.[2] A useful reference to the economic valuations of ecosystems undertaken as part of the Millennium Ecosystem Assessment and The Economics of Ecosystems and Biodiversity (TEEB) exercise is TEEB (2011) edited by Brink. Since then, a comprehensive set of background papers and sectoral and country studies have become available (Kubiszewski et al., 2013; McVittie and Hussain, 2013; Russi et al., 2013).

Despite the efforts alluded to above, valuing ecosystem services remains challenging. It is an underdeveloped field, and the kind of techniques referred to here are neither widely deployed around the world nor well integrated into assessment and evaluation exercises. Recently initiated national efforts to address these gaps (for example in France, the Netherlands and the United Kingdom) are therefore to be welcomed. Looking to the future, valuation of ecosystem services must be considered a cornerstone in any effective strategy for managing the balance between human activity and the health of the ocean. As the European Union's Marine Strategy Framework Directive states, "applying an ecosystem-based approach to the management of human activities means ensuring that the collective pressure of such activities is kept within levels compatible with the achievement of good environmental status and that the capacity of marine ecosystems to respond to human-induced changes is not compromised, while enabling the sustainable use of marine goods and services by present and future generations."

In conclusion, while the main focus of this report is on ocean-based industries and activities, it is important to also bear in mind that the ocean's natural assets and ecosystem services are an integral part of the ocean economy. The project testifies to their importance by highlighting marine ecosystem aspects throughout the report, while at the same time recognising the need to intensify efforts to better understand and value ocean ecosystems.

Notes

1. Values converted to a common set of units, namely 2007 "international" dollars/year, i.e. translated into USD values on the basis of purchasing power parity.

2. Revealed preference methods estimate the demand for an ecosystem's goods and services through statistical analysis of individuals' willingness to incur costs related to benefits from the goods and services obtained. This method includes the travel cost method (TCM), Hedonic Price (HP) approach and averting behaviour approach (Koundouri, 2009). The common underlying feature is a functional dependency of environmental benefits on the consumption of a specific market good (weak substitutability). Cultural and recreational values are often measured by using this method. The stated preference method is based on surveys and questionnaires to measure in a constructed or hypothetical market the stakeholder's willingness to pay to enjoy and/or protect an ecosystem (Koundouri, 2009). Stated preference approaches include the Contingent Valuation Method (CVM) and Choice Experiments (CE).

References

Barbier, E. et al. (2011), "The value of estuarine and coastal ecosystem services", *Ecological Monographs*, Vol. 81, No. 2, pp. 169-193, http://dx.doi.org/10.1890/10-1510.1.

Bekkers, E., J.F. Francois and H. Rojas-Romagosa (2015), "Melting ice caps and the economic impact of opening the Northern Route", *CPB Discussion Paper 307*, CPB Netherlands Bureau for Economic Policy Analysis, www.cpb.nl/en/publication/melting-ice-caps-and-the-economic-impact-of-opening-the-northern-sea-route.

Cesar, H., L. Burke and L. Pet-Soede (2003), "The economics of worldwide coral reef degradation", Cesar Environmental Economics Consulting (CEEC), Arnhem, Netherlands.

Crowder, L. and E. Norse (2008), "Essential ecological insights for marine ecosystem-based management and marine spatial planning", *Marine Policy*, Vol. 32, No. 5, September, pp. 772-778, http://dx.doi.org/10.1016/j.marpol.2008.03.012.

De Groot, R., M.A. Wilson and R.M.J. Boumans (2002), "A typology for the classification, description and valuation of ecosystem functions, goods, and services", *Ecological Economics*, Vol. 41, No. 3, pp. 393-408, http://dx.doi.org/10.1016/S0921-8009(02)00089-7.

De Groot, R. et al. (2012), "Global estimates of the value of ecosystems and their services in monetary units", *Ecosystem Services*, Vol. 1, No. 1, pp. 50-61, http://dx.doi.org/10.1016/j.ecoser.2012.07.005.

Douvere, F. (2008), "The importance of marine spatial planning in advancing ecosystem-based sea use management", *Marine Policy*, Vol. 32, No. 5, September, pp. 762-771, http://dx.doi.org/10.1016/j.marpol.2008.03.021.

Douvere, F. et al. (2007), "The role of marine spatial planning in sea use management: The Belgian case", *Marine Policy*, Vol. 31, No. 2, March, pp. 182-191, http://dx.doi.org/10.1016/j.marpol.2006.07.003.

Ecorys (2012), "Blue growth: Scenarios and drivers for sustainable growth from the oceans, seas and coasts", Third Interim Report, Rotterdam/Brussels, 13 March, available at: http://ec.europa.eu/maritimeaffairs/documentation/studies/documents/blue_growth_third_interim_report_en.pdf.

Ehler, C. and F. Douvere (2007), *Visions for a Sea Change. Report of the First International Workshop on Marine Spatial Planning, Intergovernmental Oceanographic Commission and Man and the Biosphere Programme*, UNESCO iOC, Paris.

FAO (2015), *Global Aquaculture Production Database*, www.fao.org/fishery/statistics/global-aquaculture-production/en.

German Bioeconomy Council (2015), "International bioeconomy strategies", www.biooekonomierat.de/en.

GOC (2014), "From decline to recovery, rescue package for the global ocean", Global Ocean Commission, Oxford, United Kingdom, www.globaloceancommission.org/wp-content/uploads/GOC_Report_20_6.FINAL_.spreads.pdf.

Grilo, C. (2015), "Land versus sea", note prepared for OECD project on The Future of the Ocean Economy.

IEA (2014), "World oil statistics", IEA Oil Information Statistics, http://dx.doi.org/10.1787/oil-data-en.

Kaiser, B. and J. Roumasset (2002), "Valuing indirect ecosystem services: The case of tropical watersheds", *Environment and Development Economics*, No. 4, pp. 701-714, http://dx.doi.org/10.1017/S1355770X02000426.

Koundouri, P. (ed.) (2009), *The Use of Economic Valuation in Environmental Policy: Providing Research Support for the Implementation of EU Water Policy Under Aquastress*, Routledge, Taylor and Francis Group.

Kubiszewski, I. et al. (2013), "An initial estimate of the value of ecosystem services in Bhutan", *Ecosystem Services*, Vol. 3, March, pp. e11-e21, http://dx.doi.org/10.1016/j.ecoser.2012.11.004.

Levander, O. (2015), "Towards unmanned ships", presentation for Rolls-Royce at "Ship Efficiency the Event 2015", London, 8 September 2015, www.globalmaritimehub.com/custom/domain_2/extra_files/attach_639.pdf.

Lloyd's Register (2014), "Global marine fuel trends 2030", Lloyd's Register Global Technology Centre, London, www.lr.org/en/_images/213-34172_Global_Marine_Fuel_Trends_2030.pdf.

McVittie A. and S.S. Hussain (2013), *The Economics of Ecosystems and Biodiversity – Valuation Database Manual*, The Economics of Ecosystems & Biodiversity, December.

Norse, E. and L. Crowder (eds.) (2005), *Marine Conservation Biology: The Science of Maintaining the Sea's Biodiversity*, Island Press.

OECD (2015), "*Oversupply in the shipbuilding industry*", www.oecd.org/sti/ind/shipbuilding.htm.

OECD (2014), *OECD Tourism Trends and Policies 2014*, OECD Publishing, Paris, http://dx.doi.org/10.1787/tour-2014-en.

OECD (2011), *The Space Economy at a Glance 2011*, OECD Publishing, Paris, http://dx.doi.org/10.1787/9789264111790-en.

OECD (2009), *The Bioeconomy to 2030: Designing a Policy Agenda*, OECD Publishing, Paris, http://dx.doi.org/10.1787/9789264056886-en.

OECD (2007), *Infrastructure to 2030 (Vol. 2): Mapping for Electricity, Water and Transport*, OECD Publishing, Paris, http://dx.doi.org/10.1787/9789264031326-en.

OECD and FAO (2015), *OECD-FAO Agricultural Outlook 2015*, OECD Publishing, Paris, http://dx.doi.org/10.1787/agr_outlook-2015-en.

OECD STAN, *OECD STAN Database for Structural Analysis*, http://stats.oecd.org/Index.aspx?DatasetCode=STAN08BIS&lang=en.

Park, K.S. (2014), "A study on rebuilding the classification system of the ocean economy", Center for the Blue Economy in Monterey Institute of International

Studies, Monterey, California, available at: http://centerfortheblueeconomy.org/wp-content/uploads/2014/11/10.29.14.park_.kwangseo.the_ocean_economy_classification_systemfinal_21.pdf.

Polasky S. and K. Segerson (2009), "Integrating ecology and economics in the study of ecosystem services: Some lessons learned", *Annual Review Resource Economics*, Vol. 1, pp. 409-434, http://dx.doi.org/10.1146/annurev.resource.050708.144110.

Russi, D. et al. (2013), *The Economics of Ecosystems and Biodiversity for Water and Wetlands*, IEEP, London and Brussels, Ramsar Secretariat, Gland, available at: http://doc.teebweb.org/wp-content/uploads/2013/04/TEEB_WaterWetlands_Report_2013.pdf.

SEA (2015), *2014 Market Forecast Report*, SEA Europe, Ships & Maritime Equipment Association, available at: www.seaeurope.eu/template.asp?f=publications.asp&jaar=2015.

TEEB (2011), *The Economics of Ecosystems and Biodiversity in National and International Policy Making*, edited by Patrick ten Brink, Earthscan, London and Washington.

UNIDO INDSTAT, INDSTAT 4, *ISIC Rev. 3 Database*, https://stat.unido.org.

UNSD, National Accounts Official Country Data, http://data.un.org.

Vermeulen, S. and I. Korziell (2002), "Integrating global and local values: A review of biodiversity assessment", *IIED Natural Resource Issues Paper No. 3*, *Biodiversity and Livelihoods Issues Paper No. 5*, International Institute for Environment and Development, London, available at: http://pubs.iied.org/pdfs/9100IIED.pdf.

World Bank (2013), "Fish to 2030: Prospects for fisheries and aquaculture", *Agriculture and Environmental Services Discussion Paper 03*, World Bank, Washington, DC, available at: http://documents.worldbank.org/curated/en/2013/12/18882045/fish-2030-prospects-fisheries-aquaculture.

Part I.

Global trends and macro-factors influencing the ocean economy

Chapter 2.

Global trends and uncertainties to 2030/2060

The ocean economy is key to the future welfare and prosperity of humankind. But unsustainable use of the ocean and its resources threatens the very basis on which much of that welfare and prosperity depend. This chapter briefly outlines a range of critical global factors and underlying changes which, individually and in combination with one another, are playing their part in shaping the overall context within which the balancing act between ocean use and sustainability is likely to evolve over the coming decades. It is not the aim of this chapter to forecast the future or present a particular scenario. Projections and scenarios are developed elsewhere in this report. Rather, this chapter provides a backdrop for the report's discussion of future developments in the ocean environment and the ocean economy. It draws primarily, but not exclusively, on OECD materials to discuss key demographic, economic, social, environmental, technological and governance trends, as well as major uncertainties and risks, which could influence world developments and, by extension, that of the ocean economy.

A wide range of global trends and macro-factors are set to influence the longer term development of the ocean economy. Their combined effect is expected to cut both ways. While on the one hand many of them hold out the promise of expanding economic, social and health-related opportunities through ocean use, on the other hand, they point to a further increase in the pressures already weighing on the ocean's health. The most important trends and drivers are most likely to be related to the growth, structure and settlement patterns of the world's population; to global economic developments such as growth, rising incomes and international trade; to the effects of climate change; and to advances in science, technology and innovation. However, geopolitical factors and governance are also likely to play an important part in the longer run.

World population: Still growing, urbanising and ageing

The trends

On the United Nation's 2015 medium-variant projection, the world's population is expected to expand by over 1 billion people in the next 15 years, reaching 8.5 billion by 2030, and then to increase again by more than 1 billion, reaching 9.7 billion by 2050 (UN, 2015). The increase will take place almost entirely in developing countries and some emerging economies. In the developed world, some countries' populations will grow, while others decline, but the size of the aggregate population is likely to remain largely unchanged. Africa will account for more than half of the global population growth between now and 2050, followed by Asia, and then by North America, Latin America, the Caribbean and Oceania. Europe is expected to have a smaller population by mid-century than it had in 2015.

More than half of the world's population is now living in urban areas. By the middle of the 21st century, the urban population will have doubled to almost 6.5 billion, i.e. some 66% of total world population. This growth in city populations will be spread unevenly across the planet. Almost all urban population growth will occur in cities of the developing regions of the world, with nearly 90% occurring in Asia and Africa. The fastest growing urban agglomerations are medium-sized cities and cities of less than 1 million inhabitants in Africa and Asia. In the high-income countries, by contrast, urban populations are projected to remain largely unchanged over the next two decades or so (UN, 2015).

The majority of the world's megacities (13 of the 20 most populated cities in 2005) are situated at the coasts. These port cities have high concentrations of global populations and assets and are a vital component of the global economy. Their economic importance in terms of international trade has grown markedly, particularly in developing countries, in line with globalisation and the rapid development of the newly industrialised countries (Nicholls et al., 2008).

However, population growth in coastal zones generates pressure on coastal ecosystems and natural resources through increased utilisation and pollution. Since the turn of the century, there has been a growing trend of migration towards coastal areas. The UN Atlas 2010 records that today about one in every three people on the planet lives within 100 kilometres (km) of the sea, and 44% of the world's population (more people than inhabited the entire globe in 1950) currently live within 150 km of the coast. Overall, average population density in coastal zones is three times higher than the world average, and in recent decades the overall growth of coastal populations has outstripped that of inland populations (Crawford Heitzmann, 2006). Projections suggest that these trends are set to continue in the years ahead. In deltas and flood plains, i.e. areas most exposed to flood risks, the population is expected to increase rapidly – by 50% between 2000 and 2030 according to Neumann et al. (2015).

Populations are also ageing. The share of the population over 65 years of age has been increasing in OECD countries over the past few decades. In 1960, 9% of the OECD population was over 65 years old, but the proportion rose to around 15% in 2010 (OECD, 2011a). This trend is expected to continue into the future, so that by 2050 the share of the population aged 65 or more is expected to reach 26% of the total OECD population. With rising life expectancy and improved healthcare, elderly citizens will be able to remain active longer, in many cases continuing to work well beyond the official retirement age.

Outside of the OECD area, the picture is mixed. On the whole, the less developed regions of the world still have young populations, a situation that is unlikely to change much before 2020, when ageing will become a more significant factor. Some of the larger emerging economies, however, are likely to be converging with OECD population-ageing profiles by mid-century. Projections for 2050 indicate that the share of those over 65 is heading for around 25% in the People's Republic of China (hereafter "China") and 23% in Brazil and the Russian Federation, closely followed by Argentina, Colombia and Indonesia with 18-19% (UN, 2011).

Risks and uncertainties

Long-term population projections inevitably contain an element of uncertainty, necessitating the use of numerous scenarios in order to be able to anticipate eventualities that may have a marked impact on population development over a period of say 50 years. The most widely used global population projection of the UN is the "medium" variant. But in fact, the UN develops several different scenarios which point to the possibility of very different population outcomes over the period under consideration here. For example, under the "low" variant of the UN's 2010 projections, the global population would, in fact, peak just before 2030 and start declining thereafter. The "high" variant, on the other hand, would see a very considerable increase in the global population over the coming decades (Figure 2.1).

Figure 2.1. **Total population scenario to 2050 (in hundred thousands)**

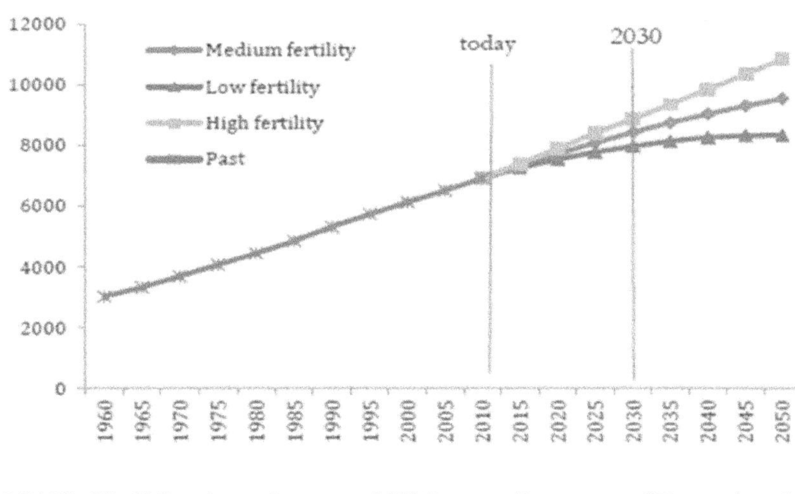

Source: UN (2011), *World Population Prospects, 2010 Revision,* Department of Economic and Social Affairs, Population Division © 2011 United Nations. Reprinted with the permission of the United Nations.

One of the key factors behind this range of projections is the different assumptions regarding fertility rates in 2025-30: 2.79 children per woman for the high-variant hypothesis, 2.29 for the medium-variant and 1.79 for the low-variant hypotheses. The result is a difference in total population between the two extremes of about 1 billion people for 2030, with almost 9 billion in the high-variant scenario and about 8 billion in the low-variant scenario.

Similarly, global shocks to the world population cannot be entirely ruled out. Pandemics are a case in point. It is not possible to predict the exact timing or nature of any future pandemic, but there seems to be agreement among experts that a new form of influenza A is the virus most likely to reach pandemic scale. The World Health Orgnization (WHO) estimates that a future H5N1 avian flu pandemic could lead to between 2 and 7.4 million deaths globally (OECD, 2011e). Needless to say, variations on the scale suggested by these examples could have important implications for food demand and the consumption of natural resources.

Some implications for the ocean economy

World population growth, urbanisation and intensifying coastal settlement (the preferred residential location for many elderly people) are all placing mounting strain on the ocean's health and state of its natural resources. Growing ocean pollution through sewage, fertiliser run-off from farming, disposal of plastic waste, increased exploitation of marine resources, etc. all weigh heavily on the ocean environment, with little prospect of a reversal of trends. By way of illustration, it is estimated that without improvements to waste management infrastructure, the cumulative quantity of plastic waste available to enter the ocean from land could increase by an order of magnitude by 2025 (Jambeck et al., 2015). At the same time, however, those very same population factors are at the heart of growth in the ocean economy, as they constitute an important driver of maritime activities. Expanding populations will need to be fed, raising demand for fish, molluscs and other marine foods; as consumers they will stimulate sea-borne freight and passenger traffic, shipbuilding and marine equipment manufacturing, as well as exploration for offshore oil and gas reserves. Ageing populations will continue to motivate the medical and pharmaceutical communities of the world to accelerate marine biotechnological research into new drugs and treatments.

Climate-ocean interactions

The trends

The Intergovernmental Panel on Climate Change (IPCC) indicates not only that there are intense physical climate-ocean interactions, but that the impact of these interactions might well have serious implications for human and economic development over the next century.

The IPCC's Fifth Assessment Report concludes that "Warming of the climate system is unequivocal, and since the 1950s, many of the observed changes are unprecedented over decades to millennia. The atmosphere and ocean have warmed, the amounts of snow and ice have diminished, sea level has risen, and the concentrations of greenhouse gases have increased" (IPCC, 2013). Specifically concerning ocean warming, the IPCC observes that "ocean warming dominates the increase in energy stored in the climate system, accounting for more than 90% of the energy accumulated between 1971 and 2010 (high confidence). It is virtually certain that the upper ocean (0-700 metres [m]) warmed from 1971 to 2010, and it likely warmed between the 1870s and 1971" (IPCC, 2013). On sea-level rise, the IPCC observes that “the rate of sea-level rise since the mid-19th century has been larger than the mean rate during the previous two millennia (high confidence). Over the period 1901 to 2010, global mean sea level rose by 0.19 [0.17 to 0.21]m” (IPCC, 2013). Views on expected changes to 2100 in ocean temperature, sea-level rise, acidification, etc. are set out in Chapter 3 of the present volume.

Without new policy action, and barring major economic setbacks, greenhouse gas (GHG) emissions are expected to continue to grow to 2050 (OECD, 2012). Energy- and industry-related emissions are projected to more than double over the same period compared to 1990 levels. Emissions from BRIICS countries (Brazil, Russian Federation, India, Indonesia, China and South Africa) will likely account for most of the increase, driven by rising populations and economic growth. In the OECD area, emissions are expected to grow at a slower pace, largely as a consequence of declining population numbers, slower economic growth and the effect of climate policies already in place. However, OECD countries will continue to lead the field in terms of emissions per capita. The OECD *Environmental Outlook to 2050: The Consequences of Inaction* notes that “A temperature increase of more than 2°C would alter precipitation patterns; increase glacier and permafrost melt; drive sea-level rise; worsen the intensity and frequency of extreme weather events such as heat waves, floods and hurricanes; and become the greatest driver of biodiversity loss” (OECD, 2012).

Against this background, the Paris Agreement at COP21 marks a historic step-change in the response to climate change. Key features of the agreement – an ambitious target for limiting the global temperature rise, a five-year review cycle, clear rules on transparency, a global goal for resilience and reducing vulnerability, and a framework for supporting developing countries – suggest a turning point has been reached. Yet, while the agreement does indeed constitute a vital framework for action, it is widely considered just the beginning of a long and hard road to a sustainable future.

Risks and uncertainties

There are massive uncertainties for the seas and oceans related to the above-cited ocean-climate interactions. Three examples are worth citing here, though there will invariably be many more. First, depending on how much and how quickly sea levels rise, there will be varied implications in coastal areas.

Secondly, depending on how much and how quickly the seas and oceans warm, there are implications for the flora and fauna in the affected regions. Some regions are already finding quite rapid species changes. For example, the threat of climate warming and the resulting diminishing ice pack on the polar bear, the world’s largest land predator, has been particularly widely reported. However, research suggests that many species around the world may be similarly affected (Doney et al., 2012). Third, implications for weather, especially extreme weather conditions in coastal areas and on the oceans, could potentially impact upon many different human activities in coastal areas and on the oceans.

However, these and other phenomena related to ocean-climate interactions are still little understood by the scientific community, and their economic implications hard to assess. Indeed, writing on the theme of ecosystem connectivity in a changing ocean, for example, Cunha (2016) notes that “the lack of knowledge of the types and patterns of connectivity make it impossible to determine the effect of climate change and/or human exploitation on marine ecosystems”.

Some implications for the ocean economy

Despite many uncertainties, the direct implications of changing ocean-climate interactions for the ocean economy invariably will be extensive. As Chapter 3 explains in more detail, the effects on ocean ecosystems and marine diversity are considerable and are resulting in biodiversity and habitat loss, changes in fish stock composition and migration patterns, and higher frequency of severe ocean weather events. The consequences are being – and will continue to be – felt by fishing and aquaculture operations, the offshore oil and gas industry, vulnerable low-lying coastal communities, shipping companies, coastal and marine tourism, and marine bio-prospecting for medical and industrial purposes.

An indirect effect of climate change on all marine industries emanates from the responses (e.g. emission targets, regulations, standards, incentives) of governments, intergovernmental agencies, industry associations, etc. to rising levels of GHG emissions, biodiversity loss and so on. Some, such as shipping, offshore oil and gas platforms and seabed mining, are very likely to see their operations continue to be the object of tighter regulation, tougher safety rules and closer monitoring of their activities. Others, such as offshore wind farms and ocean renewable energy devices, are likely to see agreements such as the recent COP21 to reduce GHG emissions as a welcome stimulus for further research and investment.

The global economy: Slower growth, geographical shifts and the rise of the middle class

The trends

Notwithstanding the impacts of recent events such as the steep decline in oil prices, the volatility on global stock markets and the weakness of economic recovery in many parts of the world, what is important for 2030 and beyond are the prospects for economic performance over the long term.

Recent OECD work on projections to 2060 (Braconier, Nicoletti and Westmore, 2014) suggests that potential real growth in individual OECD and G20 economies is set to slow through to 2060, a trend that, to some extent, will be compensated by faster growth in some of the OECD partner economies. As a result, the central scenario of the OECD work expects world GDP to grow by only 3% per annum between 2010 and 2060, compared to 3.4% over the period 1996-2010.

The emerging market economies are set to put in a more sustained performance than the OECD economies over the 50-year period. The result will be a major shift in the centre of economic gravity away from OECD countries towards emerging economies, and especially those in Asia. The share of OECD partner economies in world GDP is set to rise from 45% in 2012 to almost 70% in 2060.

However, over time, economic growth in the emerging economies will slow too, as less favourable demographics and a slowing productivity catch-up begin to take their toll. Population ageing will lead to a shrinking potential labour force, only partially compensated through rises in labour market participation rates and employment levels.

The coming decades will also see global trade integration continue apace, albeit at a slower rate than in recent decades. Key factors in this development will be continuing falls in transport costs, and lower trade barriers resulting from trade agreements already in place. The share of world trade accounted for by OECD partner economy exports could rise from 35% in 2012 to 56% in 2060 (Braconier, Nicoletti and Westmore, 2014).

Figure 2.2. **Global GDP growth set to slow over next 50 years (annual average, constant 2005 PPP)**

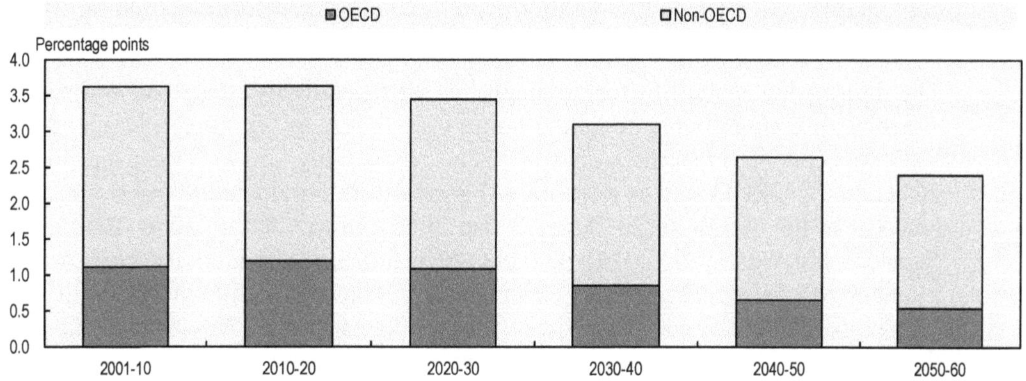

StatLink http://dx.doi.org/10.1787/888933094412

Note: The figure combines the long-term projections for 42 countries published in the *OECD Economic Outlook 95* and, for all other countries, projections from the ENV-growth model of the OECD Environmental Directorate.

Source: OECD (2014), "Long-term baseline projections, No. 95 (Edition 2014)", *OECD Economic Outlook: Statistics and Projections* (database), http://dx.doi.org/10.1787/data-00690-en.

Potential GDP per capita in the OECD area to 2060 is expected, on aggregate, to rise slightly higher than the 1.5% annual increase registered in the period immediately preceding the crisis. There will, however, be considerable variations among OECD countries. Among OECD partner economies, income growth is expected to be substantially higher than in OECD countries, averaging 4.3% per annum between 2010 and 2030, but falling quite sharply to 2.8% over 2030-60. The deterioration in GDP per capita growth is particularly pronounced in China, where it almost halves to 2030 and then halves again to 2060. In other countries, e.g. Indonesia and South Africa, incomes are expected to improve on aggregate over pre-crisis levels (Braconier, Nicoletti and Westmore, 2014).

The above findings on widespread GDP per capita increases over the coming decades are broadly in line with the projections of other institutions, some of which point to the rise of the middle classes as a particularly important economic phenomenon of the coming decades. Indeed, almost everywhere in the developing world, the middle classes are expected to expand considerably. Globally, the middle classes are currently estimated at around 1 billion people. Depending on the projection and on the definition of "middle class" used (e.g. Gros and Alcidi, 2013; Kharas, 2010), their numbers could rise to somewhere between 2 and 5 billion worldwide already by 2030, continuing to rise through to the middle of the century. Studies generally point to India and China as the countries likely to generate the steepest growth in middle classes.

Risks and uncertainties

The picture painted above represents a relatively benign view of progress in the world economy over the next 50 years or so. However, a range of economic factors – singly or in combination with one another – could act to slow or even jeopardise the future growth trajectory. These include:

- Fiscal pressures are likely to continue to build up in many countries as demographics evolve unfavourably, and spending pressures stemming from pensions, health, education and infrastructure investment intensify.
- The future pace of multifactor productivity (MFP) is highly uncertain, with some experts expressing doubts about the future growth rate of "frontier" ideas, and the ability of economies to sustain innovation and productivity levels (Fernald and Jones, 2014). In the OECD area as a whole, MFP growth is anticipated to fall from 1.1% per year in the decade to 2030 to 1.0% to 2040 and to 0.9% to 2050 (Braconier, Nicoletti and Westmore, 2014). The uncertain future of productivity, however, is a matter of considerable debate, with the discussants broadly splitting into two camps: the pessimists and the optimists. Robert Gordon and followers contend that the recent slowdown in productivity is a permanent phenomenon, arguing that the kinds of innovation that occurred in the first half of the 20th century, such as electrification, have been much more important than those taking place since (e.g. ICT) or that are likely to occur in the future. The optimists, such as Brynjolfsson and McAfee, maintain that the underlying rate of technological progress has not slowed and that, on the contrary, ICT innovations will continue to drive and transform leading-edge economies. Recent OECD work suggests that the main source of the productivity slowdown is, in fact, related more to a slowing of the pace at which innovations diffuse through economy and society rather than a matter of slowing innovation by the most globally advanced companies (OECD, 2015b).
- Climate change could prove costly to economic growth even before mid-century. Recent projections by the OECD suggest that by 2060 world GDP could be dented by as much as between 0.7% and 2.5% by a range of climate change impacts. Developing countries, rather than the advanced economies, stand to lose most in terms of (relative) economic losses, as the deteriorating environment increasingly acts as a drag on growth. In south and South-East Asia, for example, it is expected that by 2060 environmental damage could lower GDP by as much as 5% compared to the central scenario used (Braconier, Nicoletti and Westmore, 2014).

Some implications for the ocean economy

Along with population, the economy is one of the most dynamic drivers of developments in the maritime economy. Although the long-term prospects for global economic growth, and for the OECD area as a whole, remain modest, GDP per capita is expected to rise significantly over the next few decades, providing substantial impetus to a range of ocean industries. Recent projections suggest, for example, that global freight trade could grow between 330% and 380% by 2050. Since around 90% of international freight is carried by sea, the impetus to the shipping business and ports will be considerable. Much as a result, port volumes are expected to almost quadruple by mid-century (OECD and ITF, 2015). On the other hand, deterioration in the above-mentioned areas of public finances, productivity and climate change damage could act to slow global income growth.

With an expanding share of world production located in China, India and Indonesia (almost 40% by 2030 and around 50% by 2050) and concomitant increases in incomes and wealth, especially in the emerging economies and some of the rapidly developing countries, a gradual shift in trade patterns eastwards is inevitable. The consequences for ocean industries are huge. Careful consideration is already being given by shipping lines and shipbuilding companies to likely future changes in markets, routes, types of cargo and types of vessel that will be required.

Moreover, as the middle classes emerge as powerful drivers also in the emerging economies and some developing countries, important consequences for consumption patterns can be expected to materialise: e.g. higher demand for marine tourism and especially cruise tourism; big shifts in dietary habits towards higher quality fish and other marine products.

Energy: Continuing dominance of fossil fuels but a changing energy landscape

The trends

The COP21 meeting in Paris in December 2015 brought countries together to agree on an ambitious target for limiting the global temperature rise. While the agreement that was reached provides a strong framework for action towards a new pathway to a low-carbon, climate-resilient future, the intended nationally determined contributions (INDCs) to cut emissions submitted by 160 countries – even if they were to be fully enacted – still fall short of the level of emissions reduction required to hold the global average temperature rises below 2°C. Details of the actions needed to close this emissions gap still need to be worked out.

Reducing energy consumption from fossil fuel sources will likely prove extremely challenging. The global energy picture is currently dominated by fossil fuels, and will continue to be so for many years to come. This is because a significant reorientation of the world's energy system will take time, but also because fossil fuel reserves are enormous. Total proven oil reserves are estimated at around 1 700 billion barrels, equivalent to 54 years of oil production at current levels. Proven world natural gas reserves are in the order of 61 years of production at current levels. And coal reserves exceed those of oil and gas combined (IEA, 2013).

The ocean will play a key role in the transition to a more sustainable global energy system. While current global offshore wind installed capacity is in excess of 7 gigawatts (GW), projections suggest there may be potential for 40-60 GW by 2020 and growth of a further order of magnitude by 2050 (Anson, forthcoming). And while ocean power (wave, tidal, thermal conversion, salinity gradient technology) is not yet mature or operating at commercial scale, its longer term potential is considerable (Sweeney, forthcoming). Both offshore wind and ocean-based energy stand to gain considerably from future investment in the wake of the Paris COP21 agreement.

Offshore oil and gas are set to continue to play a bridging role in the transition towards a greener energy system. Some 37% of proven oil reserves are thought to be offshore, with around one-third of these in deep water (IEA, 2012). Estimates of these resources could rise further as new technologies come on stream.

Risks and uncertainties

The offshore energy sector faces tough challenges in the years ahead, on the technological, regulatory and supply chain management fronts. Growth in offshore wind capacity, for example, is critically dependent upon the industry driving down costs across all elements of the supply chain and becoming cost-effective *vis-à-vis* alternative sources of energy, including both traditional forms and alternative renewables. Similarly, for both offshore wind and ocean energy technologies, access to finance, a stable regulatory environment and government support are all considered key conditions for future large-scale development (Anson, forthcoming; Sweeney, forthcoming).

With respect to oil and gas, energy markets have been particularly volatile. Unlike earlier steep falls in oil price, the causes are both supply- and demand-driven, and appear to be more complex than in many earlier episodes. The supply from countries not part of the Organization of the Petroleum Exporting Countries (OPEC) was at record levels in 2014, and demand growth has proven unexpectedly weak. New technologies in the form of light, tight oil extraction, notably in the United States, have unlocked a vast new resource and upset the traditional balance of relations between OPEC and non-OPEC. Meanwhile, global demand for oil is undergoing profound change as China shifts to a new phase of less oil-intensive development, and the global economy more generally is becoming less fuel intensive. Globalisation of the natural gas market has accelerated recently, and concerns over climate change are leading to a rethink of energy policy in many parts of the world (IEA, 2015a).

Gas prices, by virtue of their direct and indirect linkages to oil, are impacted by the plunge in oil prices. The response of oil and gas companies has been to curb capital expenditure programmes, and further cuts are expected. Hence, growth in gas production is expected to slow. Liquefied natural gas (LNG) is particularly hard hit due to its capital-intensive nature, and many projects are being abandoned or deferred. However, looking to the medium term, LNG markets could well start to tighten by 2020 (IEA, 2015b).

Some implications for the ocean economy

Energy issues pervade the full range of maritime industries, both as energy users and energy suppliers.

Market price levels and market volatility are crucial factors in the viability of offshore oil and gas exploration and production, as underlined by recent decisions to scale back, defer or abandon several offshore projects, since they are particularly capital intensive. Nonetheless, despite low oil prices, a good number of high-profile offshore projects have seen their development continue. Economic viability varies of course by region and by project, but it is thought that oil prices of around USD 80/barrel over the long term would suffice to sustain most deep-water developments (DW, 2015).

Depending on future development costs (also in comparison to onshore production) as well as on future hydrocarbon prices and other investment conditions, offshore is projected to continue to provide for approximately 30% of the global hydrocarbons production. Total offshore crude oil production is expected to rise relatively slowly – from approximately 25 million barrels of oil-equivalent per day (mboe/d) in 2014 to around 28 mboe/d in 2040. Offshore gas, on the other hand, should see stronger growth over the same period – from slightly above 17 mboe/d in 2014 to 27 mboe/d in 2040 (Borelli, forthcoming).

In contrast to producers of hydrocarbons, consistently high oil and gas prices are an essential ingredient for the continuing progress of offshore wind and ocean renewables, as well as for the development of aquaculture-based algal biofuels. However, offshore wind is likely to continue to benefit from government subsidies in the years to come and, as capacity grows, from efforts to reduce production and running costs. Both factors should help offshore wind build more resilience to fluctuations in oil and gas markets. The global market for ocean energy systems (tidal, wave, ocean current, etc.), on the other hand, is not expected to scale up significantly in the medium term, but the longer term potential is enormous.

On the side of users, energy prices are a key determinant in the cost structure of shipping companies' operations as well as in their projections of future demand for their services. Similarly, oil prices are an important component of the costs borne by commercial fishing and marine travel and tourism. For the longer term, current experiments with new fuels (LNG, LPG, hydrogen, biofuels) and new forms of propulsion (electric) could begin to bear fruit and reduce ocean users' dependence on oil-based fuels (DNV GL, 2015).

Finally, over the coming decades, the development and changing pattern of demand will greatly influence the volumes of oil and gas that will be transported via tankers and LNG carriers. These currently account for around 30% of global seaborne trade. Recent projections suggest that further growth of the world economy, especially in Asia, will continue to drive significant growth in tanker and LNG carrier shipments. The transport of oil by sea alone is thought to increase from its current level of around 3 500 million tonnes to close to 4 500 million tonnes by 2030 (SEA, 2015). However, over the last decade or so, surplus capacity has built up, so that the oil tanker fleet requirement is expected to grow more slowly than in past years, at a rate of nonetheless just under 1% per annum (SEA, 2015) over the short to medium term.

Metals and minerals: Continuing pressures on the supply side

The trends

The main drivers behind increasing demand for natural resources remain economic growth and population. Over the last 30 years or so, global extraction of metals and minerals (including fossil fuels) has risen from less than 40 billion tonnes in 1980 to almost 70 billion tonnes in 2008, an annual increase of over 2%. Given the prospects of rising population and growing prosperity, extraction rates are expected to accelerate further over the next two to three decades, reaching around 100 billion tonnes by 2030 (Austrian Federal Ministry of Agriculture, Forestry, Environment and Water Management [BMLFUW], 2015).

For most metals and minerals, the issue is expected to be less about whether global supplies will be adequate to keep up with demand and more about the negative environmental effects associated with extraction, use and emissions, as well as about price levels and price fluctuations. The years up to 2007/08 saw the prices of precious and other metals (gold, silver, copper, zinc) peak at all-time highs, then fall back sharply as the financial crisis and recession took hold. Thereafter, prices have been prone to considerable volatility.

There is also much discussion around future demand – and possible shortages – of metals and minerals that are critical to modern economies, and especially to key high-technology products such as ICT hardware, electric vehicles and renewable energy facilities. Key technologies affected include, amongst others, nuclear energy, solar energy, wind energy, carbon capture storage and electricity grids.

Although still very much at the exploration stage, interest in seabed mining for minerals, and especially metals, has picked up in recent years, not least because of the rising demand and price increases noted above, but also due to sovereignty considerations in the case of some rare earth elements. Given limitations on some land-based mineral resources, concerns about declines in the quality of some ores and possible shortages of some rare metals (see below), interest in seabed exploration is expected to be sustained over the long-term future. Commercial interest is particularly strong in poly-metallic nodules and in seafloor massive sulphides (SMSs), which are base-metal sulphur-rich mineral deposits that precipitate from the hydrothermal fluids as these interact with the cooler ambient sea water at hydrothermal vent sites. It is estimated that thousands of underwater sulphide systems exist, and that even if only half of them are geographically viable, annual seafloor production would represent several billion tonnes of copper alone. Deposits of rare earth elements are also to be found under or on the seabed, as are methane hydrate deposits.

Risks and uncertainties

For some (in certain cases critical) metals, there is concern that supply bottlenecks could occur. The supply-side factors that could play a role in future are:

- the possibility of global demand growth surges from new uses
- short- to medium-term limitations on output expansion (e.g. due to lack of known reserves or production capacity constraints)
- market dominance of very few supplier countries
- political risk (instability, internal conflict, etc.) in major supplier countries.

Over the coming decade at least, continuing demand growth is likely to keep up the pressure on the supply side. In some cases (e.g. neodymium and dysprosium), bringing new rare earth mines to the market will prove quite difficult. These challenges will likely be compounded by high political risks due to the heavy concentration of supply in a single country, namely China (Moss et al., 2013) and, last but not least, by environmental issues associated with their extraction.

Implications for the ocean economy

Despite the expected growth in demand for ores and minerals in the decades ahead and concerns about the declining quality of some ores, it remains unclear whether deep-sea mining will come on stream any time soon on a commercial scale. The availability of alternative land-based sources, the potential for metals recycling, the unfavourable economics and environmental issues associated with deep-sea mining are among the factors behind this uncertainty (Hannington, forthcoming).

However, specifically on the environmental front, political interest is already gathering momentum. For example, the declaration from the G7 summit in Germany in 2015 identified environmental impact assessment (EIA) and scientific research as priority issues for sustainable deep-sea mining. Indeed, as the recent EcoDeep-SIP Workshop (2015) in Tokyo emphasised, the deep seabed is a particularly complex set of interconnected ecosystems that are vulnerable to disturbance, but about which scientific knowledge is very limited. EIA for deep-sea mining is highlighted as a key component for ensuring effective protection of deep-sea ecosystems.

The shipping and shipbuilding industries stand to gain considerably from the anticipated growth and continuing industrialisation of the world economy in the coming years. Demand for iron ore, bauxite/alumina and phosphate rock (as well as coal and grain) will see seaborne trade in the five main bulk categories expand strongly (SEA, 2015).

The long-term prospects with respect to rare earths are keenly debated and questions remain about the reliability of international supply chains. This could prove problematic for the development of many renewable energy systems, not least ocean-based renewables. Manufacturers of offshore wind turbines, for example, use several rare earth elements as key inputs – terbium, neodymium and dysprosium – the supply security of which appears to be uncertain.

Figure 2.3. **Global main dry bulk seaborne trade 1970-2035**

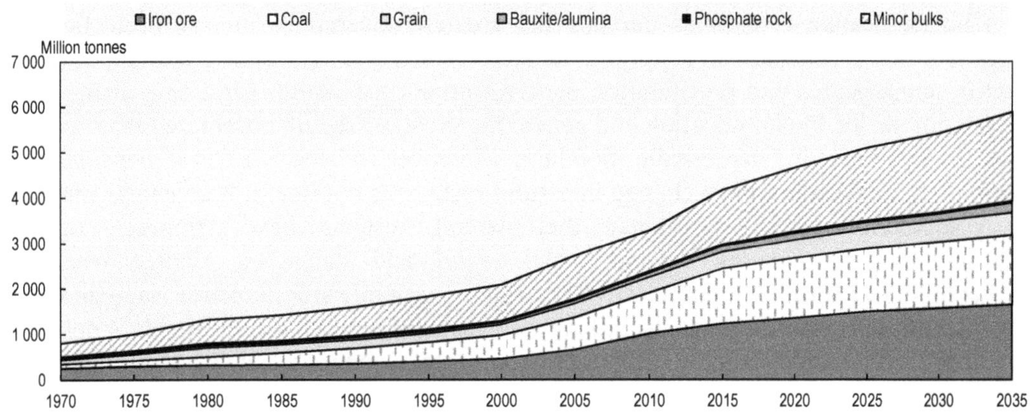

Source: SEA Europe MF.

Global food supplies: Continuing pressures and uncertainties

The trends

The issue of global food security has figured prominently on national and international agendas for some years now. Food insecurity is chiefly a concern of developing countries. The number of undernourished people currently stands at just short of 800 million. The bulk of the world's undernourished people are to be found in Asia, which accounts for almost two-thirds of the world total, followed by Africa with almost 30%. While the total number of undernourished has fallen over the last two decades, large pockets of undernourished populations remain, especially among the least-developed countries (FAO, IFAD and WFP, 2015).

Overall trends do not bode well for the future:

- First, and as noted earlier, population growth is likely to add upward of 2 billion people to the planet by 2050, with much of this expected growth to be in developing countries and cities. This is expected to place a further burden on the world's food and agricultural system, as it implies a 60% rise in food production compared to the period 2005-07 (Alexandratos and Bruinsma, 2012).
- Second, as incomes across the world increase in coming years, changes in dietary preferences are also expected to remain a key driver, notably with increasing demands on high-value animal protein, including fish and other seafood products.
- A third problem is that food production is under increasing competition from non-food crops, not least for biofuels.
- Fourthly, global food supplies are in some cases threatened by an overexploitation of resources. Concerning fish stocks, for example, despite the implementation of recovery plans, overfishing has already seen the collapse of high-profile species (such as the Northwest Atlantic cod which, at long last, are showing some signs of recovery) and today almost 30% of global fish stocks are judged to be fished at a biologically unsustainable level, i.e. overfished (FAO, 2014).

Risks and uncertainties

Climate change constitutes perhaps the greatest uncertainty in any projection of long-term future demand and supply in the area of food and agriculture. It is expected to modify temperatures and precipitation patterns around the world, triggering changes in the conditions for food production and generating greater risks of extreme weather events such as cyclones and large-scale flooding. Moreover, as the OECD *Environmental Outlook to 2050* underscores, change in natural systems is not linear. It considers there to be compelling scientific evidence that natural systems have "tipping points", i.e. biophysical boundaries beyond which rapid and damaging change becomes irreversible. Examples are biodiversity/species loss, groundwater depletion, land and soil degradation, and climate change itself. Knowledge about such critical thresholds is not well developed, nor is understanding of their environmental, economic and social implications.

Further uncertainties in projecting food supplies (apart from population growth) are dietary change as incomes rise, agricultural yield increases, and, to a lesser extent, the pace and pattern of urbanisation. Finally, at the interface of climate change, technological developments and globalisation is the risk of plant- and animal-related diseases, which may scale up to cross frontiers and even continents, and cause widespread damage to agricultural production systems and, subsequently, food supplies.

Some implications for the ocean economy

In light of the expected increase in world population to 2050 and demand for food, the ocean clearly has an important part to play in supplementing the food supplies generated by agriculture. Indeed, fish already represents 16% of all animal protein consumed globally (World Bank, 2013), and this proportion is likely to increase as consumers with rising incomes seek higher value seafood, and aquaculture production increases production in response to rising demand. However, the ocean's capacity to perform that key role is increasingly undermined by the impacts of agricultural activity, not least the run-off of fertilisers and agricultural waste into coastal and estuary zones, which threaten marine life habitats, fish stocks, molluscs and so on (see Chapter 3).

As already noted in relation to potential future shortages of fresh water – not least for agricultural purposes – a case can be made for redirecting significant amounts of food production from land to sea. An additional argument is that fish tend to have much more favourable metabolic conversion rates and produce less greenhouse gases than ruminants.

Some carnivorous farmed fish, e.g. salmon were in the past fed primarily on wild-caught fish from lower trophic levels. As demand for farmed fish expands in the next decades, pressure to reduce fish-based inputs is likely to strengthen even more. Vegetal raw materials in salmon feed in Norwegian aquaculture, for example, already account for three-quarters of all salmon feed ingredients, compared to just 11% in 1990 (Ytrestøyl, Aas and Aasgaard, 2014). Recent breakthroughs in the genetic modification of some cereals, which can be engineered to contain Omega-3 oils, also raise hopes for the future for a viable shift to plant-based fish feed.

Changing fish capture strategies may also have the potential to make for more efficient protein production for human consumption, for example, fishing at lower trophic levels for phytoplankton, zooplankton, calanus, etc. At present there is increased motivation for humans to consume foodstuff from lower trophic levels and by doing so more food can be provided. Further, the volumes of animal and phytoplankton in the seas is assumed to be enormous, relative to the stocks of fish.

Figure 2.4. **Lower trophic fishing for more efficient protein production**

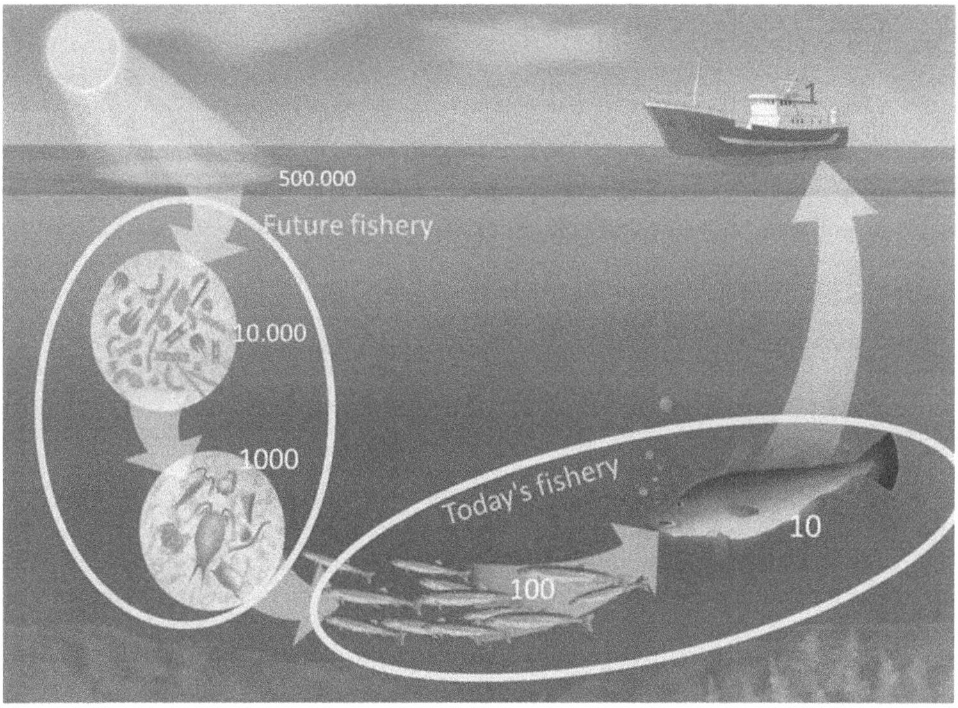

Note: Each step higher in the trophic chain is associated with a loss in energy of about 90%. In other words, the consumption of sea food from lower trophic levels entails nine times more food per unit of fish compared to the fish caught at a higher trophic level. For example, a cod of 10 kilogrammes (kg) will have consumed 100 kg of herring. One step further down the trophic level, those herrings would have eaten 1 000 kg of animal plankton which in turn would have consumed about 10 000 kg of phytoplankton, generated by 500 kilojoules of sunrays.

Source: Endal and Johnson (2014).

Finally, growing demand for food worldwide is set to benefit the shipping industry, which will be transporting agricultural and horticultural produce in dry bulk, liquid bulk and container vessels.

Technological developments

The trends

Technological innovations are expected to play a crucial role not only in helping find solutions to many of the challenges outlined above, but also in shaping the future more generally.

New ICT technologies are at the forefront of developments underpinning advances in science, and revolutionising production and the delivery of services. Machine-to-machine communication, highly sophisticated sensors, data analytics and artificial intelligence are set to bring about quite transformative changes in both products and processes. Improvements in the use and management of energy and natural resources, creation of new markets and new value chains, changes in global trade patterns and shifts in international competitiveness, will all flow from progress in ICT. Those, in turn, are set to be driven increasingly by convergence in various information and communication technologies – the Internet of Things – and by convergence with other emerging technologies such as nano- and biotechnology. Big data, data analytics, cloud computing and machine-learning algorithms are leading to new levels of artificial intelligence and thence to smart applications, autonomous machines and systems. The robots of the future are expected to be flexible, self-learning and intelligent, with applications in science, space research, mining, health and pharmaceuticals, and of course in manufacturing.

Among the new additive manufacturing processes talked about today, 3D printing probably features most frequently. It has enormous potential to enable digital transportation, storage, creation and replication of products, generate savings on the use of materials, waste and transport, and permit precision personalisation of articles. However, it is difficult to predict how fast it will spread, given the obstacles it still faces (e.g. limited number of usable materials, lack of standards, intellectual property rights issues, etc.).

Nanotechnology, with its potential to make objects lighter, stronger, cheaper, faster, more resistant or more energy efficient for example, is expected to make inroads into pharmaceuticals, chemistry, engineering, electronics, indeed across almost every economic activity, and holds out the promise of significant contributions to environmental and social challenges.

Biotechnology, which encompasses *inter alia* genomics, genetic as well as cell, tissue, protein and molecule engineering, process biotechnology and bioinformatics, is finding applications in a wide range of fields and is being driven to an important extent by concerns around climate change, natural resource depletion, energy security, agricultural production, global health issues and the sustainability of economic growth more generally. Industrial biotechnology is expected to find its way on an increasing scale into a widening range of sectors, not least pharmaceuticals, food and textiles (see Chapter 4 for a detailed discussion of science and technology advances in the ocean domain).

Risks and uncertainties

Among the greatest uncertainties is the prospect of disruptive technological innovations. At a general level, uncertainties with all of these technologies arise with respect to the speed of technological development, the impact of advances in individual technologies, and – perhaps most importantly – the convergence of ICT, sensors, robotics, nano- and biotechnology. Advances in one technology may amplify developments and outcomes of other technologies, leading to disruptive changes. This is already becoming visible in green technologies, which typically operate at the intersection of these emerging technologies, in the creation of "programmable matter", and in advances in the medical and pharmaceutical fields. Such disruptive changes not bring only benefits, they constitute serious challenges to established ways of doing things, to competitive positions, trade patterns, business models and especially to labour markets, where changes to working conditions, job losses and job displacements may result. Key in the armoury of policy makers, businesses and educational establishments alike will be the capacity to prepare for such deep-seated changes by ensuring that the workforce is equipped with the necessary skills and qualifications to handle upcoming disruptive and transformative changes (OECD, 2015a).

Implications for the ocean economy

Every sector of the ocean economy stands to be affected by these technological advances. By way of illustration: commercial shipping appears to be on the verge of the introduction of autonomous ships and greater use of new fuels, and the implementation of e-navigation is moving steadily closer; shipbuilding and fish processing in developed economies are seeing previously outsourced activities being "re-shored" as, for example, automated riveting/welding and fish-filleting become more sophisticated and cost-efficient; oil and gas and seabed mining companies are looking to robotics for their subsea operations; marine aquaculture is building on advances in biotechnology to improve fish health and welfare and reduce dependence on wild fish catches for feed; renewable ocean energies are making increasing use of advances in new materials and sensors; fisheries, maritime safety and ocean observation will continue to benefit from the great strides that are being made in satellite technologies (communications, remote sensing, navigation); and cruise tourism scales up its on-board digital facilities for passengers and crew to unprecedented levels.

Geopolitical developments: A multipolar world in flux

The trends

This chapter has already identified a range of trends and developments occurring at global level – for example, the growing importance of emerging and developing countries; the shift in centre of economic gravity towards the east and Asia and the concomitant decline in the relative economic weight of North America and Europe; the internationalisation of supply chains and networks – which already convey a shift in the distribution and balance of power and influence across the globe. What goes hand in hand with these trends is a clearly visible drift to a multipolar world. Hegemony is being gradually but decisively diluted as new national and regional players emerge on the geopolitical stage, and the cast of state actors is joined by an expanding range of non-state actors, from corporations and NGOs to megacities, foundations and terrorist organisations.

The flipside to this multipolar structure of economic power is the challenges it poses to governance and international co-operation more generally. International institutions such as the United Nations, the International Monetary Fund and the World Bank struggle to cope with this diffusion, indeed fragmentation, of power at all levels, and the growing numbers of parties with divergent views which need to be consulted and nudged to agreement. Management of ocean resources and ocean territories is no exception to this trend (see Chapters 5 and 9).

Risks and uncertainties

A survey of the literature reveals that there is no shortage of risks and uncertainties that could significantly alter our expectations of a linear trajectory of the future. The recent economic and financial crisis has highlighted the extraordinary interdependencies of the world economy and the vulnerability of economic and social systems to deeply disruptive events. Given the prospect of continuing globalisation in its many facets, possible new financial and economic crises figure prominently on many an expert's list of the main global risks of the next decades. Equally prominent are concerns about the twin nexus of climate change and tensions around natural resources such as food, energy, water and minerals. These, in turn, may be compounded by further tensions linked to urbanisation, migration and global inequalities. What makes the nature of these threats so complex and difficult to assess is the degree to which they are all inextricably interlinked, one with the other.

In light of this interdependence, there is considerable room for seemingly localised regional or national events to spill over onto the world stage and create instability. Again, the literature is rich in examples. With China set to overtake the United States in a few years as the largest economy in the world, worries abound about its ability to sustain economic growth over the long term (especially with a rapidly ageing population) and the implications for the world which might flow from that. On a slightly different note, some experts point to already existing cases of deep-seated regional instability, notably in the Middle East and south Asia, and the possibility of that instability spilling out beyond regional borders. Equally, risks have been identified with the destabilising potential of "rogue" states that are potentially able to wreak havoc with the relatively modest tools at their disposal, thanks to an interdependent world that empowers them beyond their size. On a less negative note, regions could develop in surprising ways. For example, due to its plentiful reserves of oil, natural gas and minerals, and abundant supplies of fresh water, the next three decades or so might see a rapid growth in the prosperity and power of the Arctic regions grouped around the Russian Federation, Alaska, Canada and the Nordic countries.

In this changing world, technology works as a double-edged sword. On the one hand, advanced technologies in ICT, biotechnology, life sciences, space applications and so on have the potential to reinforce the destabilising effects of many of the possible events described above. On the other, they have the potential to improve humankind's response to many of the global challenges facing the planet. Either way, they stand to reshuffle the cards in the geopolitical game in unexpected ways.

Implications for the ocean economy

Among the most serious geopolitical risks to the future ocean environment are international tensions and conflicts – both inter- and intra-state – and terrorism. International tensions often result in environmental priorities being severely neglected. A telling illustration is the plight of the South China Sea. With political attention distracted by competing claims of sovereignty and construction work on vulnerable reefs, scant attention is paid to the serious deterioration of the marine ecosystem and the potential consequences for the food security of millions of people (The Economist, 2015). The threat of serious marine pollution hangs over many situations of armed conflict. Typical of this are perhaps the concerns surrounding the fact that some of the world's most important oil tanker routes pass through areas rife with unrest and civil war. Piracy and the threat of hijack by terrorist groups (taking control of vessels physically or by breaching cyber-security defences) add to the list of concerns.

Arguably, however, an even more significant threat is the fragmentation of power and the growing difficulty of forging international consensus on global and regional issues key to the ocean environment and ocean industries. Whether this involves climate change and GHG emission levels or the governance of the high seas and area beyond national jurisdiction (ABNJ), the protection of marine biodiversity or international conventions on maritime safety, the path to international agreement appears increasingly complex and painstaking. This appears to be all the more so since, as the Global Ocean Commission (GOC, 2014) recently concluded, ocean governance is plagued by a patchwork of sectorally focused agencies and institutions hampered by weak compliance and lack of enforcement. Moreover, as Chapter 9 highlights, the situation is exacerbated by a lack of legal clarity about economic activities in the oceans beyond national jurisdiction as well as the potential of increased competition between states for access to resources in the seas.

On a brighter note, however, a number of recent successes on the global governance front deserve highlighting. These include, for example: mention of the ocean in the Paris COP21 agreement, the establishment of ocean-related Sustainable Development Goals (in particular SDG 14), and agreement of member states at the United Nations to develop a legally-binding instrument to conserve and sustainably use marine biological diversity of areas beyond their national borders.

Concluding remarks

It is impossible to say with any degree of confidence how the many drivers addressed above will eventually interact to create the future world of 2030/50. But they do provide indications as to the complex set of challenges facing the planet in the coming decades: climate change, global warming, a slowing but nonetheless significant increase in population and urbanisation, fresh water shortages, weakening productivity, slower economic growth, greater income inequalities, food security issues, sustainable energy provision – the list is long.

A central tenet of this report is that the ocean and seas are an indispensable part of the search for solutions to many if not most of those challenges. However, the driving forces shaping the longer term are also partly responsible for some of the pressures weighing on the ocean and coastal waters. For example: increasing concentrations of populations in proximity of the sea are set to place mounting strain on coastal waters in particular; rising incomes and ageing populations will see increased prosperity and leisure time combining to drive the expansion of maritime and coastal tourism; convergence of incomes and dietary attitudes in developing and especially emerging economies towards those of the developed world are expected to lead to substantial increases in demand for animal protein, including fish, thereby adding to the strains on wild fish stocks. The shift in the centre of gravity of economic activity towards emerging and developing countries is projected to raise considerably the share of South-South trade in global trade in the next two decades, resulting in significant increases in shipping in those parts of the world. Similarly, climate change, global warming and environmental pressures are all expected to influence the ocean environment in important ways. And last but not least, the legacy of largely sectoral approaches to ocean governance, at the expense of more holistic solutions, promises to remain a serious impediment to efforts aiming at more integrated ocean management.

As the following chapter will explain, these stresses and strains on the marine and coastal environment come on top of quite dramatic physical changes taking place in the ocean itself, changes which are expected to gather momentum in the coming decades, heightening the fragility of the ocean environment.

References

Alexandratos, N. and J. Bruinsma (2012), "World agriculture towards 2030/2050: The 2012 revision", *ESA Working Papers*, No. 12-03, June, Food and Agriculture Organization, Rome, www.fao.org/docrep/016/ap106e/ap106e.pdf.

Anson, S. (forthcoming), "Prospects for offshore wind to 2030", *OECD Science, Technology and Industry Working Papers*, OECD Publishing, Paris, forthcoming.

Austrian Federal Ministry of Agriculture, Forestry, Environment and Water Management (BMLFUW) (2015), www.bmlfuw.gv.at/en/fields/greentec/Wastemanagement/Ressourcedata.html.

Borelli, A. (forthcoming), "Offshore oil and gas: The new frontiers", *OECD Science, Technology and Industry Working Papers*, OECD Publishing, Paris, forthcoming.

Braconier, H., G. Nicoletti and B. Westmore (2014), "Policy challenges for the next 50 years", *OECD Economic Policy Papers*, No. 9, OECD Publishing, Paris, http://dx.doi.org/10.1787/5jz18gs5fckf-en.

Crawford Heitzmann, M. (2006), "Don't forget the coastal waters", *OECD Observer*, No. 254, OECD Publishing, Paris, March, www.oecdobserver.org/news/fullstory.php/aid/1807/Don_92t_forget_the_coastal_waters!.html.

Cunha, M.R. (2016), "Ecosystem connectivity in a changing ocean", Chapter 3, in: *Sailing through Changing Oceans: Ocean and Polar Life and Environmental Sciences on a Warming Planet*, Science Position Paper, European Science Foundation, Strasbourg, www.esf.org/fileadmin/Public_documents/Publications/sailing_through_changing_oceans.pdf.

DNV GL (2015), "The fuel trilemma: Next generation of marine fuels", DNV GLAS, Høvik, Norway, www.dnvgl.com/Images/DNV%20GL_Position%20Paper%20on%20Fuel%20Trilemma_tcm8-25973.PDF.

Doney, S.C. et al. (2012), "Climate change impacts on marine ecosystems", *Annual Review of Marine Sciences*, Vol. 4, January, pp. 11-37, http://dx.doi.org/10.1146/annurev-marine-041911-111611.

DW (2015), "Offshore prospects for 2016: Playing the waiting game?", Douglas Westwoord, www.offshoreenergytoday.com/douglas-westwood-offshore-prospects-for-2016-playing-the-waiting-game/.

Endal, A. and G. Johnson (2014), "Livet i havet" (Life in the Seas), in Leif Lundby (ed.), *Havromsteknologi* (Ocean Space Technology), Fagbokforlaget, Bergen (Norway).

EcoDeep-SIP Workshop (2015), "The crafting of seabed mining ecosystem-based management: Assessing deep sea ecosystems in the Pacific Ocean", Final Report, July, https://fbox.jamstec.go.jp/public/Meb0QAIJu8DAnyoBmgFS4jIe8L-XODrU0j0tlod7rpRP.

FAO (2014), *The State of World Fisheries and Aquaculture*, Food and Agriculture Organization, Rome, www.fao.org/3/a-i3720e.pdf.

FAO, IFAD and WFP (2015), *The State of Food Insecurity in the World: Meeting the 2015 International Hunger Targets: Taking Stock of Uneven Progress*, Food and Agriculture Organization, Rome, www.fao.org/3/a-i4646e.pdf.

Fernald, J.G. and C.I. Jones (2014), "The future of U.S. economic growth", *NBER Working Papers*, No. 19 830, January.

GOC (2014), "From decline to recovery, rescue package for the global ocean", Global Ocean Commission, Oxford, United Kingdom, www.globaloceancommission.org/wp-content/uploads/GOC_Report_20_6.FINAL_.spreads.pdf.

Gros, D. and C. Alcidi (eds.) (2013), *The Global Economy in 2030: Trends and Strategies for Europe*, Centre for European Policy Studies, Brussels, November, available at: http://europa.eu/espas/pdf/espas-report-economy.pdf.

Hannington, M. (forthcoming), "Prospects and challenges of deepsea mining", *OECD Science, Technology and Industry Working Papers*, OECD Publishing, Paris, forthcoming.

IEA (2015a), "Executive summary", *Medium-Term Oil Market Report 2015*, OECD/IEA, Paris www.iea.org/Textbase/npsum/MTOMR2015sum.pdf.

IEA (2015b), "Executive summary", *Medium-Term Gas Market Report 2015: Market Analysis and Forecasts to 2020*, OECD/IEA, Paris, www.iea.org/Textbase/npsum/MTGMR2015SUM.pdf.

IEA (2013), *World Energy Outlook 2013*, International Energy Agency, Paris, http://dx.doi.org/10.1787/weo-2013-en.

IEA (2012), *World Energy Outlook 2012*, International Energy Agency, Paris, http://dx.doi.org/10.1787/weo-2012-en.

IPCC (2013), *Climate Change 2013: The Physical Science Basis: Summary for Policymakers, technical Summary and Frequently Asked Questions*, Working Group I Contribution to the Fifth Assessment Report of the Intergovernmental Panel on Climate Change, Intergovernmental Panel on Climate Change, www.ipcc.ch/pdf/assessment-report/ar5/wg1/WG1AR5_SummaryVolume_FINAL.pdf.

Jambeck, J.R. et al. (2015), "Plastic waste inputs from land into the ocean", *Science*, 13 February 2015, Vol. 347, No. 6 223, pp. 768-771, http://dx.doi.org/10.1126/science.1260352.

Kharas, H. (2010), "The emerging middle class in developing countries", *OECD Development Centre Working Papers*, No. 285, OECD Publishing, Paris, http://dx.doi.org/10.1787/5kmmp8lncrns-en.

Moss, R.L. et al. (2013), "The potential risks from metals bottlenecks to the deployment of strategic energy technologies", *Energy Policy*, Vol. 55, April, pp. 556-564, http://dx.doi.org/10.1016/j.enpol.2012.12.053.

Neumann, B. et al. (2015), "Future coastal population growth and exposure to sea-level rise and coastal flooding: A global assessment", *PLOS ONE*, Vol. 10, No. 3, http://dx.doi.org/10.1371/journal.pone.0118571.

Nicholls, R.J. et al. (2008), "Ranking port cities with high exposure and vulnerability to climate extremes: Exposure estimates", *OECD Environment Working Papers,* No. 1, OECD Publishing, Paris, http://dx.doi.org/10.1787/011766488208.

OECD (2015a), "Enabling the next production revolution: Issues paper", DSTI/IND(2015)2, OECD, Paris, available at: www.oecd.org/officialdocuments/publicdisplaydocumentpdf/?cote=DSTI/IND%282015%292&docLanguage=En.

OECD (2015b), *The Future of Productivity*, OECD Publishing, Paris, http://dx.doi.org/10.1787/9789264248533-en.

OECD (2014), "Long-term baseline projections, No. 95 (Edition 2014)", *OECD Economic Outlook: Statistics and Projections* (database), http://dx.doi.org/10.1787/data-00690-en.

OECD (2011a), *Health at a Glance 2011: OECD Indicators*, OECD Publishing, Paris, http://dx.doi.org/10.1787/health_glance-2011-en.

OECD (2011e), *Future Global Shocks: Improving Risk Governance*, OECD Publishing, Paris, http://dx.doi.org/10.1787/9789264114586-en.

OECD and ITF (2015), *ITF Transport Outlook 2015*, OECD Publishing/ITF, Paris, http://dx.doi.org/10.1787/9789282107782-en.

SEA (2015), *2014 Market Forecast Report*, SEA Europe, Ships & Maritime Equipment Association, available at: www.seaeurope.eu/template.asp?f=publications.asp&jaar=2015.

Sweeney, E. (forthcoming), "Prospects for ocean energy to 2030", *OECD Science, Technology and Industry Working Papers*, OECD Publishing, Paris, forthcoming.

The Economist (2015), "How to catch the overfishermen: Big data allow fish to be protected as never before. Governments should take advantage of this", *The Economist*, print edition, 24 January.

UN (2015), *World Population Prospects: Key Findings & Advance Tables – 2015 Revision*, Department of Economic and Social Affairs, Population Division, United Nations, New York, http://esa.un.org/unpd/wpp/publications/files/key_findings_wpp_2015.pdf.

UN (2011), *World Population Prospects: 2010 Revision*, Department of Economic and Social Affairs, Population Division, United Nations, New York.

World Bank (2013), "Fish to 2030: Prospects for fisheries and aquaculture", *Agriculture and Environmental Services Discussion Paper 03*, World Bank, Washington, DC, http://documents.worldbank.org/curated/en/2013/12/18882045/fish-2030-prospects-fisheries-aquaculture.

Ytrestøyl, T, T.S. Aas and T. Aasgaard (2014), "Resource utilisation of Norwegian salmon farming in 2012 and 2013", Report 36/2014, Nofima, Norway, http://nofima.no/wp-content/uploads/2014/11/Nofima_report_resource_utilisation_Oct_2014.pdf.

Chapter 3.

Expected changes to the ocean environment: Impacts on the ocean economy

The aims of this chapter are to: take stock of the scientific literature on the current state of the world's ocean and its likely evolution to around 2030/50; indicate how current and future pressures and drivers, such as climate change, warming ocean water, acidification, deoxygenation, overfishing and pollution physically change the ocean environment and marine ecosystems and directly affect the economic potential of ocean-based activities; and explore some of the potential implications of those changes for biomass and biodiversity and the ocean economy as a whole. The resulting picture of the strains and stresses weighing on the ocean environment provides an important context for the subsequent chapters, which assess the future development of a range of key ocean-based industries.

Introduction

The ocean covers 71% of the planet's surface and contains 97% of the planet's water, yet more than 95% of the underwater world remains unexplored. It provides seafood, which is the primary source of animal protein in the diets of approximately 1 billion people (mostly in developing countries), and it accounts for at least 15% of the protein eaten by 60% of the planet's human population (FAO, 2014). Seafood products account for 10% of total agricultural food exports and 1% of world merchandise trade in terms of their value. The shipping industry carries approximately 90% of global trade; and the tourism industry, of which marine and coastal tourism is a major part, represents 5% of global GDP. More than 500 million people are engaged in ocean-related livelihoods (UNDP-GEF, 2012).

Marine ecosystems and their marine biodiversity also provide a variety of other services that are critical for human well-being. These services include the regulation of atmospheric and marine carbon dioxide (CO_2) concentrations, the provision of oxygen, the hydrothermal convection cycle, the hydrological cycle and coastal protection. Oceans, for example, have absorbed one-third of the anthropogenic carbon dioxide (Bijma et al., 2013).

Brander et al. (2015) estimate that the total ecosystem service benefits of achieving 10% coverage of the ocean's surface by marine protected areas (MPAs) are in the range USD 622-923 billion over the period 2015-50, and for 30% coverage range between USD 719 to 1 145 billion. The ecosystem services covered include coastal protection, fisheries, tourism, recreation and carbon storage provided by coral reefs, mangroves and coastal wetlands. Variation in benefits across scenarios is largely due to differences in the provision of services from coral reefs.

However, the anthropogenic carbon emissions caused by the burning of fossil fuels and deforestation have severely impacted the ocean. Since the industrial revolution, atmospheric CO_2 has increased from 278 to 400 parts per million (ppm) inducing ocean acidification at an unprecedented rate (ten times faster than any time in the last 55 million years) (Tripati, Roberts and Eagle, 2009; LaRiviere et al., 2012, Hönisch et al., 2012).

The overall risks confronted by the ocean and its ecosystem seem to have been significantly underestimated (UN, 2015). Already today, over 550 species of marine fishes and invertebrates are listed as threatened in the IUCN Red List. While the marine data are limited, a first IUCN Red List of Threatened Species assessment available for all known species indicated that 12% are under threat. The following subsections provide an overview of likely changes in the ocean environment up to 2050. They describe the current situation, and indicate what the situation in 2030/50 might be, what physical and biological impacts may emerge and how these changes might affect the economic potential of ocean-based activities. It is important to note the interconnections between the drivers and changes addressed in each subsection. By way of illustration, rising CO_2 emissions contribute to rising ocean acidification, which in turn affects certain marine creatures and, further compounded by e.g. ocean warming, pollution and ultimately the ocean's biomass.

Sea temperatures and sea levels

The largest increase in the storage of heat in the climate system over recent decades has been in the ocean, leading to accelerating glacial melting and rising sea levels.

Situation to date and likely future trends

Over the period from 1971 to 2010, the ocean warmed at average rates of >0.1°C per decade in the upper 75 metres (m) of the water column and 0.015°C per decade at a depth of 700 m, with regional, seasonal and inter-annual variations. The strongest warming trends have been found at high latitudes (Rhein et al., 2013). The global temperature difference between the ocean's surface and a depth of 200 m increased on average by 0.25°C from 1971 to 2010 (Levitus et al., 2009).

Ocean thermal expansion and glacier melting have been the main culprits in the rise in mean sea level in the 20th century. Observations since 1971 indicate that thermal expansion and glacier melt (excluding Antarctic glaciers peripheral to the ice sheet) explain 75% of the observed rise. The contribution of the Greenland and Antarctic ice sheets has increased since the early 1990s, partly from increased outflow induced by warming of the immediately adjacent ocean (Church et al., 2013).

Since satellite measurements began in 1993, the global sea level has risen by 3.2 millimetres a year, which is almost double the mean rate of increase over the whole of the 20th century and triple the mean rate compared to the beginning of the 20th century (Robinson, Calov and Ganopolski, 2012).

Figure 3.1 illustrates the contrasting outcomes under the highest emissions pathway, the IPCC business-as-usual scenario (RCP8.5) versus the lowest emissions pathway, the IPCC stringent emission-mitigation scenario (RCP2.6). Ocean physics and chemistry would be quite different in these two emissions scenarios, with the differences becoming ever more pronounced as we move through the 21st century.

Figure 3.1. **Projected atmospheric greenhouse gas emission pathways 2000-2100**

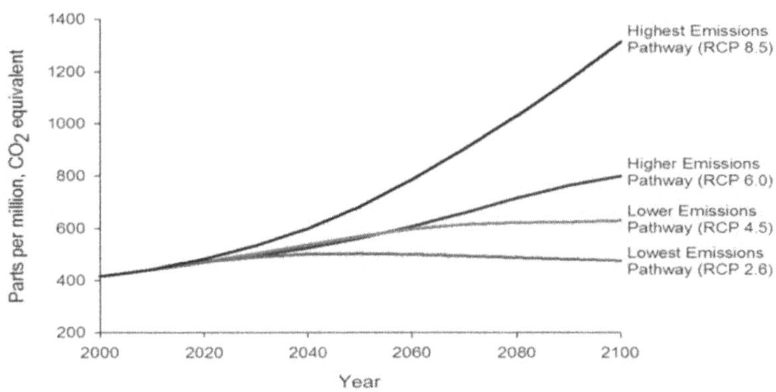

Source: Based on data from the *Representative Concentration Pathways Database* (Version 2.0.5).

By 2100, for the business-as-usual scenario, the average global increase in mean sea level is expected to be around 0.86 m, which would be 16 centimetres more than in the stringent emission-mitigation scenario (Stocker et al., 2013), although some places would experience significant deviations of local and regional sea-level change from the global average increase. The biggest sea-level rise is expected in the tropics (Perrette et al., 2013), whereas most regions located near current and former glaciers and ice sheets may experience a sea-level fall (Rhein et al., 2013).

Future ice melting will be accelerated by reduced surface reflection, which would further increase surface melting. The Arctic summer sea may disappear by 2037 or shortly thereafter (Stroeve et al., 2007). According to a recent paper (Khan et al., 2014), the ice sheet in northeast Greenland is melting faster than previously predicted. Sustained global warming greater than the threshold of 4°C compared to pre-industrial levels could lead to the near-complete loss of the Greenland ice sheet over a millennium or more, causing a global mean sea-level rise of about 7 m (Church et al., 2013). In such an extreme scenario, the increased melt water would bring an enormous amount of fresh water, changing currents, reducing salinity, increasing wave heights and altering wave directions in the Southern and Arctic Oceans (Rhein et al., 2013).

Physical and biological implications

All organisms specialise in a limited range of ambient temperatures, which affects the optimal performance of many organisms at temperatures beyond these ranges (Bijma et al., 2013). An organism in climatic conditions exceeding these limits can be affected in its growth, body size, behaviour, immune defences, feeding and reproductive success (Pörtner et al., 2014). For example, fishes in warmer waters are expected to have a smaller maximum body size and smaller size at first maturity (Kolding, Haug and Stefansson, 2008; Daufresne, Lengfellner and Sommer, 2009). Fishes with smaller bodies, as a consequence of warmer environments, are likely to suffer higher natural mortality rates (Anderson et al., 2008).

The capacity of present-day fauna and flora in marine ecosystems to compensate for, or keep up with, the rate of ongoing thermal change is limited. However, regional patterns will likely shift and genetic adaptation may occur, resulting in global redistribution of catch potential for fishes and invertebrates. The impacts of climate change on marine biodiversity have already resulted in either a loss or degradation of 50% of salt marshes, 35% of mangroves, 30% of coral reefs and 20% of sea grasses worldwide (Doney et al., 2009).

As a reaction to warming, many species – including various invertebrates, commercially important fish species and marine mammals – move to regions where the temperature is similar to that in their original habitats (Chambers et al., 2013; Jones and Cheung, 2015; Gibert and DeLong, 2014; Vergés et al., 2014), potentially causing permanent changes to ecosystems, including extinctions of some species (Jones and Cheung, 2015). By the mid-21st century, biodiversity is expected to increase at mid and high latitudes and to decrease in the tropics (Pörtner et al., 2014) due mostly to regional shifting and genetic adaptation. These shifts will continue with projected ocean warming (Pinsky et al., 2013; Jones and Cheung, 2015, Hiddink, Burrows and García Molinos, 2015).

Rising seawater temperatures may impact surface ocean stratification, which affects nutrient availability and primary productivity due to reduced biologically important mixing zones. However, outcomes may differ by region. Surface ocean stratification can minimise the transportation of oxygen-rich surface water to deeper layers, and deplete oxygen in mid-water layers, which affects the availability of nutrients (Keeling, Körtzinger and Gruber, 2010; Stramma et al., 2011; Hoegh-Guldberg and Bruno, 2010). Some observations suggest that annual primary productivity may decrease at low latitudes, in the north Pacific and in the Southern Ocean, while others suggest an increase in primary productivity in the north Atlantic and Arctic (Bijma et al., 2013).

These changes are projected to lead to a turnover of species in marine ecosystems, with regional differences of losses and invasions (Cheung et al., 2009). Some 60% of the species turnover is projected to take place in sub-polar regions, the tropics and semi-enclosed seas (Carpenter et al., 2008; Cheung et al., 2009), whereas species invasion is projected to be most intense in the Arctic and the Southern Ocean.

Whereas in the Intergovernmental Panel on Climate Change (IPCC) emission mitigation scenario the risks for marine ecosystem services are projected to be still moderate, cascading consequences would be expected in the business-as-usual scenario by 2100, notably for marine biology, including altered food web dynamics, reduced abundance of habitat-forming species, range shifts and expansion of pathogens (Hoegh-Guldberg and Bruno, 2010).

Likely effects on the ocean economy

Rising sea levels present a critical challenge, particularly in coastal areas that are inhabited by a large and growing proportion of the world's population. The projected sea-level rise could inundate low-lying areas, submerge coastal marshes and wetlands, erode beaches, exacerbate flooding and increase the salinity of rivers, bays and aquifers. With higher sea levels, coastal regions could also be subject to increased economic damages from intensified tropical storms. A threat is attributed to the potential damage to harbours and ports due to sea-level rise (IPPC, 2013), which could lead to overall economic losses of USD 111.6 billion by 2050 and USD 367.2 billion by the end of this century (Noone, Sumaila and Diaz, 2012).

On a more positive note, reducing sea ice also presents an opportunity to open new waterways for shipping (IPCC, 2014). Reductions in Arctic sea ice would facilitate new trade routes such as the Northwest Passage, possibly making trans-Arctic shipping economically viable, and oil and gas extraction, mining and tourism more accessible. However, this development is projected to increase emissions of greenhouse gases and other pollutants (Lauer et al., 2009; Corbett et al., 2010), and facilitate the invasion of non-indigenous species carried on hulls and in ballast water (Lewis, Riddle and Hewitt, 2004).

As described earlier in this section, temperature, wind patterns and productivity are projected to induce shifts in species distribution, moving towards the poles and into deeper waters. Researchers have observed that the composition of fisheries' catches is already shifting: for example, there has been a shift of 30-130 km towards the poles in the north Atlantic, Antarctic and Arctic waters, and of 3.5 m per decade into deeper waters, resulting in species gains and losses for fisheries (Gattuso et al., 2015; Beaugrand, Edwards and Legendre, 2010; Weimerskirch et al., 2012; Wassmann et al., 2011).

The changing ocean environment could cut both ways whereas the negative side likely overweighs. On the one hand, economic opportunities could emerge as a result of poleward shifts of commercial fish and invertebrate species. Increasing abundances are projected for mid-trophic levels and higher latitudes. The fishery impacts of global warming on both Iceland's and Greenland's gross domestic product are expected to be positive, with the economy of Greenland projected to benefit substantially (Arnason, 2007). On the other hand, that increased catch potential could be reduced, since these areas are also a hot spot for acidification and reduced dissolved oxygen in the ocean. Climate change research predicts that catches in high-latitude countries may increase. Hence, it is expected that fisheries in the Arctic and Southern Oceans may benefit from increased primary production, with projected revenue increasing by 14-59% by the mid-21st century relative to the present day under a high-emissions scenario (Pörtner et al., 2014).

Economic losses are expected to be the biggest in the tropics and semi-enclosed seas (e.g. Mediterranean Sea, Persian Gulf) (Jones and Cheung, 2015; Barange et al., 2014; Cheung et al., 2010) due to high rates and varying patterns of local species extinction

(Bell et al., 2013. The loss of critical habitats, such as coral reefs and mangroves, will exacerbate the impacts on tropical fisheries and hence on vulnerable human communities. Further economic losses are expected for coastal fishing due to some species shifting into deeper water.

Risk of impact on mid-latitude fisheries is more variable depending on the locations and exploited species, but it is expected to increase substantially in the business-as-usual scenario because of the combination of ocean warming, acidification and deoxygenation (Pörtner et al., 2014).

The IPCC (Wong et al., 2014) estimates that a 2°C global temperature increase by 2050 could cause global losses in landed catch value of USD 17-41 billion annually (at 2005 values), with an estimated cost of adaptation for the fisheries of USD 7-30 billion annually over a 40-year timeframe between 2010 and 2050 (Sumaila and Cheung, 2010).

In developing countries where fish catch provides jobs, livelihoods and nourishment for millions of coastal communities, turnover and an increased likelihood of infectious diseases could have serious impacts on food security (Cooley et al., 2012; Barange et al., 2014; Lam, Cheung and Sumaila, 2014; Bell et al., 2013). Ultimately, much will depend on the flexibility and response capacities of food production systems and coastal communities (Elmqvist et al., 2003; Planque, Bellier and Loots, 2011). However, the implications for the fishing industry are still poorly understood and future shifts in primary production and knock-on effects through food webs and into fisheries remain uncertain (Planque et al., 2011; Stock et al., 2011).

Sea-level rise will bring saline water into deltas and estuaries, where aquaculture commonly occurs, driving aquaculture upstream and destroying wetlands. Infectious diseases also pose a greater threat to aquaculture in a warmer ocean, with impacts observed, for example, in oysters and abalone aquaculture (Burge et al., 2014) and coastal fish farming (Garai, 2014).

Acidification

The drastic surge in anthropogenic CO_2 emissions since the industrialisation has not only resulted in the warming of the planet but has also increased the acidity of the ocean, causing a progressive increase in ocean inorganic carbon concentrations and decreased water pH and calcium carbonate saturation. Ocean acidification represents one of the major drivers of oceanophysical and biological changes.

Situation to date and likely future trends

Increasing atmospheric CO_2 levels have led to a rise in its concentration in near-surface layers of the ocean due to the constant gas exchange between the atmosphere and the ocean. The uptake of anthropogenic CO_2 by the ocean increases the partial pressure of carbon dioxide (pCO_2) and dissolves inorganic carbon. This process decreases pH and calcium carbonate minerals aragonite and calcite in seawater – both are critical drivers of solubility of shells and skeletons (Gattuso and Hansson, 2011).

The change in aragonite saturation over the industrial period has been more than five times greater than natural variability over the past millennium and over glacial-interglacial time scales (Joos and Spahni, 2008; Friedrich et al., 2012). The pH value of ocean surface water has already decreased by 0.02 pH units per decade from its pre-industrial baseline, with a steady overall decrease of 0.1 pH units since the pre-industrial period (Hoegh-Guldberg and Bruno, 2010). Seasonally under-saturated conditions of calcium carbonate minerals are already present in the north-eastern Pacific, the California upwelling system (Feely et al., 2008), the Arctic Ocean (Robbins et al., 2013) and expected for the Southern Ocean (Mattsdotter et al., 2014).

In the future, chemical and physical properties of the ocean will be quite different under business-as-usual and emission mitigation scenarios, although differences between the two trajectories will not be apparent by 2035, but rather by the end of the century (Gattuso et al., 2015, IPCC, 2014). In 2100, the ocean will have a lower pH under the business-as-usual scenario than under the emission mitigation scenario. The 21st century mean change in global surface pH alterations ranges from -0.327 to -0.333 units for the business-as-usual scenario, which would be almost 170% higher compared with preindustrial levels, compared to -0.069 to -0.071 units under the emission mitigation scenario (Gattuso et al., 2015). The volume occupied by under-saturated water that is corrosive to unprotected calcium carbonate shells and skeletons expands from 76% of the whole ocean volume in the 1990s to 91% in 2100 with the business-as-usual scenario and to 83% under the emission mitigation scenario (Gattuso et al., 2015).

Simulations show that the Arctic may see the biggest pH changes in the future since in the high latitudes waters absorb most of the CO_2 from the atmosphere (Doney et al., 2009; Laffoley and Baxter, 2009). Thus, lower pH values are spreading from the poles toward the tropics. A 24-year time series of seawater data from the Iceland Sea has revealed a 50% faster surface-water acidification rate in these Arctic waters than in subtropical regions of the Atlantic (Olafsson et al., 2009).

Ocean acidification in coastal waters is considerably larger than that in the open ocean, partly driven by upwelling (Feely et al., 2008), fresh water input (Salisbury et al., 2008), eutrophication (Cai et al., 2011) and biogeochemical processes (Borges and Gypens, 2010).

Physical and biological implications

Due to acidification, a broad range of marine organisms will experience reduced calcification, reduced rates of repair and weakened calcified structures (Kroeker et al., 2013). Rate of reproductive success, early life-stage survival, feeding rate and stress-response mechanisms may also be affected (Pörtner et al., 2014).

The reaction of CO_2 with seawater reduces the availability of carbonate ions which are necessary for marine calcifying organisms, such as corals, molluscs, echinoderms and crustaceans, to produce their shells and skeletons consisting of aragonite ($CaCO_3$) (Fabry, Brad and Feely, 2008). This leads to reductions in survival, calcification, growth, development and abundance for a broad range of marine organisms (Kroeker et al., 2013).

In general, heavily calcified organisms, including calcified algae, corals, krill, molluscs and the larval stages of echinoderms, are the most heavily impacted (Melzner et al., 2009). These organisms will experience reduced calcification, lower rates of repair and weakened calcified structures; reproductive success, early life-stage survival, feeding rate and stress-response mechanisms may also be affected (Pörtner et al., 2013). More active organisms, such as mobile crustaceans and fish, may be less sensitive to acidification (Melzner et al., 2009) whereas some fleshy algae and diatoms may marginally even benefit from the same conditions (Kroeker et al., 2013).

The biggest effect of acidification is a decrease of coral abundance. Even under the stringent emissions scenario of the IPCC which is consistent with the Paris Agreement of keeping the mean global temperature increase well below 2°C in the 21st century, warm-water corals and mid-latitude bivalves will be at high risk by 2100 and many already by 2050 (Gattuso et al., 2015). Although coral species may be able to adapt to changing environments (Hume et al., 2015, Silverstein, Cunning and Baker, 2015) the time scale of adaptation is likely to be long given the relatively lengthy generation times of corals (3-100 years) and their narrow window of temperature tolerance (Hoegh-Guldberg, 2012).

Acidification appears to have neurological effects on fish with repercussions for their behaviour. Experiments have shown that fish from CO_2 seeps may be more attracted to predator odour and exhibit bolder behaviour than fish from control reefs. Fish emerged more quickly from their hiding places after a disturbance and ventured farther from their hiding places than other fish because the change in pH induces neurological alterations, disrupting a nervous system receptor (Munday et al., 2014; Nilsson et al., 2012).

It is the interactive effects and feedback of changing seawater CO_2 chemistry with other stressors, such as warming, eutrophication, alien species and overfishing, that may potentially lead to long-term shifts in species composition (Wittmann and Pörtner, 2013; Lohbeck, Riebesell and Reusch, 2014), whereas the results of compensatory dynamics are not yet clear. Studies examining the impacts of acidification on multi-species assemblages have reported opposing responses of closely related species within the same assemblage, potentially due to compensatory dynamics among the most tolerant species (Fabricius et al., 2011; Hale et al., 2011; Kroeker et al., 2011; Porzio et al., 2011). This and other factors, such as nutritional status or source population, which could increase substantial variation in organisms' responses (Kroeker et al., 2013), should be further investigated to project future behaviour on climate change.

Likely effects on the ocean economy

The above physical and biological changes will affect income, employment and food security through their effects on capture fisheries, marine aquaculture, maritime and coastal tourism, marine biotechnology and regulatory services such as coastal protection.

The decrease in maximum body size of fish may reduce maximum catch potential by 2050 in both the North Atlantic and Northeast Pacific and result in economic losses for fish productivity (Cheung et al., 2011). If the impacts of acidification occur globally and there is a synchronous reduction in global supply of fishery products, such as oysters or mussels, demand may drive prices up, partially offsetting losses caused by reduced production. The IPCC (2014) model projections suggest a potential loss of up to 13% of annual total fishery value in the United States, or globally over USD 100 billion annually by 2100 (Cooley and Doney, 2009; Narita, Rehdanz and Tol, 2012).

With the expected changes in climate and in both the quantity and quality of marine fish catch, the economic rent generated through fishing could be altered, with the direction and magnitude of change varying across regional fishing zones. Owing to increased sea temperatures, the reduction in coral cover and its associated fisheries production is expected to lead to a potential net revenue loss of between USD 95 million and 140 million (current net revenue is USD 310 million) per year in the Caribbean basin by 2015 (Trotman et al., 2009). A World Bank report estimated the annual economic impact of climate change on the coast of Viti Levu, Fiji to be USD 0.1 million to 2 million for subsistence fisheries, and USD 0.05 million to 0.8 million for commercial coastal fisheries by 2050 (Lal, Kinch and Wickham, 2009).

Climate- and acidification-related impacts will also affect marine aquaculture, albeit varying by location, species and aquaculture method. Farmed species at higher trophic levels are expected to exhibit higher mortality rates and lower productivity under warming and acidification, with open and semi-open aquaculture and those in the tropics particularly at risk (Callaway et al., 2012, Ruckelshaus et al., 2013). Depending on the scenario, the US production of molluscs in open aquaculture could reduce by 3-13% (IPCC, 2014; Cooley and Doney, 2009; Cooley et al., 2012). A reduction of mussel production by 50% or 70% is projected in the United Kingdom under the mitigation emission scenario or business-as-usual scenario, respectively (Callaway et al., 2012). Projected declines in oyster production resulting from warming are much lower, but ocean acidification increases the risk in upwelling areas, such as the northeast Pacific (Barton et al., 2012). The global economic cost of losses in the capture and aquaculture of molluscs resulting from ocean acidification based on the high-emissions scenario could be higher than USD 100 billion by the year 2100 (Narita, Rehdanz and Tol, 2012).

Local economies derive substantial benefits from the ecosystem services that coral reefs provide including coastline and habitat protection, nitrogen fixing, sand supply, climate records, fisheries, medicine, recreation and tourism (Hoegh-Guldberg, 2012). As a result, the loss of corals would be expected to hit local economies and even wider parts of the economy due to indirect effects. Coral reefs present a source of livelihood for about 500 million people and the corresponding global asset value of coral reefs is estimated at nearly USD 797.4 billion[1] (Cesar, Burke and Pet-Soede, 2003). For about a quarter of the countries with reef-related tourism, mainly less-developed countries, this kind of tourism accounts for more than 15% of gross domestic product (Burke et al., 2011). In some tourist destinations, the value of coral reefs can be up to USD 1 million per hectare per year, as is the case for Hawaii (Cesar, Burke and Pet-Soede, 2003). In Australia, the economic value added of the Great Barrier Reef World Heritage Area for specified reef-dependent industries and activities, including tourism, recreation, commercial fishing and scientific research, was estimated to be USD 5.68 billion in 2011-12 and to have generated almost 69 000 full-time equivalent jobs (Deloitte Access Economics, 2013). The loss of coral reefs would affect indirectly wider parts of the economy. It would mean a loss of the above-mentioned ecosystem services and additionally make some islands and coastal areas more vulnerable to tsunamis, storm surges, wave impact and coastal erosion. In addition, decreases in the quality and abundance of coral reef cover are expected to negatively affect tourism. As a result, the loss of coral reefs under the emission mitigation scenario and business-as-usual scenario could cost between USD 1.9 billion and USD 12 billion per year, respectively (Chen et al., 2015). This is a conservative estimate since it includes only the estimated loss of corals to tourism; hence, the effects for the wider economy would be even higher.

Ocean as regulator of concentration of oxygen

Decreased concentration of oxygen in the ocean impacts the lives of marine organisms and related ocean-based industries.

Situation to date and likely future trends

The decrease of oxygen content is most apparent in two main forms. The first form is anoxia, a general trend of declining oxygen levels in tropical oceans and areas of the North Pacific over the last 50 years (Deutsch, Emerson and Thompson, 2005; Stramma et al., 2008; Keeling, Körtzinger and Gruber, 2010); the second form is the dramatic increase in coastal hypoxia associated with increased nutrient and phosphorus run-off from coastal eutrophication (Diaz and Rosenberg, 2008).

Anoxia is the result of decreased solubility of oxygen and enhanced stratification. Both can happen when sea waters warm and excessive rain or land runoff lead to an excessive fresh water influx. Most of the time stratification is a natural process, but long-term warming trends in the ocean, climate-related precipitation changes and altered riverine input insert a human element: a warmer ocean is more stratified, holds less oxygen and may make new regions subject to low oxygen (Levin et al., 2009). In the present climate change cycle, these low-oxygen areas are expanding (Keeling, Körtzinger and Gruber, 2010). Studies also indicate ongoing dissolved oxygen depletion and vertical expansion of the oxygen minimum zone in the tropical northeast Atlantic Ocean (Stramma et al., 2008, 2009), making habitat compression an increasingly global issue. As the expansion of oxygen minimum zones encompasses nearly all Atlantic equatorial waters, the estimated annual loss of vertical habitat (up to 1 m) resulting from continual oxygen minimum zone expansion equates with a 15% habitat loss in the upper 200 m between 1960 and 2010 (Brandt et al., 2010; Stramma et al., 2011).

Overall predictions for ocean oxygen content suggest a decline of between 1% and 4% by 2100 with the range of uncertainty linked to both the biological and physical elements of the models, including varying assumptions of climate sensitivity (Keeling, Körtzinger and Gruber, 2010). Under the business-as-usual scenario and the emission mitigation scenario, the ocean oxygen inventory is consistently projected to decrease by $-3.45 \pm 0.44\%$ or $-1.81 \pm 0.31\%$, respectively, with the largest changes occurring in the subsurface mid-latitude regions. The reduction in the level of oxygen in seawater due to climate change is practically irreversible on timescales that are relevant for human society (Gruber, 2011).

The second form of oxygen minimum zones is the dramatic increase in coastal hypoxia due to run off from land-based eutrophication, sometimes also referred to as dead zones[2] (Vaquer-Sunyer and Duarte, 2008). Multiple reports provide evidence for an unambiguous increase in the number of cases of coastal hypoxia (approximately 30% oxygen saturation) and its extension, severity and duration (Vaquer-Sunyer and Duarte, 2008; Stramma et al., 2008). The outlook for these so-called dead zones is grim. In the future, the level of nitrogen in coastal marine systems due to coastal run-off is expected to more than double (a 2.4-fold increase) between 2000 and 2050 (Tilman et al., 2001).

Increased inputs of nutrients from land are enhancing algal blooms, and the sinking of this organic matter to the seafloor and subsequent decay leads to a high oxygen demand in bottom waters (Kemp et al., 2009). Since the 1960s, the number of so-called dead zones has approximately doubled every decade, with their occurrence correlated to adjacent centres of human population and major watersheds (Diaz and Rosenberg, 2008). Areas where exchange of water is restricted, such as inland seas or estuaries, are particularly prone to these effects. Seriously affected regions include the northern Adriatic Sea, the Black Sea, the Baltic Sea, the northern Gulf of Mexico and the Chesapeake Bay (Rabotyagov et al., 2014; Elliott, Pierson and Roman, 2013). Hence, coastal hypoxia is emerging as one of the global threats to coastal ecosystems. Growth of this phenomenon is expected to continue. Hypoxia is expected to increase further due to the combined effects of increasing eutrophication and elevating sea temperatures (Stramma et al., 2009). This development enhances the respiratory oxygen demand of coastal ecosystems (Prince and Goodyear, 2006), reduces the oxygen solubility (Prince et al., 2010) and ventilation by affecting stratification patterns (Worm et al., 2005). Once a coastal marine system develops a dead zone, it can develop a new dead zone each year (Baird et al., 2004). The latest estimates indicate over 600 dead zones in the world's coastal areas covering more than 245 000 km^2 of sea bottom (Diaz and Rosenberg, 2008).

The worldwide distribution of hypoxia is related to major population centres and watersheds that export large quantities of nutrients, specifically nitrogen and phosphorus. Up to 1970, there were scattered reports of dead zones in North America and northern Europe. By the 1990s, dead zones were prevalent in North America, northern Europe and Japan. By the 2000s, there were increased reports of dead zones in South America, southern Europe and Australia. Considering the close association of coastal hypoxia and human population, it is likely that Asia and the Indo-Pacific have many unreported hypoxic areas.

Hundreds of experiments to determine thresholds of hypoxia for a range of benthic organisms have been conducted. However, proposed oxygen thresholds for hypoxia are based on limited observations of impacts on organisms. A thorough empirical assessment of the available experimental evidence is still pending. While the thresholds of hypoxia suggested in the literature range broadly from 0.28 mg O_2/litre to 4 mg O_2/litre (Paerl, 2006), most reports (55%) refer to a value of 2 mg O_2/l or lower (mean ± SE of thresholds proposed in the literature: 2.31 ± 0.10 mg O_2/litre) (Turner et al., 2005). This threshold refers to the oxygen level at which fisheries collapse; however, there is ample experimental evidence that a 2 mg O_2/litre threshold may be inadequate to describe the onset of hypoxia impacts for many organisms that experience hypoxia impacts at higher oxygen concentrations. Moreover, the diversity of behavioural and physiologic adaptations to hypoxia suggests that different species are likely to exhibit different vulnerability to hypoxia and may have, therefore, different oxygen thresholds, a possibility that is not addressed by the conventional oxygen thresholds in use (Vaquer-Sunyer and Duarte, 2008).

In addition, the increased frequency and intensity of oxygen-deprived "dead zones" along the world's coasts can negatively impact environmental conditions in far more than local waters. Scientists explain that the increased amount of nitrous oxide produced in hypoxic waters can elevate concentrations in the atmosphere, further exacerbating the impacts of global warming and contributing to ozone "holes" that increase our exposure to harmful UV radiation (Codispoti, 2010).

Physical and biological implications

The expansion of oxygen minimum zones that minimise the transportation of oxygen-rich surface water to deeper layers have a profound impact on pelagic and benthic ecosystems and on the physiological performance and distribution of marine organisms (Pörtner, 2010).

Increased nutrient run-off can result in increases in algal bloom and changes in algal species composition, leading to low-oxygen zones. These can cause a major loss in biodiversity and impact the surviving organisms through sub-lethal stresses, such as reduced growth and reproduction, physiological stress, forced migration, reduction of suitable habitat, increased vulnerability to predation and disruption of life cycles (Rabalais, Turner and Wiseman, 2002). Benthic organisms are particularly vulnerable to coastal hypoxia because they live farthest from contact with atmospheric oxygen supply and because coastal sediments tend to be depleted in oxygen relative to the overlying water column (Vaquer-Sunyer and Duarte, 2008).

Generally, large species are more sensitive to hypoxia than small ones, albeit with variations between life stages (IPCC, 2014). Large, mobile and more active fish would face a survival challenge in these oxygen-poor waters and migrate to more oxygen-rich waters, while more simple specialised organisms with a lower need for oxygen would remain and even thrive in the absence of predation from larger species. Within a species, early life stages may be more subject to oxygen stress than older life stages (Levin et al., 2009).

The magnitude of habitat loss due to oxygen minimum zones reduces the usable vertical habitat for high oxygen-demand tropical pelagic billfishes and tunas, thereby possibly increasing encounter rates between fish (Stramma et al., 2011). The impact of oxygen minimum zones may lead to a 10-50% worldwide decline of pelagic predator diversity (Worm et al., 2005), with the effect of a habitat compression likely to alter the encounter rates between these predators and their prey.

Fishing in these reduced habitat zones increases the vulnerability of tropical pelagic fishes (Stramma et al., 2011). The increased vulnerability of billfishes and many tuna species (Prince et al., 2010) raises a particular challenge with regard to the high harvest rates in expanded oxygen minimum zones taking place in global fisheries at present. Considering that fishing pressure is likely to continue at a high rate into the foreseeable future, and the expansion of oxygen minimum zones is expected to worsen with the present cycle of climate change, associated global warming and increasing atmospheric CO_2 levels, any further loss of habitat might be expected to adversely impact the sustainability of these fish stocks (Brewer and Peltzer, 2009).

Over long periods of time, hypoxia or anoxia could eliminate almost all the benthic fauna, with the result that the ecosystem becomes progressively more dominated by microorganisms. Hypoxia and anoxia might lead to mass mortality of sea life through attrition of intolerant species (Levin et al., 2009; Noone, Diaz and Sumaila, 2013).

Likely effects on the ocean economy

Coastal hypoxia can have social and economic effects on coastal communities, including loss of tourism due to restrictions on swimming and boating, beach closures, public health concerns, and consumption of fish and shellfish, which all imply negative impacts on estuarine and coastal fishery resources.

The northern Gulf of Mexico has a seasonal hypoxic zone that forms every year in late summer. In June 2015, the National Oceanic and Atmospheric Administration (NOAA) measured a "dead zone" ranging 6 474 square miles (16 760 km^2) in the Gulf of Mexico, stretching from south Texas all the way to Alabama (EPA, 2016). That seasonal dead zone poses a real threat to the gulf's seafood and tourism industry, which generates more than 600 000 jobs and USD 9 billion in wages annually. The gulf produces roughly 40% of all the seafood in the lower 48 states. The NOAA previously estimated that the dead zone costs the US seafood and tourism industries USD 82 million a year (NOAA, 2010).

Agricultural and industrial activity expanded rapidly around the Black Sea in the 1960s, especially in the Danube River watershed, resulting in increased nutrient influxes and eutrophication that lead to expanding hypoxic zones (Selman et al., 2008). In summer 1973, hypoxic zones measured 3 500 km^2. They had increased tenfold by 1978, peaking at 40 000 km^2 in the late 1980s. During this period, the fishery that once supported over 25 species of commercially valuable fish, worth roughly USD 2 billion, was reduced by 90%. The tourism sector too – dependent as it is on the recreational value of beaches and clean waters – was affected by this event. The decline in revenues from tourism was estimated at USD 500 million (Battaglini, Plonka and Merla, 2008). These losses did not include health effects, decline in recreation opportunities, biodiversity and aesthetic concerns (Rabotyagov et al., 2014).

Hypoxia also impacts marine aquaculture, since decreased oxygen concentration impairs larval growth (Miller et al., 1995), and adult fishes reduce food intake and growth when oxygen falls to 60-70% of saturation (Pichavant et al., 2000).

Ocean currents and circulation patterns

Major ocean currents transport enormous amounts of water with its physical and chemical characteristics around the globe. However, melting glaciers and increasing CO_2 in the atmosphere might lead to alterations of water currents and circulation patterns.

Situation to date and likely future trends

Ocean currents and circulation patterns play a significant role in the thermohaline circulation system. The thermohaline circulation spans the globe like a giant conveyor belt. It pulls the dense water of the pole regions downward. At a depth of around 2 000 m, the water flows across the ocean floor halfway around the globe into the North Atlantic and Southern Ocean.[3] Even the Gulf Stream and its branches are driven by convection and thermohaline circulation.

The Atlantic thermohaline circulation is an important feature of the climate system, since it is responsible for most of the northward heat transport in the North Atlantic (up to 1015 watts) (Ganachaud and Wunsch, 2000). A collapse of the thermohaline circulation is widely discussed as one of a number of "low probability – high impact" risks associated with global warming (Rahmstorf et al., 2005).

Depending on scenario, current and wind trajectory is expected to experience substantial transformation as the global sea temperature rises. The IPCC (Rhein et al., 2013) projects climate change to increase fresh water run-off from the melting glaciers to the sea by 2050, which could create changes to convection and thermohaline circulation, potentially increasing the incidence of hypoxic and anoxic conditions (Chan et al., 2008; Roegner, Needoba and Baptista, 2011).

Figure 3.2. **The world ocean currents of the thermohaline circulation system**

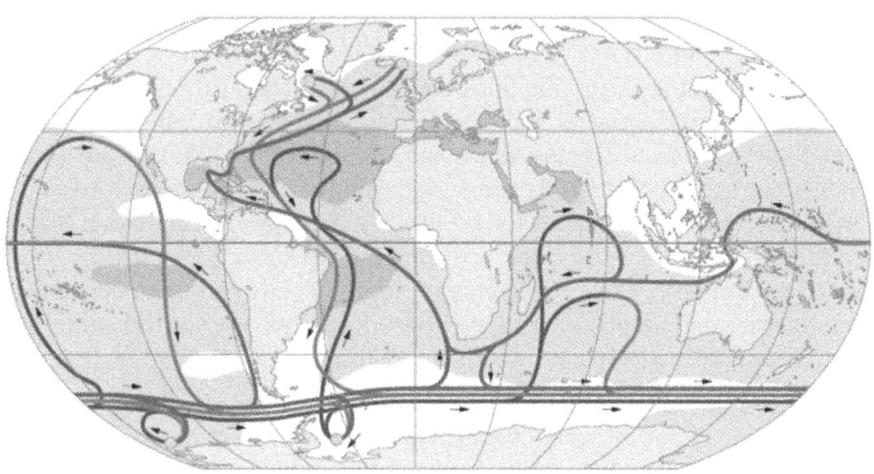

Source: Maribus (2010).

Physical and biological implications

In case of increased glacier melting, enormous amounts of fresh water would be brought into the ocean circulation. In such an extreme scenario, the increased melt water input from Greenland and high-Arctic glaciers might slow down the conveyor belt effect with major repercussions for the Gulf Stream. The increased water volume would alter patterns of ocean mixing by down welling water masses, weakening the oxygen transport to the deep sea. Moreover, the altered patterns of ocean mixing by down welling water masses could reduce nutrient availability in surface water layers (Steinacher et al., 2010), and increase stratification of the ocean in low to mid-latitudes with a growing incidence of hypoxic and anoxic conditions (Chan et al., 2008; Roegner, Needoba and Baptista, 2011). Evidence was found from marine Arctic ecosystems where rising temperatures resulting in freshening of surface waters from melting glaciers were able to initiate significant changes in lower/middle trophic food chains, and alter the quantity and quality of food supply to upper trophic levels (Wassmann et al., 2011).

The IPCC (2014) points out that climate change-induced intensification of ocean upwelling in some eastern boundary systems, as observed in the last decade, may lead to regional cooling rather than warming of surface waters, the total effects of which are still uncertain. This phenomenon could enhance productivity. On the other hand, ocean upwelling could also worsen hypoxia and acidification, and lead to associated biomass reduction in fish and invertebrate stocks. Due to these contradictory observations, there is currently no certainty about the future trends of major upwelling systems and how their drivers, such as enhanced productivity, acidification and hypoxia, will shape ecosystem characteristics.

Likely effects on the ocean economy

The effects on the ocean economy have still hardly been identified. New opportunities for fisheries could be opened from enhanced river run-off and increased precipitation, which may result in a shift from marine to more brackish and even fresh water fish communities (Kirby and Beaugrand, 2009). Nevertheless, changes in the thermohaline circulation and upwelling systems could affect commercially valuable fish stocks as ocean currents and temperature influence the dispersal of larvae, which determines the connectivity of fish populations (O'Conner et al., 2007).

In addition, renewable energy facilities could be affected due to the interdependencies between sea-surface temperature anomaly, local wind-energy input, and changes in currents and surface waves (Huang and Qiao, 2009; Spall, 2006). More (less) wind-energy input decreases (increases) the sea surface temperature. In other words, more wind energy input can result in stronger vertical mixing. Stronger mixing can transport more heat from the surface to the subsurface, affecting the sea surface temperature and oceanic circulation. For example, large wind-energy input at low latitudes can enhance the meridional overturning circulation and poleward heat flux via vertical mixing (Huang, Huang and Wang, 2007; McPhaden and Zhang, 2002).

In addition, it is thinkable that the fresh water increase of melting glaciers in the Southern and Arctic Oceans entering the ocean, and thus decreasing salinity, might affect salinity-gradient or osmotic power stations. Altering currents in high latitudes might affect the location of renewable energy platforms, such as ocean-wave energy and ocean-current power plants. However, in light of high infrastructure costs, it is questionable if renewable energy platforms will be installed in these regions.

Ocean and the hydrological cycle

The ocean plays a major role in the hydrological cycle. Thus, changes in the ocean environment might also lead to changes in the hydrological cycle, affecting precipitation and fresh water resources.

State to date and likely future trends

The IPCC expects changes in precipitation worldwide. In regions with snowfall, climate change has already altered stream flow seasonality. For example, in countries of the northern hemisphere, warming has reduced the maximum snow depth in spring and brought forward snow melt seasons and the spring maximum of snowmelt discharge (Hartmann et al., 2013).

All projections for the 21st century show continued mass loss from glaciers leading to increased total melt water. Normally, glaciered catchment run-off reaches an annual maximum in summer. However, researchers indicate the Arctic could break earlier during the year, and glacier-fed rivers melt. The hydrological regime of the Arctic is particularly susceptible to warming because of the dominance of the thermally sensitive permafrost zone and its controlling zone of the water cycle.

Physical and biological implications

The IPCC considers that there is a medium confidence that the changing hydrological cycle will reduce fresh water resources in the 21st century, which will lead to intensified droughts in some seasons and in most dry subtropical regions due to reduced precipitation and/or increased evapotranspiration, whereas wet regions and seasons could become wetter (IPCC, 2012; Sun et al., 2012). In most dry subtropical regions, the changed precipitation patterns might lead to decreasing renewable surface water and groundwater resources with a higher extent and frequency of soil moisture droughts. It is likely that rainfall in subtropical latitudes, particularly in the Mediterranean, Mexico and Central America and parts of Australia will decrease. This could lead to less surface water and groundwater in most dry subtropical regions. For a range of scenarios, soil moisture droughts lasting 4-6 months could double in extent and frequency, and droughts longer than 12 months could become three times more common, between the mid-20th century and the end of the 21st century. This contrasts developments in higher latitudes, notably in India and parts of central Asia, where water resources may increase (Hartmann et al., 2013).

Likely effects on the ocean economy

As pointed out earlier, critical factors driving changes in the ocean environment are interdependent and interacting. Hence, increased water temperature; increased sediment, nutrient and pollutant loadings from heavy rainfall and river runoff; and increased concentration of pollutants during droughts, as well as disruption of treatment facilities during floods, create economic impacts that are not easy to quantify. The direct damages to assets due to global weather- and climate-related disaster losses since 1980 have ranged from a few billion to over USD 200 billion (in 2010 dollars).[4]

The IPCC (2012) points out that the prolonged drought in the Syrian Arab Republic – in its fourth consecutive year by 2011 – had affected around 1.3 million people; moreover, the loss of the 2008 harvest had accelerated migration to urban areas and increased levels of extreme poverty (UN, 2009, 2011; Sowers, Vengosh and Weinthal, 2011). Approximately 70% of the 200 000 affected farmers in the rain-fed areas have produced minimal to no yields because seeds were not planted due to poor soil moisture conditions or failed germination (USDA, 2008; FAO, 2009b). Herders in the region were reported to have lost around 80% of their livestock due to barren grasslands, and animal feed costs rose by 75%, forcing sales at 60-70% below cost (FAO, 2008). Many farmers and herders sold off productive assets (FAO, 2009b), eroding their source of livelihoods, which has triggered an unprecedented wave of refugees to countries in the northern hemisphere.

The contribution of the oceans' food production could be much increased, shifting a large share of global food production away from the land to the sea. The high quantities of protein – up to half of their weight – make algae one of the most interesting emerging food sources. Algae are simple, single-cell organisms that can grow very rapidly at sea, in polluted water and in places that would normally not generate food crops, ranging from giant seaweeds and kelps to microscopic slimes. Algae would be a cost-effective, land- and climate-neutral alternative to meat proteins while at the same time fixing large amounts of CO_2 from the atmosphere. The nutraceutical omega-3 fatty acids and carotenoids found in seaweeds may constitute the main source of future protein-rich fish feed for marine aquaculture. Already now, more than half of all aquatic species of harvested algae for human consumption are produced by aquaculture. With aquaculture expected to grow extensively in the next 15 years, the need for protein in aqua feed may possibly follow that trend. Thus, the oceans could present an opportunity to meet the increasing demand for protein, a challenge that will grow in the next decades due to at best stagnant harvest of capture fisheries.

Algal biomass can be used also in a wide range of other applications, including biofuels, fertilisers, cosmetics and wastewater treatment. Microalgae are productive photosynthetic organisms on this planet that can double biomass on a daily basis. Under optimum conditions, commercial algae farms can produce 5 000-10 000 gallons (equivalent to around 19 000-38 000 litres) of oil per acre, compared to just 350 gallons (about 1 300 litres) of ethanol biofuel per acre grown with crops like maize. Replacing all US biofuel production with algae oil would need around 2 million acres (almost 8 100 km^2) of desert; however, it would potentially allow 40 million acres (equivalent to around 161 874 km^2) of cropland to be planted with human food, and save billions of litres of irrigation water a year (Brennan and Owende, 2010; Chen et al., 2015; Milledge, 2011).

Unsustainable fishing

Illegal, unreported and unregulated (IUU) fishing, as well as unused catch and other forms of unsustainable fishing add pressures to the sustainability of marine ecosystems.

State to date and likely future trends

Unsustainable catch stems from a failure to adequately constrain fishing effort and the manner in which it is applied. Illegal, unreported and unregulated (IUU) fishing, and discarded catch (by-catch, also called unused catch) are part of this problem and are all potential threats to the sustainability of fisheries (FAO, 2014). In addition to this, a growing world population, rising incomes and evolving diets have resulted in demand for fish continuously increasing, putting stocks under even greater pressure. The FAO (2014) states that global fish production is increasing at an average annual rate of 3.2%, outpacing world population growth at 1.6% (FAO, 2014). However, the bulk of this growth now stems from aquaculture production, as the volume of landings generated by capture fishery is stagnating.

Stocks are considered to be biologically overfished when they are reduced to levels that prevent them from producing their maximum sustainable yield (MSY) (FAO, 2014). Figure 3.2 shows that in 2011, 28.8% of stocks monitored by the FAO were overfished, depleted or recovering; 61.3% were fully exploited (fully fished); and 9.9% were underexploited (FAO, 2014). It is estimated that between 11 and 26 million tonnes of fish are caught by IUU fishing annually, representing 18% of global catches across all fisheries (Agnew et al., 2009). This represents a substantial pressure on fish stocks, above what would be considered as desirable. Discarded catch is an additional issue, as 7.2 million tonnes of non-target fish (8% of global fish landings) are subsequently dumped back into the sea dead after capture as a consequence of factors such as market or regulatory constraints (FAO, 2014). However, it is claimed that the number of economically overfished stocks is even higher than the number that is biologically overfished (e.g. Pauly and Zeller, 2016).

Although the general trend toward overfishing and depletion of fish stocks has yet to be reversed, many depleted stocks have been or are being rebuilt and many fisheries are now being managed sustainably. In New Zealand, the percentage of fish stocks above the overfishing threshold declined 7 percentage points from 25% in 2009 to 18% in 2013. The European Union reported that up to 70% of assessed stocks were either fished at decreasing rates or were showing increased stock abundance (Fernandes and Cook, 2013). Similar examples of success also exist in many other fisheries around the world (FAO, 2014).

Physical and biological implications

There are abundant data to suggest that overexploitation[5] of fish stocks affects not only target stocks but also communities of organisms, ecological processes and entire marine ecosystems. Though the list of marine endangered and threatened species pales in comparison to that of terrestrial and fresh water systems, marine biodiversity is being lost at an alarming rate as genetically unique populations of marine organisms become extinct (Dayton et al., 1995). Currently, over 550 species of marine fishes and invertebrates are listed as threatened in the IUCN Red List. While the marine data are limited, a first IUCN Red List of Threatened Species assessment available for all known species of marine shore fish, marine mammals, sea turtles, sea birds, corals, mangroves and sea grasses in a major marine biogeographic region of tropical eastern Pacific indicated that 12% are under threat.

Researchers (e.g. Agardy, 2000) suggest that entire marine ecosystems can be affected by unsustainable fishing methods. The nature and extent of fishing impacts depends upon a range of factors and are influenced by the type of fishing gear used and how and when it is applied. Long-lining and bottom trawling may cause the death of seabirds, turtles and other non-commercial species, and alter habitats by raking plants and other species at the sea bottom (Auster, 1998, Dayton et al., 1995). The catchability and market value of certain species can also influence fishery impact as they are factors that influence fishing behaviour. For example, once fisheries have depleted the large, typically higher value, predatory fish at the top of the food web, they have been seen to then progressively redirect effort towards smaller, often less valuable, species at lower trophic levels (Pauly et al., 1998). This situation, referred to as fishing down the food web, can also be associated with increased fishing intensity to offset the lower value of the smaller species, which can further negatively affect diversity and productivity (see Folke et al., 2004; Frank et al., 2005; Pauly et al., 1998). On the other hand, fishing at lower trophic value can also present an opportunity since it could increase the output of food supply (see Garcia et al., 2012; Zhou et al., 2010) compared to similar food consumption of terrestrial sources (see Endal and Johnson, 2014).

Figure 3.3. **Global trends in the state of world marine fish stocks, 1974-2011 (in percent)**

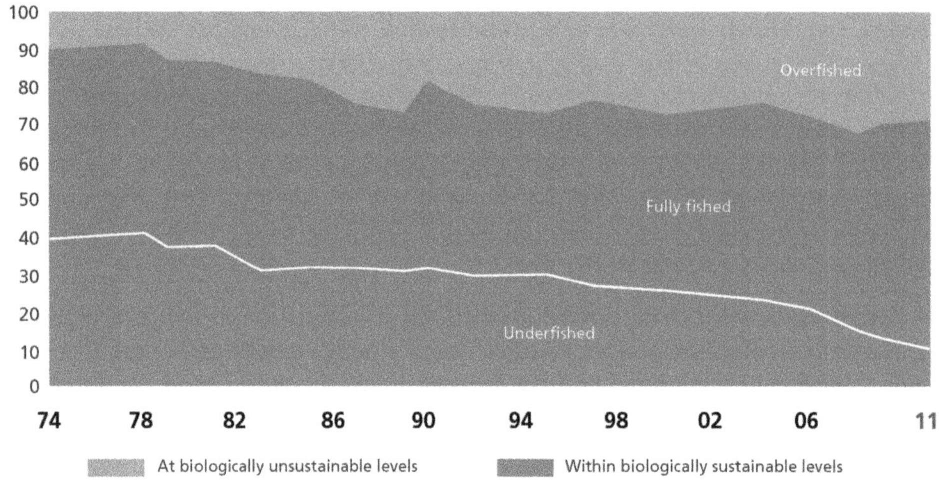

Note: The white line divides the stocks within biologically sustainable levels into two sub-categories: fully fished (above the line) and under-fished (below the line).

Source: FAO (2014).

Regime shifts are also increasingly the result of overfishing, the effects of climate change, and pollution including land-use change. Once these effects take place, an ecosystem might lose its resilience and become more vulnerable (Folke et al., 2004; Troell et al., 2005; Eriksson et al., 2010). Once an ecosystem has shifted, the process may be difficult to reverse (Scheffer and Carpenter, 2003; Scheffer, Carpenter and de Young, 2005). An example is the Eastern Scotian Shelf ecosystem that suffered from overfishing of cod and other ground fish, and consequently became dominated by crustacean and small planktivorous fish in the early 1990s (Frank et al., 2011). Despite the ban on fishing since 1993, the ecosystem on the Eastern Scotian Shelf has failed to recover to its former composition of fish. Thus, both fisheries and climatic perturbations may have important consequences for the composition in ecosystems, including the seabed community composition and biodiversity (Worm et al., 2005).

Likely effects on the ocean economy

Unsustainable fishing is responsible for the net economic benefits of marine fisheries in the order of USD 50 billion per year lower than they could be in an industry with an annual landed catch value of USD 68 billion (TEEB, 2011). These losses occur at two levels: depleted fish stocks imply that the cost of finding and catching the fish is higher that it needs to be and fleet overcapacity means that the economic benefits of fishing are dissipated due to redundant investment and operating costs. The cumulative economic loss to the global economy over the last three decades associated with overfishing is estimated to be in the order of USD 2 trillion (FAO, 2009a). In the future, the cost of declining fishing yields is expected to continue to rise to USD 88.4 billion by 2050 and USD 343.3 billion by 2100 (Noone, Sumaila and Diaz, 2012). The negative effects are projected to be most significant in the developing nations of tropical regions. But a joint study by the World Bank and the FAO (World Bank and FAO, 2009) also argues that these losses could be turned into sustainable economic benefits for millions of fishers and coastal communities though better management of marine fisheries.

It is estimated that rebuilding overfished stocks could raise fishery production by 16.5 million tonnes and increase annual rent by USD 32 billion, which would certainly increase the contribution of marine fisheries to the food security, economies and well-being of coastal communities (FAO, 2014).

Pollution

There are several sources of pollution in the ocean since the oceans and their sediments have long been a sink for wastes from numerous human activities. Concurrently, pollution from land-based sources including marine litter is threatening species and marine habitats. Climate change compounds these effects, altering both the thermal and chemical characteristics of the ocean.

State to date and likely future trends

The most damaging marine pollution is agriculture run off of nutrient and phosphorus that leads to eutrophication and dramatic increases in coastal hypoxia as outlined above. Eighty-five per cent of the sewage discharged in the Mediterranean Sea is untreated, leading to eutrophication (WWF, 2015) and, if left unchecked, to the creation of dead zones.

In addition, plastic pollution has spread throughout the world's seas and oceans. Plastic pollution moves more easily between oceanic gyres and between hemispheres than previously assumed (Lebreton, Greer and Borrero, 2012). It is of particular concern due to its abundance and persistence in the environment more generally. Plastic pieces in the ocean were estimated to be over 5 trillion, and weighing over 250 000 tonnes (Eriksen et al., 2014), with the world's largest floating "island" of trash in the north Pacific Ocean. The polluted area, known as the "Great Pacific Garbage Patch", covers approximately 8 million square kilometres (km^2). However, the ultimate fate of buoyant micro plastics is not at the ocean surface. UV degradation, biodegradation, fouling with marine life and sediment can cause items to sink to the seabed (Barnes et al., 2009). It has been suggested that quantities on the seabed may exceed 10 000 items per hectare, reaching more than 1 000 m below the ocean surface, and including even inverted plastic bags. Quantitative data on the abundance of debris on the seabed are still very limited, but there are concerns that degradation rates in the deep sea will be especially slow because of darkness and cold (Barnes et al., 2009; Ryan et al., 2009). In the future, it is likely that the problem of ocean pollution with plastics and other man-made debris from land-based sources could worsen as consumer-orientated societies grow (Coe and Rogers, 1997).

Chemical pollution – with more than 300 chemical substances classified as dangerous for the marine environment – adds to the pressures already weighing on the ocean environment (OSPAR, 2010). Some chemical pollutants – e.g. heavy metals and persistent organic substances – have been entering the seas for decades, not least due to the fact that chemical weapons from the Second World War are still located on the sea floor (Bearden, 2007; Beddington and Kinloch, 2005).

In addition, there is also nuclear radiation in the ocean that can cause genetic changes, reproductive disorders and cancer due to its accumulation along food chains. However, average doses affecting marine organisms and humans are well below international thresholds, except in the case of pollution from incidents such as the Fukushima disaster, and eventually new sources of radioactive material, such as decommissioned nuclear vessels (AMAP, 2010; WBGU, 2013). However, most contamination comes from natural sources (UNEP and GPA, 2006; Livingston and Povinec, 2000), which can be up to 1 000 times higher than the current anthropogenic contribution.

Underwater noise due to military activities, seabed mapping and shipping creates large-scale changes in the acoustic environment which are of particular concern for marine mammals, since they rely on sound as their primary sensory mode for echolocation and communication (Tyack, 2008). Noise may lead to physiological stress (Wright et al., 2007; Rolland et al., 2012) and changes in behaviour (Nowacek et al., 2007) including evasive tactics (Christiansen et al., 2010) and heightened vocalisation frequency (Parks, Clark and Tyack, 2007), rate or duration. The cumulative cost of these responses can alter the animals' activity budget and energy balance, which may have downstream consequences for individual vital rates, population dynamics and disorientation leading to animals stranding at beaches.

Oil pollution presents an additional threat to the marine environment. Although oil spills are usually devastating in the severity of their impact on the environment, they only account for roughly 12% of oil in the sea. Oil enters primarily from diffuse sources, such as leaks during oil extraction, illegal tank-cleaning operations at sea or discharges into the rivers which are then carried into the sea (WWF, n.d.). The International Tanker Owners Pollution Federation (ITOPF) estimated that between 1970 and 2012, approximately 5.75 million tonnes of oil were lost as a result of tanker incidents. While seaborne oil trade has been increasing (ITOPF, 2015), the number of oil spills has been decreasing since the mid-1980s. Nevertheless, the weak international regulations, especially in developing regions of the world (Rochette, 2014), are of a concern since offshore exploration and development is growing fast in Africa and Brazil, where sometimes basic environmental requirements are hardly met.

Additionally, the introduction of non-native marine species into marine ecosystems constitutes another change to the ocean environment. Around 7 000 marine species are carried around the world due to the release of ballast water from commercial shipping operations every day (WWF, 2009), which can lead to challenges for native species. For example, the American lobster, which has been invading as a stowaway in ballast tanks on board Europe-bound vessels, is eradicating the local lobster in the Oslo fjord.

As the quality of deposits of minerals and metals on land deteriorates and as technology progressively makes digging and drilling activities on and under the seafloor more feasible, extracting this mineral wealth is attracting commercial interest, although the prospects for the large-scale development of seabed mining by 2030 are controversial. It is widely acknowledged that future commercial-scale exploitation would have significant direct and indirect effects on ocean ecosystems on the seabed, endangering unique habitats and affecting the overlying water column. Seabed mining activities would likely release contaminated water and suspend downslope transmission of sediment-laden plumes (GOC, 2013a), which would reduce light penetration and temperature through increased turbidity resulting in reduced plankton growth with knock-on effects for the whole food chain. However, impacts differ significantly between each specific deposit (Ecorys, 2014; Van Dover, 2011; Thiel et al., 2001; Bluhm, 2001). By the time seabed mining becomes commercial, improved technologies may be able to mitigate the risk of environmental damage.

Although tourism can be an opportunity for sustainable development, poorly planned development of hotels and resorts in coastal areas can result in habitat destruction, pollution and other negative impacts on biodiversity. In addition, cruise ships are a major source of marine pollution through the dumping of garbage and untreated sewage at sea, and the release of other shipping-related pollutants (Copeland, 2008).

Physical and biological implications

Marine pollution and invasive species can change the physical, chemical and biological characteristics of the ocean and coastal zones, affecting the quality, productivity and resilience of marine ecosystems.

As indicated before, pollution, oil spills and persistent heavy metals can enter marine ecosystems with far-ranging impacts on multiple levels of marine life by disrupting ocean food web dynamics (Clark, Frid and Attrill, 1997). Toxic chemicals and plastic can bio-accumulate in fish, disrupt hormone balances, endanger fish reproduction and alter food web dynamics, ecosystem functions and biodiversity. Due to their durability, persistent organic pollutants can be transported by air and sea currents to regions located far away from the pollution sources.

In sum, pollutants may undermine the immune and reproduction systems of marine species, and weaken resilience to other anthropogenic stressors (Noone, Sumaila and Diaz, 2012).

Finally, the introduction of non-indigenous species, when induced by climate-shifting interactions, may promote the displacement of ecotypes and shifts in ecosystem functioning.

Likely effects on the ocean economy

Overall, marine pollution can result in sizable economic effects. The theoretical economic welfare losses may occur in many different forms: e.g. losses from harvest closures-restrictions or from consumption of unsafe seafood and healthcare costs. For example, bacterial pollution on beaches has been driving up healthcare costs, estimated to range from USD 21 million to USD 414 million per year in southern California (NOEP, 2009). Other effects included sport fishing and beach use, and decreasing property prices of waterfront real estate adjacent to contaminated water (Ofiara and Seneca, 2006). As in the case of California, the expenditures on its six-year cleaning initiative of beaches in an attempt to reverse the decline in tourism revenues triggered by polluted beaches were estimated at around USD 51 million. Estimates of the economic cost of pollution from oil spill range from USD 1.2 billion to USD 23.5 billion per year (Costanza et al., 2010).

If different forms of marine pollution continue, the impressive rate of discovery of genetic resources from marine organisms is likely to slow down, leading to a loss of option value from marine ecosystems (GOC, 2013b). Thanks to their high biological diversity, marine ecosystems are particularly suited for bioprospecting, a process that aims to identify and isolate natural compounds from genetic material. Marine bioprospecting has increased rapidly in recent years due to the discovery of genetic resources from marine organisms useful in pharmacology and human health, agriculture, food, cosmetics and industrial applications. Since 1999, the number of patents on genetic material from marine species has increased at the rate of 12% per year (Arrieta, Arnaud-Haond and Duarte, 2010), while it is expected that many more genetic sequences are yet to be discovered, in particular marine species that live in extreme environments such as hydrothermal vents and seamounts that are also interesting for seabed mining (de la Calle, 2009). However, if marine pollution proceeds at present rates, new discovery of genetic resources will become more challenging and compromise medical and economic opportunities if newly explored species that had been positively identified for medical therapies and used in cancer therapy and in the treatment of viral infections were found to be extinct once scientists endeavoured to further progress their research.

Last but not least, the loss of biodiversity affects also maritime tourism. A continuous loss of coral reefs and marine biodiversity would put at risk marine resources, threatening large economic benefits. The value of marine biodiversity for recreation and leisure purposes is an economically important factor, with 898 million arrivals in 2007 and an annual growth of about 5% worldwide (PISCO, 2002). Diving is the activity which has the highest value among all recreational activities. A meta-analysis of 52 coral reef valuation studies showed an average value of USD 184 per visit (Fenical, 2002).

Conclusion

The combined pressures of increasing sea temperatures, acidification, stratification, changes in ocean currents and the hydrological cycle, eutrophication from coastal run-off and other forms of pollution, overfishing and habitat destruction will define how productive and efficient the future ocean will be.

Relatively little is known about the inter-related effects of environmental factors and the complexity of the marine food web, and so it is considered premature to make ecosystem-wide projections (UN, 2015). Investigations of single drivers, such as rising sea temperature and acidification, can produce misleading inferences about organismal responses in a multivariate natural environment because interactive (additive, synergistic or antagonistic) effects are often not predictable from single driver studies. This is a major source of uncertainty for projections. Changes in temperature, and pH, such as those projected in the IPCC business-as-usual scenario for the year 2100, can have synergistic negative effects on species growth, survival, fitness, calcification and development (Gobler et al., 2014; Mackenzie et al., 2014; Madeira et al., 2014; Rosa et al., 2014). In some cases, hypoxic conditions can mediate negative effects of ocean acidification (Frieder et al., 2014), whereas ocean acidification and hypoxia increase heat sensitivity and vice versa (Pörtner et al., 2014), and oxygen loss combined with warming is likely to decrease the size and quality of habitats of marine animals (Deutsch et al., 2015). The interactions with other environmental factors can markedly alter the biological effects of warming, ocean acidification and hypoxia (Richier et al., 2014; Ko et al., 2014).

However, should global temperature increases exceed 2°C compared to pre-industrial levels, the business-as-usual scenario suggests that the ocean environment would experience far-reaching changes in terms of regional biodiversity patterns, trophic linkages, nutrient cycling and habitat provision, and pose considerable challenges for the future development of ocean-based industries.

Among many other effects, rising sea temperatures, decreasing oxygen levels and pollution would lead to global losses in fisheries and tourism revenues, as well as to rising health costs. Should the growth trends of different types of marine pollution persist, the impressive rate of discovery of genetic resources from marine organisms is likely to slow, leading to a loss of option value from marine ecosystems. On the other hand, these changes may mean new opportunities, such as shorter international shipping routes due to ice-free summers in the Arctic and increased fish catches in higher latitudes.

Further, these changes could affect the wider economy by altering resources and increasing risks to public health, human development, well-being and security. Changes in the accessibility of these marine resources might lead to increasing geopolitical and governance challenges to the management of resources in exclusive economic zones and in the high seas. Missing these transformation goals under the UNEP Convention on Biological Diversity (see targets 6,7,10,11 and 12) (UNEP, 2016), the UN Sustainable

Development Goal (UN, 2016), which devotes an entire goal to conserve and sustainably use the oceans, seas and marine resources (goal 14), as well as the goals of the recent COP21 meeting in Paris in December 2015, may result in further additional economic and societal costs that will be unevenly distributed, creating heavier burdens especially for developing countries where fish catch and tourism revenues provide jobs, livelihoods and nourishment for millions of coastal communities. This elevates the expected changes in the ocean environment to 2030/50 and their resultant impacts to a matter of global concern beyond the North/South divide. The sustainable use of the ocean cannot be achieved unless the management of all sectors of human activities affecting the ocean is coherent.

Notes

1. This was calculated at a 3% discount rate and over a 50-year timeframe.
2. Dead zones – a term that was first applied to the northern Gulf of Mexico, which is related to excess agricultural and municipal nutrients discharged from the Mississippi and Atchafalaya Rivers (Rabalais, Turner and Wiseman, 2002). When fishers trawl in these zones little to nothing is caught.
3. Before sinking, the water absorbs enormous amounts of gases such as carbon dioxide at the sea surface and then transports them rapidly to much greater depths. From the time of sinking into the deep until its return to the surface, a period of several hundred or even up to 1 000 years passes.
4. Loss estimates are lower bound estimates because many impacts, such as loss of human lives, cultural heritage and ecosystem services, are difficult to value and monetise, and thus they are poorly reflected in estimates of losses. With respect to measuring the value of ecosystems, several initiatives have started, e.g. in France (Évaluation française des écosystèmes et des services écosystémiques, EFESE), the Netherlands, the United Kingdom and the European Union (mapping and assessment of ecosystem and their services).
5. Overexploitation means harvesting species from the wild at rates faster than natural populations can recover. Overfishing and overhunting are both types of overexploitation.

References

Agardy, T. (2000), "Effects of fisheries on marine ecosystems: A conservationist's perspective", *ICES Journal of Marine Science*, Vol. 57, No. 3, pp. 761-765, http://dx.doi.org/10.1006/jmsc.2000.0721.

Agnew, D.J. et al. (2009), "Estimating the worldwide extent of illegal fishing", *PLOS ONE*, Vol. 4, No. 2, http://dx.doi.org/10.1371/journal.pone.0004570.

AMAP (2010), "AMAP assessment 2009: Persistent organic pollutants (POPs) in the Arctic", *Science of the Total Environment Special Issue*, No. 408, pp. 2 851-3 051, www.amap.no/documents/doc/amap-assessment-2009-persistent-organic-pollutants-pops-in-the-arctic/45.

Anderson, C.N.K. et al. (2008), "Why fishing magnifies fluctuations in fish abundance", *Nature*, Vol. 452, pp. 835-839, http://dx.doi.org/10.1038/nature06851.

Arnason, R. (2007), "Climate change and fisheries: Assessing the economic impact: Conserving the ocean's genetic resources in Iceland and Greenland", *Natural Resource Modeling*, Vol. 2, pp. 163-197.

Arrieta, J.M., S. Arnaud-Haond and C.M. Duarte (2010), "What lies underneath: Conserving the oceans' genetic resources", *Proceedings of the National Academy of Sciences of the United States of America*, Vol. 107, No. 43, pp. 18 318-18 324, http://dx.doi.org/10.1073/pnas.0911897107.

Auster, P. (1998), "A conceptual model of the impacts of fishing gear on the integrity of fish habitats", *Conservation Biology*, Vol. 12, No. 6, December, pp. 1 198-1 203, www.jstor.org/stable/2989837.

Baird, D. et al. (2004), "Consequences of hypoxia on estuarine ecosystem function: Energy diversion from consumers to microbes", *Ecological Applications*, Vol. 14, No. 3, June, pp. 805-822, http://dx.doi.org/10.1890/02-5094.

Barange, M. et al. (2014), "Impacts of climate change on marine ecosystem production in societies dependent on fisheries", *Nature Climate Change*, Vol. 4, pp. 211-216, http://dx.doi.org/10.1038.nclimate2119.

Barnes, D.K.A. et al. (2009), "Accumulation and fragmentation of plastic debris in global environments", *Philosophical Transactions of the Royal Society B*, Vol. 364, No. 1 526, pp. 1 985-1 998, http://dx.doi.org/10.1098/rstb.2008.0205.

Barton, A. et al. (2012), "The Pacific oyster, *Crassotrea gigas*, shows negative correlation to naturally elevated carbon dioxide levels: Implications for near-term ocean acidification effects", *Limnology and Oceanography*, Vol. 57, No. 3, pp. 698-710, http://dx.doi.org/10.4319/lo.2012.57.3.0698.

Battaglini, E., B. Plonka and A. Merla (2008), "Europe and Central Asia Region", in: World Bank, *Environment Matters*, Annual Review, July 2007-June 2008, http://sitere

sources.worldbank.org/INTENVMAT/Resources/3011340-1238620444756/5980735-1238620476358/13ECA.pdf (accessed 18 September 2015).

Bearden, D.M. (2007), "U.S. disposal of chemical weapons in the ocean: Background and issues for Congress", *CRS Report for Congress*, Congressional Research Service.

Beaugrand, G., M. Edwards and L. Legendre (2010), "Marine biodiversity, ecosystem functioning, and carbon cycles", *Proceedings of the National Academy of Sciences of the United States of America*, Vol. 107, No. 22, pp. 10 120-10 124, http://dx.doi.org/10.1073/pnas.0913855107.

Beddington, J. and A. Kinloch (2005), "Munitions dumped at sea: A literature review", *Imperial College Consultants*, Vol. 01/2005, June, London.

Bell, J.D. et al. (2013), "Mixed responses of tropical Pacific fisheries and aquaculture to climate change", *Nature Climate Change*, Vol. 3, pp. 591-599.

Bijma, J. et al. (2013), "Climate change and the oceans – What does the future hold?", in: *Marine Pollution Bulletin*, Vol. 74, No. 2, September, pp. 495-505, http://dx.doi.org/10.1016/j.marpolbul.2013.07.022.

Bluhm, H. (2001), "Re-establishment of an abyssal mega benthic community after experimental physical disturbance of the sea floor", *Deep Sea Research, Part II: Topical Studies in Oceanography*, Vol. 48, No. 17, pp. 3 841-3 868, http://dx.doi.org/10.1016/S0967-0645(01)00070-4.

Borges, A.V. and N. Gypens (2010), "Carbonate chemistry in the coastal zone responds more strongly to eutrophication than to ocean acidification", *Limnology and Oceanography*, Vol. 55, No. 1, January, pp. 346-353, http://dx.doi.org/10.4319/lo.2010.55.1.0346.

Brander, L. et al. (2015), "The benefits to people of expanding marine protected areas", IVM Institute for Environmental Studies, Amsterdam, Netherlands, May, available at: http://ivm.vu.nl/en/Images/R15-05_Final_report___App_C_tcm234-454652.pdf.

Brandt, P. et al. (2010), "Changes in the ventilation of the oxygen minimum zone of the tropical North Atlantic", *Journal of Physical Oceanography*, Vol. 40, No. 8, pp. 1 784-1 801, http://dx.doi.org/10.1175/2010JPO4301.1.

Brennan, L. and P. Owende (2010), "Biofuels from microalgae – A review of technologies for production, processing, and extractions of biofuels and co-products", *Renewable Sustainable Energy Reviews*, Vol. 14, No. 2, pp. 557-577, http://dx.doi.org/10.1016/j.rser.2009.10.009.

Brewer, P. and E. Peltzer (2009), "Limits to marine life", *Science*, Vol. 324, No. 5 925, pp. 347-348, http://dx.doi.org/10.1126/science.1170756.

Burge, C.A. et al. (2014), "Climate change influences on marine infectious diseases: Implications for management and society", *Annual Review of Marine Science*, Vol. 6, pp. 249-277, http://dx.doi.org/10.1146/annurev-marine-010213-135029.

Burke, L.M. et al. (2011), *Reefs at Risk Revisited*, World Resources Institute, Washington, DC, pp. 114.

Cai, W.-J. et al. (2011), "Acidification of subsurface coastal waters enhanced by eutrophication", *Nature Geoscience*, Vol. 4, pp. 766-770, http://dx.doi.org/10.1038/ngeo1297.

Callaway, R. et al. (2012), "Review of climate change impacts on marine aquaculture in the UK and Ireland", *Aquatuatic Conservation: Marine and Freshwater Ecosystems*, Vol. 22, No. 3, pp. 389-421, http://dx.doi.org/10.1002/aqc.2247.

Carpenter, K.E. et al. (2008), "One-third of reef-building corals face elevated extinction risk from climate change and local impacts", *Science*, Vol. 321, No. 5 888, July, pp. 560-563, http://dx.doi.org/10.1126/science.1159196.

Cesar, H., L. Burke and L. Pet-Soede (2003), "The economics of worldwide coral reef degradation", Cesar Environmental Economics Consulting (CEEC), Arnhem, Netherlands.

Chambers, L.E. et al. (2013), "Phenological changes in the southern hemisphere", *PLOS ONE*, Vol. 8, No. 10, http://dx.doi.org/10.1371/journal.pone.0075514.

Chan, F. et al. (2008), "Emergence of anoxia in the California current large marine ecosystem", *Science*, Vol. 319, No. 5 865, pp. 920, http://dx.doi.org/10.1126/science.1149016.

Chen, P.-Y. et al. (2015), "Evaluating the economic damage of climate change on global coral reefs", *Global Environmental Change*, Vol. 30, January, pp. 12-20, http://dx.doi.org/10.1016/j.gloenvcha.2014.10.011.

Cheung, W.W.L. et al. (2011), "Integrating ecophysiology and plankton dynamics into projected maximum fisheries catch potential under climate change in the Northeast Atlantic", *ICES Journal of Marine Science*, Vol. 68, No. 6, pp. 1 008-1 018, http://dx.doi.org/10.1093/icesjms/fsr012.

Cheung, W.W.L. et al. (2010), "Large-scale redistribution of maximum fisheries catches potential in the global ocean under climate change", *Global Change Biology*, Vol. 16, No. 1, January, pp. 24-35, http://dx.doi.org/10.1111/j.1365-2486.2009.01995.x.

Cheung, W.W.L. et al. (2009), "Projecting global marine biodiversity impacts under climate change scenarios", *Fish and Fisheries*, Vol. 10, No. 3, September, pp. 235-251, http://dx.doi.org/10.1111/j.1467-2979.2008.00315.x.

Christiansen, F. et al. (2010), "Effects of tourist boats on the behaviour of Indo-Pacific bottlenose dolphins off the south coast of Zanzibar", *Endangered Species Research*, Vol. 11, No. 1, pp. 91-99, http://dx.doi.org/10.3354/esr00265.

Church, J.A. et al. (2013), "Sea level change", Chapter 13, in: *Climate Change 2013: The Physical Science Basis*, Contribution of Working Group I to the Fifth Assessment Report of the Intergovernmental Panel on Climate Change, Cambridge University Press, Cambridge, United Kingdom and New York, New York, www.climatechange2013.org/images/report/WG1AR5_Chapter13_FINAL.pdf.

Clark, R.B., C. Frid and M. Attrill (1997), *Marine Pollution*, Fourth edition, Oxford University Press, Oxford.

Codispoti, L. (2010), "Interesting times for marine N_2O", *Science*, Vol. 327, No. 5 971, pp. 1 339-1 340, http://dx.doi.org/10.1126/science.1184945.

Coe, J.M. and D.B. Rogers (1997), "Land-based sources of marine debris", in: Coe, J.M. and D.B. Rogers (eds.), *Marine Debris: Sources, Impacts, Solutions*, Springer-Verlag, New York, pp. 289-291.

Cooley, S.R. and S.C. Doney (2009), "Anticipating ocean acidification's economic consequences for commercial fisheries", *Environmental Research Letters*, Vol. 4, http://dx.doi.org/10.1088/1748-9326/4/2/024007.

Cooley, S.R. et al. (2012), "Nutrition and income from molluscs today imply vulnerability to ocean acidification tomorrow", *Fish and Fisheries*, Vol. 13, No. 2, June, pp. 182-215, http://dx.doi.org/10.1111/j.1467-2979.2011.00424.x.

Copeland, C. (2008), "Cruise ship pollution: Background, laws and regulations, and key issues", CRS Report for Congress, Congressional Research Service, Washington, DC, available at: www.cep.unep.org/publications-and-resources/databases/document-database/other/cruise-ship-pollution-background-laws-and-regulations-and-key-issues.pdf/at_download/file.

Corbett, J.J. et al. (2010), "Arctic shipping emissions inventories and future scenarios", *Atmospheric Chemistry and Physics*, Vol. 19, pp. 9 689-9 704, http://dx.doi.org/10.5194/acp-10-9689-2010.

Costanza, R. et al. (2010), "The perfect spill: Solutions for averting the next Deepwater Horizon", *Solutions*, 16 June, www.thesolutionsjournal.com/node/629.

Daufresne, M., K. Lengfellner and U. Sommer (2009), "Global warming benefits the small in aquatic ecosystems", *Proceedings of the National Academy of Sciences of the United States of America*, Vol. 106, No. 1, pp. 12 788-12 793, http://dx.doi.org/10.1073/pnas.0902080106.

Dayton, P. et al. (1995), "Environmental effects of marine fishing", *Aquatic Conservation: Marine and Fresh water Ecosystems*, Vol. 5, No. 3, September, pp. 1-28, http://dx.doi.org/10.1002/aqc.3270050305.

De la Calle, F. (2009), "Marine genetic resources, a source of new drugs: The experience of the biotechnology sector", *International Journal of Marine and Coastal Law*, Vol. 24, No. 2, pp. 209-220, http://dx.doi.org/10.1163/157180809X421743.

Deloitte Access Economics (2013), *Economic Contribution of the Great Barrier Reef*, Great Barrier Reef Marine Park Authority, Townsville, Australia, www.environment.gov.au/system/files/resources/a3ef2e3f-37fc-4c6f-ab1b-3b54ffc3f449/files/gbr-economic-contribution.pdf.

Deutsch, C., S. Emerson and L. Thompson (2005), "Fingerprints of climate change in North Pacific oxygen", *Geophysical Research Letters*, Vol. 32, No. 16, August, http://dx.doi.org/10.1029/2005GL023190.

Deutsch, C. et al. (2015), "Climate change tightens a metabolic constraint on marine habitats", *Science*, Vol. 348, No. 6 329, pp. 1 132-1 135, http://dx.doi.org/10.1126/science.aaa1605.

Diaz, R.J. and R. Rosenberg (2008), "Spreading dead zones and consequences for marine ecosystems", *Science*, Vol. 321, No. 5 891, pp. 926-929, http://dx.doi.org/10.1126/science.1156401.

Doney, S. et al. (2009), "Ocean acidification: The other CO_2 problem", *Marine Science*, Vol. 1, pp. 169-192, http://dx.doi.org/10.1146/annurev.marine.010908.163834.

Ecorys (2014), "Study to investigate the state of knowledge of deep-sea mining", Final Report under FWC MARE/2012/06 – SC E1/2013/04, DG Maritime Affairs and Fisheries, Rotterdam/Brussels, available at: https://webgate.ec.europa.eu/maritimeforum/sites/maritimeforum/files/FGP96656_final_rep._formatted._november_2014.pdf.

Elliott, D.T., J.J. Pierson and M.R. Roman (2013), "Copepods and hypoxia in Chesapeake Bay: Abundance, vertical position and non-predatory mortality", *Journal of Plankton Research*, pp. 1027-1034, http://dx.doi.org/10.1093/plankt/fbt049.

Elmqvist, T. et al. (2003), "Response diversity, ecosystem change, and resilience", *Frontiers in Ecology and the Environment*, Vol. 1, No. 9, November, pp. 488-494, http://dx.doi.org/10.1890/1540-9295(2003)001[0488:RDECAR]2.0.CO;2.

Endal, A. and G. Johnsen (2014), Livet i havet in Havromteknologi ed. Leif Lundby, NTNU og Fagbokforlaget.

EPA (2016), Northern Gulf of Mexico Hypoxic Zone, United States Environmental Protection Agency, available at: www.epa.gov/ms-htf/northern-gulf-mexico-hypoxic-zone.

Eriksen, M. et al. (2014), "Plastic pollution in the world's oceans: More than 5 trillion plastic pieces weighing over 250,000 tons afloat at sea", *PLOS ONE*, Vol. 9, No. 12, http://dx.doi.org/10.1371/journal.pone.0111913.

Eriksson, B.K. et al. (2010), "Major changes in the ecology of the Wadden Sea: Human impacts, ecosystem engineering and sediment dynamics", *Ecosystems*, Vol. 13, No. 5, August, pp. 752-764, http://dx.doi.org/10.1007/s10021-010-9352-3.

Fabricius, K.E. et al. (2011), "Losers and winners in coral reefs acclimatized to elevated carbon dioxide concentrations", *Nature Climate Change*, Vol. 1, pp. 1-5, http://dx.doi.org/10.1038/nclimate1122.

Fabry, V.J., A.S. Brad and R.A. Feely (2008), "Impacts of ocean acidification on marine fauna and ecosystem processes", *ICES Journal of Marine Science*, No. 65, No. 3, pp. 414-432, http://dx.doi.org/10.1093/icesjms/fsn048.

FAO (2014), *The State of World of Fisheries and Aquaculture 2014: Opportunities and Challenges*, Food and Agriculture Organization, Rome, www.fao.org/3/a-i3720e.pdf.

FAO (2009a), *The State of World Fisheries and Aquaculture 2008*, Food and Agriculture Organization, Rome, www.fao.org/docrep/011/i0250e/i0250e00.htm.

FAO (2009b), "FAO's role in the Syria Drought Response Plan 2009", Food and Agriculture Organization, Rome, www.fao.org/fileadmin/user_upload/emergencies/docs/app_syria drought2009.pdf.

FAO (2008), *The State of Food Insecurity in the World 2008: High Food Prices and Food Security – Threats and Opportunities*, Food and Agriculture Organization, Rome, available at: ftp://ftp.fao.org/docrep/fao/011/i0291e/i0291e00.pdf.

Feely, R.A. et al. (2008), "Evidence for upwelling of corrosive 'acidified' water onto the continental shelf", *Science*, Vol. 320, No. 5 882, pp. 1 490-1 492, http://dx.doi.org/10.1126/science.1155676.

Fenical, W. (2002), "Accessing marine biodiversity for drug discovery", in: Committee on Marine Biotechnology, *Marine Biotechnology in the Twenty-First Century: Problems, Promise, and Products*, National Research Council, Washington, DC, pp. 45-47.

Fernandes, P.G. and R.M. Cook (2013), "Reversal of fish stock decline in the northeast Atlantic", *Current Biology*, Vol. 23, No. 15, pp. 1 432-1 437, http://dx.doi.org/10.1016 /j.cub.2013.06.016.

Folke, C. et al. (2004), "Regime shifts, resilience and biodiversity in ecosystem management", *Annual Review of Ecology, Evolution and Systematics*, Vol. 35, pp. 557-581, http://dx.doi.org/10.1146/annurev.ecolsys.35.021103.105711.

Frank, K.T. et al. (2011), "Transient dynamics of an altered large marine ecosystem", *Nature*, Vol. 477, pp. 86-89, http://dx.doi.org/10.1038/nature10285.

Frank, K.T. et al. (2005), "Trophic cascades in a formerly cod-dominated ecosystem", *Science*, Vol. 308, No. 5 728, pp. 1 621-1 623, http://dx.doi.org/10.1126/science.1113075.

Frieder, C.A. et al. (2014), "Can variable pH and low oxygen moderate ocean acidification outcomes for mussel larvae?", *Global Change Biology*, Vol. 20, No. 3, pp. 754-764, http://dx.doi.org/10.1111/gcb.12485.

Friedrich, T. et al. (2012), "Detecting regional anthropogenic trends in ocean acidification against natural variability", *Natural Climate Change*, Vol. 2, pp. 167-171, http://dx.doi.org/10.1038/nclimate1372.

Ganachaud, A. and C. Wunsch (2000), "Improved estimates of global ocean circulation, heat transport and mixing from hydrographic data", *Nature*, Vol. 408, pp. 453-457, http://dx.doi.org/10.1038/35044048.

Garai, J. (2014), "The impacts of climate change on the livelihoods of coastal people in Bangladesh: A sociological study", Chapter 11, *International Perspectives on Climate Change*, W. Leal Filho, pp. 151-163, http://dx.doi.org/10.1007/978-3-319-04489-7_11.

Garcia, S. et al. (2012), "Reconsidering the consequences of selective fisheries", *Science*, Vol. 335, No. 6 072, pp. 1 045-1 047, http://dx.doi.org/10.1126/science.1214594.

Gattuso, J.-P. and L. Hansson (2011),"Ocean acidification: Background and history", in: Gattuso, J.-P. and L. Hansson (eds.), *Ocean Acidification*, Oxford University Press, Oxford, pp. 1-20.

Gattuso, J.-P. et al. (2015), "Contrasting futures for ocean and society from different anthropogenic CO_2 emissions scenarios", *Science*, Vol. 3, No. 6 243, http://dx.doi.org/10.1126/science.aac4722.

Gibert J.P. and J.P. DeLong (2014), "Temperature alters food web body-size structure", *Biology Letters*, Vol. 10, No. 8, August, http://dx.doi.org/10.1098/rsbl.2014.0473.

Gobler, C.J. et al. (2014), "Hypoxia and acidification have additive and synergistic negative effects on the growth, survival, and metamorphosis of early life stage bivalves", *PLOS ONE*, Vol. 9, No. 1, http://dx.doi.org/10.1371/journal.pone.0083648.

GOC (2013a), "Policy options paper #5: Strengthening deep seabed mining regulation", prepared for: Third Meeting of the Global Ocean Commission, November, www.globaloceancommission.org/wp-content/uploads/GOC-paper05-seabed-mining.pdf.

GOC (2013b), "Policy options paper #4: Bioprospecting and marine genetic resources in the high seas", prepared for the Third Meeting of the Global Ocean Commission, November, www.globaloceancommission.org/wp-content/uploads/GOC-paper04-bioprospecting.pdf.

Gruber, N. (2011), "Warming up, turning sour, losing breath: Ocean biogeochemistry under global change", *Philosophical Transactions of the Royal Society A*, Vol. 369, No. 1 943, pp. 1 980-1 996, http://dx.doi.org/10.1098/rsta.2011.0003.

Hale, R. et al. (2011), "Predicted levels of future ocean acidification and temperature rise could alter community structure and biodiversity in marine benthic communities", *Oikos*, Vol. 120, No. 5, pp. 661-674, http://dx.doi.org/10.1111/j.1600-0706.2010.19469.x.

Hartmann, D.L. et al. (2013), "Observations: Atmosphere and surface", Chapter 2, in: *Climate Change 2013: The Physical Science Basis*, Contribution of Working Group I to the Fifth Assessment Report of the Intergovernmental Panel on Climate Change, Cambridge University Press, Cambridge, United Kingdom and New York, New York, www.climatechange2013.org/images/report/WG1AR5_Chapter02_FINAL.pdf.

Hiddink, J.G., M.T. Burrows and J. García Molinos (2015), "Temperature tracking by North Sea benthic invertebrates in response to climate change", *Global Change Biology*, Vol. 21, No. 1, January, pp. 117-129, http://dx.doi.org/10.1111/gcb.12726.

Hoegh-Guldberg, O. (2012), "The adaptation of coral reefs to climate change: Is the Red Queen being outpaced?", *Scientiae Marina*, Vol. 76, No. 2, pp. 403-408, http://dx.doi.org/10.3989/scimar.03660.29A.

Hoegh-Guldberg, O. and J.F. Bruno (2010), "The impact of climate change on the world's marine ecosystems", *Science*, Vol. 328, No. 5 985, pp. 1 523-1528, http://dx.doi.org/10.1126/science.1189930.

Hönisch, B. et al. (2012), "The geological record of ocean acidification", *Science*, Vol. 335, No. 6 072, pp. 1 058-1 063, http://dx.doi.org/10.1126/science.1208277.

Huang, C. and F. Qiao (2009), "The relationship between sea surface temperature anomaly and wind energy input in the Pacific Ocean", *Progress in Natural Science*, Vol. 19, No. 10, pp. 1 409-1 412, http://dx.doi.org/10.1016/j.pnsc.2009.03.004.

Huang, R.X., C.J. Huang and W. Wang (2007), "Dynamical roles of mixed layer in regulating the meridional mass/heat fluxes", *Journal of Geophysical Research*, Vol. 112, No. C5, May, http://dx.doi.org/10.1029/2006JC004046.

Hume, B.C.C. et al. (2015), "*Symbiodinium thermophilum* sp. nov., a thermotolerant symbiotic alga prevalent in corals of the world's hottest sea, the Persian/Arabian Gulf", *Scientific Reports*, Vol. 5, Article 8 562, http://dx.doi.org/10.1038/srep08562.

IPCC (2014), "Summary for policymakers", *Climate Change 2014: Impacts, Adaptation, and Vulnerability*, Part A: Global and Sectoral Aspects, Contribution of Working Group II to the Fifth Assessment Report of the Intergovernmental Panel on Climate Change, Cambridge University Press, Cambridge, United Kingdom and New York, New York, pp. 1-32, https://ipcc-wg2.gov/AR5/images/uploads/WG2AR5_SPM_FINAL.pdf.

IPCC (2012), "Managing the risks of extreme events and disasters to advance climate change adaptation", *A Special Report of Working Groups I and II of the Intergovernmental Panel on Climate Change* [Field, C.B. et al. (eds.)]. Cambridge University Press, Cambridge, United Kingdom, and New York, New York.

ITOPF (2015), Oil Tanker Spill Statistics 2015, www.itopf.com/knowledge-resources/data-statistics/statistics.

Jones, M.C. and W.W.L. Cheung (2015), "Multi-model ensemble projections of climate change effects on global marine biodiversity", *ICES Journal of Marine Science*, Vol. 72, No. 3, pp. 741-752, http://dx.doi.org/10.1093/icesjms/fsu172.

Joos, F. and R. Spahni (2008), "Rates of change in natural and anthropogenic radiative forcing over the past 20,000 years", *Proceedings of the National Academy of Sciences of the United States of America*, Vol. 105, No. 5, pp. 1 425-1 430, http://dx.doi.org/10.1073/pnas.0707386105.

Keeling, R.F., A. Körtzinger and N. Gruber (2010), "Ocean deoxygenation in a warming world", *Annual Review of Marine Science*, Vol. 2, pp. 199-229, http://dx.doi.org/10.1146/annurev.marine.010908.163855.

Kemp, W.M. et al. (2009), "Temporal responses of coastal hypoxia to nutrient loading and physical controls", *Biogeosciences*, Vol. 6, pp. 2 985-3 008, http://dx.doi.org/10.5194/bg-6-2985-2009.

Khan, S.A. et al. (2014), "Sustained mass loss of the northeast Greenland ice sheet triggered by regional warming", *Nature Climate Change*, Vol. 4, pp. 292-299, http://dx.doi.org/10.1038/nclimate2161.

Kirby, R.R. and G. Beaugrand (2009), "Trophic amplification of climate warming", *Proceedings of the Royal Society B: Biological Sciences*, Vol. 276, No. 1 676, pp. 4 095-4 103, http://dx.doi.org/10.1098/rspb.2009.1320.

Ko, G.W.K. et al. (2014), "Interactive effects of ocean acidification, elevated temperature, and reduced salinity on early-life stages of the Pacific oyster", *Environmental Science & Technology*, Vol. 48, No. 17, pp. 10 079-10 088, http://dx.doi.org/10.1021/es501611u.

Kolding, J., L. Haug and S. Stefansson (2008), "Effect of ambient oxygen on growth and reproduction in Nile tilapia (*Oreochromis niloticus*)", *Canadian Journal of Fisheries and Aquatic Sciences*, Vol. 65, No. 7, pp. 1 413-1 424, http://dx.doi.org/10.1139/F08-059.

Kroeker, K. et al. (2013), "Impacts of ocean acidification on marine organisms: Quantifying sensitivities and interaction with warming", *Global Change Biology*, Vol. 19, No. 6, pp. 1 884-1 896, http://dx.doi.org/10.1111/gcb.12179.

Kroeker, K. et al. (2011), "Divergent ecosystem responses within a benthic marine community to ocean acidification", *Proceedings of the National Academy of Sciences of the United States of America*, Vol. 108, No. 35, pp. 14 515-14 520, http://dx.doi.org/10.1073/pnas.1107789108.

Laffoley, D.d'A. and J. Baxter (2009), "Ocean acidification: The facts. A special introductory guide for policy advisers and decision makers", European Project on Ocean Acidification (EPOCA), www.us-ocb.org/publications/oa_guide_english.pdf.

Lal, P.N., J. Kinch and F. Wickham (2009), *Review of Economic and Livelihood Impact Assessments of, and Adaptation to, Climate Change in Melanesia*, Secretariat of the Pacific Regional Environment Programme, Apia, Samoa, www.sprep.org/att/publication/000743_Review_of_economic_and_livelihood.pdf.

Lam, V.W.Y., W.W.L. Cheung and U.R. Sumaila (2014), "Marine capture fisheries in the Arctic: Winners or losers under climate change and ocean acidification?", *Fish and Fisheries*, early view, http://dx.doi.org/10.1111/faf.12106.

LaRiviere, J.P. et al. (2012), "Late Miocene decoupling of oceanic warmth and atmospheric carbon dioxide forcing", *Nature*, Vol. 486, pp. 97-100, http://dx.doi.org/10.1038/nature11200.

Lauer, A. et al. (2009), "Assessment of near-future policy instruments for oceangoing shipping: Impact on atmospheric aerosol burdens and the Earth's radiation budget", *Environmental Science & Technology*, Vol. 43, No. 15, pp. 5 592-5 598.

Lebreton, L., S. Greer and J. Borrero (2012), "Numerical modeling of floating debris in the world's oceans", *Marine Pollution Bulletin*, Vol. 64, No. 3, pp. 653-661, http://dx.doi.org/10.1016/j.marpolbul.2011.10.027.

Levin, L.A. et al. (2009), "Effects of natural and human-induced hypoxia on coastal benthos", *Biogeosciences*, Vol. 6, pp. 2 063-2 098, http://dx.doi.org/10.5194/bg-6-2063-2009.

Levitus, S. et al. (2009), "Global ocean heat content 1955-2008 in light of recently revealed instrumentation problems", *Geophysical Research Letters*, Vol. 36, available at: www.oco.noaa.gov/resources/Documents/Levitus_GRL_Heat2008.pdf.

Lewis, P.N., M.J. Riddle and C.L. Hewitt (2004), "Management of exogenous threats to Antarctica and the sub-Antarctic islands: Balancing risks from TBT and non-indigenous marine organisms", *Marine Pollution Bulletin*, Vol. 49, No. 11-12, pp. 999-1 005.

Livingston, H.D. and P.P. Povinec (2000), "Anthropogenic marine radioactivity", *Ocean & Coastal Management*, Vol. 43, No. 8-9, pp. 689-712, http://dx.doi.org/10.1016/S0964-5691(00)00054-5.

Lohbeck, K.T., U. Riebesell and T.B.H. Reusch (2014), "Gene expression changes in the coccolithophore *Emiliania huxleyi* after 500 generations of selection to ocean acidification", *Proceedings of the Royal Society B: Biological Sciences*, Vol. 281, No. 1 786, http://dx.doi.org/10.1098/rspb.2014.0003.

Mackenzie, C.L. et al. (2014), "Ocean warming, more than acidification, reduces shell strength in a commercial shellfish species during food limitation", *PLOS ONE*, Vol. 9, No. 1, http://dx.doi.org/10.1371/journal.pone.0086764.

Madeira, D. et al. (2014), "Synergy of environmental variables alters the thermal window and heat shock response: An experimental test with the crab *Pachygrapsus marmoratus*", *Marine Environmental Research*, Vol. 98, July, pp. 21-28, http://dx.doi.org/10.1016/j.marenvres.2014.03.011.

Maribus (2010), "World Ocean Review 1 – Mit den Meeren leben", Maribus, Hamburg, Germany.

Mattsdotter, B. et al. (2014), "Ocean acidification state in western Antarctic surface waters: Controls and interannual variability", *Biogeosciences*, Vol. 11, pp. 57-73, http://dx.doi.org/10.5194/bg-11-57-2014.

McPhaden, M.J. and D. Zhang (2002), "Slowdown of the meridional overturning circulation in the upper Pacific ocean", *Nature*, Vol. 415, pp. 603-608, http://dx.doi.org/10.1038/415603a.

Melzner, F. et al. (2009), "Physiological basis for high CO_2 tolerance in marine ectothermic animals: Preadaptation through lifestyle and ontogeny?", *Biogeosciences*, Vol. 6, pp. 2 313-2 331, http://dx.doi.org/10.5194/bg-6-2313-2009.

Milledge, J.J. (2011), "Commercial application of microalgae other than as biofuels: A brief review", *Reviews in Environmental Science and Bio/Technology*, Vol. 10, No. 1, pp. 31-41, http://dx.doi.org/10.1007/s11157-010-9214-7.

Miller, D.C. et al. (1995), "Effects of hypoxia on growth and survival of crustaceans and fishes of Long Island Sound", in: McElroy, A. and J. Zeidner (eds.), *Proceedings of the Long Island Sound Research Conference: Is the Sound Getting Better or Worse*, New York Sea Grant Institute, Stony Brook, New York, pp. 1-92.

Munday, P.L. et al. (2014), "Behavioural impairment in reef fishes caused by ocean acidification at CO_2 seeps", *Nature Climate Change*, Vol. 4, pp. 487-492, http://dx.doi.org/10.1038/nclimate2195.

Narita, D., K. Rehdanz and R.S.J. Tol (2012), "Economic costs of ocean acidification: A look into the impacts on global shellfish production", *Climatic Change*, Vol. 113, No. 3-4, pp. 1 049-1 063, http://dx.doi.org/10.1007/s10584-011-0383-3.

Nilsson, G.E. et al. (2012), "Near-future carbon dioxide levels alter fish behaviour by interfering with neurotransmitter function", *Nature Climate Change*, Vol. 2, pp. 201-204, http://dx.doi.org/10.1038/nclimate1352.

NOAA (2010), "Fisheries economics of the US 2008", US Department of Commerce, National Marine Fisheries Service, NOAA Tech. Memo, NMFS-F/SPO-109.

NOEP (2009), "State of the US ocean and coastal economies", National Ocean Economics Program.

Noone, K., R.J. Diaz and U.R. Sumaila (2013), *Managing Ocean Environments in a Changing Climate: Sustainability and Economic Perspectives*, Elsevier Press, Burlington, Massachusetts, available at: www.sciencedirect.com/science/book/9780124076686.

Noone, K., R. Sumaila and R.J. Diaz (2012), *Valuing the Ocean*, Stockholm Environment Institute (SEI), Stockholm, www.sei-international.org/publications?pid=2064.

Nowacek, D. et al. (2007), "Responses of cetaceans to anthropogenic noise", *Mammal Review*, Vol. 37, No. 2, pp. 81-115, http://dx.doi.org/10.1111/j.1365-2907.2007.00104.x.

O'Conner, M.I. et al. (2007), "Temperature control of larval dispersal and the implications for marine ecology, evolution, and conservation", *Proceedings of the National Academy of Sciences of the United States of America*, Vol. 104, No. 4, pp. 1 266-1 271, http://dx.doi.org/10.1073/pnas.0603422104.

Ofiara, D.D. and J.J. Seneca (2006), "Biological effects and subsequent economic effects and losses from marine pollution and degradations in marine environments: Implications from the literature", *Marine Pollution Bulletin*, Vol. 52, No. 8, pp. 844-864.

Olafsson, J. et al. (2009), "Rate of Iceland Sea acidification from time series measurements", *Biogeosciences*, Vol. 6, pp. 2 661-2 668, www.biogeosciences.net/6/2661/2009/bg-6-2661-2009.pdf.

OSPAR (2010), "Hazardous substances" in: OSPAR Commission (ed.), *Quality Status Report 2010*, OSPAR Commission, London, pp. 37-52.

Paerl, H.W. (2006), "Assessing and managing nutrient-enhanced eutrophication in estuarine and coastal waters: Interactive effects of human and climatic perturbations", *Ecological Engineering*, Vol. 26, No. 1, January, pp. 40-54, http://dx.doi.org/10.1016/j.ecoleng.2005.09.006.

Parks, S.E., C.W. Clark and P.L. Tyack (2007), "Short- and long-term changes in right whale calling behavior: The potential effects of noise on acoustic communication", *Journal of the Acoustical Society of America*, Vol. 122, No. 6, pp. 3 725-3 731, http://dx.doi.org/10.1121/1.2799904.

Pauly, D. and D. Zeller (2016), "Catch reconstructions reveal that global marine fisheries catches are higher than reported and declining", *Nature Communications*, Vol. 7, Article 10 244, http://dx.doi.org/10.1038/ncomms10244.

Pauly, D. et al. (1998), "Fishing down marine food webs", *Science*, Vol. 279, No. 5 352, pp. 860-863, http://dx.doi.org/10.1126/science.279.5352.860.

Perrette, M. et al. (2013), "A scaling approach to project regional sea level rise and its uncertainties", *Earth System Dynamics*, Vol. 4, pp. 11-29, http://dx.doi.org/10.5194/esd-4-11-2013.

Pichavant, K. et al. (2000), "Effects of hypoxia on metabolism and growth in juvenile turbot", *Aquaculture*, Vol. 188, No. 1, pp. 103-114, http://dx.doi.org/10.1016/S0044-8486(00)00316-1.

Pinsky, M.L. et al. (2013), "Marine taxa track local climate velocities", *Science*, Vol. 341, No. 6 151, pp. 1 239- 1242, http://dx.doi.org/10.1126/science.1239352.

PISCO (2002), *The Science of Marine Reserves*, Partnership for Interdisciplinary Studies of Coastal Oceans.

Planque, B., E. Bellier and C. Loots (2011), "Uncertainties in projecting spatial distributions of marine populations", *ICES Journal of Marine Science*, Vol. 68, No. 6, pp. 1 045-1 050, http://dx.doi.org/10.1093/icesjms/fsr007.

Planque, B. et al. (2011), "Understanding what controls the spatial distribution of fish populations using a multi-model approach", *Fisheries Oceanography*, Vol. 20, No. 1, pp. 1-17, http://dx.doi.org/10.1111/j.1365-2419.2010.00546.x.

Pörtner, H-O. (2010), "Oxygen- and capacity-limitation of thermal tolerance: A matrix for integrating climate-related stressor effects in marine ecosystems", *Journal of Experimental Biology*, Vol. 213, No. 6, pp. 881-893, http://dx.doi.org/10.1242/jeb.037523.

Pörtner, H.-O., M. Langenbuch and B. Michaelidis (2005), "Synergistic effects of temperature extremes, hypoxia, and increases in CO_2 on marine animals: From Earth history to global change", *Journal of Geophysical Research*, Vol. 110, http://dx.doi.org/10.1029/2004JC002561.

Pörtner H.-O. et al. (2014), "Ocean systems", Chapter 6, in: *Climate Change 2014: Impacts, Adaptation, and Vulnerability*, Part A: Global and Sectoral Aspects, Contribution of Working Group II to the Fifth Assessment Report of the Intergovernmental Panel on Climate Change, Cambridge University Press, Cambridge, pp. 411-484, https://ipcc-wg2.gov/AR5/images/uploads/WGIIAR5-Chap6_FINAL.pdf.

Porzio, L et al. (2011), "Macro algal communities of gas vents near Ischia island in the Mediterranean sea, 2011", Supplement to: Porzio, Lucia; Buia, Maria-Cristina; Hall-Spencer, Jason M (2011): "Effects of ocean acidification on macro algal communities", *Journal of Experimental Marine Biology and Ecology*, Vol 400, No. 1-2, pp. 278-287.

Prince, E.D. and C.P. Goodyear (2006), "Hypoxia-based habitat compression of tropical pelagic fishes", *Fisheries Oceangraphy*, Vol. 15, No. 6, pp. 451-464, http://dx.doi.org/10.1111/j.1365-2419.2005.00393.x.

Prince, E.D. et al. (2010), "Ocean scale hypoxia-based habitat compression of Atlantic istiophorid billfishes", *Fisheries Oceangraphy*, Vol. 19, No. 6, pp. 448-462, http://dx.doi.org/10.1111/j.1365-2419.2010.00556.x.

Rabalais, N.N., R.E. Turner and W.J. Wiseman Jr. (2002), "Gulf of Mexico hypoxia, aka 'The dead zone'", *Annual Review of Ecology and Systematics*, Vol. 33, pp. 235-263, http://dx.doi.org/10.1146/annurev.ecolsys.33.010802.150513.

Rabotyagov, S.S. et al. (2014), "The economics of dead zones: Causes, impacts, policy challenges, and a model of the Gulf of Mexico hypoxic zone", *Review of Environmental Economics and Policy*, Vol. 8, No. 1, pp. 1-22, http://dx.doi.org/10.1093/reep/ret024.

Rahmstorf, S. et al. (2005), “Thermohaline circulation hysteresis: A model intercomparison”, *Geophysical Research Letters*, Vol. 32, No. 23, December, http://dx.doi.org/10.1029/2005GL023655.

Representative Concentration Pathways Database (Version 2.0.5), http://tntcat.iiasa.ac.at:8787/RcpDb/dsd?Action=htmlpage&page=download.

Rhein, M. et al. (2013), “Observations: Ocean”, Chapter 3, in: *Climate Change 2013: The Physical Science Basis*, Contribution of Working Group I to the Fifth Assessment Report of the Intergovernmental Panel on Climate Change, Cambridge University Press, Cambridge, United Kingdom and New York, New York, pp. 255-315, available at: www.ipcc.ch/pdf/assessment-report/ar5/wg1/WG1AR5_Chapter03_FINAL.pdf.

Richier, S. et al. (2014), “Phytoplankton responses and associated carbon cycling during shipboard carbonate chemistry manipulation experiments conducted around northwest European shelf seas”, *Biogeosciences*, Vol. 11, pp. 4 733-4 752, http://dx.doi.org/10.5194/bg-11-4733-2014.

Robbins, L.L. et al. (2013), “Baseline monitoring of the western Arctic Ocean estimates 20% of Canadian basin surface waters are undersaturated with respect to aragonite”, *PLOS ONE*, Vol. 8, No. 9, http://dx.doi.org/10.1371/journal.pone.0073796.

Robinson, A., R. Calov and A. Ganopolski (2012), “Multistability and critical thresholds of the Greenland icesheet”, *Nature Climate Change*, Vol. 2, pp. 429-432, http://dx.doi.org/10.1038/nclimate1449.

Rochette, J. (2014), “La délimitation des espaces maritimes en Méditerranée: Entre enjeux stratégiques nationaux et exigencies de conservation de la biodiversité”, Perin, C. (ed.), *Un littoral sans nature? L'avenir de la Méditerranée face á l'urbanisation*, École Français de Rome, pp. 29-35.

Roegner, G.C., J.A. Needoba and A.M. Baptista (2011), “Coastal upwelling supplies oxygen-depleted water to the Columbia River estuary”, *PLOS ONE*, Vol. 6, No. 4, http://dx.doi.org/10.1371/journal.pone.0018672.

Rolland, R.M. et al. (2012), “Evidence that ship noise increases stress in right whales”, *Proceedings of the Royal Society B: Biological Sciences*, Vol. 279, No. 1 737, pp. 2 363-2 368, http://dx.doi.org/10.1098/rspb.2011.2429.

Rosa, R. et al. (2014), “Differential impacts of ocean acidification and warming on winter and summer progeny of a coastal squid (*Loligo vulgaris*)”, *Journal of Experimental Biology*, Vol. 217, pp. 518-525, http://dx.doi.org/10.1242/jeb.096081.

Ruckelshaus, M. et al. (2013), “Securing ocean benefits for society in the face of climate change”, *Marine Policy*, Vol. 40, July, pp. 154-159, http://dx.doi.org/10.1016/j.marpol.2013.01.009.

Ryan, P.G. et al. (2009), “Monitoring the abundance of plastic debris in the marine environment”, *Philosophical Transactions of the Royal Society B*, Vol. 364, No. 1 526, pp. 1 999-2 012, http://dx.doi.org/10.1098/rstb.2008.0207.

Salisbury, J. et al. (2008), “Coastal acidification by rivers: A new threat to shellfish?”, *Eos*, Vol. 89, No. 50, p.513, http://dx.doi.org/10.1029/2008EO500001.

Scheffer, M. and S.R. Carpenter (2003), “Catastrophic regime shifts in ecosystems: Linking theory to observation”, *Trends in Ecology and Evolution*, Vol. 18, No. 12, pp. 648-656, December, http://dx.doi.org/10.1016/j.tree.2003.09.002.

Scheffer, M., S. Carpenter and B. de Young (2005), "Cascading effects of overfishing marine systems", *Trends in Ecology and Evolution*, Vol. 20, No. 11, November, pp. 579-581, http://dx.doi.org/10.1016/j.tree.2005.08.018.

Selman, M. et al. (2008), "Eutrophication and hypoxia in coastal areas: A global assessment of the state of knowledge", *WRI Policy Note*, World Resources Institute, available at: http://pdf.wri.org/eutrophication_and_hypoxia_in_coastal_areas.pdf.

Shi, D. et al. (2010), "Effect of ocean acidification on iron availability to marine phytoplankton", *Science*, Vol. 327, No. 5 966, pp. 676-679, http://dx.doi.org/10.1126/science.1183517.

Sowers, J., A. Vengosh and E. Weinthal (2011), "Climate change, water resources and the politics of adaptation in the Middle East and North Africa", *Climate Change*, Vol. 104, No. 3, pp. 559-627, http://dx.doi.org/10.1007/s10584-010-9835-4.

Spall, M. (2006), "Effect of sea temperature-wind stress coupling on baroclinic instability in the ocean", *Journal of Physical Oceaonagraphy*, Vol. 37, pp. 1 092-1 097, http://dx.doi.org/10.1175/JPO3045.1.

Steinacher, M. et al. (2010), "Projected 21st century decrease in marine productivity: A multi-model analysis", *Biogeosciences*, Vol. 7, pp. 979-1 005, http://dx.doi.org/10.5194/bg-7-979-2010.

Stock, C.A. et al. (2011), "On the use of IPCC-class models to assess the impact of climate on living marine resources", *Progress in Oceanography*, Vol. 88, No. 1-4, pp. 1-27, http://dx.doi.org/10.1016/j.pocean.2010.09.001.

Stocker, T.F. et al. (2013), "Technical summary", in: *Climate Change 2013: The Physical Science Basis*, Contribution of Working Group I to the Fifth Assessment Report of the Intergovernmental Panel on Climate Change, Cambridge University Press, Cambridge, United Kingdom, pp. 33-115, available at: www.climatechange2013.org/images/report/WG1AR5_TS_FINAL.pdf.

Stramma, L. et al. (2011), "Expansion of oxygen minimum zones may reduce available habitat for tropical pelagic fishes", *Nature Climate Change*, Vol. 2, pp. 33-37, http://dx.doi.org/10.1038/nclimate1304.

Stramma, L. et al. (2009), "Deoxygenation in the oxygen minimum zone of the eastern tropical north Atlantic", *Geophysical Research Letters*, Vol. 36, No. 20, http://dx.doi.org/10.1029/2009GL039593.

Stramma, L. et al. (2008), "Expanding oxygen-minimum zones in the tropical oceans", *Science*, Vol. 320, No. 5 876, pp. 655-658, http://dx.doi.org/10.1126/science.1153847.

Stroeve, J. et al. (2007), "Arctic sea ice decline: Faster than forecast", *Geophysical Research Letters*, Vol. 34, No. 9, http://dx.doi.org/10.1029/2007GL029703.

Sumaila, U.R. and W.W.L. Cheung (2010), "Cost of adapting fisheries to climate change", *World Bank Discussion Paper 5*, The World Bank, Washington, DC, www-wds.worldbank.org/external/default/WDSContentServer/WDSP/IB/2010/09/20/000334955_20100920035715/Rendered/PDF/566630NWP0D1CC10Box353730B01PUBLIC1.pdf.

Sun, Y.D. et al. (2012), "Lethally hot temperatures during the early Triassic greenhouse", *Science*, Vol. 338, No. 6 105, pp. 366-370, http://dx.doi.org/10.1126/science.1224126.

TEEB (2011), *The Economics of Ecosystems and Biodiversity in National and International Policy Making*, edited by P. ten Brink, Earthscan, London and Washington.

Thiel, H. et al. (2001), "The large-scale environmental impact experiment DISCOL – reflection and foresight", *Deep Sea Research Part II: Topographic Study Oceanography*, Vol. 48, No. 17-18, pp. 3 869-3 882, http://dx.doi.org/10.1016/S0967-0645(01)00071-6.

Tilman, D. et al. (2001), "Diversity and productivity in a long-term grassland experiment", *Science*, Vol. 94, No. 5 543, pp. 843-845, http://dx.doi.org/10.1126/science.1060391.

Tripati, A., C. Roberts and R. Eagle (2009), "Coupling of CO_2 and ice sheet stability over major climate transitions of the last 20 million years", *Science*, Vol. 326, No. 5 958, pp. 1 394-1 397, http://dx.doi.org/10.1126/science.1178296.

Troell et al. (2005), Regime shifts and ecosystem service generation in Swedish coastal soft bottom habitats: when resilience is undesirable, *Ecology and Society* Vol. 10, No. 1: 30, available at: http://www.ecologyandsociety.org/vol10/iss1/art30/

Trotman, A. et al. (2009), "Policy responses to GEC impacts on food availability and affordability in the Caribbean community", *Environmental Science & Policy*, Vol. 12, No. 4, pp. 529-541, http://dx.doi.org/10.1016/j.envsci.2009.02.001.

Turner, R.E. et al. (2005), "Summer hypoxia in the northern Gulf of Mexico and its prediction from 1978 to 1995", *Marine Environmental Research*, Vol. 59, No. 1, pp. 65-77, http://dx.doi.org/10.1016/j.marenvres.2003.09.002.

Tyack, P. (2008), "Implications for marine mammals of large-scale changes in the marine acoustic environment", *Journal of Mammalogy*, Vol. 89, No. 3, pp. 549-558, http://dx.doi.org/10.1644/07-MAMM-S-307R.1.

UN (2016), "Goal 14: Conserve and sustainably use the oceans, seas and marine resources", UN Sustainable Development Goals, www.un.org/sustainabledevelopment/oceans.

UN (2015), "Summary of the first Global Integrated Marine Assessment", United Nations General Assembly, 22 July 2015, A/70/112, www.un.org/ga/search/view_doc.asp?symbol=A/70/112.

UN (2011), "General Assembly Report of the Special Rapporteur on the right to food", Oliver De Schutter, Mission to the Syrian Arab Republic, United Nations, New York, New York.

UN (2009), "Syria Drought Response Plan", United Nations, New York, New York, http://reliefweb.int/report/syrian-arab-republic/syria-drought-response-plan.

UNDP-GEF (2012), *International Waters: Delivering Results*, United Nations Development Program, New York, New York, www.undp.org/content/undp/en/home/librarypage/environment-energy/water_governance/international-waters--delivering-results.html.

UNEP (2016), "Aichi Biodiversity Targets", Convention on Biological Diodiversity, www.cbd.int/sp/targets.

UNEP and GPA (2006), *The State of the Marine Environment: Trends and Processes*, United Nations Environment Programme, Nairobi, www.unep.org/regionalseas/globalmeetings/9/global_soe_trends.pdf.

USDA (2008), "Syria: Wheat production in 2008/09 declines owing to season-long drought", US Department of Agriculture, Foreign Agricultural Service, Washington, DC, www.pecad.fas.usda.gov/highlights/2008/05/Syria_may2008.htm.

Van Dover, C. (2011), "Tighten regulations on deep-sea mining", *Nature*, Vol. 470, pp. 31-33, http://dx.doi.org/10.1038/470031a.

Vaquer-Sunyer, R. and C.M. Duarte (2008), "Thresholds of hypoxia for marine biodiversity.", *PNAS*, Vol 105, No. 40, pp. 15452-15457.

Vergés, A. et al. (2014), "The tropicalization of temperate marine ecosystems: Climate-mediated changes in herbivory and community phase shifts", *Proceedings of the Royal Society B: Biological Sciences*, Vol. 281, No. 1 789, http://dx.doi.org/10.1098/rspb.2014.0846.

Wassmann, P. et al. (2011), "Footprints of climate change in the Arctic marine ecosystem", *Global Change Biology*, Vol. 17, No. 2, pp. 1 235-1 249, http://dx.doi.org/10.1111/j.1365-2486.2010.02311.x.

WBGU (2013), *World in Transition: Governing the Marine Heritage*, German Advisory Council on Global Change, Berlin, Germany, available at: www.wbgu.de/en/flagship-reports/fr-2013-oceans.

Weimerskirch, H. et al. (2012), "Changes in wind pattern alter albatross distribution and life-history traits", *Science*, Vol. 335, No. 6 065, pp. 211-214, http://dx.doi.org/10.1126/science.1210270.

Wittmann, A.C. and H.-O. Pörtner (2013), "Sensitivities of extant animal taxa to ocean acidification", *Nature Climate Change*, Vol. 3, pp. 995-1 001, http://dx.doi.org/10.1038/nclimate1982.

Wong, P.P. et al. (2014), "Coastal systems and low-lying areas", Chapter 5, in: *Climate Change 2014: Impacts, Adaptation, and Vulnerability*, Part A: Global and Sectoral Aspects, Contribution of Working Group II to the Fifth Intergovernmental Panel on Climate Change, Cambridge University Press, Cambridge, United Kingdom and New York, New York, pp. 361-409, https://ipcc-wg2.gov/AR5/images/uploads/WGIIAR5-Chap5_FINAL.pdf.

World Bank and FAO (2009), *The Sunken Billions: The Economic Justification for Fisheries Reform*, The World Bank, Washington, DC, http://siteresources.worldbank.org/EXTARD/Resources/336681-1224775570533/SunkenBillionsFinal.pdf.

Worm, B. et al. (2005), "Global patterns of predator diversity in the open oceans", *Science*, Vol. 308, No. 5 739, pp. 1 365-1 369, http://dx.doi.org/10.1126/science.1113399.

Wright, A. et al. (2007), "Do marine mammals experience stress related to anthropogenic noise", *International Journal of Comparative Psychology*, Vol. 20, No. 2, pp. 274-316.

WWF (2015), *Living Blue Planet Report: Species, Habitats and Human Well-being*, Tanzer, J. et al. (eds.), WWF International, Gland, Switzerland, www.worldwildlife.org/publications/living-blue-planet-report-2015.

WWF (2009). "Silent invasion: The spread of marine invasive species via ships' ballast water", WWF International, Gland, Switzerland, www.wwf.de/fileadmin/fm-wwf/Publikationen-PDF/Study_Silent_Invasion.pdf.

WWF (n.d.), "Marine problems: Pollution", World Wildlife Federation, wwf.panda.org/about_our_earth/blue_planet/problems/pollution.

Zhou, S. et. al. (2010), "Ecosystem-based fisheries management requires a change to the selective fishing philosophy", Proceedings of the National Academy of Sciences of the United States of America, Vol. 107, No. 21, pp. 9 485-9 489, http://dx.doi.org/10.1073/pnas.0912771107.

Part II.

Critical factors influencing the emerging ocean-based industries

Chapter 4.

Science, technology and innovation in tomorrow's ocean economy

This chapter considers one of the most important drivers behind the development of ocean industries: science, technology and innovation. Specifically, it assesses the role of science and new knowledge about the oceans; recent and upcoming developments in incremental and disruptive technologies which are enabling and accelerating the growth of the ocean economy; and the fostering of innovation in the ocean domain through such avenues as leveraging technology synergies among maritime sectors, promoting innovation through maritime industry clusters and technology incubators, and encouraging ocean economy foresight. Rather than adopting a sector-by-sector perspective, the chapter favours a cross-cutting approach that emphasises many of the interdependencies and interactions among maritime activities which are a key feature of the ocean economy.

One of the most dynamic drivers of development in the ocean economy of the future is science and technology. New knowledge and a growing range of technologies are gradually pervading every maritime sector, where they are adopted and adapted, triggering yet further innovation. Indeed, many of the scientific and technological advances in the pipeline are expected to have a transformational impact. Particularly striking are the potential innovation benefits to be reaped from combining different ocean technologies, constructing multi-purpose ocean platforms, co-locating ocean-based activities from different sectors, and seeking synergies from collaboration among different ocean industries. To this end, initiatives are proposed to create international forums that would bring together, for example, maritime clusters, or innovation laboratories and centres of ocean excellence, to foster multi-sectoral and multi-functional innovation in the ocean domain.

Almost 70 years ago, Shepard (1948) observed that "Man's perpetual curiosity regarding the unknown has opened many frontiers. Among the last to yield to the advance of scientific exploration has been the ocean floor. Until recent years much more was known about the surface of the moon than about the vast areas that lie beneath three-fourths of the surface of our own planet". This statement continues to hold true and is repeated by scientists countless times. Arguably, nowhere on Earth have science and technology so strongly driven economic development as in the seas and oceans, and this inter-relationship continues to drive new economic activity.

Similarly, the pace of technology development has also persisted over the decades. Where science has opened up new potential, it is technology that has made human activities in the oceans possible. In some cases, the application of such technologies, individually and jointly, is set to bring about significant incremental and step-change innovation to all maritime sectors; in other cases, they hold out the prospect of transformative and sometimes even highly disruptive change – to products and processes, to business models, and to goods and labour markets. Importantly, many of the scientific and technological advances stem from other marine and maritime activities, demonstrating the ocean economy's capacity for cross-fertilisation of knowledge and applications.

Together new knowledge and technology development have pushed innovation at a remarkable pace. The oceans are being used more intensively than ever before, with studies suggesting that a point is being reached at which the pace of change will accelerate beyond the physical capacities of the ocean to cope. Specifically, the Global Ocean Commission (GOC, 2014) has recently identified five interconnected drivers of ocean decline, all of which are related to economic development: rising demand for resources; technological advances[1]; decline of fish stocks; climate change, biodiversity and habitat loss; as well as weak high seas governance. The commission and many observers agree that more innovation is needed if humankind wishes to continue to raise the productivity of the oceans while protecting its ecological integrity.

This chapter examines the issues of science, technology and innovation. Specifically, it assesses the role of new knowledge about the oceans, recent technology developments which have enabled the growth of the ocean economy, emerging and potentially disruptive technologies and, finally, what innovation, including disruptive developments, might be needed to address the challenges of the future.

Rather than adopting a sector-by-sector perspective, the chapter favours a cross-cutting approach that emphasises many of the interdependencies and interactions among maritime activities which are a key feature of the ocean economy.

Science: Knowledge for the ocean economy

Science has been, and will continue to be, a powerful driver of economic development in the seas and oceans. Oceanographic investigations have uncovered, for example, that climate-ocean interlinkages are inextricably linked to agricultural productivity. Biological investigations have discovered a vast array of life forms, with new discoveries being made all the time. Chemical investigations have uncovered nutrient cycles and chemical processes found nowhere else on Earth. Geological investigations have given us an unprecedented understanding of our Earth as well as the mineral resources available. Indeed, even recently, new scientific knowledge about the seas and oceans and their importance to human development and our understanding of the oceans have been the subject of a variety of reports. This includes the discovery of new organisms below the ocean floor (Bojanowski, 2015).

The lack of knowledge about the oceans has inspired the development of various large-scale and long-term efforts at reaching a more comprehensive level of knowledge. One recent example is the Census of Marine Life, which ran from 2000-10, and raised in excess of USD 1 billion in funding from private and public sources. It significantly increased the estimate of known marine species: every second specimen collected from abyssal waters deeper than 3 000 metres (m) was new to science and previously undescribed (Rogers et al., 2015). In short, there is still much that is not known about the oceans. And, by extension, the economic value of what we do know has not been calculated.

There is a similar lack of knowledge about the physical seafloor. While the seafloor has been completely mapped, the scale for the vast proportion remains at a resolution of approximately 5 square kilometres (km^2) (Witze, 2014). According to the National Oceanic and Atmospheric Administration (NOAA), less than 5% of the seafloor has been explored in greater detail. When it comes to managing economic exploitation, this lack of knowledge leaves governments without even basic tools, such as a geological map of the seafloor – a tool at the centre of every land-based minerals regulatory system – or data to make cost-benefit analyses of different exploitation patterns.

More fundamentally, a scientific understanding of the ocean – its properties and behaviour, its health, role in climate change and influence on weather, etc. – is essential for understanding and managing ocean ecosystems. Equally, it is a vital pre-requisite for the sustainable operation of all ocean-based industries. Ocean observation therefore is a cornerstone of ocean science. A raft of infrastructures is required to perform modern ocean observation, including *inter alia*: ocean-going research vessels; satellite remote sensing, communications and global positioning; floating, submersible and fixed platforms and systems; modelling and computational infrastructure, as well as big data storage and management. Much of the investment in the research, data collection and infrastructure comes from public money. While numerous ocean observation initiatives have evaluated the effectiveness of their contribution to scientific fields of endeavour (such as ocean meteorology, measuring acidification, etc.), little to no effort has been undertaken to assess the economic value of the data produced. Yet, knowledge of that economic value could help generate much greater interest and financial participation in ocean research, and also help direct, and in some cases help prioritise, research efforts.

One effort in this direction is the new AtlantOS project, which has been funded by the European Union through its Horizon2020 research framework programme. With EUR 21 million over a period of four years, AtlantOS has been tasked to set up a more integrated, more effective and more sustainable observing of the Atlantic Ocean. In total,

62 partners, including research institutions, universities and private companies from Europe, Brazil, Canada, South Africa and the United States have joined the project to co-operate in improving current observation systems. AtlantOS is co-ordinated by the GEOMAR Helmholtz Centre for Ocean Research Kiel (Germany). Researchers from around the world already co-operate in the Global Ocean Observing System (GOOS), which co-ordinates global sustained ocean observations including satellites, freely drifting floats, fixed observatories, as well as ship-based systems. However, a lot of measurements are still made on a short-term basis or are restricted to a single issue with the data not necessarily being compatible with other measurements and, in some cases, not freely available. Furthermore, data from the deep oceans are still scarce. On the observatories side, knowledge of the interactions between the physics, chemistry and ecology, but also between open-ocean and coastal observing, is still weak. While focused on the Atlantic Ocean, it is hoped that AtlantOS can develop a best practices model of global relevance on how to mobilise the observation communities and governments to develop and support more integrated and sustainable observation systems that are embedded in wider value chains of supply and demand.

One aspect that needs to be considered more extensively in long-term science initiatives is the possible contribution of the private sector. In the case of seabed mapping, this is particularly important given the vast quantities of data being collected by, for example, the oil and gas as well as fisheries industries (see below). In other fields, public-private collaboration is already well developed. This includes the broad area of biological and genetic resources, with many research projects having been launched between universities, research centres and pharmaceutical companies. Areas of co-operation include the discovery and analysis of genetic materials, preclinical and clinical research as well as patent applications and ownership. The extent of this interaction has been highlighted in ongoing deliberations under the UN Convention on Biological Diversity to prepare for an international agreement on the access to and use of biological resources in areas beyond national jurisdiction. (See, for example, the presentations made at Intersessional Workshops on marine genetic resources at the UN General Assembly Ad Hoc Open-ended Informal Working Group to study issues relating to the conservation and sustainable use of marine biological diversity beyond areas of national jurisdiction[2]).

Incremental technology development in the ocean economy

In the course of the next couple of decades, a string of enabling technologies promises to stimulate improvements in efficiency, productivity and cost structures in many ocean activities, from scientific research and ecosystem analysis to shipping, energy, fisheries and tourism. These technologies include imaging and physical sensors, satellite technologies, advanced materials, ICT, big data analytics, autonomous systems, biotechnology, nanotechnology and subsea engineering.

Advanced materials

Metallic, ceramic, polymeric and composite materials are increasingly finding their way into marine activities. Their benefits reside largely in their capacity to make structures stronger, tougher and more durable. As offshore oil and gas operations move increasingly into deeper water, the liaison from seabed to surface, and especially to floaters, is subject to much more stress on mooring systems (anchor cables, for instance), power cables and umbilicals. The use of composite materials such as aramid polyester and kevlar in cable is attracting much interest, also for use on armour production risers and gas injection risers. Similarly, stronger, more durable moorings are required as offshore wind turbines (static and floating) also move into greater water depths, and marine aquaculture makes increasing use of high-density polyethylene for collar cages in exposed sites. In the case of tidal energy, a better understanding of the behaviour of carbon fibre tidal blades has resulted in a more optimised design, reducing the need for costly over-engineering (Anson, forthcoming; Borelli, forthcoming; Sweeney, forthcoming). And in the search for lighter cost-saving structures, there appears to be an increasing appetite for composites – polymer matrix composites, carbon-fibre reinforced plastics – to replace steel in selected applications (Lloyd's Register, 2015).

Nanotechnology

Although nanotechnology is mostly related to materials science, this enabling technology has a vast range of possible applications. More and more materials are being designed at the nano-scale and finding application, for example, as self-diagnostic, self-healing and self-cleaning materials, in coatings, in energy storage and in nano-electronics. These include treating surfaces to prevent fouling; the development of new biomolecules to obtain enhanced oil recovery (EOR); and biocatalysts for bioremediation of oil. In shipping, new nano-scale materials offer surfaces corrosion protection as well as self-repairing properties (Lloyd's Register, 2015). The amount of publications, patents and market applications around nanotechnology has exploded during the last ten years and appears set to have a significant impact on the development of the marine/maritime industries. As a general indication, the average annual number of nanotechnology patents filed in the 1990s was 300. Between 2000 and 2012, that number jumped to 1 800 (OECD, 2016).

Biotechnology

Biotechnology (genetics included) is another enabling technology that has evolved enormously during the last 30 years and that will continue to have a pervasive impact in the future on most if not all domains of the ocean economy. Commercial scale aquaculture has for many years been dependent upon this enabling technology, for example in breeding of species, vaccine and feed development, etc. The development of new marine biochemical substances for pharmaceutical, cosmetic, food and feed use is based upon the genetic characteristics. The future of algal bio-fuels as well as new biomarine industries such as those based on biomimetics are likely to be shaped decisively by further developments in biotechnology.

Subsea engineering and technology

As many of the maritime industries – offshore oil and gas, ocean renewable energy, offshore wind, marine aquaculture, seabed mining and potentially carbon capture and storage (CCS) – evolve in the coming years, common challenges are expected to emerge ever more clearly. These include improving underwater grid technology, developing power transmission to and from onshore, designing subsea power systems, improving pipeline safety, and developing moorings and anchorings for stationary and floating structures.

Given its long history offshore, the oil and gas industry has been the front-runner in subsea innovation. The objective for the future is to install subsea the maximum amount of the functions required to produce the hydrocarbons from the field, the ultimate goal being to be able to produce an oil field without a floater, and entirely with subsea equipment remotely controlled from the shore or the export facility. Moreover, the longer term vision is to move towards entirely electric powered subsea equipment that has no need for other sources of energy. The challenge is considerable: to operate a subsea field with all-electric boosting and separation on the seafloor is thought to require power in the order of 50 megawatts (MW) (and even more if the water treatment is also located subsea) (Borelli, forthcoming).

In ocean energy and offshore wind, too, technological innovations offer scope for greatly improving the industry cost profile. Foremost amongst them are support structures that allow access to deeper waters and a fully integrated grid based on a high-voltage direct current (HVDC) transmission network. Support structures designed for deeper waters enable development in sites with greater average wind speeds and more consistent wind. Both of these increase annual energy output, although development in such deep waters is not without its own challenges. There is significant hope that floating foundations will unlock further opportunities after that. Importantly, both Japan and the United States would be reliant upon floating foundations to build a domestic industry, given the volume of their offshore wind resources that are located in depths greater than 100 m. Grid integration, including cross-border interconnection, will need to be based upon HVDC transmission as distances from shore and the amounts of power being transferred increase. Such interconnection has the benefits of increasing the security of energy supply by reducing the variability of aggregate wind power and hence balancing costs (Anson, forthcoming).

Sensors and imaging

Sensors and imaging are benefiting considerably from the drive for miniaturisation and automation, the growing demand for low-power, low-cost devices for the measurement and graphic display of the physical environment, and moves to endow the sensor itself with "intelligence".

In ocean observation, new smart sensors, techniques and platforms are emerging that are bringing about significant improvements in sensitivity, accuracy, stability and resistance to the stresses and strains of ocean conditions, and since the 1990s there have been impressive advances in automated sensing of key physical features such as current, salinity and temperature. These have formed the basis for global observation projects such as ARGO and OceanSites, providing datasets which support the GOOS. The last decade saw the emergence of novel sensors able to monitor nitrate and methane and also micro-nutrients. Efforts are now focusing on the autonomous *in situ* biological and chemical measurement of marine biodiversity, but also more generally on reducing sensors' power requirements and developing miniaturised micro-sensors that can be carried by gliders and buoys, and even aquatic animals (European Marine Board, 2013).

Not only the scientific community but also industry and business stand to benefit from future advances in sensing and imaging. Seabed mining companies are currently developing undersea remote sensing techniques that allow quantification not only of the spatial extent but also the depth of seafloor massive sulphide deposits (see the next subsection). In the oil and gas sector, new geophysical tools are under development, including improved sub-salt and sub-basalt imaging, very high resolution 3-D (and even 4-D) seismic imaging systems, and more sophisticated well-head sensors. In deeper water and harsher climate conditions, technologies for identifying geohazards and environment risks are increasingly important. In the Arctic, climate and environment will be major determinants of the speed of economic development in the region. One of the main problems facing economic actors there, however, is the availability of good, comprehensive, reliable data on the climate and environment, which would enable them to plan their future investments and the operation of the facilities. However, because of global warming and receding ice cover, historical data are proving a poor baseline for predicting crucial climate and weather conditions, such as ice movements, storm frequencies and so on. There will, therefore, be a premium on scientific and technological tools that enhance knowledge and understanding of the Arctic climate. For example, many experts are of the view that extreme weather conditions (notably polar storms) will increase in frequency and intensity, presenting a real hazard to shipping, oil and gas activities, fishing, etc. Also, it is hard to predict how the ice structure may change. The movement of "fragile" Arctic ice (first- and second-year ice), for instance, appears to be very susceptible to strong winds, moving faster and less predictably than older, more stable ice, and posing a potential threat to exploration and drilling.

Commercial shipping is set to see on-board data increasingly collected autonomously by the deployment of a network of remote sensors capable of real-time communication and data transmission. Development of robust wireless networking architecture for the shipping industry will require sensors exhibiting a variety of features, from self-calibration, fault tolerance and eco-disposability to ultra-low energy consumption and miniaturised scale (Lloyd's Register, 2015).

Satellite technologies

The various functionalities of satellites – communication, navigation, positioning, remote sensing and tracking – are already well established as critical infrastructure for all dimensions of the ocean economy, from marine science, ocean-environment monitoring and seabed mapping, to long-range vessel identification and tracking, fisheries surveillance and communication with offshore facilities. For the coming years, further innovations in satellite technology are in the pipeline. Improvements are expected, for instance in optics, imagery, resolution of sensors, quality and quantity of satellite-transmitted data, etc. but also in satellite coverage as more satellite systems are put into orbit (e.g. Copernicus, Galileo) and the deployment of small, micro- and nano-satellites allows more and more tailored, high-precision observation and tracking (OECD, 2014).

Such improvements will support gradual changes in many areas. For example: 1) in realising more comprehensive information exchange between systems (such as those deployed by new groups of users in shipping; between on-board and onshore systems for navigation and corrective action; for delegation by ship masters and ship owners of supervisory tasks); 2) in combining multiple satellite capabilities (radar, ship tracking with automatic identification system [AIS] and VMS, and communication) to build a more complete "maritime picture"/"maritime domain awareness" or, for instance, to provide an integrative approach to find and identify non-reporting ships; 3) in developing multiple spectral bands to enhance the monitoring of optically complex coastal waters, and improved resolution for polar orbiting observations; 4) pairing satellites with UAVs and drones for high-resolution observation, mapping, environmental and bio-diversity analysis and so on.

Computerisation and big data analytics

As data-processing techniques and applications improve through the introduction of smart machine technologies and computing systems that process information in ways akin to the human brain, it is anticipated that their capacity to handle the extraordinary increases in data generation expected in the coming years will grow; this is set to provide innovative and cost-effective ways to make better sense of complex phenomena, enhance insight into intricate interactions, and improve decision making in many different domains of the maritime economy.

In the oil and gas industry, for instance, a huge amount of data is collected at all stages of exploration, production, transport, refining and distribution. The capacity to interconnect and analyse these data is an essential step to enable significant improvements in business decisions regarding exploration and production investments, inventory location, production planning, safety and so on.

By way of illustration, improvements in data processing and virtual imaging have made possible major progress in reservoir monitoring and management.

In offshore wind technology, new software tools are driving multivariable optimisation of wind-farm array layout. And in the field of ocean renewable energy, advances in ICT are assisting in the development of array electrical systems and array interaction analysis, and the subsea interconnection of multiple devices to reduce cost. In marine tourism, offshore connectivity for crew and passengers has so far proven to be a daunting technical challenge. But major cruise companies have now begun to invest heavily in upgrading on-board broadband, by taking advantage of emerging satellite technology that uses closer-to-Earth orbits than conventional satellites, or by building a "hybrid" approach using satellite and terrestrial networks multiple access technologies (Murphy, 2014).

Autonomous systems

In the marine environment, the deployment of autonomous underwater vehicles (AUVs), remotely operated underwater vehicles (ROVs), autonomous and semi-autonomous surface vehicles (ASVs), drones, stationary data-collection and -relay stations, is set to expand considerably. Moreover, as demands on safety, security and productivity increase, and further progress is made in miniaturisation, motion control and cognition sensing, it is expected that the use of robots will expand in the fields of on- and off-board inspection, repair and maintenance. Shipbuilding and marine equipment manufacturing is also expected to offer fertile ground for autonomous systems by 2030 – e.g. higher levels of automation; use of intelligent algorithms to convert 2D to 3D and accelerate the design process; additive manufacturing (3D printing) to provide greater design freedom and permit the manufacture of products with complex geometry that would be too costly to produce traditionally (Lloyd's Register, 2015). And modern ports are already experiencing partial to full automation of cargo handling. Rotterdam's Maasvlakte II terminal, for example, which opened in April 2015, has no personnel at all inside its cargo-handling section (EIU, 2015).

Combined with other technologies, such as high-performance satellite systems, AUVs, ROVs and ASVs hold out the promise not of incremental but of quite radical innovations in some fields. These and other potentially disruptive technological innovations are the subject of the next section.

Disruptive and step-change innovations combining multiple technologies

In addition to the incremental innovations set out above, there is the prospect of different technologies emerging and converging to bring about quite fundamental shifts in knowledge acquisition and marine industry practices. Rather than present an exhaustive list, this section contents itself with four illustrative examples of such disruptive or at least step-change innovations, describing how their impacts reach across multiple ocean industries. The four examples are ocean floor mapping, e-navigation and smart shipping, sustainable strategies for tackling offshore oil-spills, and the traceability of fish stocks and fish products.

Case 1: Ocean floor mapping

A major impediment to our understanding and monitoring of environmental changes due to climate change, of the dynamics of marine ecosystems and of the ocean environment more generally, is lack of knowledge of the topography, composition and other features of the ocean floor. Recent advances in satellite altimeter technology and data management have made it possible to map the planet's entire seafloor. The resolution of this global data, however, is low – 1.5 kilometres – so while they provide an overall general picture of the ocean bed, detail is very limited. Nonetheless, satellite technology and gravity models are powerful tools for mapping tectonic structures, especially in the deep ocean basin. Sandwell et al. (2014), for example, combined new radar altimeter measurements from satellites CryoSat-2 and Jason-1 with existing data, to construct a global marine gravity model that is twice as accurate as previous models, allowing the identification of extinct undersea ridges and thousands of previously uncharted seamounts.

In the same vein, Dutkiewicz et al. (2015) report on progress towards creating the world's first digital map of the seafloor's geology. Coupling the digital map to large oceanographic data sets, and thereby quantifying, for instance, the link between the seafloor and the sea surface, is expected ultimately to result in more robust reconstructions and predictions of climate change and its impact on the ocean environment.

High-resolution mapping for much greater detail is a different matter. To date, only about 5% of the global ocean has been mapped in high resolution (usually by modern multi-beam sonar systems). Yet, high-resolution seafloor mapping is a critical tool in many respects: for detecting and observing at finer scales and at greater accuracies the undulations and composition of the seafloor; acquiring more detailed knowledge of entire marine ecosystems; protecting and tracking marine life; identifying natural resources, and regulating subsea resource exploration, extraction and equipment, etc.

The acoustic and optical technologies used for high-resolution mapping are evolving rapidly. Acoustics, for example, can be used at virtually any depth, but they become more efficient the deeper the water. Typical acoustic systems are from ships, small boats or even AUVs. Acoustics are also very effective for mapping in areas which are too cloudy with sediment for optical systems (Battista, 2012).

High-resolution mapping is especially important for many of the emerging ocean industries dealt with in this report. For the siting and anchoring of offshore wind turbines, ocean energy devices and marine aquaculture, for example, precise knowledge of the characteristics of the ocean floor are critical for the stability, durability and operational efficiency of the projects. In the case of offshore oil and gas exploration and production, new reservoir monitoring and management techniques are coming on stream, in particular seismic imaging and interpretation: for instance, 4-D seismic reservoir monitoring and management (i.e. 3-dimensional seismic imaging associated to time intervals), in-field drilling analysis based on 4-D results, the fitting of well sensors for real-time permanent monitoring and so on.

In the field of deep-sea mining, among the most expensive and challenging tasks is simply the delineation of the resources. A typical nodule claim of 75 000 km^2 will take years to map, let alone survey in detail to establish the environmental baseline. A sulphide claim typically amounts to no more than 10 000 km^2 and so is a more manageable undertaking. However, a typical high-resolution AUV mapping programme can cover no more than about 10 km^2 per day for a single vehicle, requiring 1 000 days to survey a sulphide claim in its entirety. Vastly more efficient means of surveying are required. Nautilus Minerals, for example, has been able to apply emerging high-resolution geo-survey techniques to seabed massive sulphide (SMS) delineation, achieving a very high success rate in converting exploration targets into high-grade SMS prospects. However, it does not appear that such advanced technologies are being applied routinely (Hannington, forthcoming).

AUVs offer considerable flexibility in that they can carry various types of sensors working at various scales of resolution, and their adoption is considered crucial for keeping up with the geo-survey requirements of a rapidly expanding portfolio of exploration targets.

Current marine geo-physical technologies have proven effective at mapping the lateral spatial extent of SMS deposits, but less so in surveying their depth. That has had to be performed through drilling programmes conducted by ROVs, which are costly and time consuming and cannot provide a comprehensive view of the deposit's depth. 3-D seismic technology is expected to be of considerable help in the future, reducing drilling costs and providing higher quality geological and geotechnical information (Stevenson, Lowe and Plunkett, 2010).

There remains the question, however, of how long it is likely to take to map in high-resolution the remaining 95% of the ocean floor. To put this in perspective, rough calculations suggest that an average modern mapping research vessel, equipped with current technologies and working alone, would need 1 042 years for the task. Using 104 dedicated vessels would take about 10 years. Data management, processing and interpretation also pose a major challenge: the average mapping research vessel using modern technology would probably generate around 267 000 000 terabytes of data (Casavant et al., 2015).

The scale of the task suggests at least two courses of action. First, more international co-operation will be required. A pointer to the future is offered by the first trans-Atlantic sea-floor mapping survey that will take place under the Atlantic Ocean Research Alliance with the deployment of the Irish research vessel, RV Celtic Explorer. The work will be performed by a multinational team made up of US, Canadian and European ocean mapping experts, with 2020 as the target completion date.[3]

Case 2: E-navigation, sea traffic management and smart shipping[4]

Progress in information and communication technologies as well as in big data analytics should see the exchange of data among the key stakeholders in the shipping industry multiply. They should be able to acquire customised information and data around the clock, raising commercial and regulatory effectiveness to new levels, and transforming the business model of the industry. For example, Lloyd's Register (2015) predicts that:

- "Classification societies will have access to data for safety and classification purposes, or for other additional services as driven by client demand.
- Ship owners will have access to the full material state of the ship.
- Operators will have full control of operational and performance data.
- Cargo owners will have full access to the material state of their cargoes and schedules.

- Regulatory authorities such as flag states will be able to obtain full statutory compliance information.
- Port states will have access to safety, cargo and personnel information."

In parallel, the digitalisation of navigation is fully underway as satellite applications, mobile communications, visualisation techniques, remote sensing and radar technologies converge around the management of the maritime sector. As a result, recent years have seen important developments in a number of ship- and shore-based technologies that improve situational awareness and decision making. These include AIS, Electronic Chart Display and Information System (ECDIS), Integrated Bridge Systems/Integrated Navigation Systems (IBS/INS), automatic radar plotting aids (ARPA), radio navigation, long-range identification and tracking (LRIT) systems, Vessel Traffic Service (VTS) and the Global Maritime Distress Safety System (GMDSS). Moreover, ships now carry global satellite navigation systems (GNSS) and will soon all have reliable ECDIS.

Regional initiatives are emerging that aim to bring about fundamental improvement in sea traffic management. Europe's Mona Lisa 2.0 project, for example, is aimed at improving the safety, environment and efficiency of the industry. A cornerstone in the strategy is Route Exchange, which will significantly enhance safety by complementing data already available to deck officers (e.g. their own route, position, speed, etc.) with information about other ships' routes, helping to avoid collisions and other possibly dangerous situations. Also on the horizon are sea traffic co-ordination centres (STCC) that will be able to monitor traffic and assist the vessels with up-to-date local information, helping the vessels detect movements outside intended routes and suggesting alternative routes to avoid drifting containers, traffic congestion and environmentally sensitive areas. Similar initiatives to improve maritime situational awareness are underway in other parts of the world (e.g. Australia, Korea).

The enormous benefits of these transformational initiatives, however, can only be reaped fully at global scale if systems are compatible. This is currently not the case, neither for the technology systems (for instance, the on-board deployment of GNSS and ECDIS is not fully integrated and harmonised with other systems and those of other ships and shore-based facilities) nor for the regional plans described above. If current technological advances continue without proper co-ordination, there is a risk that the future development of marine navigation systems will be hampered through a lack of standardisation onboard and ashore, incompatibility between vessels and an increased and unnecessary level of complexity. This is where e-navigation comes into the picture.

E-navigation is a major initiative of the International Maritime Organisation (IMO) to harmonise and enhance navigation systems. It is expected to have a significant impact on the future of marine navigation.

E-navigation is defined as: "the harmonised collection, integration, exchange, presentation and analysis of maritime information onboard and ashore by electronic means to enhance berth to berth navigation and related services, for safety and security at sea and protection of the marine environment" (IMO NAV 53/13, 2007).

In 2014, the IMO approved the e-navigation Strategy Implementation Plan (SIP) (IMO, 2014), which sets out a list of tasks to address five prioritised e-navigation solutions during the period 2015-19. These are:

- improved, harmonised and user-friendly bridge design
- means for standardised and automated reporting

- improved reliability, resilience and integrity of bridge equipment and navigation information
- integration and presentation of available information in graphical displays received via communication equipment
- improved communication of VTS Service Portfolio (not limited to VTS stations).

Case 3: Sustainable strategies for dealing with offshore oil spills[5]

Most oil spills are quite small (usually less than 7 tonnes), but make up around 90% of total petroleum hydrocarbon discharges to the environment worldwide. Large-scale spills, in contrast, contribute only a quite small proportion – less than 10%. However, they are usually dramatic and very high-profile events and attract massive media attention, as demonstrated by recent accidents on offshore platforms such as in Australia (2009), the United States (2010), the People's Republic of China (2011; hereafter "China") and Brazil (2012). They also raise public awareness about the way offshore oil exploration and production is moving into ever deeper waters. Evidence from the Gulf of Mexico indicates that the number of incidents correlates with water depth: on average, for every 30 m of additional depth, the probability of an incident increases by more than 8%. As the water depth of operations increases, so does the risk of future accidents. Hence, major efforts worldwide have gone into developing strategies for minimising accidental spills and designing new remedial technologies.

What stands out is the highly diverse range of different technologies that are increasingly being brought to bear on the problem. Indeed, technological innovations in the pipeline would appear to militate in favour of what some researchers denote as a "paradigm shift" in oil spill research to enable operational readiness prior to the next large oil spill, rather than attempting to develop solutions during a spill (Figure 4.1).

The role of smart software-based tools in contingency planning is growing rapidly. Where disaster responders benefit from effective emergency decision support systems (DSSs), environmental damage can be reduced. Such software systems may also include management science and operational research tools. Mathematical tools are also deployed to support decision making in emergency situations. While proving useful, they do suffer from drawbacks, e.g. lengthy computing times and low response rates. Recent innovations, however, hold out possibilities to overcome these through the use of "intelligent" methods such as artificial neural networks (ANNs), increasingly used in environmental applications, and oil spill emergency preparedness tools incorporating intelligent mathematical model systems – case-based reasoning (CBR), genetic algorithms (GA) and ANN.

Satellite data are critical to timely and appropriate oil spill response. Synthetic aperture radar (SAR) on satellites has become an important tool in oil spill monitoring: it has the advantage of wide area coverage, day and night deployment, and insensitivity to adverse weather. Its weaknesses – e.g. difficulty in differentiating oil spills from algal blooms, or slicks from sheens – are increasingly being rectified by improved visible satellite sensors. Examples are the AVIRIS hyperspectral approach to measure oil thickness (first used during the Deepwater Horizon incident) and rapid response products, such as the Ocean Imaging expert system and MODIS (a sophisticated digital camera).

Figure 4.1. **Windows of opportunity oil spill response management decision-making system**

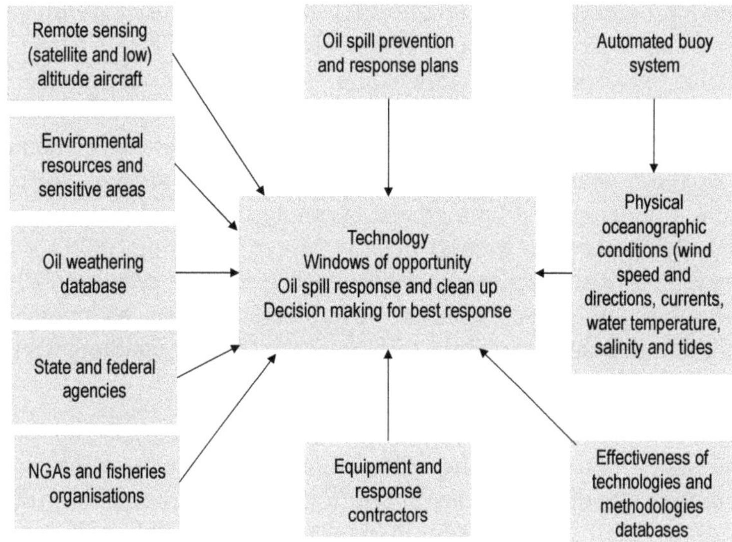

Source: Adapted from Ornitz and Champ (2002).

In terms of remediation, there are currently four main types of technology response: 1) chemical treatment (dispersants, emulsion breakers); 2) *in situ* burning; 3) mechanical recovery (booms, skimmers, oil-water separators, adsorbents); and 4) bioremediation. A combination of clean-up technologies is usually required. Bioremediation is of particular interest here. Microorganisms occurring naturally in almost all marine ecosystems have an enormous capacity to decompose petroleum hydrocarbons. The bulk of the tens of thousands of chemical compounds from which crude oil is made up are vulnerable to attack by these bacterial populations.

Bioremediation methods are not effective in all situations. However, among the clean-up technologies available, they are considered the more sustainable and cost-effective. And through the addition of fertilisers, they are able to accelerate the rate of oil biodegradation in some situations. Moreover, and looking further ahead, a rich and growing range of genome-wide (-omics) technologies, biosensors and so-called "ecogenomics" is becoming available which have the potential to greatly improve bioremediation in the field.

Case 4: Traceability of fish stocks and fish products[6]

It is indisputable that much improved governance of our oceans is required to preserve and rebuild fish stocks and in particular to combat illegal, unreported and unregulated (IUU) activities. Science and technology can contribute in important ways to more effective enforcement and conservation of fisheries through the identification and monitoring of wild fish populations and traceability of fish and fish products. Recent years have seen some noteworthy innovations in this respect, which have the potential to revolutionise wild fish stock management on a geospatial scale and make serious inroads into IUU prevention. They bring together a cluster of technologies ranging from DNA sequencing, bio-informatics and microchemistry to satellite technologies and web-based geo-visualisation techniques.

So far, one of the biggest hurdles blocking progress towards sustainable fish stock management and prosecution of IUU activities were the limitations of geographically defined stocks as an indicator of the regional provenance of fish. In just a few years, access to so-called "next-generation sequencing" has radically changed the situation. By virtue of the identification of thousands of genetic differences at numerous genes, it has been made possible to design hundreds to thousands of new genetic markers. The unique combinations of these genetic variations now allow the assignment of fish to specific populations from more areas and with greater certainty than previously possible, attaining standards which can be used in a court of law. Moreover, using otolith (fish ear stone) microchemistry, it has also become possible to differentiate between fish species and between populations within each species: new image analysis techniques are used to photograph, digitise and analyse subtle differences in shape, enabling fish to be traced back to their home area.

Selected genetic characteristic information can be accessed publicly through a map-based interface – a geographic visualisation platform – which points to the biological characteristics of the species in relation to their environment (ocean currents, temperature, salinity, etc.) and puts them in geographic context. Hence, data and findings can be made available on a continuous basis to the scientific community and other stakeholders for use as a management and regulation decision support tool – not least by the relevant control and enforcement authorities.

The control and enforcement authorities are gaining additional support from developments in satellite technologies. For example, a new monitoring system – a "virtual watch room" – has been developed by the United Kingdom's Satellite Applications Catapult in collaboration with the Pew Foundation, to cross-check information on tens of thousands of fishing boats operating around the world. The data are provided by ships' AIS, mandatory for commercial vessels, fishing boats included, with a gross tonnage of more than 300, and by VMS (vessel monitoring system). Switching off either system draws the attention of the watch room to potentially suspicious activity. Satellites equipped with synthetic-aperture radar can detect a vessel's position no matter what the weather conditions. Even if a ship has switched off its AIS or VMS system, its fishing pattern can be logged and more closely investigated. With the advent of nano-satellites, the watch-room system is set to become even more effective, with the capacity to launch swarms of small satellites to observe likely IUU at ever lower cost.

From the point of view of traceability and sustaining wild fish stocks, the watch room system promises to be useful to supermarkets keen to protect their supply chains, and their reputations, for not handling IUU products.

Promoting innovation for a sustainable ocean economy

While new and sometimes disruptive technologies can bring about massive changes, they often remain embedded in the existing patterns of "business-as-usual". As highlighted in Chapter 3, business-as-usual will, however, likely not solve the problems facing the oceans. There are some indications that in the scientific and business communities this is being recognised and efforts are being made to look at innovative approaches to developing the ocean economy. These emphasise: the importance of science taking a more integrated approach to understanding the oceans; the benefits of leveraging technology synergies; the need for academia and business to help drive a new culture of education and skills; and the need for more foresight analyses of the ocean.

Towards a more integrated understanding of the oceans

The need for more interdisciplinary or transdisciplinary studies to tackle complex societal challenges that emerge out of the nexus of a variety of long- and short-term trends is a major theme in science policy (Stirling, 2014). With no external pressure to address the oceans in an integrated manner, disciplinary boundaries in the marine and maritime sciences tend to be well entrenched. Such pressure, however, is beginning to grow. A recent study summarised the need as follows:

> As intensified development proceeds seawards towards the ocean-edge of the Margin, we are reminded of the unsustainable exploitation of ecosystems that has already occurred and continues along the landward edge of the Margin and in shallow seas. A new, pluralistic scientific agenda is needed as the Great Acceleration unfolds on this new frontier to prevent repeating mistakes of the past. Specifically, innovative research … is needed to inform policy and practice and lead to societal actions that foster ocean and coastal sustainability. (Glavovic et al., 2015)

Markus, Huhn and Bischof (2015) make a similar point.

Doing more with less – Leveraging technology synergies among ocean sectors

The notion that different ocean-based activities might be pulled together in a single location has been debated for some time already (Lacroix and Pioch, 2011). The reasoning behind such initiatives stems from the potential benefits that could be reaped in terms of lower costs from shared common infrastructure, a reduced impact on the marine environment, and more effective planning of the use of limited ocean space.

Inter-sectoral technology synergies

To begin with, at least, proposals for capturing potential synergies of ocean-based activities focused mainly on energy production – offshore wind and offshore oil and gas operations – but the idea of associating forms of marine aquaculture with offshore structures soon gained ground as well, to be followed by ideas around leisure and tourism, marine research and marine biotechnology.

A surprisingly high degree of potential interaction exists, for example, between offshore wind and a multitude of other ocean-based activities (Figure 4.2).

Commonalities in infrastructure requirements represent an opportunity for offshore wind and the oil and gas industry to find mutually beneficial efficiencies. These include making more productive use of vessels and port infrastructure, as well as learning through research, design and development (RD&D). The latter might include effective and safe operations and maintenance techniques in the marine environment, construction and subsea engineering, as well as improved knowledge in areas such as seabed mapping. Indeed, pre-engineering surveys, including the metocean conditions of the site and the detailed bathymetry and geotechnical information on the first few tens of metres below the seafloor, are a pre-requisite to both types of developments. Shallow water offshore construction methods and tools including marine supports are often complementary and can be used on both offshore oil and gas and renewables projects: already today, some of the most efficient construction marine supports, jack-up platforms, heavy lift capacity ships, or cable lay and burial ships, work for both industries with minor mobilisation costs. In contrast, however, methods and equipment in deep water are different from shallow water (requiring, for example, systematic dynamic positioning, remote intervention technology, etc.) and so generally fewer synergies are to be found (Borelli, forthcoming).

The two industries could benefit from the development of more and stronger energy clusters, including R,D&D bases, a highly competitive supply chain and access to a skilled labour market. Of course, such co-location would inevitably mean competition for resources, which may temper some of these potential benefits (Anson, forthcoming).

Figure 4.2. **Offshore wind potential interactions with other marine users**

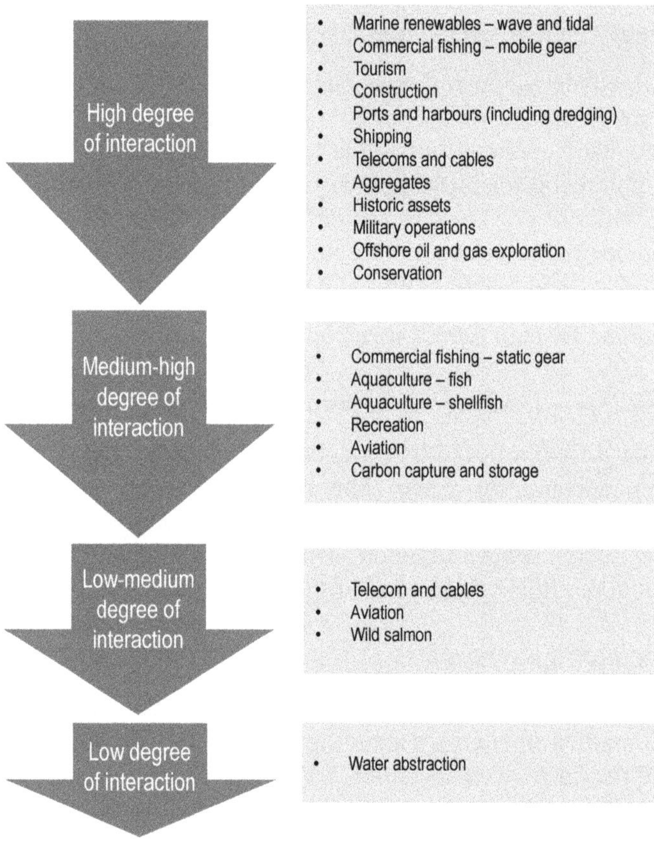

Source: Adapted from Anson (forthcoming).

Many of the above-mentioned synergies also apply to the development of ocean renewables where, for example, economies of scale might also be achieved through shared grid connections. Proximity of development would strengthen the arguments for some of the more innovative, interconnected grid designs mentioned earlier in this chapter. However, as Borelli (forthcoming) points out, mixing electrical power generation from renewable marine sources and oil and gas production fields is not always straightforward. The energy required to develop a field of 150 000-200 000 boe/d (barrels of oil-equivalent per day) is typically in the range of a continuous 50-100 MW. This is the same order of magnitude as the total output of a typical offshore wind farm – output, however, which by nature is irregular and needs to be associated with some storage method to deliver a stable average flow of energy. Hence, in the general case, use of associated gas to feed a centralised power production plant is likely to be judged more economical. Nonetheless, depending upon the configuration of the field, and the distance from primary energy production source, it is possible that a local production of energy in the vicinity of an isolated well or marginal field could be competitive compared to a permanent cable link.

A further advantage would lie in reducing variability in energy supply. While wave energy is primarily a wind-driven phenomenon, at a particular location and time, the energy levels in the wind and waves may be different. More ambitiously, there has also been speculation around the possibility of integrating other marine renewables with offshore wind. Such "hybrid" designs would share the same substructure or foundation with the offshore wind turbine. This shared cost would, in turn, lead to an important cost reduction, given the importance of the substructure within an offshore project. An additional advantage may reside in the smaller environmental impact that combined production would be expected to have compared to the separate alternative (Anson, forthcoming). It does appear increasingly clear, however, that the future development of the wave and tidal energy sectors will be linked with developments in other sectors, such as offshore wind energy, oil and gas, and hydropower. There are significant opportunities for co-location of technologies, e.g. for wave, tidal and offshore wind energy, and for utilising common platforms. Mutual learning processes, shared infrastructure and innovations from a shared supply chain will be of benefit to the future expansion of both the ocean energy sector and related sectors. Research carried out by the SI Ocean consortium partner JRC indicates that offshore wind and wave and tidal projects could have component and project synergies of up to 40%. Industry co-operation initiatives can also pave the way for increased cross-supply chain co-operation and knowledge sharing with other marine sectors (Sweeney, forthcoming).

With respect to renewables and aquaculture, joint development of offshore wind farms with open ocean aquaculture is currently under consideration (Wever, Krause and Buck, 2015). The specific infrastructure and environmental conditions at an offshore wind farm will determine the type of aquaculture that can be undertaken. Little information is available at present on the feasibility of co-locating finfish culture with offshore wind farms. However, the culture of aquaculture species such as mussels on offshore wind infrastructure has been shown to be, in theory, biologically and economically feasible if suitable management measures are followed (Michler-Cieluch and Krause, 2008; Buck and Krause, 2012). Seaweed cultivation is a further possibility, with the aim to harvest biomass for producing fish and animal feed, biofuels and energy. Since offshore wind farm areas may often be closed for shipping and commercial fishing (either by law or a proxy-closure), the conditions for aquaculture could be favourable, as too could be the designation of the park as a sort of marine conservation area. Fish are likely to be attracted to the seaweed fields and use them for shelter or as a nursery. In addition, the seaweed could provide nutrients and energy (Ecofys, 2012; Fredheim and Reve, forthcoming). Furthermore, integrating offshore aquaculture with wind farms helps provide the necessary structural support that aquaculture operations need, whilst wind farms have the potential to benefit from maintenance activities carried out by aquaculture workers if given proper training (Allard, 2009).

On the downside, wind turbine bases are finely tuned to withstand the particular forces of the ocean environment while keeping costs in check. It may therefore prove problematic to add any physical connection between the installations. Moreover, offshore wind farms are often located far from the shore, leading to long transport distances which can be economically challenging for the marine aquaculture operations.

Notwithstanding these potential hurdles, the potential benefits of co-locating offshore wind turbines with aquaculture are substantial, especially if the objective of multi-purpose use were to be built into the design, development and construction process right from the outset. Artificial habitats to support ecological functions such as protection, breeding, spawning and feeding, could be designed as an integral part of the infrastructure and its surroundings, generating greater diversity along the structure from the surface (best suited mainly for post-larvae and juveniles) to the seabed (for adult specimens) and stimulating biodiversity and biomass development throughout the whole wind farm area (Lacroix and Pioch, 2011).

Of course, any form of co-location will in practice rely on the implementation of an effective regulatory framework that specifies official planning and decision-making responsibilities as well as trialling existing equipment in offshore locations, technological improvements and detailed consideration of the practical, health, safety, liability, economic, operational, legal and commercial issues (DEFRA, 2015). In addition, developers also need to be convinced that the potential returns outweigh the risks associated with it (Fredheim and Reve, forthcoming).

With respect to possible synergies between deep-water oil and gas projects and deep-sea mining projects, the picture is mixed. First, there are the elements of architecture, engineering and surveying to consider. In deep-sea mining, the reserves to be exploited are on the seafloor or near the bottom surface, whereas with oil and gas, reserves are often several thousand metres below the seafloor and require extensive subsurface facilities (wells and associated services). Architecture of the projects may therefore be very different. But there are strong similarities in terms of engineering methods and survey requirements. Pre-engineering surveys, including ocean weather and condition of the sea surface and water column, the detailed bathymetry and geotechnical information about the first few tens of metres below the seafloor, are key elements for both activities. They also share the basic principles of dividing the facilities into subsea production system, risers (including production line, cables and umbilicals) and floaters, supporting production, accommodation and export systems. Second, there are the construction methods and equipment. Potential synergies apply here to the need for dynamically positioned ships equipped with construction, lifting and handling equipment as well the need for remote intervention technology, including inspection, precision measurements and telemetry (Borelli, forthcoming).

There may also be synergies with marine tourism. Looking to onshore impacts, a study in the South Baltic region (Stiftung Offshore-Windenergie, 2013) found that there could be positive impacts from offshore wind on tourism. They report that the fascination with offshore wind technology, its character and its contribution to environmental protection were the main drivers of this increased attraction to tourists. Additionally, the region profits from the value creation generated by the offshore wind industry. These factors can improve the general attractiveness of a region and create a niche in the competitive tourism market (Anson, forthcoming).

Finally, there is great potential at local scale and at ocean scale for subsea cabled observatories combining under-sea cable systems with monitoring and sensory functions (suites of sensors including biosensors) to enhance deep-sea observation, seabed mapping and similar activities. This may present considerable opportunities to synergise with telecom and power cables. Indeed, several such seafloor observatories are already in operation, such as those run by Japan (DONET and DONET 2) and Canada (NEPTUNE). Moreover, the United States Ocean Observatories Initiative (NSF-OOI) is planning a network of seafloor observatories deploying highly sophisticated sensors and imagery, instrumented moorings, submarine robots and gliders, etc., interconnected by fibre-optic cables spread across the northern and southern hemispheres in the Atlantic and Pacific Oceans. The observatory will be breaking new ground by streaming real-time data and images on the seafloor and water column on an ongoing basis (OOI, 2015).

Innovation through networks of maritime industry clusters

The last couple of decades have seen the emergence of maritime industry clusters at national level, and also at regional level (notably in Europe). In addition to representing the interests of the various member industries, many maritime clusters act as agents of cross-sectoral technology transfer and stimulators of innovation synergies, not least among small and medium-sized enterprises (SMEs). However, many clusters only encompass a small part of all the maritime sub-industries; some are public, others private or mixed; some clusters have little interaction among sectors and cannot perform the tasks of co-ordination and cross-sectoral exchange; yet others have no remit to pursue cross-industry science and technology innovation initiatives. Moreover, many countries and regions around the world have no active maritime industry cluster at all. Given the right conditions, government policy can help create, strengthen, sustain and expand maritime industry clusters. There is no one-size-fits-all policy approach, and much depends on local and national circumstances, but the potential to leverage such structures for the promotion of technological innovation and exchange in the maritime domain can be considerable.

Multiple-use platforms

A more advanced, more complex version of joint location of offshore industries is stirring considerable interest in ocean engineering and ocean management, namely the concept of common-use or multiple-use ocean platforms. At the core of the idea is system integration that builds on capturing the synergies offered by the use of different ocean-based technologies – renewable energy (wind, wave, etc.), marine aquaculture, maritime transport and logistics, marine research, biotechnology – deployed on the same site (see, for example, Karmakar and Guedes Soares, 2015).

Explorations are underway into the opportunities that may arise for sustainable economic growth and ocean utilisation from mixing different sectors, technologies and functions on the same platform. The European Union, for example, has set in motion several such multi-use ocean platform projects. These include TROPOS, H2OCEAN, MERMAID, ORECCA and MARINA (see Annex 4.A1).

Figure 4.3 is a diagrammatic representation of the process implementation of H2OCEAN, which provides first insights into the complexities of the concepts underlying such integrated platforms.

Multi-functional platforms will need to be developed also in a number of specific under-sea activities. In seabed mining, for example, the pre-mining phase necessitates the capture and measurement of a multiplicity of parameters. This will require the development of a multiplatform (fixed and mobile) system with a large variety of sensors and imaging devices suitable for adaptive monitoring and adaptive management, enhanced by versatile sensors with analytical (*in situ*) and sampling capacity for a number of elements. (IFREMER, for example, is currently developing and testing such instruments together with its industrial partners.) Concerning hydrothermal vents and ferro-manganese crusts, Japan's JAMSTEC has been mapping naturally occurring "smoker" plumes using geological sensors (acoustic, turbidity, electrometer) and investigating ferromanganese crust environments using bathymetric data, information on tidal direction and velocities, videos, etc. For the future, however, there much more integrated work across a range of disciplines will be required (EcoDeep-SIP, 2015).

Figure 4.3. **H2OCEAN multi-use platform process**

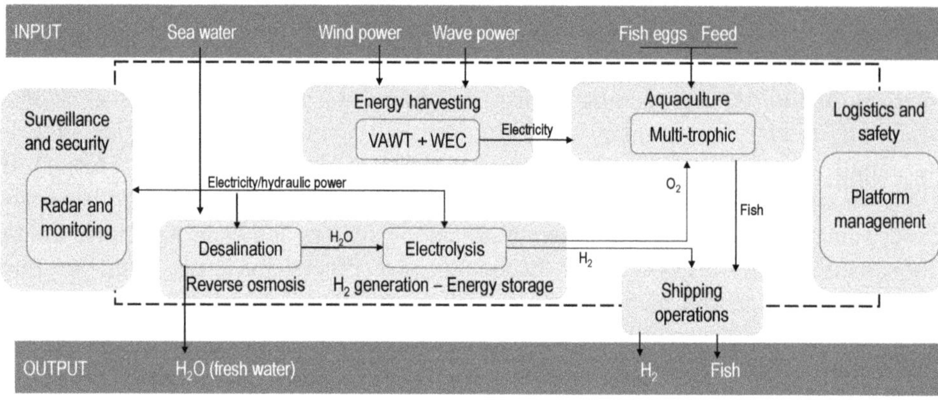

Source: Koundouri (2014).

Centres of excellence, S&T incubators and marine tech labs

Looking more to the future, recent years have seen the emergence of numerous initiatives (many still at the planning stage) around the world to create specific centres of excellence aimed at leveraging the potential synergies of technological innovations across and even beyond maritime industries, often in liaison with maritime clusters. These initiatives include, for example, the Sealab Innovation Centre (Mediterranean), the San Diego Blue Tech Incubator (United States), the Ocean Space Centre (Norway) and the Ocean Technology Alliance (Canada). Many take the form of public-private partnerships, opening up opportunities for governments to promote innovation in the maritime sector in a variety of different ways.

The Sealab Innovation Center, for example, is a collaborative innovation platform – still in progress – designed to accelerate synergy building from the integration of innovative technological elements of R&D projects developed in French competitiveness clusters, and innovative products from companies. The Norwegian Ocean Space Centre aims to become a knowledge centre for future ocean-space technology. It will be the hub of national efforts in the development of ocean-space technology and infrastructure, and will provide for extensive interactions and networking with national and international research institutions and industrial participants.

A new culture of training and education

If the ocean economy of the future is to be skills and knowledge based, then more of an effort must be made to link academia with industry. In Europe this link was made in the European Commission's (2014) report on "Innovation in the blue economy", which stresses the potential job and growth opportunities for marine and maritime sectors. It is recognised that a majority of marine graduates will move from academia into the wider job market. Marine graduate training of the future must also work across academia, industry and wider stakeholders and stimulate attractive career pathways across existing and emerging blue sectors. A recent communication by the European Marine Board (2016) on its planned publication of a *Future Science Brief on Marine Graduate Training* noted that, to bridge the culture gap between disciplines, marine and maritime sectors, and to create an interdisciplinary and adaptable workforce that can tackle holistic ocean issues, marine graduate training needs to:

- identify and provide the necessary skills and competences needed by graduates entering the job market
- promote internationalisation
- foster active partnerships between academia, policy and industry
- promote life-long learning for marine graduates
- foster long-term funding commitment to marine training
- enhance recruitment and branding
- enhance the attractiveness of academic careers.

Foresight studies of the ocean economy

While there are more and more scientific studies and market analyses of the oceans and the ocean economy, there are few if any fora that exist to analyse current developments in ocean affairs and their potential impacts on the future or to debate different normative visions for what the ocean economy ought to look like in the future. Given the fragmented nature of ocean governance (see Chapter 9) and if the aim is to realise a sustainably-managed global ocean economy, then a forum that engages in foresight might have a useful role in the future.

Foresight is often explicitly intended to establish networks of knowledgeable agents, who can respond better to policy and other challenges. As Hanus (2012) indicates, such an approach comprises five key elements: systematic gathering of anticipatory intelligence about the future; a participative, interactive and iterative process; building networks of knowledgeable agents; generation of common visions of the future; and establishment of the implications for present-day decisions and actions.

Overall, there remains a clear gap between the concrete strategic-level co-operation among education, research, technology and industrial communities on the one hand, and the expectations articulated by, for example, the Global Oceans Commission on the other. Bringing these communities together in the context of a long-term foresight forum might offer an innovative context in which ocean economy value chains are assessed and debated with a view to identifying those that hold out the greatest potential to create growth and jobs, and to establish exactly where the potential for economic activity lies in a global context. In their 2014 "Global value chains" report the OECD, World Trade Organization and World Bank showed that value chains covering the various bases from education through to commercialisation are powerful drivers of growth and productivity and support job creation (OECD, WTO and World Bank Group, 2014).

But much remains to be done in the maritime sectors. For example, in the field of marine observation and data there are large-scale scientific plans, companies developing commercial applications and public sector assessments on the need for a better understanding of ocean dynamics, ecosystems values, and impacts of climate change and human activities. However, no strategic analysis exists of where public and private sector investments would be best made to service these different needs as well as creating a basis for altogether new opportunities. Similarly, in the environmentally vulnerable and commercially interesting Arctic region, data and figures exist for individual commercial sectors – e.g. transport growth, possible environmental impacts (e.g. soot), oil and gas reserves – however, there is no integrated analysis on what new skills, scientific and education services or technology applications would be derived from public funding in the region. A similar lack of strategic cost-benefit analyses exists also in fields related to the use of marine biodiversity and marine biotechnologies for new products and applications.

A long-term "forum" for foresight in ocean affairs could serve a variety of concrete purposes, including, for example:

- identifying specific marine economic activities which hold substantial commercial and job creation potential and the corresponding regional value chains from basic research and/or education to market
- assessing value chains in terms of potential for new science, new skills and commercial success and employment
- assessing the challenges and opportunities of further investing in these areas in the global context
- debating the possible contributions of ocean science and technology to ocean governance.

Concluding remarks

The trends identified and illustrated in this chapter depict a maritime economy that is in the throes of remarkable scientific and technological change. Innovation is moving fast in all of the domains covered here, spilling over into and interacting with each other, and thereby triggering yet further innovations. As entire industries undergo transformation and globalise yet further, and as patterns of ocean use and resource extraction shift, regulation – in particular at international level – is called upon to respond in ways which create and preserve a sustainable framework for such rapid development while protecting ocean ecosystems and human welfare. But can regulation evolve rapidly enough in the coming years to keep pace? That is the subject of the next chapter.

Notes

1. For example, increasingly sophisticated fish finding devices, or greatly improved seafloor mapping and analysis to support seabed mining.
2. Available at: www.un.org/depts/los/biodiversityworkinggroup/documents/BBNJ_Worshops.pdf.
3. For more information, see: www.thefishsite.com/fishnews/25497/transatlantic-ocean-floor-to-be-mapped-in-international-effort/#sthash.lzJRxVeM.dpuf.
4. This case study is drawn from: www.imo.org/en/OurWork/Safety/Navigation/Pages/eNavigation.aspx.
5. This case study is drawn from Ivshina et al. (2015).
6. This case study is drawn from Carvalho, MacAoidh and Martinsohn (2011) and The Economist (2015).

Annex 4.A1.
EU multi-use ocean platform projects[1]

The TROPOS project aims to:

- explore the relations and integration into the platform of a broad range of sectors including energy, aquaculture and related maritime transport
- research the relations between oceanic activities, including wind energy, aquaculture, transport solutions for shipping, and other additional services
- determine the optimal locations for multi-use offshore platforms in Mediterranean, sub-tropical and tropical latitudes
- develop novel, cost-efficient, floating and modular multi-use platform designs that enable optimal coupling of the various services and activities
- study the logistical requirements of the novel multi-use platform
- assess the economic feasibility and viability of the platform
- develop a comprehensive environmental impact methodology and assessment
- configure at least three complete solutions, for the Mediterranean, sub-tropical and tropical areas.

H2OCEAN aims at:

- Developing an economically and environmentally sustainable multi-use open-sea platform on which wind and wave power will be harvested. Part of the generated energy will be used for multiple applications on-site, including the conversion of energy into hydrogen that can be stored and shipped to shore, and a multi-trophic aquaculture farm. Launched in January 2012 for two years, H2OCEAN involves industrial and academic partners from five countries.

MERMAID aims at:

- Developing novel innovative design concepts for offshore platforms to address different physical conditions (from deep water to shallow and inner waters) in order to make the best use of the ocean space. Launched in January 2012 for three years, MERMAID gathers 28 partners from 13 countries.

ORECCA signifies:

- Offshore Renewable Energy Conversion platforms – Co-ordination Action and aims to create a framework for knowledge sharing and to develop a roadmap for research activities in the context of offshore renewable energy which is a

1. This annex is based on www.troposplatform.eu/tropos-european-collaborative-project/Other-Platforms.

relatively new and challenging field of interest. In particular, the project will stimulate collaboration in research activities leading towards innovative, cost-efficient and environmentally benign offshore renewable energy conversion platforms for wind, wave and other ocean energy resources, for their combined use as well as for the complementary use such as aquaculture e.g. biomass and fishes and monitoring of the sea environment e.g. marine mammals, fish and bird life.

MARINA will:

- Establish a set of equitable and transparent criteria for the evaluation of multi-purpose platforms for marine renewable energy (MRE). Using these criteria, the project will produce a novel, whole-system set of design and optimisation tools addressing, *inter alia*, new platform design, component engineering, risk assessment, spatial planning, platform-related grid connection concepts, all focused on system integration and reducing costs. The multi-purpose renewable energy platforms will be brought to the level of preliminary engineering designs with estimates for energy output, material sizes and weights, platform dimensions, component specifications and other relevant factors. This will allow the resultant new multi-purpose MRE platform designs, validated by advanced modelling and tank-testing at reduced scale, to be taken to the next stage of development, which is the construction of pilot-scale platforms for testing at sea.

References

Allard, J. (2009), "Symbiotic relationship: Aquaculture and wind energy?", *Ecological Aquaculture Studies and Reviews*, University of Rhode Island, Kingston, Rhode Island, available at: http://ecologicalaquaculture.org/Allard(2009).pdf.

Anson, S. (forthcoming), "Prospects for offshore wind to 2030", *OECD Science, Technology and Industry Working Papers*, OECD Publishing, Paris, forthcoming.

Battista, T. (2012), "Technology: Using mapping technology to improve our understanding of the ocean floor", NOAA Ocean Science Blog, 1 April, https://noaaoceanscience.wordpress.com/2012/04/01/technology-using-mapping-technology-to-improve-our-understanding-of-the-ocean-floor.

Bojanowski, A. (2015), "Forscher entdecken Lebewesen 2500 Meter tief im Meeresgrund", *Spiegel Online*, 23 July, www.spiegel.de/wissenschaft/natur/lebewesen-in-2-5-kilometer-tiefe-entdeckt-a-1045022.html.

Borelli, A. (forthcoming), "Offshore oil and gas: The new frontiers", *OECD Science, Technology and Industry Working Papers*, OECD Publishing, Paris, forthcoming.

Buck, B.H. and G. Krause (2012), "Short expertise on the potential combination of aquaculture with marine-based renewable energy systems", in: *Welt im Wandel: Menschheitserbe Meer, Expertise für das WBGU-Hauptgutachten "Welt im Wandel: Menschheitserbe Meer"*, Wissenschaftlicher Beirat der Bundesregierung Globale Umweltveränderungen (WBGU), Berlin, www.wbgu.de/fileadmin/templates/dateien/veroeffentlichungen/hauptgutachten/hg2013/Expertise_Buck.pdf.

Carvalho, G., E. MacAoidh and J. Martinsohn (eds.) (2011), "Traceability of fish populations and fish products: Advances and contribution to sustainable fisheries", FishPopTrace Consortium, available at: https://fishpoptrace.jrc.ec.europa.eu/c/document_library/get_file?uuid=c21ccbef-029f-43da-b1cd-ade11e743301&groupId=10226.

Casavant, A. et al. (2015), "The other 95 percent: A campaign to map the world's oceans", *Okeanos Explorer*, National Oceanic and Atmospheric Administration, 2 June, http://oceanexplorer.noaa.gov/okeanos/explorations/ex1503/logs/jun2/jun2.html.

DEFRA (2015), "United Kingdom multiannual national plan for the development of sustainable aquaculture", Department for Environment, Food and Rural Affairs, October.

Dutkiewicz, R. et al. (2015), "Census of seafloor sediments in the world's ocean", *Geology*,Vol. 43, No. 9, pp. 795-798, http://dx.doi.org/10.1130/G36883.1.

EcoDeep-SIP (2015), "The crafting of seabed mining ecosystem-based management: Assessing deep sea ecosystems in the Pacific Ocean", Final report, EcoDeep-SIP Workshop, 29 June-1 July, Tokyo.

Ecofys (2012), "Ecofys launches test module for seaweed cultivation in offshore wind farms", Press release, 5 March, www.ecofys.com/en/press/ecofys-launches-trial-module-for-seaweed-cultivation-in-offshore-wind-farm.

EIU (2015), "A turning point: The potential role of ICT innovations in ports and logistics", report for DP World prepared by The Economist Intelligence Unit, http://web.dpworld.com/wp-content/uploads/2015/11/ICT-innovations-DP-World_Eng.pdf.

European Commission (2014), "Innovation in the blue economy: Realizing the potential of our seas and oceans for jobs and growth", COM(2014)254 final/2, Communication from the Commission to the European Parliament, the Council, the European Economic and Social Committee and the Committee of the Regions, Brussels, http://cor.europa.eu/en/activities/stakeholders/Documents/COM(2014)254%20final.pdf.

European Marine Board (2016), "Marine graduate training: Training the 21st century ocean scientists", www.marineboard.eu/marine-graduate-training.

European Marine Board (2013), "Navigating the future IV", *Position Paper 20*, European Marine Board, Ostend, Belgium.

Fredheim, A. and T. Reve (forthcoming), "Future prospects of marine aquaculture", *OECD Science, Technology and Industry Working Papers*, OECD Publishing, Paris, forthcoming.

Glavovic, B.C. et al. (2015), "Living on the margin in the anthropocene: Engagement arenas for sustainability research and action at the ocean-land interface", *Current Opinion in Environmental* Sustainability, Vol. 14, June, pp. 232-238, http://dx.doi.org/10.1016/j.cosust.2015.06.003.

GOC (2014), "From decline to recovery: A rescue package for the global ocean", Global Ocean Commission, Oxford, United Kingdom, www.globaloceancommission.org/wp-content/uploads/GOC_Report_20_6.FINAL_.spreads.pdf.

Hannington, M. (forthcoming), "Prospects and challenges of deep-sea mining", *OECD Science, Technology and Industry Working Papers*, OECD Publishing, Paris, forthcoming.

Hanus, J. (2012), "Preliminary definitional report and review of existing foresight processes relevant to JPI Oceans", JPI Oceans, Brussels.

IMO NAV 53/13 (2007), "Development of an e-navigation strategy", Subcommittee on Safety of Navigation, International Maritime Organization.

Ivshina, I.B. et al. (2015), "Oil spill problems and sustainable response strategies through new technologies", *The Royal Society of Chemistry. Environmental Science, Processes and Impacts*, Vol. 17, pp. 1 201-1 219.

Karmakar, D. and C. Guedes Soares (2015), "Review of the present concepts of multi-use offshore platforms", in: Guedes Soares, C. (ed.), *Renewable Energies Offshore*, CRC Press.

Koundouri, P. (2014), "The ocean of tomorrow", presentation, www.aueb.gr/users/koundouri/resees/uploads/Athens%20presentation.pdf.

Lacroix, D. and S. Pioch (2011), "The multi-use in wind farm projects: More conflicts or a win-win opportunity?", *Aquatic Living Resources*, Vol. 24, pp. 129-135.

Lloyd's Register (2015), *Global Marine Technology Trends 2030*, Lloyd's Register.

Markus, T., K. Huhn and K. Bischof (2015), "The quest for sea-floor integrity", *Nature Geoscience*, Vol. 8, March, pp. 163-164.

Michler-Cieluch, T. and G. Krause (2008), "Perceived concerns and possible management strategies for governing 'wind farm-mariculture integration'", *Marine Policy*, Vol. 32, No. 6, pp. 1 013-1 022, http://dx.doi.org/10.1016/j.marpol.2008.02.008.

Murphy, C. (2014), "Broadband demand hits the high seas", *Information Week*, 21 November, www.informationweek.com/strategic-cio/digital-business/broadband-demand-hits-the-high-seas/a/d-id/1317631.

OECD (2016), *OECD Patent Statistics,* database, https://stats.oecd.org/Index.aspx?DataSetCode=PATS_IPC.

OECD (2014), *The Space Economy at a Glance 2014*, OECD Publishing, Paris, http://dx.doi.org/10.1787/9789264217294-en.

OECD, WTO and World Bank Group (2014), "Global value chains: Challenges, opportunities, and implications for policy", report prepared for submission to the G20 Trade Ministers Meeting Sydney, Australia, 19 July, www.oecd.org/tad/gvc_report_g20_july_2014.pdf .

OOI (2015), Ocean Observatory Initiative", http://oceanobservatories.org/about.

Ornitz, B.E. and M.A. Champ (2002), "The technology windows-of-opportunity oil spill response strategy", in: Ornitz, B.E. and M.A. Champ, *Oil Spills First Principles: Prevention and Best Response*, Elsevier Science, Netherlands.

Perkins, R. (2015), "New species discovered beneath the ocean", *USC News*, 15 January. http://news.usc.edu/73851/new-species-discovered-beneath-ocean-crust.

Rogers, A.D. et al. (2015), "Delving deeper: Critical challenges for 21st century deep-sea research", *Position Paper 22*, European Marine Board, Ostend, Belgium, www.marineboard.eu/sites/marineboard.eu/files/public/publication/EMB_PP22_Web_v4.pdf.

Sandwell, D.T. et al. (2014), "New global marine gravity model from CryoSat-2 and Jason-1 reveals buried tectonic structure", *Science*, Vol. 346, No. 6 205, pp. 65-67, http://dx.doi.org/10.1126/science.1258213.

Shepard, F.P. (1948), *Submarine Geology*, Harper & Brothers, New York.

Stevenson, I., J. Lowe and S. Plunkett (2010), "New technologies for deep-ocean seafloor resource exploration", *Sea Technology Magazine*, October, www.sea-technology.com/features/2010/0910/seafloor_exploration.php.

Stiftung Offshore-Windenergie (German Offshore Wind Energy Foundation) (2013), "The impact of offshore wind energy on tourism: Good practices and perspectives from the South Baltic region", Varel, Germany, www.offshore-stiftung.com/60005/Uploaded/Offshore_Stiftung|2013_04SBO_SOW_tourism_study_final_web.pdf.

Stirling, A. (2014), "Disciplinary dilemma: Working across research silos is harder than it looks", *The Guardian Online*, 11 June 2014, www.theguardian.com/science/political-science/2014/jun/11/science-policy-research-silos-interdisciplinarity.

Sweeney, E. (forthcoming), "Prospects for ocean energy to 2030", *OECD Science, Technology and Industry Working Papers*, OECD Publishing, Paris, forthcoming.

The Economist (2015), "Combating illegal fishing. Dragnet: A new satellite-based surveillance system will keep a sharp eye on those plundering the oceans", *The Economist*, 24 January, www.economist.com/news/science-and-technology/21640306-new-satellite-based-surveillance-system-will-keep-sharp-eye-those.

Wever, L., G. Krause and B. Buck (2015), "Lessons from stakeholder dialogues on marine aquaculture in offshore wind farms: Perceived potentials, constraints and research gaps", *Marine Policy*, Vol. 51, pp. 251-259, http://dx.doi.org/10.1016/j.marpol.2014.08.015.

Witze, A. (2014), "Gravity map uncovers sea-floor surprises", *Nature*, 2 October, www.nature.com/news/gravity-map-uncovers-sea-floor-surprises-1.16048.

Witze, A. (2013), "Marine science: Oceanography's billion-dollar baby", *Nature,* 25 September, www.nature.com/news/marine-science-oceanography-s-billion-dollar-baby-1.13803.

Chapter 5.

International maritime regulation and emerging ocean-based industries

This chapter provides a forward view of the changing regulatory landscape affecting ocean industries. It describes briefly how the traditional composition of the maritime sector has been transformed over time by the emergence of new ocean-based activities, and some of the difficulties encountered by the existing regulatory frameworks to adapt to these new industries. Regulatory frameworks are nonetheless evolving. The chapter explores some of the regulatory changes that can be expected in the coming years, selecting three areas for particular attention: the ocean environment and protection of biodiversity, prevention and mitigation of pollution, and maritime safety. Ocean industries and the protection of marine biodiversity are addressed through the lens of gaps in regulatory instruments identified several years ago by the International Union for Conservation of Nature (IUCN), some of which still remain. Regulation of pollution is approached from the aspect of CO_2, NO_x and SO_x emissions from maritime activities, as well as the potential problems still posed by oil spills and discharge of waste, not least in the extremely vulnerable environment of the Arctic. And upcoming regulatory changes in maritime security are explored with a special focus on maritime cybersecurity.

The maritime industry landscape has been undergoing a profound transition. Long considered the traditional domain of shipping, shipbuilding, fishing, and – since the 1960s – offshore oil and gas, new activities are emerging: offshore wind, tidal and wave energy, offshore aquaculture, seabed mining, marine biotechnology, etc. These are fast-developing and reshaping and diversifying the maritime economy, while at the same time becoming increasingly interconnected both with one another and with traditional maritime sectors. At the same time, the world has witnessed a serious decline in the health of its oceans. In spite of long-standing efforts by a range of international organisations, regulatory regimes at global and regional level have found it difficult to adjust to these new circumstances and effectively integrate issues arising from the growing presence of emerging ocean industries. The result has tended to be a piecemeal approach to adjusting existing regulations, which will continue to hamper future efforts to improve ocean management.

There is broad agreement across the business community and among policy makers that ocean industries benefit from a clear, coherent, stable regulatory framework so as to be able to plan ahead long term and unleash the investments needed to develop their activities. However, that objective has become increasingly difficult to attain in a fast-changing and increasingly complex, interdependent world. In particular, and as noted in Chapter 4, technological innovation is moving very fast.

Despite long-standing efforts of existing institutions (e.g. International Maritime Organization [IMO], Food and Agriculture Organisation [FAO], International Labour Organisation [ILO], International Seabed Authority [ISA], Intergovernmental Science-Policy Platform on Biodiversity and Ecosystem Services [IPBES], International Union for Conservation of Nature [IUCN], Census of Marine Life) the regulatory regimes at global, regional – and indeed at state – levels have struggled to keep abreast of these real-world changes, especially in respect of emerging ocean industries. A large number of traditional players have already developed their own regulatory systems, and well-established schemes for maritime safety, pollution prevention, etc. exist thanks to efforts by UN agencies with a specific mandate for such matters. But as emerging ocean industries have grown in importance and have spread across the globe, the challenge has become how to integrate them into existing regulatory structures. For indeed, there is no agency for ocean issues. Since they are not specifically covered by one single set of regulations, they have been integrated piece by piece into existing legislation when deemed necessary. This piecemeal approach to integrating emerging ocean industries into existing traditional legal instruments is set to continue. The following section selects three domains of ocean-related regulation – environment and biodiversity, pollution prevention, and maritime safety – and explores them with a view to gaining a sense of what is in the "pipeline" in terms of international and regional regulations that will affect ocean industries, both established and emerging, in the coming years.

Protection of marine biodiversity

In 2008, the IUCN performed a "gap analysis" to identify and summarise regulatory and governance gaps at global and regional level in the international regime for the conservation and sustainable use of marine biodiversity in areas beyond national jurisdiction (ABNJ) (Gjerde et al., 2008). The study's target was the conservation and sustainable use of marine biodiversity. But its findings warrant reproducing here, because many of the gaps and weaknesses identified in the regime also have repercussions on the operation and economic viability of most, if not all, ocean-based industries and activities, from fisheries and deep-sea mining to subsea cable laying and marine bio-prospecting.

The IUCN interpreted regulatory gaps as "substantive and/or geographical gaps in the international legal framework, i.e. issues which are currently unregulated or insufficiently regulated at a global, regional or sub-regional level." (In contrast, governance gaps are defined by the IUCN as "gaps in the international institutional framework, including the absence of institutions or mechanisms at a global, regional or sub-regional level and inconsistent mandates of existing organizations and mechanisms.")

As Box 5.1 shows, the IUCN's list of gaps in 2008 was long and diverse. They range from inadequate mechanisms for the implementation of conservation principles and lack of assessment and management tools, to the absence of detailed internationally agreed rules and standards for established and emerging ocean activities, and lack of effective compliance and enforcement instruments.

Box 5.1. Gaps in international ocean regulation

Regulatory gaps identified in the IUCN study include:

- The absence of an instrument or mechanism to ensure that modern conservation principles building on the general obligations contained in treaties such as the United Nations Convention on the Law of the Sea [UNCLOS], the Convention on Biological Diversity (CBD) and the United Nations Fish Stocks Agreement (UNFSA), such as the ecosystem approach and the precautionary approach, are consistently incorporated and/or applied in all existing global and regional instruments that apply to areas beyond national jurisdiction (ABNJ).
- The absence of detailed international rules and standards to implement modern conservation principles for existing activities (marine scientific research [MSR], bio-prospecting, laying of cables and pipelines and construction of various types of installations); unregulated fisheries (e.g. some discrete high seas fish stocks, sharks), and new and emerging activities (e.g. ocean fertilisation, climate change mitigation techniques, and potential construction and operation of floating energy and aquaculture facilities).
- The lack of regulation to manage increasing impacts from traditional uses such as shipping, MSR and military activities (e.g. underwater noise, weapons testing) in line with modern conservation principles.
- The lack of specific requirements for modern conservation tools such as environmental impact assessments (EIAs), monitoring and reporting, area-based measures, networks of representative marine protected areas (MPAs), strategic environmental assessments (SEAs) and marine spatial planning to apply to the full range of ocean-based human activities in or having an effect on ABNJ.
- The lack of effective compliance and enforcement mechanisms at global and regional levels for all human activities and measures.
- The absence of legally binding instruments in all ocean regions to provide integrated coverage at the regional level for fisheries and biodiversity conservation.
- The lack of rules or a process to co-ordinate regulation of interactions between activities occurring in the high seas water column and those occurring on the extended continental shelf of coastal states.

Source: Gjerde et al. (2008).

This is not to say that prior to 2008 little had been done in this respect. In fisheries for example, some 17 regional fisheries management organisations (RFMOs) were established between the 1950s and 2006, covering wide areas of open seas and charged *inter alia* with fisheries conservation and management measures. Moreover, the FAO has done considerable work on establishing regulations and promoting best practices on fisheries and other issues related to biodiversity. Examples include the Code of Conduct for Responsible Fisheries or guidelines to reduce by-catch and also extensive work on IUU related topics.

Since 2008, there has been some progress on a number of fronts, as the following examples illustrate:

- In 2015, member states at the United Nations agreed to develop a legally binding instrument to conserve and sustainably use marine biological diversity of areas beyond their national borders. The 193-member UN General Assembly agreed to establish a preparatory committee, open to all countries, to negotiate the new instrument over 2016-17. The committee will report back to the General Assembly on its progress at the end of 2017. The negotiations will cover, among other issues, the sharing of benefits related to the use of marine genetic resources, MPAs and EIAs, as well as the transfer of marine technology (UN, 2015).
- More regions are beginning to adopt marine ecosystem approaches and are strengthening their ocean assessment, evaluation and management toolboxes. For example, in recent years the European Union has adopted two instruments, the 2002 EU Recommendation on Integrated Coastal Zone Management and the 2008 Marine Strategy Framework Directive, which offer a comprehensive and integrated approach to the management of all European coasts and marine waters, and set medium- and long-term objectives (to 2020 and beyond) for member states for managing their ocean activities. Somewhat more limited in scope are UNEP's Regional Seas programmes, which function through an Action Plan that is nonetheless underpinned with a strong legal framework in the form of a regional convention and associated protocols on specific issues such as MPAs. OSPAR brings together 15 governments and the European Union to co-operate in protecting the marine environment of the north-east Atlantic, working in close co-operation with the North-East Atlantic Fisheries Commission (NEAFC) particularly on conservation issues on the high seas. East Asia has its Partnerships in Environmental Management for the Seas of East Asia (PEMSEA), an international organisation focused on coastal and ocean governance in east Asia, scaling up integrated coastal management initiatives and aiming to improve technical co-operation in ecosystem-based management of watersheds, estuaries and adjacent coastal seas.

Nonetheless, many of the regulatory and governance gaps identified in the 2008 IUCN analysis remain. In addition to the lack of protection that such gaps afford the ocean environment and its biodiversity, they create a decision-making vacuum for many ocean industries, notably in respect of future investment. By way of illustration, the negotiations around the implementation of the UN agreement to protect marine biodiversity promise to usher in a period of considerable uncertainty for those ocean industries operating in the high seas. The establishment of MPAs in the high seas will probably directly affect fisheries, displacing the fishing activity to other areas, potentially increasing journey costs and altering the species composition of their catch; EIAs may influence the plans of deep-sea mining companies, the oil and gas industry, and subsea cable-laying businesses with respect to potential future operations in the ABNJ; and sharing marine genetic resources may have consequences for marine biotechnology and bio-prospecting.

International and regional environmental legislation may have pervasive implications, especially for emerging ocean industries. The following overview illustrates the impact of international and European instruments on all the key development stages of offshore renewable energy deployment.

As the EWEA (2012) emphasises, while instruments exist that focus on, for instance, fishery and shipping, none explicitly treats offshore renewable energy. Yet most of them may have an immediate impact on the space that is available for offshore renewable energy deployment.

Table 5.1. **Impact of legislation on the different phases of offshore renewable energy development**

Phase of project development	Instrument	Relevant elements influencing offshore renewable energy deployment
Shipping and navigation	UNCLOS	– Offshore renewable energy installations may be built anywhere within the economic exclusion zone (EEZ) with a safety buffer of 500 metres.
	IMO	– Sea-lanes and traffic separation schemes regulated by the IMO are considered as excluded zones in the sea. – Particularly sensitive sea area (PSSA) introduced the principle to deviate shipping routes.
	Regional fisheries management organisations (RFMO)	– RFMOs establish fishing limits and controlled zones for sustainable fisheries. This can conflict with offshore renewables activities.
	Convention on Biological Diversity (CBD)	– Under the CBD, parties can establish marine protected areas (MPAs) inside and outside national jurisdiction (including EEZ). The designation of MPAs under the CBD (a legally binding treaty) may influence the location; meanwhile possible compatibilities need to be clarified.
	Birds and Habitat Directive	– The Birds Directive calls for the establishment of special protected areas for birds. The Habitats Directive calls for the establishment of special areas of conservation for habitats or species. The protected areas defined by these directives are legally binding and restrict or forbid certain human activities. Member states must put measures into place to achieve the conservation goals for each site. – The directives allow for industrial developments inside the areas, including offshore wind, as long as they have no significant impacts on those goals. Potential projects are evaluated in this regard through a thorough screening procedure and, if necessary, must provide a positive environmental impact assessment. – Possible synergies between user and environmental goals need to be studied.
	CFP, GFCM, NEAFC	– Currently, there are no regulatory restrictions between fisheries and offshore renewable energy establishment activities such as wind farms. The CFP aims to ensure a sustainable exploitation of fish resources. This means reducing the number of fishing vessels and the duration of the fishing period, the establishment of open and closed fishing seasons and areas. These influence the location and some operational phases of offshore renewables. Meanwhile, the compatibility between fisheries and offshore renewables infrastructure should be clarified.
	Barcelona Convention	– RFMO establishes fishing limits and controlled zones, for sustainable fisheries. This can conflict with offshore renewables activities.
	Espoo Convention	– The Espoo Convention promotes consultation and cross-border co-operation in the planning process of various sea activities. It outlines specific conditions to be incorporated into national environmental impact assessment (EIA) procedures.

Table 5.1. **Impact of legislation on the different phases of offshore renewable energy development** (*continued*)

Phase of project development	Instrument	Relevant elements influencing offshore renewable energy deployment
Permitting and licensing	SEA Directive, EIA Directive	– Offshore renewables activities require an EIA according to the SEA and EIA Directives. The results of the EIA are presented in an environmental statement and are submitted together with licence and consent applications.
	OSPAR	– The OSPAR Commission is a legally binding regulation requiring member states to adopt procedures and actions related to marine environment protection. This can influence the licensing and permitting procedure for the development phase of offshore renewable energy projects. – OSPAR serves as a platform for information exchange and plays an important role in starting discussions on new marine-related issues. Under OSPAR, parties are obliged to carry out regular marine environmental assessments.
	UNCLOS	– UNCLOS creates obligations to protect the marine environment and to carry out environmental monitoring and assessment.
Monitoring	UNCLOS	– A coastal state cannot control cable laying carried out by other states passing through its EEZ. UNCLOS preserves the freedom to do so (Art. 58). However delineation of cables is subject to the consent of the coastal state (Art 79). Within the territorial sea, the coastal state has more comprehensive control on cable and pipeline laying, and can impose restrictions.
	OSPAR	– The OSPAR Commission adopts legally binding regulation requiring member states to introduce procedure and actions related to marine environment protection.
Construction and operation	Bonn Agreement	– Chapter 8 of the Bonn Agreement *Counter-Pollution Manual* sets out the considerations for problems that appear to be related to wind farms. It uses the polluter pays principle.
	CFP, GFCM, NEAFC	– Construction and maintenance activities could be influenced or restricted during fishing.
	UNCLOS	– UNCLOS (Art. 60) states the principle of removing abandoned or disused offshore renewables installations.
Removal/ decommissioning	IMO	– In 1989, the IMO adopted guidelines and standards for the removal of offshore renewables installations and structures on the Continental Shelf and in the EEZ.
	CFP, GFCM, NEAFC	– Removal planning could be modified or restricted during particular fishing periods.
	OSPAR	– The OSPAR Commission adopted in 1998 a legally binding regulation for the disposal of disused offshore renewables installations. Parties have the obligation to foresee the disposal of discussed offshore installations.

Notes: CFP: Common Fisheries Policy; GFCM: General Fisheries Commission for the Mediterranean; NEAFC: North-East Atlantic Fisheries Commission. Some of the detailed observations in the table are debatable. For example: it includes the Barcelona Convention that covers protection of the Mediterranean against pollution, but not HELCOM and the Bonn Agreement for the North Sea and the Baltic; PSSAs are, in fact, not regulated by an IMO convention – rather, it is an IMO resolution that currently regulates the designation. Nonetheless, the table presents a useful broad overview of the complexities of legislative impact on different phases of offshore renewable energy development.

Source: Adapted from EWEA (2012).

Pollution (air and ocean)

Air emissions from shipping are significant

Different studies estimate CO_2 emissions from shipping at around 2-3% of total global emissions, SO_x emissions at 5-10% and NO_x emissions at 17-31%, depending on methodology used (OECD, 2014). Shipping emissions are projected to increase over the coming decades. The IMO, for example, indicates that shipping-related carbon dioxide emissions would double or triple by 2050 (IMO, 2014). Among the biggest obstacles to progress is that, to date, no practicable method exists for assigning the emissions from a transnational voyage to an individual country. Moreover, international vessels enjoy a great deal of flexibility with respect to country of registration and choice of the national flag they fly on-board, which in turn often determines the regulations to which it is required to comply.

However, progress is being made – especially under the auspices of the IMO – and further measures are on the not-too-distant horizon, which will oblige shipping companies to step up their efforts to reduce future greenhouse gas (GHG) emissions, not least by pushing for energy efficiency. For example:

- In 2012, the IMO adopted a new package of "Regulations on Energy Efficiency for Ships", including two measures that came into force in early 2013 affecting all vessels over 400 GT (gross tonnage): first, the Energy Efficiency Design Index, which involves the gradual phasing in of stringent criteria into the building standards for different types and sizes of ships; second, the Ship Energy Efficiency Management Plan, which is a plan for benchmarking and improving operable ships and bringing owners and operators to periodically review and upgrade their energy performance (UNCTAD, 2014; OECD and ITF, 2015).
- The IMO is also working on regulations aimed at reducing emissions of other toxic substances from using fuel oil, notably NO_x and SO_x. (Bunker oil is considered a particularly toxic fuel.) January 2016 was the date set for implementation of "tier III" NO_x standards in existing emission control areas (ECAs), and as of 2020 the global sulphur cap will be reduced further to 5 000 ppm (Marpol Convention, Annex VI).
- Regarding ECAs, the legislative requirements are laid down in Annex VI to the MARPOL (Marine Pollution) Convention. Despite the fact that levels of SO_x and particulate matter are not expected to increase by 2050 thanks to regulations that are being enacted in the coming years, substantial decreases of both types of emissions would be within reach if the boundaries of existing ECAs were to be extended, and more such zones introduced (OECD and ITF, 2015). However, the new Marpol Annex VI agreement could well turn out to be quite costly for participants in the shipping industry (Notteboom, 2011). Higher fuel costs will, in turn, put the spotlight on energy efficiency. As Cullinane and Bergqvist (2014) suggest: "The future imposition of more stringent limits on both SO_x and NO_x emissions, together with greater geographical applicability, will put energy use and other efficiency measures high on the agenda for shipping companies. This may result in the wider use of measures such as speed differentiation that, in turn, may enable shipping companies to better absorb the price changes arising from the ECA regulations. The large socio-economic benefits of the ECA regulations, combined with the global challenges related to pollution in densely populated areas such as the Mediterranean and Asia, emphasize the importance of designating more regions as ECAs." It follows from the above that powerful drivers are at work which could lead to a significant shift to new environmentally friendlier fuels. In its report on future marine fuels, Lloyd's Register (2014) models a "Global Commons" scenario in which a more aggressive carbon policy combined with a moderate hydrogen price (both specified in the Global Commons scenario) leads to a significant expansion in the use of hydrogen and liquefied natural gas (LNG) around 2025 (see Figure 5.1).

Accidental oil spills make up only a small share of total releases of oil into the environment, around 5-10%. For tankers, accidental oil spills of 100 tonnes or more from vessels have been on the decline worldwide for many years, much as a result of progress in reducing oil discharges from routine oil tanker operations (Farrington, 2013). Steep declines are also recorded for large spills (i.e. over 700 tonnes) from tankers since the 1970s.

Figure 5.1. **Shift in fuel mix for all major ship types combined, 2010-30 (in percent)**

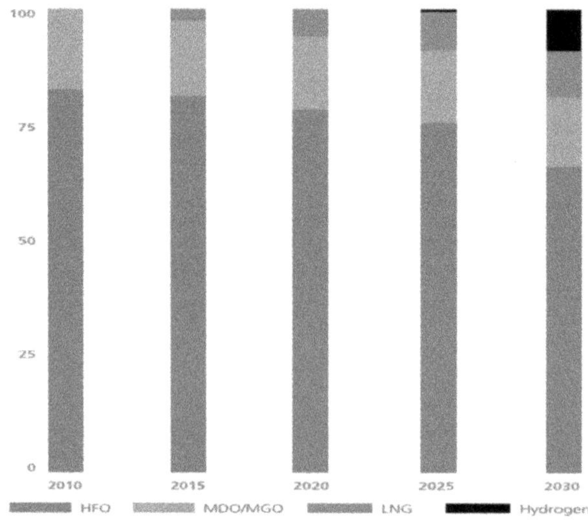

Note: HFO: heavy fuel oil; MDO/MGO: marine diesel oil/marine gas oil; LNG: liquefied natural gas.

Source: Lloyd's Register (2014).

As new destinations open up, however, regulators need to act quickly to introduce appropriate new packages of measures. For the Arctic, considerable progress has been made in recent years on a Polar Code. There is now agreement on a mandatory code for ships operating in polar waters which applies to passenger and cargo ships of 500 GT and above, and which covers the full range of protection matters, including those of pollution prevention and environmental protection (UNCTAD, 2014).

Part II of the Polar Code, adopted by the IMO's Marine Environment Protection Committee (MEPC) and due to enter into force in 2017, includes mandatory provisions in chapters covering the following topics:

- "prevention of pollution by oil, including discharge restrictions prohibiting any discharge into the sea of oil or oily mixtures from any ship, as well as structural requirements including protective location of fuel-oil and cargo tanks
- control of pollution by noxious liquid substances in bulk, prohibiting any discharge into the sea of noxious liquid substances, or mixtures containing such substances
- prevention of pollution by sewage from ships, prohibiting the discharge of sewage except for comminuted and disinfected sewage under specific circumstances, including a specified distance from ice
- prevention of pollution by garbage from ships, adding additional restrictions to the permitted discharges (under MARPOL Annex V, discharge of all garbage into the sea is prohibited, except as provided otherwise). Food wastes shall not be discharged onto the ice and discharge into the sea of comminuted and ground food wastes is only permitted under specific circumstances including at a not less than 12 nautical miles from the nearest land, ice-shelf or fast ice. Only certain

cargo residues, classified as not harmful to the marine environment, can be discharged."

But the advance of offshore oil and gas exploration and production especially into deeper waters and harsher environments raises concerns about future risks of major oil spills from offshore installations (see, for example, Schroeder-Hinrichs et al., 2013). Many observers see little prospect of a global agreement on this matter over the short or medium term. No specific international institution seems inclined to champion efforts to secure global conventions on safety or liability and compensation. Moreover, many states are currently able to rely on regional organisations to make inroads into more effective regulation of offshore drilling activities in their respective geographic areas. The numerous regional seas programmes are a case in point. The next few years could see other regional intergovernmental organisations stepping into the breach, notably on safety issues. In addition to existing regional agreements (e.g. in the ROPME Sea Area or north-east Atlantic), others have just entered into force (in the Mediterranean) or are currently being elaborated (in Western, Central and Southern Africa and the western Indian Ocean; Rochette, 2014).

Pollution of the ocean may also arise from seabed activities such as dredging for aggregates and seabed mining for metals and minerals, potentially resulting in sediment disturbance and discharge of mineral waste and waste water into the water column or on to the seabed. As Hannington (forthcoming) points out in his contribution to the November 2014 OECD workshop on seabed mining, international environmental regulation for deep-sea mining in the area is still in its infancy:

> Even the most careful deep-sea mining will disturb the marine environment. The generally held view is that industrial-scale mining will inflict a range of harm that will irreversibly alter the deep oceans, but as yet there is no clear picture of what those impacts might be. "Serious harm" referred to in the ISA regulations still has not been defined. This contrasts with regulations on land, which in most mining jurisdictions are very specific (e.g. EPA regulations for metals in surface water). The footprint of any individual mining operation may be small, but nobody knows how large or what influence it might have on marine ecosystems, and the nature of the impacts will vary according to the type of mining and the technology used. For the mining of nodules, initial calculations by the EU MIDAS project suggest that the direct areal footprint of mining on the seabed will be much larger than land-based equivalents (…). Because nodules are distributed only on the seafloor's surface, commercial extraction could impact tens to hundreds of square kilometres. The fallout from a sediment plume produced during these operations may be even larger. From a commercial point of view, these details must be known in order to assess whether the operational cost of environmental protection will exceed the value of the project (…). Recommendations arising from environmental risk assessments need to be integrated with a full accounting of the costs and legal constraints of the proposed operations, but so far this has not been done.
>
> In the nodule areas of the Clarion Clipperton Zone (CCZ), an expert-driven process has already been used to delineate a network of sites for protection that have the same general characteristics as the planned exploitation areas ("areas of particular environmental interest") (…). However, the designated areas are so far not permanent and no information is available as to their geological, physical, chemical or biological attributes, let alone any baseline measurements as reference for monitoring impact. There is still only very limited knowledge of the marine habitats that are likely to be

affected, including basic information on species composition and distribution ranges, natural variability and dynamics, connectivity, and the many factors that affect community diversity (…). It is difficult to know what regulatory regime should be put in place to address environmental impacts in areas that have never been mapped or even visited to protect them against harm that is still largely unknown and might not happen for decades to come (Hannington, forthcoming).

In light of the many unknowns and uncertainties associated with the potential environmental impacts of deep-sea mining, pressure is growing to step up efforts to gather much more scientific data and strengthen regulation ahead of the commencement of wider scale mining activity. Participants at the EcoDeep-SIP workshop in 2015, for example, call amongst other things for:

- holistic strategic environmental assessments incorporating a comprehensive ecosystem-based approach
- decision making based on the precautionary principle
- strategic networks of marine protected areas taking into account connectivity
- limiting the spread of plumes from return water and those generated by mining tools to specific amounts and specific distances from the mining site
- identification of thresholds and triggers associated with significant impact
- clear and well-defined decision rules about the extent of changes in monitored parameters before mining starts.

Maritime safety

A very large part of the world's shipping fleet involved in international activities is fairly well regulated from a safety point of view. However, maritime safety is facing numerous challenges as it heads towards 2030. New maritime activities are coming to the fore along with new actors; the seas are becoming increasingly crowded as shipping and offshore activities gain momentum; potentially hazardous freight (e.g. LNG) is growing as seaborne trade expands; new destinations (such as the Arctic) are emerging for commercial shipping, cruise tourism, oil and gas exploration and extraction, fisheries and aquaculture; and big technological changes are looming on the horizon in the form of e-navigation and autonomous and unmanned vessels. (There are other significant threats in the shape of civil war, interstate conflict, piracy, tensions around sovereign claims to seabed rights and natural resources on the continental shelf, etc.; these are addressed briefly in Chapter 2.)

As the ocean environment becomes more complex, the international regulatory system under the leadership of the IMO (and also the ILO) becomes more and more complex too. It is continually having to adjust to changing patterns of sea use, refocusing on existing safety gaps, responding to special demands of certain ship types, taking account of new technologies and new environmental risks. In some cases this is happening in timely fashion, in others more slowly.

Safety of fishing vessels, for instance, is an area of slower progress, even though fatality rates among fishermen tend to be much higher than the national average. The Torremolinos Convention, the first-ever global instrument of its kind to address specifically the safety of fishing vessels, was adopted by the IMO several decades ago, yet its provisions have not entered into force internationally. However, renewed efforts are now under way to establish a globally binding regime that is both robust and workable in addressing and enhancing fishing vessel safety. Even the recently implemented International Convention on Standards of Training, Certification and Watchkeeping for Fishing Vessel Personnel (which introduced mandatory standards for the certification and minimum training of crews of seagoing fishing vessels) is not comprehensive in functional or geographic coverage, as it applies only to vessels of at least 24 metres in length, and involves only 17 member states, representing less than 5% of the world fishing fleet. Other recent efforts to improve international standards have been more successful.[1]

In the area of offshore renewables, too, international regulation on safety matters is slow to materialise. Offshore wind energy is a case in point. While there are internationally well-established technical and design standards (e.g. IEC 61400), there is no internationally applicable mandatory regulation, and the IMO does not have the mandate to look into these matters. Consequently, individual coastal states have had to develop their own legal frameworks. However, the development of guidelines and practices has often been up to the industry itself, leaving manufacturers, developers and operators to tailor their approach to each country or project. Part of the difficulty arises from the very different ocean environments in which offshore wind farms are sited and operated around the world. As Sirnivas et al. (2014) point out:

> The IEC 61400 standards are well established in the wind industry internationally and are the primary standards that govern the design of land-based and offshore wind turbines. These standards have been used successfully on most European offshore wind installations in conjunction with local regulations, standards and class guidelines for offshore wind turbines on fixed foundations. However, IEC 61400 standards do not cover several critical areas of an offshore wind turbine project. Moreover, the current IEC standards do not yet provide a comprehensive assessment of how to address tropical (and extratropical) events, fresh water ice or deeper water deployments requiring floating structures, which are important for offshore wind plant development in US waters. Nonetheless, several standards and guidelines are being developed to address these deficiencies. (Sirnivas et al., 2014)

Moreover, as Sirnivas et al. further indicate, future standards and guidelines for offshore wind energy development also stand to benefit from the vast collection of existing regulations, guidelines and standards in other offshore industries – e.g. oil and gas, marine equipment, the shipping industry.

In the absence of international regulation, voluntary standards are filling the void. For example, the ISO's new international standard, ISO 29400:2015, "Ships and marine technology – Offshore wind energy – Port and marine operations", aims to support development of the industry by improving the safety and accessibility of the sites. It sets out "requirements and guidance for the planning, design and analysis of the components, systems, equipment and procedures required to perform port and marine operations, as well as the methods or procedures developed to carry them out safely".[2]

At regional level, various initiatives are underway, notably in Europe which is leading the way on offshore wind. For example, perhaps the most important legislative development today is the 2012 release of the latest version of the European 50308 wind turbine standard (EN 50308, rev 1, Wind turbines – Safety requirements for design, operation and maintenance), which takes proper account of offshore wind for the first time, and aims to integrate safety considerations right from the outset of the turbine life cycle. Also on the health and safety front, a more unified approach is emerging among European turbine manufacturers, developers, operators, trade associations and other interested parties. Plans include the sharing of incident data and agreeing on consistent European standards for safety training. In a more focused initiative, the Global Wind Organisation (GWO), which brings together manufacturers like Vestas and Siemens along with operators such as SSE Renewables and Vattenfall, is concentrating on a single issue: setting common standards for safety training across Europe (Lawson, 2011).

Also lacking is a dedicated regulatory framework for offshore wind vessels. The operation of vessels working on the construction and operation of offshore wind facilities is very different from those deployed in the offshore oil and gas industry. In the absence of specific offshore wind vessel regulations in Europe, classification societies have been developing rules for stakeholders to follow, for example most recently on hull structures, loading gears on offshore installations and classification rules for "Crew Boats and Offshore Wind Farm Service Craft" (Earls, 2013). The IMO is exploring the possibility of such a framework covering installation vessels, crew boats and categorisation of offshore personnel.

A similar picture emerges with other ocean renewable energy sources such as energy wave, tidal current, etc., although here it must be borne in mind that these technologies are much further from maturity and commercialisation scale than offshore wind. As Elefant (2009) indicates:

> Unfortunately, international regulatory processes for siting marine renewables have not kept pace with technological advancements. In many countries, deployment-ready projects face costly and protracted permitting procedures by multiple agencies, each with their own unique legal and regulatory requirements. Few regimes provide an expedited system for deploying smaller or early stage commercial arrays. In addition, most marine renewables find themselves in a "Catch-22" situation: regulatory bodies are reluctant to grant authorizations without information about project impacts, but developers cannot provide this information without first getting projects into the water to gather data on impacts. (Elefant, 2009)

Advances in ICT, combined with other emerging technologies, are ushering in a new era of automation in shipping and offshore activities (see Chapter 4). In particular, the progressive move from traditional navigation practices to e-navigation, and in parallel that from manned vessels to automated and then autonomous ships, will place heavy demands on ship-to-ship and ship-to-shore communication as well as data exchange and analysis. (It will also require new regulation on a risk-based approach.) To date, the security of networks and information systems in the maritime sector has received but scant attention. As a result, awareness of cyber security needs and challenges in the maritime sector is currently low to non-existent (ENISA, 2011). The ENISA report goes on to point out the risks of ICT complexity and the lack of consideration given to cybersecurity matters:

> Due to the high ICT complexity and the use of specific technologies, there are particular challenges to ensure adequate security provisions in maritime systems. The fast technology development and the struggle towards complete automation in the maritime sector have, in cases, reduced the focus on the security features.
>
> One relevant example is the continuously increasing number of port operational ICT infrastructure elements (e.g. SCADA devices) connected to the Internet without due consideration to making them more secure, and even no real need to be connected. The vulnerabilities created by these security gaps of the ICT systems

within the maritime sector may affect not only the services supported by these systems, but also the commonly shared infrastructure layers (e.g. databases, systems hosting sensitive information, etc.).

In the current regulatory context for the maritime sector on global, regional and national levels, there is very little consideration given to cyber security elements. Most security related regulation only includes provisions relating to safety and physical security concepts, as can be found in the International Ship and Port Facility Security (ISPS) Code and other relevant maritime security and safety regulations, such as Regulation (EC) No 725/2004 on enhancing ship and port facility security. These regulations do not consider cyber-attacks as possible threats of unlawful acts (ENISA, 2011).

Similar concerns about cyber threats to the maritime sector have been voiced recently by the NCC, which put the vulnerabilities of ECDIS connectivity and software under the spotlight (NCC Group, 2014). And in January 2015, the US Coast Guard held an interagency meeting in Washington, DC to take comments on the development of cybersecurity assessment methods for vessels and facilities regulated by the US Coast Guard.[3]

At international regulatory level, the theme of cybersecurity is only just entering the stage. The IMO's Maritime Safety Committee (MSC) 94th session, held on November 2014, discussed the adoption of a proposal to develop voluntary guidelines on cybersecurity practices to protect and enhance the resiliency of cyber systems supporting the operations of ports, vessels, marine facilities and other elements of the maritime transportation system.[4]

As with emerging cyber threats to other critical infrastructures, until international regulation is put in place, the onus for action will first and foremost be on industry itself to establish protection of its networks and operations.

Concluding remarks

The above illustrations of progress that can be expected in the international regulation of selected maritime industries in the coming years suggest that advances in science and technology in the maritime domain are moving much faster than international regulatory co-operation. This applies in particular to the emerging ocean industries, but also – albeit to a lesser extent – to the established industries. The regulatory vacuum is being filled at least to some extent by initiatives of stakeholders, be it industry, voluntary standards organisations or certification agencies. However, as worldwide ocean activity intensifies in the future and the pressure on ocean space and natural resources increases, the need for better stewardship will likely add more momentum to international collaboration on regulatory matters. These and other related considerations are taken up again in Chapter 9 on governance and ocean management to 2030.

Notes

1. See Lloyd's Register Marine, "Future IMO Legislation" for examples at: www.lr.org/en/_images/213-35746_Future_IMO_legislation.pdf.
2. Available at: www.iso.org/iso/catalogue_detail?csnumber=60906.
3. http://mariners.coastguard.dodlive.mil/2015/01/23/1232015-guidance-on-maritime-cyber-security-standards-part-3-cyber-command-remarks.
4. www.imo.org/MediaCentre/PressBriefings/Pages/37-MSC-94-preview.aspx#.VPJF9vmUf14.

References

Cullinane, K. and R. Bergqvist (2014), "Emission control areas and their impact on maritime transport", *Transportation Research Part D: Transport and Environment*, Vol. 28, May, pp. 1-5, http://dx.doi.org/10.1016/j.trd.2013.12.004.

Earls, E. (2013), "Steering a course through offshore energy regulations", *Worldwind Technology*, 14 August, www.windpower-international.com/features/featuresteering-a-course-through-offshore-wind-energy-regulations.

Elefant, C. (2009), "Overview of global regulatory processes for permits, consents and authorization of marine renewables", in: *Ocean Renewable Energy Coalition (OREC) Annual Report 2009*, http://lawofficesofcarolynelefant.com/renewablesoffshore/wp-content/uploads/2010/04/CE_IEA_Rpt.pdf.

ENISA (2011), "Analysis of cyber security aspects in the maritime sector", European Network and Information Security Agency, November, Heraklion, Greece, www.enisa.europa.eu/activities/Resilience-and-CIIP/critical-infrastructure-and-services/dependencies-of-maritime-transport-to-icts/cyber-security-aspects-in-the-maritime-sector-1/at_download/fullReport.

EWEA (2012), "Delivering offshore electricity to the EU: Spatial planning of offshore renewable energies and electricity grid infrastructures in an integrated EU maritime policy", Seanergy 2020, Final Project Report, May, www.ewea.org/fileadmin/ewea_documents/documents/publications/reports/Seanergy_2020.pdf.

Farrington, J.W. (2013), "Oil pollution in the marine environment I: Inputs, big spills, small spills, and dribbles", *Environment*, Vol. 55, No. 6, http://dx.doi.org/10.1080/00139157.2013.843980.

Gjerde, K.M. et al. (2008), "Regulatory and governance gaps in the international regime for the conservation and sustainable use of marine biodiversity in areas beyond national jurisdiction", Marine Series No. 1, *IUCN Environmental Policy and Law Papers*, IUCN, Gland, Switzerland, https://cmsdata.iucn.org/downloads/iucn_marine_paper_1_2.pdf.

Hannington, M. (forthcoming), "Prospects and challenges of deepsea mining", *OECD Science, Technology and Industry Working Papers*, OECD Publishing, Paris, forthcoming.

IMO (2014), *Third IMO GHG Study 2014*, International Maritime Organisation, London.

Lawson, J. (2011), "Offshore wind still at sea over safety regulation", *Power Engineering International*, 1 November, www.powerengineeringint.com/articles/print/volume-19/issue-10/features/offshore-wind-still-at-sea-over-safety-regulation.html.

Lloyd's Register (2014), "Global marine fuel trends 2030", Lloyd's Register Global Technology Centre, London, www.lr.org/en/_images/213-34172_Global_Marine_Fuel_Trends_2030.pdf.

NCC Group (2014), "Preparing for cyber battleships – Electronic chart display and information system security", NCC Group, www.nccgroup.trust/globalassets/our-research/uk/whitepapers/2014-03-03_-_ncc_group_-_whitepaper_-_cyber_battle_ship_v1-0.pdf.

Notteboom, T. (2011), "The impact of low sulphur fuel requirements in shipping on the competitiveness of roro shipping in Northern Europe", *WMU Journal of Maritime Affairs*, Vol. 10, No. 1, pp. 63-95, http://dx.doi.org/10.1007/s13437-010-0001-7.

OECD (2014), *The Competitiveness of Global Port-Cities*, OECD Publishing, http://dx.doi.org/10.1787/9789264205277-en

OECD and ITF (2015), *ITF Transport Outlook 2015*, OECD Publishing, Paris/ITF, Paris, http://dx.doi.org/10.1787/9789282107782-en.

Rochette, J. (2014), "International regulation of offshore oil and gas activities: Time to head over the parapet", *Policy Briefs*, No. 06/2014, Iddri.

Schroeder-Hinrichs, J.U. et al. (2013), "Sustainable ocean development in the Arctic: Making a case for marine spatial planning in offshore oil and gas exploration", in: Chircop, A., S. Coffen-Smout and M. McConnell (eds.), *Ocean Yearbook 27*, Martinus Nijhoff Publishers, pp. 503-530, http://dx.doi.org/10.1163/22116001-90000171.

Sirnivas, S. et al. (2014), "Assessment of offshore wind system design, safety, and operation standards", Technical Report NREL/TP-5000-60573, January, National Renewable Energy Laboratory.

UN (2015), Development of an international legally-binding instrument under the United Nations Convention on the Law of the Sea on the conservation and sustainable use of marine biological diversity of areas beyond national jurisdiction, UN General Assembly, A/69/L.65, www.un.org/ga/search/view_doc.asp?symbol=A/69/L.65.

UNCTAD (2014), *Review of Maritime Transport 2015*, United Nations Conference on Trade and Development, New York and Geneva, http://unctad.org/en/PublicationsLibrary/rmt2015_en.pdf.

Chapter 6.

Measuring the global economic contribution of ocean-based industries

The ocean economy encompasses ocean-based industries and the ocean's ecosystems. However, ecological accounting to value the ocean's ecosystem services and natural assets at global level still requires much further research. This chapter therefore restricts itself to estimating the value of the world's ocean-based industries, until the opportunity arises to perform further work on valuing ocean ecosystems. It begins with observations on current measurement issues before describing the OECD Ocean Economy Database, *its sectoral composition, and the sources and data used. The remainder of the chapter is devoted to reporting some of the findings of this new database, notably estimates of the overall global value of the ocean economy on the basis of the ocean industries selected, approximate employment levels in the different industries, and a breakdown by sector and broad geographic regions.*

The calculations of value added and employment in selected ocean-based industries are based on the OECD *Ocean Economy Database* which was developed specifically for this project. It consists of 169 coastal countries and aims to improve the coherency and consistency of the assumptions, indicators and measurement methods used to estimate the size of the ocean economy. The database draws heavily on UN and OECD sources to collect industry-specific data on physical capital stock, employment and value added for those ocean-based industries defined in ISIC Rev.3 (International Standard Industrial Classification of All Economic Activities). Where official data were patchy, proxies were used based on national reports and secondary sources (for details on the methodology, see OECD, forthcoming). The economic contribution of the ten ocean-based industries selected here on the basis of their economic importance and data availability was estimated at USD 1.5 trillion in direct value added in 2010 (or about 2.5% of world value added). The industries that accounted for the major share of global value added were offshore oil and gas exploration and production, maritime and coastal tourism, port activities and maritime equipment. Direct employment was estimated at more than 31 million full-time equivalent jobs (this is roughly equal to France's entire labour force in 2010). Alone, industrial fisheries made up a third of that employment.

There are many reasons for wishing to put a value on ocean-based industries, be it at national, regional or global level. It raises public awareness of the importance of the industries, offering them higher visibility; it raises awareness among policy makers, rendering the industries more amenable to policy action; it enables progress in their development to be tracked over time; it also enables their contribution to the overall economy to be tracked in monetary and employment terms; and finally, it lends weight to the perception of ocean-based industries as a set or cluster of activities whose defining common denominator is the ocean, its use and its resources.

Over the last 15 years or so, a large number of countries have attempted to place a value on the national ocean economy as measured by the contribution of ocean-based industries to the economy (see Annex 6.A1). What is striking about the results in Table 6.A1.1 is that the range of the estimates is extraordinarily wide – the share of national gross domestic product (GDP) accounted for by their ocean-based industries varies between less than 1% and 26%. The wide variations are partly explained by the differences in the importance and data availability of ocean-based activities among the countries surveyed; partly by considerable variations in methodology, definitions, year of the assessment and the scope of the study in terms of which ocean industries were included and which excluded; and partly by differences in the quality of sources (official, semi-official, private) from which the statistics were drawn.

It becomes immediately clear that to obtain a global estimate of ocean-based industries' contribution to the world economy, one cannot simply add up the various national estimates.

The OECD *Ocean Economy Database*

The OECD *Ocean Economy Database* provides the basis for measuring the economic contribution of ocean-based industries to world economic output in terms of gross value added (GVA) and employment. In light of the need to have as complete a set of international official statistics as possible, the baseline year has been fixed at 2010.

So far, the following economic activities are included in the database:

- Water transport: the transportation of freight and passengers through the ocean commonly referred to as shipping. However, it does not include the building and repair of vessels.
- Port activities: operations and management, such as storing, loading and unloading activities. Port development and construction are also included in this sector, measuring the investment and maintenance in ports.
- Maritime and coastal tourism: ocean-related tourism and leisure activities, including the cruise industry and new destinations (e.g. Arctic and Antarctica).
- Industrial fish processing: the processing of seafood.
- Industrial capture fisheries: the catches of wild fisheries.
- Industrial marine aquaculture: the production of seafood.
- Offshore oil and gas: the exploration and production of offshore oil and gas, including the operation and maintenance of equipment related to this activity. (This does not include the actual value of the crude oil, which would be substantially higher.)
- Offshore wind: the production of electric power from offshore wind.
- Shipbuilding and repair: the building, repair and maintenance of ships, boats, offshore platforms and offshore supply vessels.
- Marine equipment: the manufacturing of marine equipment and materials, such as machinery, valves, cables, sensors, ship materials, aquaculture supplies and so on.

Availability of data permitting, the above list of ocean-based activities could be further extended by other ocean-based industries, such as marine business services, marine biotechnology, ocean energy, seabed mining and maritime surveillance. (Annex 1.A1 details the full scope of what can be considered ocean industries. The group of industries selected in this chapter is smaller due to data limitations.)

Sources and data used

The following calculations are based on the OECD *Ocean Economy Database* developed specifically for this project. It consists of 169 coastal countries, makes greater use of coherent official statistics and draws on best-available quality semi-official sources where official data are lacking. UN and OECD sources are used to collect industry-specific data on physical capital stock, employment and value added for those ocean-based industries defined in ISIC Rev.3, namely, fisheries (capture fisheries and aquaculture), fish processing, water transport (i.e. shipping), and shipbuilding and repair (excludes marine equipment). More specifically, the United Nations System of National Accounts (UNSNA), the International Yearbook of Industrial Statistics from the United Nations Industrial Development Organization (UNIDO) and OECD STAN (Structural Analysis) were used to collect data for the four industries above. Value added from shipbuilding and repair was collected from the IHS database (HIS, 2016) to include more countries from the lower- and middle-income group. Data on industries that are not defined in ISIC Rev.3 were collected from industry reports of other international organisations and industry associations. Data on offshore oil and gas and offshore wind were gathered mainly from the International Energy Agency (IEA) and the European Wind Energy Association (EWEA). Data on marine and coastal tourism were estimated from data on tourism expenditure collected from *Tourism Trends and Policies* (OECD, 2014). See Liebender et al. (forthcoming) for details.

Data from different layers were collected.

- The bottom layer data were collected from international institutions, such as the UNSNA and the International Yearbook of Industrial Statistics from UNIDO.[1]
- The second layer consists of OECD data, which replace UN data when there is an overlap.
- The third layer is the secondary sources encompassing individual country reports, industry reports and global trade associations. Data from these secondary sources replace the OECD and UN data on the latest available data for specific activities.

Data for ocean-based industries were selected from ISIC Rev.3, which is managed and issued by the UN. Most countries adopt the ISIC as a national statistical system. For future research, it would be helpful if more countries were to use ISIC Rev.4 as the statistical classification system for the ocean economy. This would allow a more detailed comparison of the ocean economy among countries. However, not every sector that is relevant and included in the ocean economy is defined as such within the ISIC and national statistical accounts. The 3- and 4-digit level ISIC codes are not detailed enough to list all the ocean-based industries mentioned above. For this analysis, ISIC data from Rev.3 were used since there are more countries reporting to Rev.3 than to the newer version Rev.4 (see Annex 6.A1 for estimating the value added and employment of ocean-based industries that were defined by ISIC Rev.3 based on a Cobb-Douglas function).

Estimates of global value added and employment in the ocean economy overall

The preferred measure of the economic contribution of an industry to the overall economy (and to compare an industry's contribution to the economy in different countries) is GVA[2] rather than GDP. The System of National Accounts (SNA) recommends using GVA at basic prices for this purpose. The difference between total industry GVA and total GDP is taxes less subsidies on products, which varies across countries. This adjustment is made at the aggregate (total economy) level because, while time series of taxes less subsidies on products may be available by product, they are not generally available by industry. In estimating the economic contribution – i.e. value added and employment – of ocean-based industries to the global economy in 2010, the following questions were asked.

- What was the direct value added of the selected ocean-based industries to the global economy in 2010?
- What was the number of direct jobs in ocean-based industries in 2010?

In summary, in 2010 the ocean-based industries selected here contributed a total value added of USD 1.5 trillion (in 2010 USD) or approximately 2.5% of world GVA (which was around USD 59 billion). Asia and Europe contributed around two-thirds of the total GVA. Offshore oil and gas accounted for almost 34% of total value added of the ocean-based industries, followed by maritime and coastal tourism (26%; Figure 6.1). In third place are port activities – measured as the direct value added of global port throughput – which accounted for 13%, followed by marine equipment (11%), water transport (5%), industrial fish processing of global seafood production (5%), and shipbuilding and repair (4%). Smaller shares were registered for industrial capture fisheries (1%), industrial marine aquaculture (0.3%) and offshore wind (0.2%). Inclusion of estimates of the value added generated by artisanal capture fisheries (mainly in Africa and Asia) would add further tens of billions of USD to the capture fisheries total.

Figure 6.1. **Value added of the ocean-based industries in 2010 by industry**

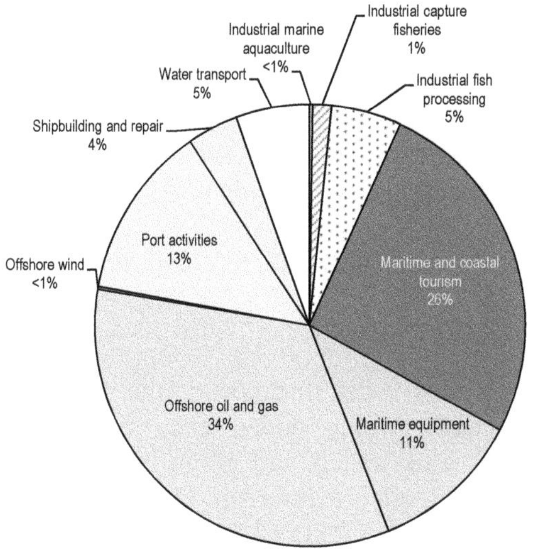

StatLink http://dx.doi.org/10.1787/888933334614

Note: Artisanal fisheries are not included in this overview.

Source: Authors' calculations based on OECD STAN, UNIDO INDSTAT, UNSD, World Bank (2013); IEA (2014); OECD (2014a, 2014b); and various industry reports.

The ocean-based industries contributed some 31 million direct full-time jobs in 2010, equivalent to around 1% of the global work force or around 1.5% of the economically active workforce (assuming a total labour force participation rate of 63%). As Figure 6.2 indicates, the largest employers were industrial capture fisheries (36%) and maritime and coastal tourism (23%). The remaining industries accounted for shares of between less than 1% and 8%.

Figure 6.2. **Employment in the ocean-based industries in 2010 by industry**

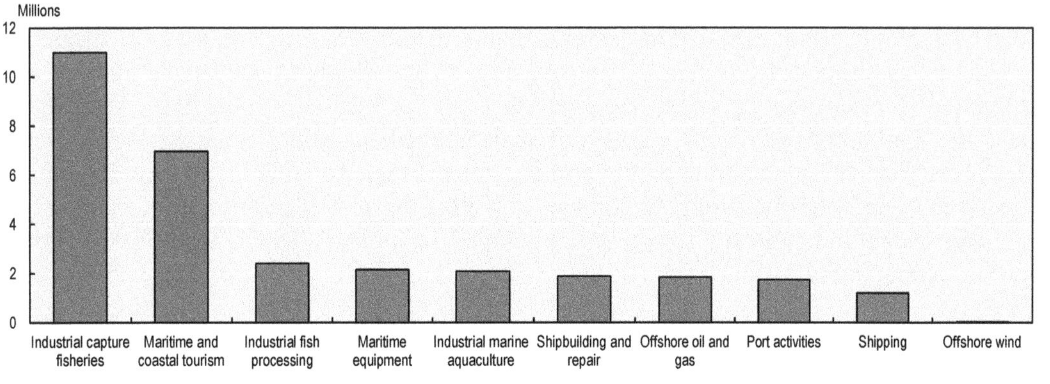

StatLink http://dx.doi.org/10.1787/888933334627

Note: Artisanal fisheries are not included in this overview.

Source: Authors' calculations based on OECD STAN, UNIDO INDSTAT, UNSD, World Bank (2013); IEA (2014); OECD (2014a, 2014b); and various industry reports.

A number of qualifying remarks are in order here. First, the percentage share of total employment accounted for by capture fisheries would increase markedly if total jobs in artisanal fisheries were to be included, adding around 100 million fishers for capture fisheries and aquaculture (including inland activities) to the overall total. Second, in addition to industrial fish processing, there are millions of people (mainly women) involved in artisanal fish processing. (See later sections in this chapter on capture fisheries, aquaculture and fish processing for more detail.)

Estimates of value added and employment in selected ocean industries

Sea and coastal water transport (shipping)

ISIC Rev.3 code "6110" defines water transport as the "transport of passengers or freight over water"[3] and indicates value added and employment where shipping companies are registered. The value added and employment in cruise tourism were excluded from water transport and added to tourism. On this basis, global value added from sea and coastal shipping was around USD 60 billion in 2010. It should be noted that consistent sets of official data for value added and employment were only available for OECD countries; data for emerging and developing states were patchy. However, using data solely from companies registered in OECD economies would have led to a bias in the calculations. In order to correct for this, approximations needed to be undertaken. These were performed by calculating a "representative" weighted average ratio of value added per tonne of freight[4] and then applying that ratio to key large OECD shipping partner economies (Brazil, the People's Republic of China, India, Indonesia, the Russian Federation, Singapore and Thailand) (see Liebender et al. [forthcoming] for details). The corrective procedure increases value added in shipping by USD 23 billion, raising the global total to around USD 83 billion.

Full-time employment in shipping companies registered in these countries was estimated at around 293 000 in 2010. (The estimate includes regular employment but not dispatched workers under a sub-contract.) However, due to limited official data, this figure does not include seafarers from OECD partner economies, estimated by the International Chamber of Shipping at a further 200 000 full-time officers and more than 700 000 ratings (unlicensed deck crew). Total employment in shipping is therefore estimated at around 1.2 million. The majority of the shipping industry's ratings are recruited from developing countries, especially the Far East and South East Asia. India and the Philippines are very significant maritime labour supply nations, with many seafarers from these countries enjoying employment opportunities on foreign flag ships operated by international shipping companies. China has also seen a large increase in the number of seafarers, but at the moment most of these work on the Chinese fleet, meeting domestic requirements.

Shipbuilding and repair

In 2010, 96.4 million GT (gross tonnage) were completed, with the biggest part of it resulting from container, bulker and tanker construction equalling around 77 million GT. The total economic contribution of the vessels completed in 2010 was estimated to be around USD 58 billion. Asia was estimated to have the biggest market share with 47%, followed by Europe (25%) and North America (23%) (Figure 6.3). Nevertheless, it should be noted that 2010 was in the middle of a period of unusually high levels of shipbuilding resulting in subsequent overcapacity.

Figure 6.3. **Value added of shipbuilding and repair by region in 2010**

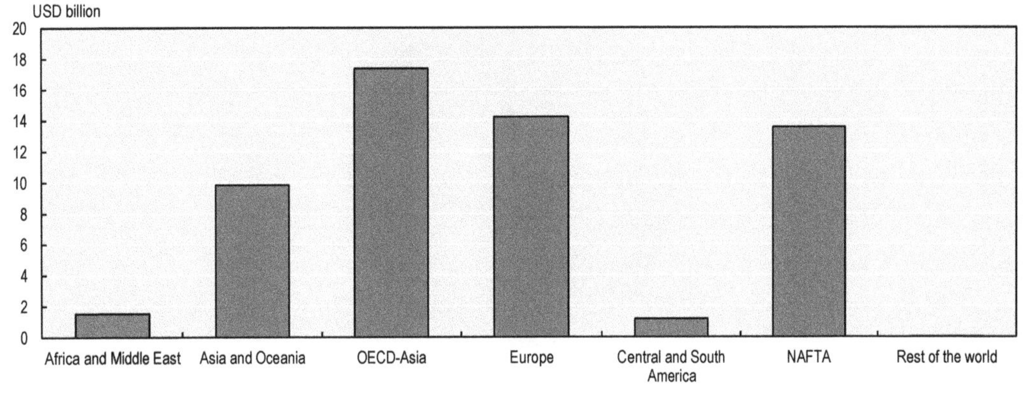

StatLink http://dx.doi.org/10.1787/888933334657

Source: Authors' calculations based on IHS Global Insights.

In 2010, shipbuilding and repair accounted for approximately 1.9 million jobs. As most of the shipyards are located in Asian countries, most jobs are in this region, notably in China, Indonesia, Japan and Korea. These countries accounted for almost 60% of jobs in global shipbuilding and repair. Europe and North American shipyards together accounted for 0.6 million jobs, approximately 30% of global employment in the industry (Figure 6.4).

Figure 6.4. **Employment in shipbuilding and repair by region in 2010**

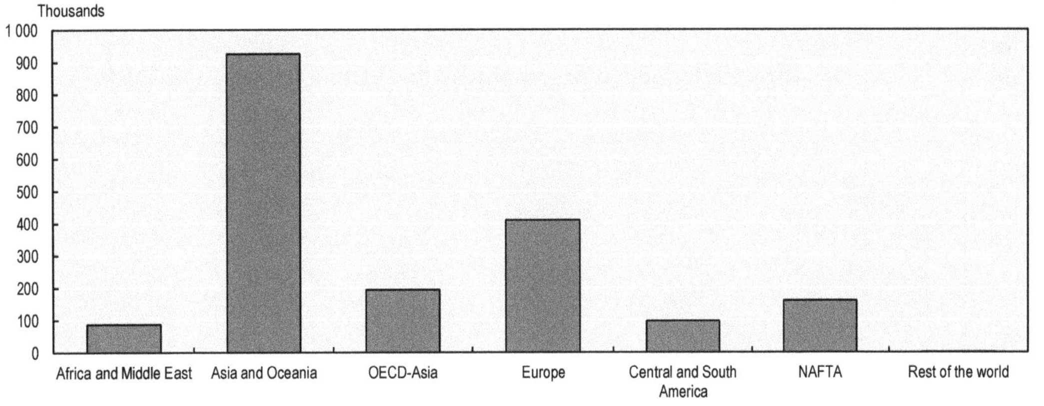

StatLink http://dx.doi.org/10.1787/888933334662

Source: Authors' calculations based on OECD STAN.

Marine equipment

Global value added in marine equipment in 2010 was estimated to be USD 168 billion, with the biggest share in Asia. Asia accounted for over three-quarters of the global market, with China and Korea alone making up more than half. Japan, rest of Asia, EU-28 and the rest of the world each accounted for 12% (Figure 6.5). Based on data approximated from BALance Technology Consulting (2014), marine equipment provided 2.1 million full-time jobs in 2010.[5]

Figure 6.5. **Value added of marine equipment by region in 2010**

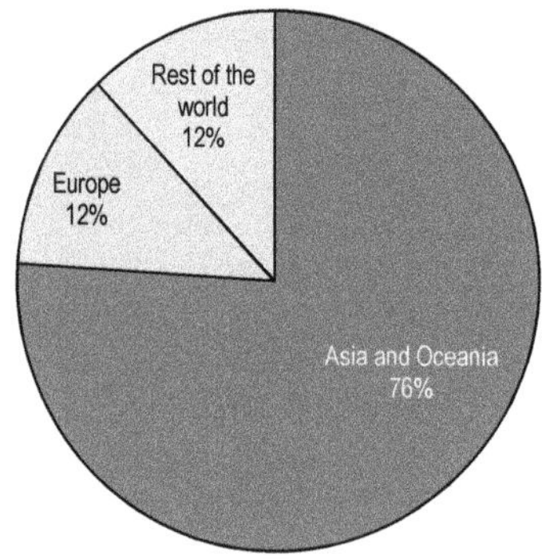

StatLink http://dx.doi.org/10.1787/888933334670

Source: Authors' calculations based on BALance Technology Consulting (2014).

Port activities

Based on the OECD's ITF Database of Global Port Activities, which comprises the 830 largest ports in the world in terms of tonnage and almost 100% of cargo handling worldwide, the direct value added of global port throughput was estimated at around USD 193 billion in 2009. Figure 6.6 shows that more than half of the global value added of port activities is estimated to have occurred in Asia, contributing roughly USD 102 billion to the global economy. Asia accounted for 53% of global ports' volume, followed by Europe (23%), NAFTA (10%) and South America (6%), Oceania (5%) and Africa (3%). Direct employment from total global port activities was estimated at more than 1.7 million full-time jobs in 2009 (see Liebender et al. [forthcoming] for details).

Figure 6.6. **Direct value added of global port throughput by region in 2009**

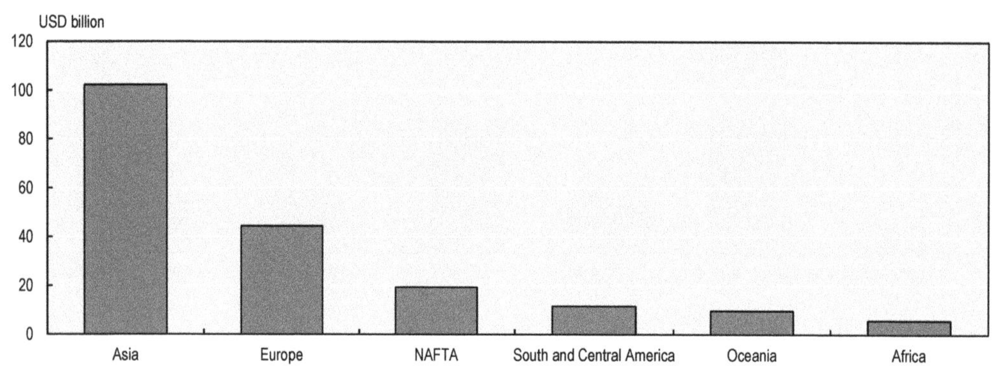

StatLink http://dx.doi.org/10.1787/888933334685

Source: Authors' calculations based on OECD ITF data; OECD (2014b).

Maritime and coastal tourism

Based on country-specific tourism consumption (OECD, 2014a) and a breakdown of maritime and coastal tourism compared to total tourism, global direct value added in marine and coastal tourism was estimated at USD 390 billion (Figure 6.7). Europe generated the biggest share of value added, contributing 35% of the total, followed by

Asia and Oceania (30%), NAFTA (19%), Africa (9%), and Central and South America (6%). Direct employment in 2013 was around 7 million full-time jobs in maritime and coastal tourism (WTTC, 2014).

Figure 6.7. **Value added of marine and coastal tourism by region in 2010**

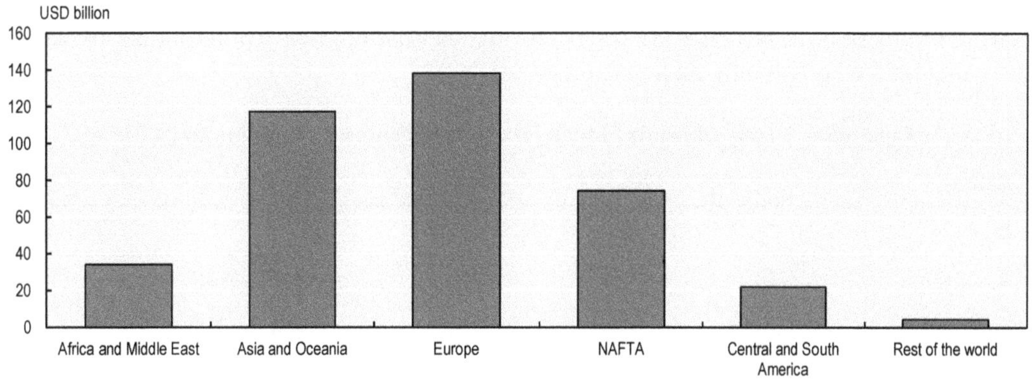

StatLink http://dx.doi.org/10.1787/888933334699

Source: Authors' calculations based on OECD (2014), World Bank (2013), World Bank WDI (n.d), UNWTO (2011).

According to the UNWTO (2011), Europe had the highest number of total international tourist arrivals (including land-based tourism), around 480 million, followed by Asia and the Pacific sharing 205 million international tourist arrivals between them. The share of international tourist arrivals for Europe was 51%, and 22% for Asia and the Pacific, respectively. In addition, outbound tourism was highest for Europe, accounting for approximately 509 million international departures.

Based on data on the regional distribution of value added (European Cruise Council, 2010), it was estimated that in 2010, cruise tourism contributed around USD 17.8 billion in direct value added and 150 000 employees. However, this does not include the indirect effects of the cruise industry, which would be substantially higher.

Industrial capture fisheries

Total global value added of industrial capture fisheries was estimated at around USD 21 billion in 2010. NAFTA accounted for the biggest share of the global value added of industrial capture fisheries (more than USD 6 billion), followed by Europe and Asia (Figure 6.8).

Industrial capture fisheries account for approximately 11 million full-time jobs globally. The regions with the highest employment figures in 2010 were Asia and Oceania combined with almost 7 million full-time employees.

The above figure of value added and employment only includes industrial capture fisheries which are registered by official statistics. That presents an underestimate for two reasons: first, artisanal marine fisheries are not captured by official statistics. Second, as Pauly and Zeller (2016) point out, official statistics do not include illegal fishing activities, since they cannot be registered as official landings. The magnitude of artisanal fishing is considerable. Based on estimates of the Food and Agriculture Organization (FAO), artisanal fishing comprises 90% of all fishing jobs worldwide, approximately 45% of the world's fisheries, and nearly a quarter of the world catch, leading to a value added of artisanal capture fisheries of around USD 18 billion annually, mostly in Africa and Asia, where most of the artisanal fishery activities take place. Hence, adding these estimates for employment and value added from artisanal capture fisheries to the industrial fishing activities and official data would make a significant difference in absolute numbers. Employment in artisanal fisheries would add approximately a further 35 million full-time jobs in capture fisheries, although this figure contains both inland and marine production. Based on FAO (2014) estimates, that number would double if fishers were included who fish only on a part-time basis.

Figure 6.8. **Value added of industrial capture fisheries by region in 2010**

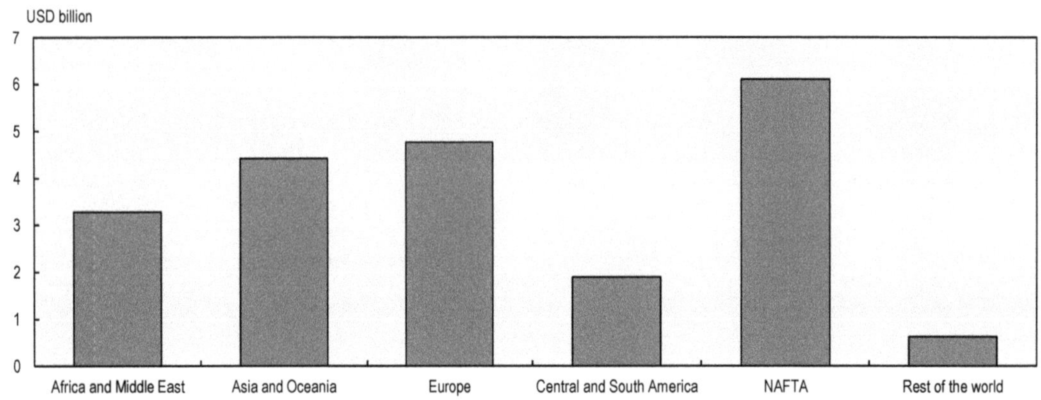

StatLink http://dx.doi.org/10.1787/888933334707

Source: Authors' calculations based on UNSTAT, OECD STAN and World Bank (2013).

Industrial marine aquaculture

Asia was the biggest operator of marine aquaculture in 2010. The region produced approximately 83% of the entire world marine aquaculture output, followed by 9% for Europe, and 7% for the NAFTA region and Central and South America combined. The global ratio of the volume of marine aquaculture relative to total aquaculture production (marine and inland aquaculture, industrial and artisanal) was 38%. Region-wise, that ratio was 81% for Europe, 62% for North and South America combined, 35% for Asia and 1% for Africa. In other words, even though Africa consists of 48 countries and 5 island nations, of which most are practising some form of aquaculture, most of the production in Africa is based on inland aquaculture.

Figure 6.9 shows that the global value added of industrial marine aquaculture in 2010 is estimated at around USD 3.6 billion. Asia was the biggest producer. Value added in Asia was approximately USD 1.4 billion, followed by NAFTA, accounting for around USD 1.2 billion.

Total employment in industrial aquaculture in 2010 was estimated at around 2 million jobs. In correlation with high Asian production, 92% of the jobs were in Asia and Oceania, followed by Europe with 5%, and NAFTA and South and Central America combined with almost 3% of total employment. Inclusion of artisanal aquaculture – mainly in Africa, Asia and Latin America – would add around 65 million jobs to the total, although this figure contains both inland and marine production.

Figure 6.9. **Value added of industrial marine aquaculture by region in 2010**

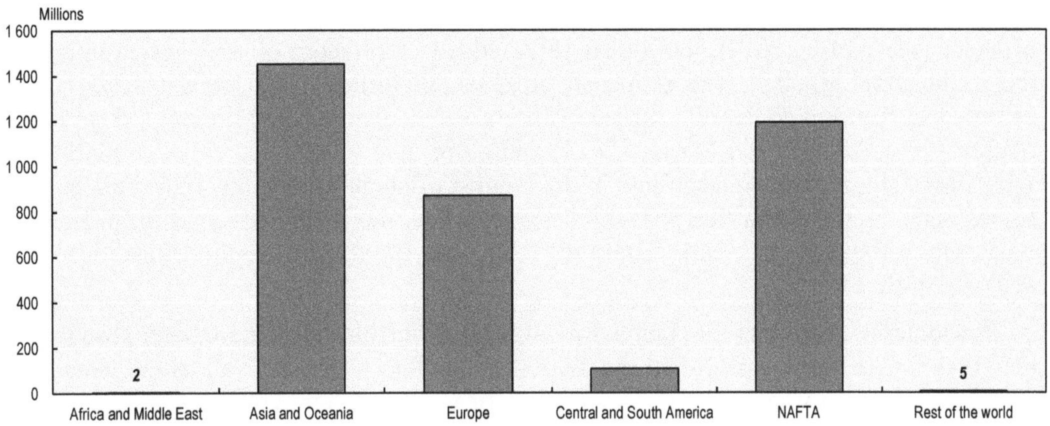

StatLink http://dx.doi.org/10.1787/888933334717

Source: Authors' calculations based on UNSTAT, OECD STAN, World Bank (2013); FAO (2015).

Fish processing

The global value added of fish processing in 2010 is estimated at around USD 79 billion. Figure 6.10 shows that combined with a strong aquaculture and capture fisheries production, Asia generated the highest value added, accounting for 54% of the global value added in fish processing, Africa and the Middle East combined 16% and Europe 14%.The largest processors in the world were China, Indonesia, India, Viet Nam, Peru, the United States, Myanmar, the Russian Federation, Japan, Bangladesh, Norway, the Philippines and Thailand.

Figure 6.10. **Value added of fish processing by region in 2010**

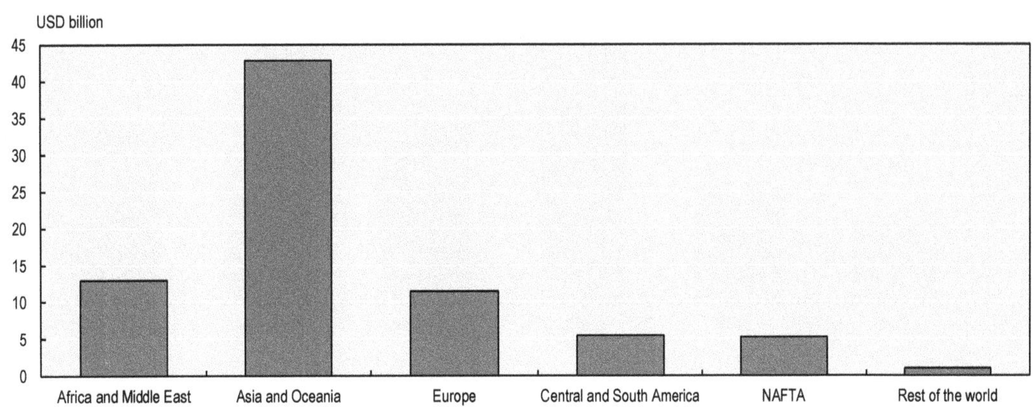

StatLink http://dx.doi.org/10.1787/888933334722

Source: Authors' calculations based on UNSTAT, OECD STAN, World Bank (2013); FAO (2015).

Total industry-specific employment for fish processing in 2010 was around 2.4 million full-time jobs. Asia, the key fish-processing region, generated the bulk of employment. Africa, with 0.5 million full-time jobs, had approximately the same level of employment as Latin America and North America combined. In addition to industrial fish processing, there are millions of people (mainly women) who are involved in artisanal fish processing.

Offshore oil and gas

Based on the assumption that approximately 32% of global oil and gas activities were offshore (see APEC, 2014), the global value added of offshore oil and gas exploration and production in 2010 was estimated at USD 504 billion. The largest shares were captured by Europe by North America (Figure 6.11). Around 270 floating oil and gas platforms (Lloyds Register Marine, 2013) and more than 9 000 fixed offshore platforms were operating, mainly concentrated in the biggest offshore oil and gas-rich sedimentary basins, such as the North Sea, the Mediterranean Sea, the Arab-Persian Gulf, West and East Africa, North and South America, India, the North and South China Sea and West Australia.[6]

It should be noted that the figures for value added include exploration and production activities for the more established production in shallow waters as well as the emerging production in deep waters. Based on estimates of world offshore crude oil production by physiographical location and region published in the IEA *World Energy Outlook 2012* (IEA, 2012), shallow-water production accounted for 93% of total output, compared to 7% for deep-water production. A much simplified calculation suggests therefore that shallow-water offshore oil and gas production generated value added in the order of around USD 468 billion, whereas deep-water offshore oil and gas production gave rise to approximately USD 35 billion in value added.

Global employment in the offshore oil and gas industry was estimated at approximately 1.8 million jobs in 2010.[7] Attracted by the lower labour costs, jobs are shifting from north and west to east and south, leading to high levels of employment in Latin America, notably Brazil, which generates 24% of global offshore oil and gas jobs, followed by Europe (19%), Asia (17%) and North America (16%).

Figure 6.11. **Value added of offshore oil and gas by region in 2010**

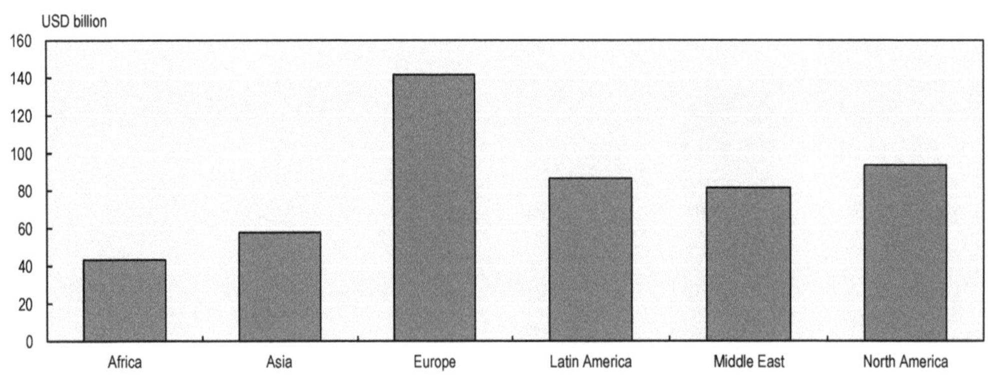

StatLink http://dx.doi.org/10.1787/888933334733

Source: Authors' calculation, based on IEA (2014); EIA (2015).

Offshore wind

The industry-specific value added for the offshore wind industry was estimated at around USD 2.9 billion in 2010. Some 887 offshore wind turbines (Lloyd's Register Marine, 2013) contributed to around 340 gigawatts (GW) capacity of offshore wind. Figure 6.12 shows that the majority of the industry activity took place in Europe, with 91% of GW capacity, followed by China producing 9% of the global offshore wind capacity. In 2010, global industry-specific employment was around 38 000 jobs.[8]

Figure 6.12. **Value added of offshore wind production by region in 2010**

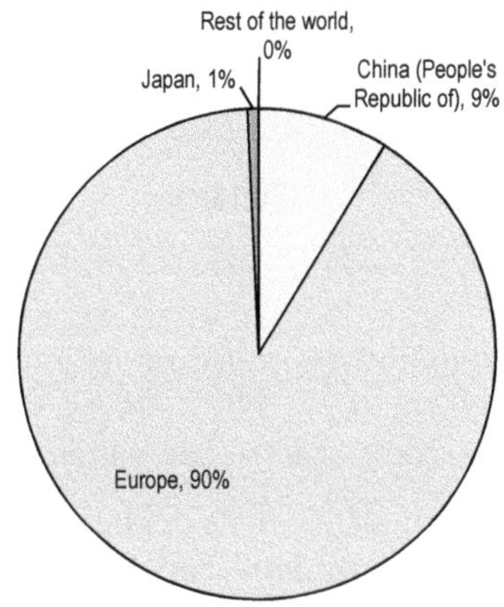

StatLink http://dx.doi.org/10.1787/888933334749

Source: Authors' calculations based on IEA (2014); APEC (2014), BTM Consulting (2010).

Concluding remarks

The above estimates underline the significance of ocean-based industries to the world economy in terms both of their contribution to economic growth and to employment worldwide. Moreover, it should be borne in mind that the estimates are highly conservative. First, they measure economic activity at industrial scale. For several sectors (e.g. capture fisheries, aquaculture and shipping), this means excluding economic activity in the artisanal and/or self-employed category which in many parts of the world generates significant value added and employment. Second, several important ocean-based activities are not captured in the database. This is due in part to difficult access to data at international level (e.g. in the case of marine business such as finance, brokerage and insurance, or maritime safety, monitoring and surveillance), and in part due to the fact that some activities have not yet developed to commercial scale at world level (e.g. marine biotechnology, ocean renewable energy, seabed mining). Thirdly, in applying approximations of missing data, the authors have chosen to err on the side of caution in most cases.

All the above issues point to the need for greatly increased efforts to improve data quality, data coverage and measurement techniques in order to arrive at a more accurate assessment of ocean-based industries and their potential for the future. In particular, it would be helpful if more countries were to use ISIC Rev.4 as the statistical classification system for the ocean economy, including also emerging ocean-based industries, and separating ocean-based from land-based activities.

Finally, as noted at the beginning of this report, to capture a fuller picture of the true size and nature of the ocean economy, much more needs to be done to calculate the global economic value of the ocean's natural assets and ecosystem services more systematically.

Notes

1. The data on industry activities are collected via a joint OECD/UNIDO questionnaire at a very detailed level (4-digit) of ISIC. However, differing survey practices across countries tend to weaken somewhat the international data comparability.

2. The link between GVA and GDP can be defined as: GVA at current basic prices plus taxes on products (available by products) less subsidies on products (available at whole economy level only) equals GDP (at current market prices; available at whole economy level only).

3. The ISIC Rev.3 code "6110" for water transport (shipping) contains the transport of passengers and freight, which also includes cruise tourism. Consequently, value added and employment in cruise tourism were estimated and excluded from water transport in order to avoid double counting.

4. The representative weighted average ratio of value added over freight volume was calculated based on official data for value added and freight volume for east European countries for which data were available (Estonia, Poland and Slovenia).

5. Due to patchy data for the maritime equipment industry, the ratio of value added and employment per unit of production for Europe was used from BALance Technology Consulting (2014). A proxy was calculated for Asia and the rest of the world, leading to a likely overestimation of value added and underestimation of employment in these regions. For further explanation see Liebender et al. (forthcoming).

6. Countries were included in the analysis where they reported either on the total of their offshore oil and gas production or on the ratio of their offshore production relative to the total oil and gas production.

7. The majority of the data collected are from 2010, although some of the country-specific productions were only available for 2009 or 2011.

8. The employment figures for Asian producers are estimated on the basis of the data for Europe, and are likely to be underestimated. Conversely, the figures for Asian value added are likely to be overestimated.

Annex 6.A1.
Current value estimation

Two different approaches are developed to estimate the current value of the ocean economy for two sets of ocean-based industries: ocean-based industries defined by the ISIC Rev.3 and ocean-based industries that are not defined by the ISIC Rev.3.

A Cobb-Douglas production function is used for those industries that are defined by ISIC Rev.3. These industries are fisheries, water transport, shipbuilding and repair, and fish processing. The following notations are introduced in the estimation process.

Denote with i=1, 2,…, I, the different sectors of the established ocean-based industries (in this case I=4). Denote with j=1, 2,…, J, the different countries (in this case J=215). Then, $GVA_{i,j,t}$ represents the gross value added from sector I in country j in year t. $GVA_{j,t}$ denotes the gross value added from all established industries in country j in year t, while $GVA_{i,t}$ represents the global gross value added of industry i in year t. The country- and industry-specific level of the remaining components of Cobb-Douglas production function, namely capital stock, employment, human capital and multi-factor productivity, are denoted analogously as $K_{i,j,t}$, $L_{i,j,t}$, $h_{i,j,t}$ and $A_{i,j,t}$, respectively.

The estimation procedure consists of the following steps:

- Collect the level of $GVA_{i,j,2010}$, $K_{i,j,2010}$, $L_{i,j,2010}$, and $h_{i,j,2010}$ for the reporting countries.
- For extrapolation purposes (see Chapter 7), collect the country level of $GDP_{j,2010}$,$K_{j,2010}$, and $L_{j,2010}$
- To estimate the multi factor productivity $A_{i,j,2010}$, transform the Cobb-Douglas production function in the following manner, and solve for $A_{i,j,2010}$.

  $$GVA_{i,j,2010} = A_{i,j,2010} \times K^{\alpha}_{i,j,2010} \times \left(h_{i,j,2010} \times L_{i,j,2010}\right)^{1-\alpha}$$

  $$A_{i,j,2010} = \frac{K^{\alpha}_{i,j,2010} \times \left(h_{i,j,2010} \times L_{i,j,2010}\right)^{1-\alpha}}{GVA_{i,j,2010}}$$

  The output elasticity α is assumed to be equal to 1/3 throughout this study.
- Calculate the income-group-specific weighted averages of the following ratios,$\frac{GVA_{i,j,t}}{GDP_{j,t}}$, $\frac{L_{i,j,t}}{L_{j,t}}$,$\frac{K_{i,j,t}}{K_{j,t}}$, and substitute this average for the non-reporting countries in order to estimate country- and industry-specific level of the respective factor of production.

This approach is based on the Solow growth model, augmented to include human capital. The same framework has been used in numerous empirical papers to analyse and project the growth of national economy, see for example Duval and de la Maisonneuve (2009), Klenow and Rodriguez-Clare (1997). The framework has been adapted to model multiple industries, following the literature on multi-sector growth models such as Hulten (1992; 1978); Greenwood, Hercowitz and Krusell (1997); and Ngai and Samaniego (2009).

Due to the lack of official data, an industry-specific method has been constructed for the ocean-based industries that are not defined by the ISIC Rev.3. These industries cannot be estimated using the Cobb-Douglas production function, notably due to lack of data on physical capital stock. Instead, production value is used to approximate for the non-reporting countries. Denote with $Y_{i,j,t}$ the country- and industry-specific production.

The estimation procedure consists of the following steps.

- Collect the country-specific level of $Y_{i,j,t}$, $GVA_{i,j,t}$, and $L_{i,j,t}$ for the industries through secondary sources. If the data do not exist on country-specific level, collect the entire industry level of $GVA_{i,t}$, and $L_{i,t}$ for each industry.
- $GVA_{i,j,t}$ and $L_{i,j,t}$ of non-reporting countries are extrapolated based on production ratios within the group of income-specific country groups.
- As a final step, all sector-specific projections estimates of value added and employment are aggregated into one figure to represent the ocean economy.

For details, see Liebender et al. (forthcoming).

National-level studies on ocean-based industries

In recent years a few attempts have been made to estimate the value of the ocean economy at regional and global level: the EC commissioned work on blue growth (Ecorys, 2012), and at global level the World Wide Fund in conjunction with the Boston Consulting Group recently released their estimates of the current value of the ocean economy (Hoegh-Guldberg et al., 2015).

National-level studies are more numerous. Over the last 15 years or so a large number of countries have attempted to place a value on the national ocean economy as measured by the contribution of ocean-based industries to the economy. For example: Pugh and Skinner (2002) and Pugh (2008) estimated marine-related activities in the United Kingdom; Australia produced two studies as part of its National Ocean Policy, with Allen Consulting Group (2004) examining the economic contribution of marine-based industries to the economy; France developed a national study in 2009 (Kalaydijan et al., 2009) which was updated in 2011 and 2014; and in 2006 New Zealand conducted a study to see how the marine environment is utilised to generate economic activity. Additionally, the United States' National Ocean Economics Program released its report on the "State of the US ocean and coastal economy" in June 2009 with regular updates since then. Recently, Belgium, China, Ireland, Korea and Portugal have all devoted considerable efforts to measuring their national ocean economy.

Table 6.A1.1. **Selected estimates of value of ocean-based industries, by country, region and world**

Country	Author	Date of study	Date of data	Contribution of ocean sectors to GDP or GVA	% of GDP or GVA	Employment (total FTE)
Australia	Allen Consulting Group	2004	1996-2003	AUD 26.7 bn GVA	3.6% GVA	253 130
Belgium	Flander's Maritime Cluster	2011	2010	..	10% GDP	..
Canada	Gardner Pinfold Consulting	2009	2006	CAD 17.7 bn GDP	1.2% GDP	171 365
	Acton and White Associates	2001	1998	CAD 10.4 billion GDP	1.4% GDP	120 000

Table 6.A1.1. **Selected estimates of value of ocean-based industries, by country, region and world** (*continued*)

Country	Author	Date of study	Date of data	Contribution of ocean sectors to GDP or GVA	% of GDP or GVA	Employment (total FTE)
China (People's Republic of)	APEC	2014	2012	..	9.6% GDP	..
	Jiang et. al.	2014	2000-11	..	13.83% GDP	..
	CMIEN	2013	2012	CNY 5 0087 tn GDP	9.6% GDP	34 0240 000
	Zhao, Hynes and He	2013	2010	CNY 239.09 bn GVA	4.3% GDP	9 000 000
Dubai	Gujarat Maritime Board	2014	2013	..	4.6% GDP	..
France	Kalaydjian et al.	2009	2007	EUR 28 bn GVA	1.4% GDP	484 548
	Kalaydjian et al.	2011	2009	EUR 26 122 bn GVA	2.5% GDP	460 163
	Kalaydjian et al.	2014	2012	EUR 30 252 bn GVA	2.75% GDP	460 396
Hong Kong (China)	Gujarat Maritime Board	2014	2013	..	25% GDP	..
Iceland	Sigfusson and Gestsson	2012	2010	..	26% GDP	ca. 30 000
Ireland	Vega, Hynes and O'Toole	2015	2012	EUR 1.3 bn GVA	0.7% GDP	17 425
	Vega, Hynes and Corless	2013	2010	EUR 1.2 bn GVA	0.7% GDP	16 614
Japan	Nomura Research Institute	2009	2005	JPY 7 863 bn GVA	1.6% GDP	981 234
Korea	APEC	2014	2005	..	8% GDP	..
	Hwang et al.	2011	2008	KRW 13 435 bn GVA	4.9% GDP	919 314
Netherlands	Maritime by Holland	2014	2012	EUR 21 bn GVA	3.3% GNP	224 000
New Zealand	Statistics New Zealand	2006	1997-2002	NZD 3.3 bn GVA	2.9% GDP	21 000
Portugal	DGPM	2013	2010	..	2.5% GVA	..
Singapore	MPA – Maritime Singapore	2014	..	..	7% GDP	..
United Kingdom	Pugh (2008)	2008	2005-06	GBP 46 041 bn GVA	4.2% GDP	890 416
United States	Kildow et. al. (2014)	2014	2010	USD 258 bn GDP	4.4% GDP	2.8 million
Europe	Ecorys	2012	2011	EUR 495 bn GVA	..	5.6 million
Worldwide	Hoegh-Guldberg et al.	2015	2011-14	USD 2.5 trillion "gross marine product"	3.2% GDP	..

Notes: .. = data not available. The German study focuses only on maritime technology and ocean engineering. FTE = full-time equivalent. The value added of Iceland and the China Marine Statistical Yearbook include also indirect effects on the economy.

Source: Individual reports by country and region.

References

Acton White & Associates (2001), "Economic study of Canada's marine and ocean industries", National Research Council Canada.

Allen Consulting Group (2004), "The economic contribution of Australia's marine industries, 1995-96 to 2002-03", The Allen Consulting Group Pty Ltd, www.environment.gov.au/system/files/resources/ce4cf41d-8ffe-470b-898a-2c0f84eac483/files/marine-economic.pdf.

APEC (2014), "Marine sustainable development report", APEC Ocean and Fisheries Working Group, Asia-Pacific Economic Cooperation, http://publications.apec.org/publication-detail.php?pub_id=1552.

BALance Technology Consulting (2014), "Competitive position and future opportunities of the European marine supplies industry", European Commission, http://ec.europa.eu/DocsRoom/documents/4233/attachments/1/translations/en/renditions/native.

BTM Consulting (2010), *International Wind Energy Development: World Market Update 2010*, Navigant Consulting.

CMIEN (China Marine Information Economic Network) (2013), "Statistical bulletin of China's ocean economy 2012", January.

DGPM (Directorate General for Maritime Policy) Government of Portugal (2013), *The National Ocean Strategy 2013 – 2020 – Annex A – The Sea Economy in Portugal*, www.dgpm.mam.gov.pt/Documents/ENM_Final_EN_V2.pdf.

Duval, R. and C. de la Maisonneuve (2009), "Long-run GDP growth framework and scenarios for the world economy", *OECD Economics Department Working Papers*, No. 663, OECD Publishing, Paris, http://dx.doi.org/10.1787/227205684023.

Ecorys (2012), "Blue growth: Scenarios and drivers for sustainable growth from the oceans, seas and coasts", Third Interim Report, Rotterdam/Brussels, 13 March, http://ec.europa.eu/maritimeaffairs/documentation/studies/documents/blue_growth_third_interim_report_en.pdf.

EIA (2015), "International energy data and analysis", Energy Information Agency, www.eia.gov/beta/international (accessed on 18 February 2016).

European Cruise Council (2010), "The cruise industry in 2010", prepared by BREA (Business Research & Economic Advisors) for the European Cruise Council.

FAO (2015), *Global Aquaculture Production Database*, www.fao.org/fishery/statistics/global-aquaculture-production/en.

FAO (2014), *The State of World Fisheries and Aquaculture*, Food and Agriculture Organization, Rome, available at: www.fao.org/3/a-i3720e.pdf.

Flander's Maritime Cluster (2011), *The genesis of a maritime cluster,* Presentation for the European Maritime Day, Gdansk, Poland, https://ec.europa.eu/maritimeaffairs/maritimeday/sites/mare-emd/files/dekock_en.pdf.

Gardner Pinfold Consulting (2009), "Economic impact of Marine Related Activities in Canada", http://www.dfo-mpo.gc.ca/ea-ae/cat1/no1-1/no1-1-eng.htm.

Greenwood, J., Z. Hercowitz and P. Krusell (1997), "Long-run implications of investment-specific technological change", *American Economic Review*, Vol. 87, No. 3, pp. 342-362, www.jstor.org/stable/2951349.

Gujarat Maritime Board (2014), *Roadmap of the development of maritime cluster in Gujarat*, www.gujaratmaritimecluster.com/Road-Map-Report.pdf.

Hoegh-Guldberg, O. et al. (2015), *Reviving the Ocean Economy: Action Agenda for 2015*, WWF International, Geneva. https://www.wwf.de/fileadmin/fm-wwf/Publikationen-PDF/WWF-Report-Reviving-the-Ocean-Economy-Summary.pdf

Hulten, C.R. (1992), "Growth accounting when technical change is embodied in capital", *American Economic Review*, Vol. 82, No. 4, pp. 964-980, www.jstor.org/stable/2117353.

Hulten, C.R. (1978), "Growth accounting with intermediate inputs", *Review of Economic Studies*, Vol. 45, No. 3, pp. 511-518, www.jstor.org/stable/2297252.

Hwang, K.H. et al. (2011), "Assessment of gross ocean products in Korea", Korea Institute of Marine Science and Technology Promotion.

IEA (2014), "World oil statistics", IEA Oil Information Statistics, http://dx.doi.org/10.1787/oil-data-en.

IEA (2012), *World Energy Outlook 2012*, OECD Publishing, Paris, http://dx.doi.org/10.1787/weo-2012-en.

IHS (2016), *IHS Global Insights Database*, https://globalsso.ihs.com/KeystoneSTS/SSOLogin/Login.aspx?theme=IGI&ReturnUrl=https%3a%2f%2fglobalsso.ihs.com%2fKeystoneSTS%2fKSFed%2fDefault.aspx%3ftheme%3dIGI.

Jiang, X.-Z. et al. (2014), "China's marine economy and regional development", *Marine Policy*, Vol. 50, Part A, December, pp. 227-237, http://dx.doi.org/10.1016/j.marpol.2014.06.008.

Kalaydjian, R. et al. (2014), *French Maritime Economic Data 2014*, Marine Economics Department, Ifremer, Paris.

Kalaydjian, R. et al. (2011), *French Maritime Economic Data 2011*, Marine Economics Department, Ifremer, Paris.

Kalaydjian, R. et al. (2009), *French Maritime Economic Data 2009*, Marine Economics Department, Ifremer, Paris.

Kildow, J. et al., (2014): "State of the U.S. Ocean and Coastal Economies 2014". *Publications.* Paper 1, http://cbe.miis.edu/noep_publications/1

Klenow, P. and A. Rodriguez-Clare (1997), "The neoclassical revival in growth economics: Has it gone too far?", in: Bernanke, B.S. and J. Rotemberg (eds.), *NBER Macroeconomics Annual 1997*, Vol. 12, National Bureau of Economic Research, Inc, pp. 73-114, www.nber.org/chapters/c11037.pdf.

Liebender, A.-S. et al. (forthcoming), "Measuring the global economic contribution of ocean-based industries – Methodology paper", *OECD Science, Technology and Industry Working Papers*, OECD Publishing, Paris, forthcoming.

Lloyd's Register Marine (2013), "Global marine trends 2030", Lloyd's Register Marine.

Marine Southeast England (2004), "Economic impact of the marine industries within South East England", Marine Southeast, Southampton, www.marinesoutheast.co.uk.

Maritime by Holland (2014), *The Dutch Maritime Cluster – High Tech, Hands On, Monitor 2014 summary*, www.maritimebyholland.com/download-link.php?file=/wp-content/uploads/2015/03/150227-NML003-samenvatting-los_UK.pdf.

MPA Maritime Singapore (Maritime and Port Authority of Singapore) (2014), "Opening remarks by Mrs Josephne Teo, Senior Minister of State, Ministry of Finance and Ministry of Transport", Speech at the opening ceremony of the smart port hackathon 2015 on 14 August 2015 at Singapore Polytechnic, www.mpa.gov.sg/web/portal/home/media-centre/news-releases/detail/69c7fe28-cafd-4a2c-8e09-3219192f5a59.

Ngai, L.R. and R.M. Samaniego (2009), "Mapping prices into productivity in multisector growth models", *Journal of Economic Growth*, Vol. 14, No. 3, pp. 183-204, http://dx.doi.org/10.1007/s10887-009-9044-z.

Nomura Research Institute (2009), "The report on of Japan's marine industry".

OECD (2014a), *OECD Tourism Trends and Policies 2014*, OECD Publishing, Paris, http://dx.doi.org/10.1787/tour-2014-en.

OECD (2014b), The Competitiveness of Global Port-Cities, OECD Publishing, http://dx.doi.org/10.1787/9789264205277-en.

Pauly, D. and D. Zeller (2016), "Catch reconstructions reveal that global marine fisheries catches are higher than reported and declining", *Nature Communications*, Vol. 7, Article 10 244, http://dx.doi.org/10.1038/ncomms10244.

Pugh, D. (2008), *Socio-economic Indicators of Marine-related Industries in the UK Economy*, The Crown Estate, London, www.thecrownestate.co.uk/media/5774/socio_economic_uk_marine.pdf.

Pugh, D. and L. Skinner (2002), "A new analysis of marine-related activities in the UK economy with supporting science and technology", *IACMST Information Document No. 10*, Inter-Agency Committee on Marine Science and Technology, Southampton Oceanography Centre, Southampton, United Kingdom, www.oceannet.org/library/publications/documents/marine_related_activities.pdf.

Rongzi, L. (2003), "An analysis of the contribution of ocean economy to the national economic development of China", *Tropical Coasts*, Vol. 16, pp. 71-79.

Sigfusson, T. and H. Gestsson (2012), *Iceland's Ocean Economy*, http://sjavarklasinn.is/en/wp-content/uploads/2014/11/2.-IcelandsOceanEconomy2011low.pdf.

Statistics New Zealand (2006), "New Zealand's marine economy 1997-2002", Experimental Series Report, Statistics New Zealand, www.stats.govt.nz/~/media/Statistics/browse-categories/environment/natural-resources/marine/nz-marine-economy-1997-2002.pdf.

UNWTO (2011), *Tourism Towards 2030/Global Overview*, Advanced edition presented at UNWTO 19th General Assembly, 10 October, World Tourism Organization, www.e-unwto.org/doi/book/10.18111/9789284414024.

Vega, A., Hynes, S. and Corless, R. (2013), *Ireland's Ocean Economy: Reference Year 2010*, NUI Galway, Ireland, www.nuigalway.ie/semru/documents/irelands_ocean_economy_report_series_no2.pdf.

Vega, A., Hynes, S. and O'Toole, E. (2015), *Ireland's Ocean Economy: Reference Year: 2012*, Ryan Institute Research Day, September, Galway, Ireland, www.nuigalway.ie/semru/documents/semru__irelands_ocean_economy__web_final.pdf.

World Bank (2013), "Fish to 2030: Prospects for fisheries and aquaculture", *Agriculture and Environmental Services Discussion Paper 03*, World Bank, Washington, DC, http://documents.worldbank.org/curated/en/2013/12/18882045/fish-2030-prospects-fisheries-aquaculture.

World Bank WDI (n.d.), Country and lending groups, http://data.worldbank.org/about/country-and-lending-groups (accessed 17 January 2016).

WTTC (2014), "Travel & tourism: Economic impact 2014: World", World Travel & Tourism Council, London, www.wttc.org/-/media/files/reports/economic%20impact%20research/regional%20reports/world2014.pdf.

Zhao, R., S. Hynes and G.S. He (2013), "Defining and quantifying China's ocean economy", *Marine Policy*, Vol. 43, January, pp. 164-173, http://dx.doi.org/10.1016.j.marpol.2013.05.008.

Part III.

Perspectives on and projections of the future of the ocean economy

Chapter 7.

Growth prospects, challenges and uncertainties for selected ocean industries

This chapter is concerned with the future of the ocean-based industries over the next couple of decades, as seen through the eyes of a range of international organisations, agencies, industry associations and research institutions. It reviews a large number of recent sectoral projections, with a view to gaining a sense of which industries are considered by experts to have strong growth prospects over the period under study, which are expected to perform less well, and what particular challenges and uncertainties the industries face. The sectors covered are capture fisheries; offshore oil and gas; shipping; shipbuilding; offshore wind; marine aquaculture; marine tourism; maritime surveillance and safety; ocean renewable energy; deep-sea mining; and marine biotechnology.

The following is a brief review of a selection of recent sector-specific projections on various ocean industries, prepared by a variety of intergovernmental agencies, industrial associations, research institutions and consultancy companies. They offer interesting perspectives on experts' views about the uncertainties, challenges, opportunities and prospects for growth and employment, allowing a first preliminary assessment of the longer term future for a range of traditional and emerging ocean industries. The review suggests that the latter can be divided broadly into three groups: those sectors whose long-term prospects for business and employment growth are considered to be only moderate; those sectors for which global business and employment growth over the longer term is expected to be quite high; and those sectors that have significant potential but are not expected to reach commercial scale for some time yet.

Sectors with prospects for modest business and employment growth

Capture fisheries

Growth in total global production of capture fisheries has been more or less flat since the mid-1990s, hovering consistently around the 90 million tonnes mark (80 million tonnes for marine fish). Since the beginning of the Food and Agriculture Organization's (FAO) stock assessments, the proportion of assessed marine fish stocks exploited within biologically sustainable levels declined from 90% in 1974 to 71% in 2011; the proportion of over-exploited stocks has risen from around one-tenth in 1974 to below one-third in 2011. Fully fished stocks accounted for 61% and under-fished stocks for just under 10% (FAO, 2014). Against this background, the latest projections by the FAO/OECD to 2024 suggest that the current plateauing of total capture fisheries production is expected to continue at least over the coming ten years (OECD and FAO, 2015).

In addition, there is the problem of illegal, unreported and unregulated (IUU) fishing, which is estimated to have reached a global annual value of EUR 10-20 billion. This compares with the estimated annual EUR 55-60 billion of legally conducted fishing. There is currently no clear solution to IUU fishing in sight, but it has reached such a scale that it is thought that it can lead to the uncontained depletion of fish stocks. This does not bode well for the future given the precarious state of many of the world's fisheries.

Looking somewhat further ahead than the OECD/FAO report, the World Bank's baseline projection sees practically zero growth in capture fisheries output through to 2030.

Figure 7.1. **Global fish production: Data and projections, 1984-2030**

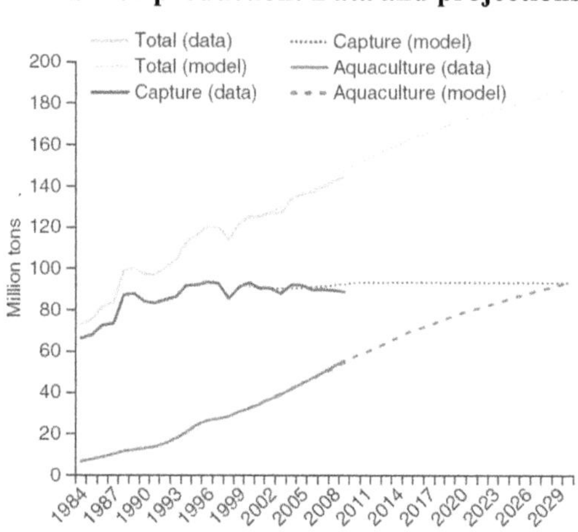

Source: World Bank (2013).

Perhaps the largest long-term threat to global capture fisheries is climate change. As Chapter 3 of this report depicts in some detail, ocean warming, rising sea levels, acidification and declining biodiversity all present a threat to wild fish stocks.

Offshore oil and gas production in deep and ultra-deep water and in the Arctic

The sector of offshore oil and gas in deep water and other extreme locations figures among those ocean-based industries which, while operating at the cutting edge of science and technology, face numerous challenges both in the short and long term. In the case of offshore oil and gas, these range from weak market demand and oversupply and concerns about safety and the ocean environment, to the new momentum gathering behind efforts to decarbonise the economy, as most recently demonstrated by the COP21 agreement. The sector's future therefore is hard to judge.

In the International Energy Agency's (IEA's) New Policies Scenario, oil and gas are expected to continue to provide approximately 50% of the energy mix in 2040, down from 52% at present. Their growth rates, however, are likely to differ significantly: oil at +0.4% per year and gas at +1.5% per year. Moreover, offshore operations are expected to continue to account for approximately 30% of global hydrocarbons production. Offshore crude oil production could thus see a significant increase in deep-water activities, at least over the medium term (50% growth in 15 years), adding to a slight decrease in production from shallow-water fields, with total production varying between approximately 25 million barrels of oil-equivalent per day (mboe/d) in 2014 and 28 mboe/d in 2040 (IEA, 2014). Strong growth in gas extraction is expected both in shallow and deep water, from slightly above 17 mboe/d in 2014 to 27 mboe/d in 2040. Total hydrocarbons (gas and oil) from offshore are expected to grow at about 3.5% per year up to 2030 (IEA, 2014). The extent to which the current persistence of low oil and gas prices will affect these projections remains to be seen, not least because ultra-deep water exploration and production come at a high cost and are often among the first projects to be shelved or deferred. By way of illustration, Douglas-Westwood (2016) has recently revised down its forecast of deep-water investment for 2016-20 to USD 137 billion, a 35% decline compared to its 2015 forecast.

Moreover, offshore costs are also affected by the fact that the new discoveries being made are getting smaller as time goes by. The average lifetime of the field is shrinking from around 25 to 15 years, and in some cases even less. So instead of having to find and produce the equivalent of 4% of total offshore hydrocarbons each year, the figure has climbed to about 7%, i.e. each year the industry must find and put into production the equivalent of roughly 3 million barrels per day just to maintain production at its current level. As a result, the industry is increasingly obliged to explore new frontiers to find new competitive hydrocarbon reserves, frontiers that all harbour their own particular challenges (Borelli, forthcoming). According to Borelli, the possible options open for the period 2015-30 are:

- increase the recovery rate from the reservoir
- develop offshore gas production, treatment and export
- develop unproduced geology plays in shallow, deep and ultra-deep water (beyond 1 500 metres [m])
- develop new areas in remote and extreme environments, such as Arctic fields
- develop unconventional hydrocarbons, such as extra-heavy oil or shale oil and gas
- pursue, over the longer term, offshore gas (methane) hydrates production.

As Borelli (forthcoming) notes, progress on each of these avenues varies considerably. For example:

- With respect to increasing the recovery rate of reserves, the objective is to advance extraction from an average of 35-40% of the total reserve in place to 60%, mainly through reservoir management and enhanced oil recovery/intelligent oil recovery techniques.
- The Arctic is thought to hold some 30% of the world's undiscovered gas and 13% of its undiscovered oil. While most of the offshore drilling would be in less than 500 m of water, the conditions in the Arctic are extremely hostile and environmental safety is written large in such a pristine environment. It is very likely that exploration and production in the Arctic will move forward fastest on the Yamal Peninsula and in the Barents and Kara Seas, and at the Arctic Circle (Borelli, forthcoming). However, the technical and operational challenges increase rapidly as operations move closer to the pole. Although the industry is working hard at resolving the challenges, many experts consider it unlikely that exploration and production of hydrocarbons at a commercially viable price can be undertaken in these regions in the near future. Moreover, the vulnerability of the Arctic's ecosystems to human activity, especially in the summer months when frequented by migratory birds, marine mammals, fish, etc., raises the likelihood of strong opposition to hydrocarbon production in the region. And in the aftermath of the COP21, the widely anticipated gearing-up of climate change policies could further dampen the outlook for oil and gas exploration in the region.
- As for methane hydrates, the technology to deliver a viable supply of natural gas from methane hydrates is still in its infancy. Successful tests have been conducted in onshore permafrost areas (e.g. Canada and Alaska [United States]), and offshore long-term production tests have been running in Japan since 2014. However, after the scientific study phase, methane hydrate exploration and production will have to be studied from a technological and industrial standpoint to enable operators to arrive at the conclusion of where and when this resource can be developed in economic conditions. In general, it seems the methane hydrates commercial exploitation is unlikely to start before 2030 in view of the challenges involved, not least the task of addressing the potential environmental consequences.

Hence, growth prospects in this sector are clouded. In addition, with increasing use of automation and remote management, employment creation is expected to continue to drift upstream from exploration and production towards supplies, equipment, and research and development (R&D).

Sectors with prospects for high long-term growth of business and employment

Shipping

At a global scale, developments in seaborne trade are closely associated with changes in real gross domestic product (GDP). Generally, a 1% increase in real GDP corresponds to a 1.1% growth in seaborne trade (as measured in tonnes). On that basis, seaborne trade is expected to grow by 4.3% in 2016, 4.1% per year over the period 2017-19, 4.0% per annum on average over 2020-29, and 3.3% between 2030 and 2040. Long-term growth in container traffic is expected to be broadly in line with that for total seaborne trade, while below average growth is expected in tanker and bulk cargos. Very fast growth, on the other hand, is foreseen in the category "others", which comprehends such types as LPG/LNG, passenger roll-on/roll-off transport, cruise and other seaborne passenger traffic.

Figure 7.2. **Seaborne trade projection, 1985-2040 (in million tonnes)**

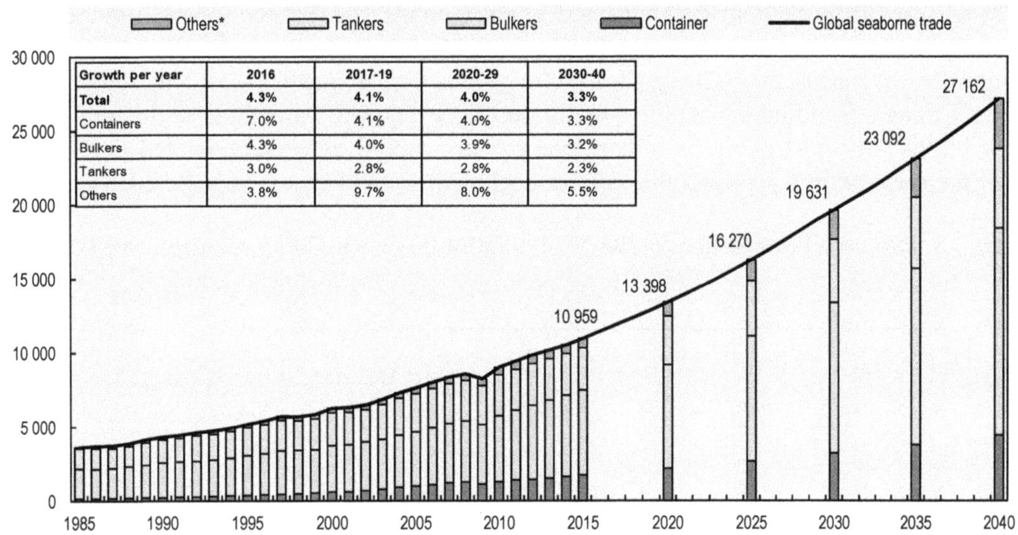

Growth per year	2016	2017-19	2020-29	2030-40
Total	**4.3%**	**4.1%**	**4.0%**	**3.3%**
Containers	7.0%	4.1%	4.0%	3.3%
Bulkers	4.3%	4.0%	3.9%	3.2%
Tankers	3.0%	2.8%	2.8%	2.3%
Others	3.8%	9.7%	8.0%	5.5%

Source: OECD (2015b).

Shipbuilding

The significant long-term growth expected in seaborne trade is projected to be reflected in shipbuilding. Shipbuilding growth is influenced by a range of factors such as underlying global trade expansion, energy consumption and prices, vessel age profiles, ship retirement/scrapping and replacement, changes in cargo types and trade patterns, etc. But to a very large extent, it also depends on existing capacity. In recent years, there has been a considerable build-up of overcapacity: in the last ten years, the global shipping fleet (measured in dwt) grew at an average rate of 7% per year by far outstripping the 3.8% p.a. notched up by world seaborne trade (tonnes). By 2013, as a consequence, cumulative oversupply had reached an estimated 83 million gross tonnage (GT) in tankers, 113 million GT in bulk carriers and 48 million GT in container vessels (equivalent to more than one-quarter of the entire container fleet worldwide). Depending on assumptions made, oversupply in the global shipbuilding market could persist until 2020 or even 2030 (OECD, forthcoming). Despite that overhang, the next 20 years could see significant growth in new building requirements. Forecasting models provide rough indications that new build gross tonnage could roughly double between 2015 and 2030.

In addition to shipbuilding's dependence on future trends in seaborne trade, there are of course strong linkages to developments in other maritime sectors, notably offshore oil and gas, offshore wind, cruise tourism, capture fisheries and marine aquaculture. Despite the current low oil prices, the demand for drillships, semi-submersibles, floating production units (FPSOs), etc. is expected to hold up at least over the medium and long term, and production of supply and maintenance vessels for platforms, anchor handling, offshore wind farms, etc. is expected to grow markedly through to 2025/30 (SEA, 2015). Indeed, expectations are for an increase in demand of almost 4% per year for all offshore vessel types between 2014 and 2025, driven over the longer term by growing offshore oil and gas supply in deep offshore fields (OECD, 2015a). On the strength of rising demand in marine tourism, extra cruise ship new building requirements are expected to be in the range of six to eight vessels per year between 2015 and 2031 (SEA, 2015). Finally, despite the difficult overall global context (fish stock depletion, a likely rise in fish quota restrictions and a likely decrease in the world fishing fleet size), demand for new fishing vessels (measured both in compensated gross tonnage (CGT) and vessel numbers) is expected to increase quite strongly in the next 20 years, from around 175 vessels per annum in the period 2016-20 to about 346 vessels a year in 2031-35. This will be due mainly to an expanding aquaculture sector and fleet renewal. Nonetheless, the number of new builds will most likely be outstripped by the amount of vessels deleted from fleets over the same period, resulting in a further decline in world fleet size (SEA, 2015).

Figure 7.3. **Past vessel completions (1995-2014) and future new building requirements (2015-35)**

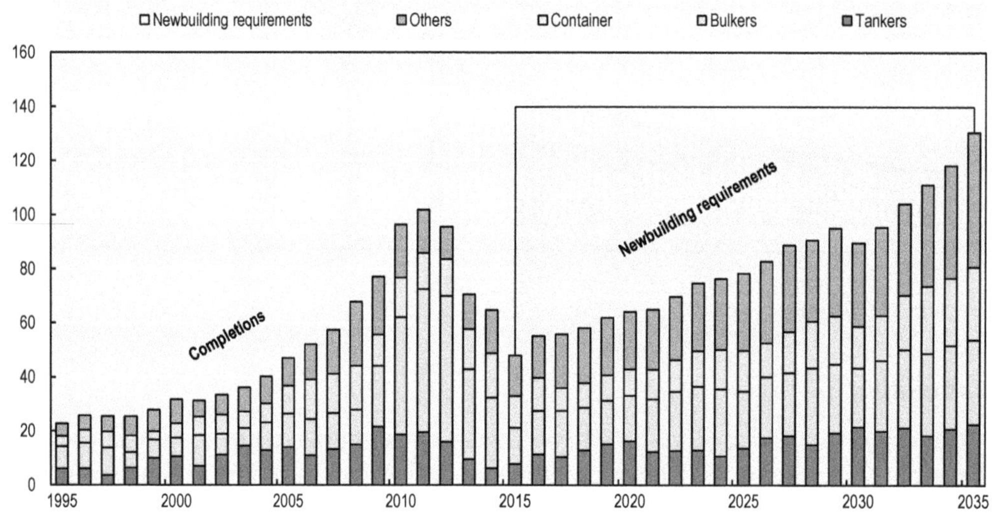

Source: OECD (2015b).

Offshore wind

Over the last 20 years, the offshore wind sector has progressed from the first small pilot project to a nascent industry with the potential for significant further growth. Current global installed capacity is greater than 7 gigawatts (GW), while projections suggest there is potential for 40-60 GW by 2020 and growth of a further order of magnitude by 2050.

There are a number of existing projections from different sources regarding the likely growth of the sector. They span varying timescales and are developed upon differing fundamental assumptions (e.g. the need to meet specified objectives, such as decarbonising the global economy), meaning that immediate comparisons are only partially possible. While none of the projections are inherently more robust or accurate than the others, they are broadly compatible in expecting offshore wind to have accrued a sizeable market share by 2050. In the more optimistic scenarios, it is predicted there could be almost 400 GW of offshore wind installed by 2030 and approximately 900 GW by 2050.

Such growth is dependent upon the industry driving down costs across all elements of the supply chain and becoming cost-effective *vis-à-vis* alternative sources of energy, including both traditional forms (most notably oil and gas) and alternative renewables.

Projections indicate that there is considerable future potential for global job creation from offshore wind. As with deployment figures, the bulk of offshore wind employment is expected to be concentrated in the People's Republic of China (hereafter "China"), the European Union, India and the United States. Projections for Europe alone suggest the creation of around 170 000 jobs by 2020 and 300 000 jobs by 2030. Projections are, however, about gross impacts and do not account for wider macroeconomic effects such as job losses/gains in other energy-related sectors.

Marine aquaculture

Global demand for fish food is expected to continue to rise over the next decades, as a consequence of increased world population, growing purchasing power and more people entering the middle class. The optimistic scenario in the FAO's (FAO, 2014) recent publication assumes an aquaculture production increase of 58% by 2022 (4.3% per year). Indeed, it is expected that most of the future growth in seafood production will be through aquaculture, making it an increasingly important component of global food security and a major driver of change in the fisheries and aquaculture sector.

Looking further ahead, the World Bank's baseline projection also expects aquaculture to continue to grow over the period to 2030, albeit at a decelerating rate, falling to below 2% per year by 2030. Nonetheless, in terms of food fish production, it would account for 62% of the global supply destined for direct human consumption by the end of the projection period (World Bank, 2013).

Marine aquaculture accounts for about one-half of total global aquaculture production. It can roughly be divided by species into four groups; finfish, crustaceans, molluscs and aquatic plants. Aquatic plants and molluscs are produced in far higher quantities than finfish, with finfish accounting in 2013 for only 10% of the marine aquaculture production volume (in tonnes) and aquatic plants for more than 50%. When viewed in terms of production value on the other hand, the relative value of finfish was almost two-fifths of total marine aquaculture, while aquatic plants accounted for less than 10% (FAO, 2015). The expected expansion in aquaculture production capacity will occur largely in the ocean.

It is conceivable that marine aquaculture could be sustained at a higher rate than projected in the above studies. However, this would require significant progress on a number of fronts, including reduction of the environmental impact of fish farms in coastal regions, improved disease management, significantly higher proportions of non-fish feed for carnivorous species, and more rapid advances in the engineering and technologies required to establish offshore aquaculture operations.

Marine tourism

Despite occasional shocks, international tourist arrivals have shown steady growth over the past six decades, from 25 million in 1950 to 1 087 million in 2013 (UNWTO, 2011). International tourist arrivals worldwide are expected to increase by 3.3% a year from 2010 to 2030, to reach 1.4 billion by 2020 and 1.8 billion by 2030. This implies an annual average increase of around 43 million international tourists globally. Up to 2030 at least, international tourist arrivals in the emerging economy destinations of Asia, Latin America, Central and Eastern Europe, eastern Mediterranean Europe, the Middle East and Africa will grow at double the rate (+4.4% a year) of that in advanced economy destinations (+2.2% a year). The market share of emerging economies will increase from 47% in 2013 to 57% by 2030 (UNWTO, 2011).

While lack of international statistics make it difficult to estimate the share of marine tourism in the overall total (guestimates are in the range of 10%, see Dwyer, forthcoming), recent developments suggest that marine tourism is set to grow at faster rates than international tourism as a whole. Cruise tourism is a case in point.

Economic modelling of the economic impact of cruise tourism for 2013 estimated that 114.87 million onshore visits by cruise lines, passengers and crew generated USD 52.31 billion in direct cruise sector expenditures at destinations and source markets around the world. In total, these expenditures generated total (direct, indirect and induced) global output of USD 117.15 billion. The production of this output required the employment of 891 009 full-time equivalent employees who earned USD 38.47 billion in income (BREA, 2014).

Projections by the Korean Ministry of Oceans and Fisheries see world cruise tourist numbers climbing from 21 million in 2013 to 37 million in 2020, an increase of around 10% per annum. Asia is set to register quite spectacular cruise tourism growth rates, from 1.3 million in 2013 to 7 million in 2020 (Lee, H.-J., 2015). In a similar vein, the SEA (2015) projects global cruise passenger numbers to almost triple between 2010 and 2035, from 19 million passengers in 2010 to over 54 million in 2035, implying annual growth rates of well over 7%.

Figure 7.4. **Projected growth in global cruise tourism to 2035**

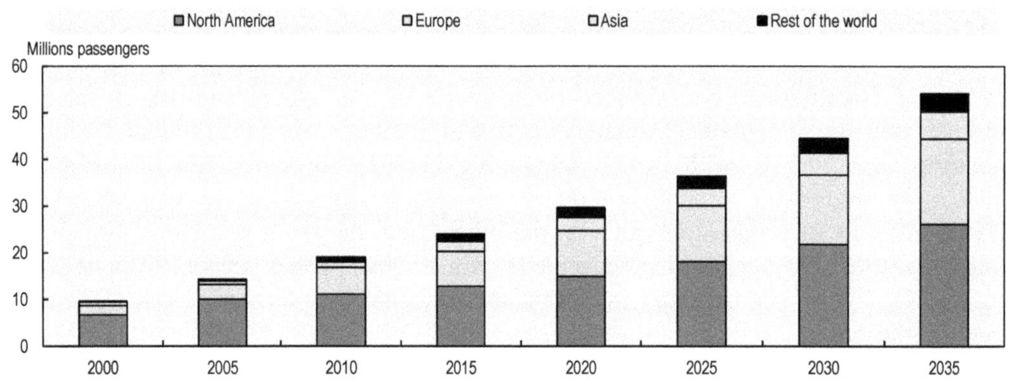

Source: SEA (2015).

Maritime surveillance and safety

Over the last few decades, the panorama of risks and challenges needing to be addressed by the maritime safety industry has changed enormously. Ships have grown ever bigger (the largest container ship built in 1968 was 1 530 TEU; 2018 could see the launch of the first 22 000 TEU container vessel); trade flows of potentially hazardous freight (e.g. liquefied natural gas) are growing apace; cases of intra-state conflict and civil war have multiplied; piracy has become a major concern in several regions of the world; new destinations in hostile but pristine areas of the globe (such as the Arctic) are emerging as likely game-changers for world shipping; new uses of the ocean (e.g. ultra-deep water oil and gas, wind turbines, aquaculture, renewable ocean energy) are multiplying; environmental issues are a growing challenge to all ocean users; and disruptive technologies are already clearly discernible on the horizon (e-navigation, autonomous and unmanned vessels, remote operation of offshore platforms, etc.). These and other factors are set to act as drivers behind the expansion of the maritime surveillance and safety industry.

Definitions of the maritime safety industry vary considerably, making valuations and forecasts extremely difficult. It can include maritime safety devices and equipment, ICT infrastructures and applications, marine accident prevention services, and maritime rescue and salvage and pollution response services. On a broader definition, maritime security is considered to encompass, among others, LNG tanker and LNG ports security, satellite-based maritime tracking, piracy mitigation, coast guard missions, container screening and Ship Automatic Identification System. On that basis, the size of the global maritime security market was expected to amount to around USD 13 billion by 2014 (HSRC, 2009). Estimates suggest the global maritime and border security market is expected to be worth USD 15.6 billion in 2015, rising to USD 23.7 billion by 2025 (some USD 9 billion of which would be accounted for by maritime surveillance and detection). This would constitute a compound annual average growth rate in the order of well over 4% (SDI, 2015).

Sectors with significant long-term potential but not operating at commercial scale for some time to come

Ocean renewable energy

The ocean contains a massive source of potential energy waiting to be harnessed. In many countries, ocean energy – tidal, wave, current, osmosis, ocean thermal energy conversion (OTEC) – is regarded as an important future source of power generation for the transition to a low-carbon future. Commercial interest in ocean energy is growing significantly at a global level, and according to the Ocean Energy Systems Implementing Agreement (OES), there is the potential worldwide to develop 337 GW of wave and tidal energy by 2050, and possibly as much again from OTEC. The OES "International vision" (2012) suggests that, in addition to generating large amounts of renewable power, deployment of ocean energy can also provide sizable benefits in terms of employment – up to 1.2 million direct jobs by 2050. Moreover, experience with early large-scale prototype construction shows that widely distributed industries are involved in the supply chain for components. In Europe, the ocean energy supply chains are pan-European. Examples include the manufacture of tidal turbines, hydro-turbines and steel spare parts (for power plants) in Austria; wave power plants and generators in Germany; and wave power attenuators and over-topping devices in Denmark. Hence, large engineering conglomerates are actively involved in many of the large-scale prototype projects being undertaken internationally. They see the development of this sector as providing significant opportunities to grow markets, utilising their core industrial capabilities (Sweeney, forthcoming).

However, many obstacles stand in the way of its development to full potential. Indeed, ocean energy technologies are still in an early demonstration phase of single units, largely involving short-duration testing deployments, with only a few prototypes initiating the first steps towards the commercialisation phase. Research efforts and funding are spread over many different wave and marine current energy concepts, and there is still no technology convergence, in contrast to wind energy. Investment costs are high, and in times of low oil and gas prices (as is currently the case), operational viability compares unfavourably with alternative power sources. Especially in Western economies, technologies are developing only slowly. Consequently, the 2020 global installed capacity will be relatively small. Game-changing technological breakthroughs, however, could lead to rapid increases in gigawatt capacity thereafter.

Deep-sea mining

The mineral resource potential of the deep sea is generally considered, even among sceptics, to be huge. However, the extent of that potential is extremely difficult to assess with any accuracy. The oceans cover more than 360 million square kilometres (km^2), and only a fraction has been explored.

All offshore mining today is in shallow water – generally less than 300 m of water depth – on the continental shelf areas. There is the potential for current offshore mining to expand into deeper water, but it is thought unlikely that this type of mining will extend beyond the limits of the continental shelf. Conversely, most targets for deep-sea mining are at far greater water depths. However, some deep-sea resources are within claims to the extended continental shelf areas, and their development could potentially overlap with areas currently occupied for other uses (Hannington, forthcoming).

Deep-sea mining is mainly concerned with three classes of mineral deposits: manganese nodules, cobalt-rich ferromanganese crusts and seafloor massive sulphide (SMS) deposits. They occur in all of the world's oceans, but they are not evenly distributed.

Although exploration licenses have been granted for all three types of deep-sea mineral resources, the main projects continue to be focused on nodules. More than 80% of the currently known manganese nodule fields (by area) are located beyond national jurisdictions. Only about 15% of the fields are in economic exclusion zones (EEZs) and another 5% may be included in current applications for extensions of the continental shelf (Hannington, forthcoming).

Considerable interest has been raised recently by reports of high concentrations of rare earth elements (REE) in deep-sea clays of the Pacific. Japanese and Korean scientists have tested the resource potential and, although the processing of the muds by hydrometallurgical methods is technically feasible, there have been no reports of a meaningful resource potential. None of the REE is present in any deep-sea mineral deposits at concentrations higher than can be found in land-based ores. In the case of deep-sea muds, many millions of tonnes of mud would have to be mined and processed per year to impact the REE markets.

UNCLOS established the International Seabed Authority (ISA) to supervise deep-sea mining in the areas beyond national jurisdiction (the "Area"). There are currently no commercial deep-sea mining operations under way in the Area, only exploration activities. These are conducted under contract to the ISA, and there are currently 26 active exploration licenses or pending applications for exploration of deep-sea minerals. Twenty-two applications have been approved: 14 for manganese nodules, 5 for SMS deposits and 3 for cobalt-rich crusts. Most of the exploration projects are located in the Clarion Clipperton Zone (CCZ) of the east-central Pacific. Collectively they cover an area of more than 1 million km^2. The remaining projects are located in the Indian Ocean (4), the Atlantic Ocean (2) and the northwest Pacific Ocean (2). Importantly, six of the exploration licenses in the CCZ will expire in 2016, but no exploitation/mining licenses have been issued (Hannington, forthcoming).

It is more difficult to track exploration licenses within national jurisdictions, as there is no single organisation or database where this information is collected. Recent reports and anecdotal evidence indicate that at least 26 projects may be active in EEZ areas. Two commercial companies (Nautilus Minerals and Neptune Minerals) hold a large proportion of the exploration licenses within EEZs, almost exclusively in the southwest Pacific, and all for SMS deposits. Although the sizes of the areas granted for exploration or under application in EEZs are not fully known, an estimated 800 000-900 000 km^2 have been granted or have pending applications in at least 10 different countries. Much larger areas are being explored by government agencies in Japan. In Europe, there have been three applications for SMS exploration projects (one in Italy, one in Norway and one in the Azores), but the details are not available. There is anecdotal evidence that projects may have started in South America, Africa, China and the Russian Federation, but it is expected that the number of projects in these jurisdictions is limited.

Among the major drivers of deep-sea mining are the perceived shortages of metals from land-based mining and the prospects of new resources from the oceans. But despite a doubling of the global population in recent decades and more intensive use of energy and mineral resources, reserves have grown steadily with consumption. There is no indication that the availability of conventional resources cannot continue to keep pace with growth. This applies also to the metals of interest in deep-sea mineral deposits. It is highly improbable that long-term shortages will occur up to 2050, even with an increase in world population of another 30-35%. Therefore, there is no reason to move into deep-sea mining because we are running out of resources (Hannington, forthcoming).

For some countries, the goals are increased security of supply of raw materials for their manufacturing industries. Still other countries have large service sectors for the marine industries that see the opportunity to benefit from demand for new technology (e.g. survey technologies, robotics, geophysical applications, heavy lifting and other marine equipment). The notion that smaller countries with access to those resources could benefit financially from their exploitation is also an important motivation, although few have the capability to properly manage future mining projects.

A fundamental challenge for operators and regulators in assessing that potential is that there are still no examples of deep-sea mining that could serve as benchmarks for analysis – production of minerals has not yet started, even in the most prospective areas of the oceans. As a result, there are no economic data (revenues, capital expenditures, job creation, etc.) to report or consider.

National governments holding exploration licenses are likely, wherever possible, to use national companies to perform the needed activities. In this way jobs and knowledge are created at home. In addition to future "mines", service and maintenance will be required that will create additional employment among marine contractors. However, according to Hannington (forthcoming), the lack of infrastructure compared to land-based mining activities and the high degree of automation expected in deep-sea mining is unlikely to result in significant employment (hundreds rather than thousands of new jobs for a new "mine").

The problematic economic outlook for wider-scale deep-sea mining is further complicated by the environmental issues surrounding the extraction of minerals from the seabed. As Chapter 5 of this report indicates in more detail, there is great concern about the potential disturbance and damage that could be inflicted on ocean-floor and deep-water ecosystems about which very little is known. What does seem to be certain is that deep-sea ecosystems are highly vulnerable and interconnected, and environmental assessment and precautionary approaches are therefore increasingly advocated.

Marine biotechnology

Marine biotechnology has the potential to address a raft of major global challenges such as sustainable food supplies, human health, energy security and environmental remediation, and to make a significant contribution to green growth in many industrial sectors. At the same time, marine bio-resources also provide a number of important ecosystem services for the planet and its inhabitants which must be maintained. Notwithstanding difficulties of definition, the global market for marine biotechnology products and processes is a significant and growing opportunity. In 2010 it was estimated at around USD 2.8 billion and, on the basis of quite conservative assumptions, is projected to grow to around USD 4.6 billion by 2017 (OECD, 2013).

Figure 7.5. **Depth ranges of possible future mining activities and jurisdictions in the deep sea**

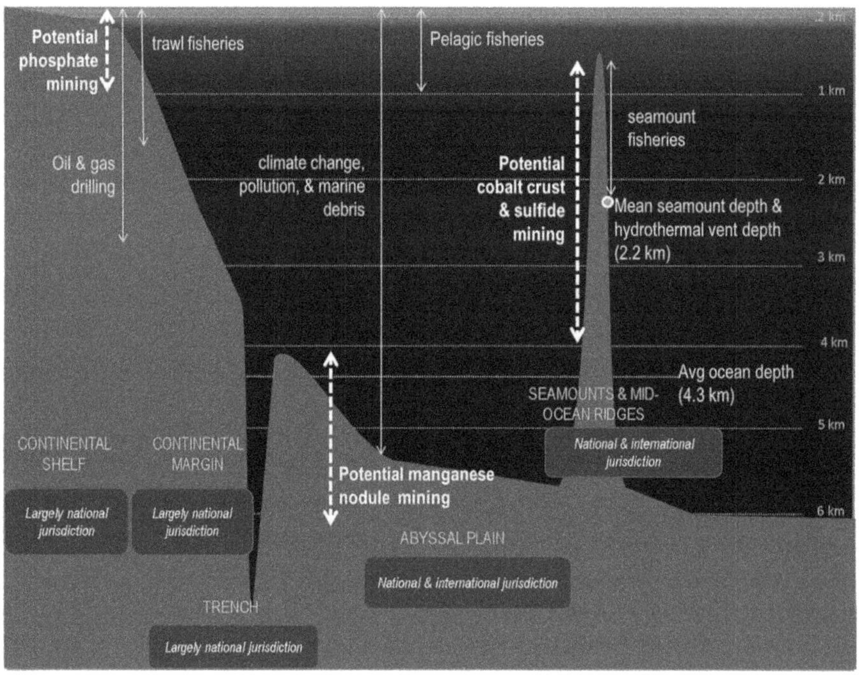

Source: Mengerink et al. (2014).

On the health front, there has been increasing interest in marine microbes, particularly bacteria, with studies demonstrating that they are a rich source of potential drugs. Antimicrobial resistance has been identified by the World Health Organization (WHO) as one of the three greatest threats to human health, so finding new strains to develop drugs is a high priority. There is also optimism about the prospects of marine bio-based cancer treatments. The complex marine ecosystem, with its large number of yet undiscovered microbial species and undiscovered properties even of known marine species, presents a rich and largely untapped resource base. That resource base is growing. Poccia (2015), for example, notes that "in a 2010 survey there were 4 approved pharmaceuticals, 2 in Phase III testing, 7 in Phase II and 4 in Phase I. Five years later, this list had grown to 7 approved, 2 Phase III, 6 Phase II, 3 Phase I/II and 14 Phase I. Thus in 5 years the number of approved pharmaceuticals and total pharmaceuticals in the medical testing pipeline has almost doubled." One area in which marine biotechnology may make a critical contribution is the development of new antibiotics. Other promising areas include biomedical products such as anti-bacterial and anti-fungal properties, as well as nutraceuticals and cosmeceuticals.

Marine biotechnology has also displayed widespread commercial potential in industrial products and processes, and in the life sciences industry as a novel source of enzymes and polymers. It is providing a source of synthetic substitutes for many high-value chemicals derived from fossil raw materials, and is being extensively applied in environmental monitoring, bioremediation and prevention of bio-fouling. Despite these successes, limited knowledge of marine genetic diversity still constrains the potential development of industrial applications and innovations.

On the energy front, algal biofuels appear to offer quite bright prospects. According to the European Science Foundation Marine Board (2010), a theoretical production volume of 20 000-80 000 litres of oil per hectare per year can be achieved from micro-algal culture, whereby only the lower end of the band seems to be achievable with the current technology. (This is nonetheless considerably higher than biofuel from terrestrial crops.) Cost-competitive, high-volume algae biofuel production is still some ways off and will require more long-term research, development and demonstration. Nonetheless, in recent years quite remarkable progress has been made towards demonstrating the feasibility of large-scale micro-algal biodiesel production (Lee, 2015).

Carbon capture and storage

Carbon capture and storage (CCS) is widely considered a potentially game-changing set of technologies in reducing CO_2 emissions. Interest is growing in storing CO_2 in saline aquifers due to their enormous storage capacity, and several demonstration projects are in operation or in the pipeline. It is also claimed to have considerable employment-creating potential.[1] However, there is still a very long way to go to establishing CCS on a significant scale. Among the main hurdles that need to be overcome are the lack of a legal and regulatory framework and wider public support. Above all, however, there does not yet appear to be a clear business case for CCS investment nor robust economic incentives (Leung, Caramanna and Maroto-Valer, 2014). Indeed, as the IEA points out: "… Climate policies in all but a couple of countries have yet to make an economic case for CO_2 storage that compensates for the up-front costs of exploration and storage site development, let alone the costs of capturing CO_2" (IEA, 2015). The recent COP21 agreement may, however, provide some of the necessary stimulus to step up investment.

Concluding observations

While the above review provides useful indications as to the long-term growth prospects of the maritime industries, it does so in a very disparate fashion. In particular, in order to assess the prospects of the maritime economy as a coherent whole, it is not meaningful to simply aggregate the different projections. They are built on different macroeconomic assumptions, apply different timelines, draw to a large extent on non-official data sources and deploy different methodologies. Merely aggregating the projections would run the risk of double counting, would ignore important interlinkages among industries and sectors, and would neglect changes in productivity which are important for the development trajectories of many of the industries. In order to overcome or at least mitigate the severity of these problems, the project team has developed a model – in collaboration with several other OECD departments – which permits a more coherent and consistent projection of a large set of ocean-based industries. The model and the preliminary findings are presented in Chapter 8.

1. See, for example, for the United Kingdom: www.theguardian.com/environment/2010/mar/17/carbon-capture-and-storage-strategy.

References

Borelli, A. (forthcoming), "Offshore oil and gas: The new frontiers", *OECD Science, Technology and Industry Working Papers*, OECD Publishing, Paris, forthcoming.

BREA (2014), "The global economic contribution of the cruise tourism 2013", report prepared for CLIA, Business Research & Economic Advisors, Exton, Pennsylvania, www.cruising.org/docs/default-source/research/global_cruise_impact_analysis_2013.pdf?sfvrsn=2.

Douglas-Westwood (2016), *World Deepwater Market Forecast 2016-2020,* Douglas-Westwood.

Dwyer, L. (forthcoming), "The future of marine and coastal tourism", *OECD Science, Technology and Industry Working Papers*, OECD Publishing, Paris, forthcoming.

European Science Foundation Marine Board (2010), "Marine biotechnology: A new vision and strategy for Europe", *Position Paper 15*, September, Marine Board-ESF, Ostend, Belgium, www.esf.org/fileadmin/Public_documents/Publications/marine_biotechnology_01.pdf.

FAO (2015), *Global Aquaculture Production* (database), updated to 2013, Summary information, www.fao.org/fishery/statistics/global-aquaculture-production/query/en.

FAO (2014), *The State of World Fisheries and Aquaculture*, Food and Agriculture Organization, Rome, www.fao.org/3/a-i3720e.pdf.

Hannington, M. (forthcoming), "Prospects and challenges of deep sea mining", *OECD Science, Technology and Industry Working Papers*, OECD Publishing, Paris, forthcoming.

HSRC (2009), *Global Maritime Security Technologies & Markets – 2010-2014*, Homeland Security Research Corporation, Washington, DC.

IEA (2015), *Energy Policy Perspectives 2015*, OECD Publishing, Paris, http://dx.doi.org/10.1787/energy_tech-2015-en.

IEA (2014), *World Energy Outlook 2014*, International Energy Agency, Paris, http://dx.doi.org/10.1787/weo-2014-en.

Lee, C.-G. (2015), "Marine (microalgal) biotechnology from engineering perspectives", presentation at OECD workshop on "The Long-term Potential of Marine Biotechnology", Plentzia, Basque Country (Spain), 29-30 September.

Lee, H.-J. (2015), "Cruises seen as new profit engine", *Korea JoongAng Daily*, 8 May, http://koreajoongangdaily.joins.com/news/article/article.aspx?aid=3003921.

Leung, D.Y.C., G. Caramanna and M.M. Maroto-Valer (2014), "An overview of current status of carbon dioxide capture and storage technologies", *Renewable and*

Sustainable Energy Reviews, Vol. 39, November, pp. 426-443, http://dx.doi.org/10.1016/j.rser.2014.07.093.

Liebender, A.-S. et al. (forthcoming), "Measuring the global economic contribution of ocean-based industries – Methodology paper", *OECD Science, Technology and Industry Working Papers*, OECD Publishing, Paris, forthcoming.

Mengerink, K. et al. (2014), "A call for deep-ocean stewardship", *Science*, Vol. 344, 16 May, www.iris.no/environment/pdf/Mengerink%20et%20al_%202014.pdf.

OECD (2015a), "Shipbuilding and the offshore industry", C/WP6(2015)5/FINAL, OECD, Paris, www.oecd.org/sti/ind/Shipbuilding-and-offshore-industry.pdf (accessed 1 February 2016).

OECD (2015b), "Oversupply in the shipbuilding industry", www.oecd.org/sti/ind/shipbuilding.htm.

OECD (2013), *Marine Biotechnology: Enabling Solutions for Ocean Productivity and Sustainability*, OECD Publishing, Paris, http://dx.doi.org/10.1787/9789264194243-en.

OECD and FAO (2015), *Agricultural Outlook 2015*, OECD Publishing, Paris, http://dx.doi.org/10.1787/agr_outlook-2015-en.

OES (2012), "An international vision for ocean energy", brochure, Ocean Energy Systems, www.ocean-energy-systems.org/documents/81542_oes_vision_brochure_2011.pdf.

Poccia, D. (2015), "Human health, basic research, and marine stations", Extended abstract prepared for the OECD workshop on "The Long-term Potential of Marine Biotechnology", Plentzia, Basque Country (Spain), 29-30 September.

Schlumberger (2015), presentation at Scotia Howard Weil Energy Conference, March.

SDI (2015), *The Global Maritime and Border Security Market 2015-2025*, August, Strategic Defence Intelligence.

SEA (2015), *2014 Market Forecast Report*, SEA Europe, Ships & Maritime Equipment Association, www.seaeurope.eu/template.asp?f=publications.asp&jaar=2015.

Sweeney, E. (forthcoming), "Prospects for ocean energy to 2030", *OECD Science, Technology and Industry Working Papers*, OECD Publishing, Paris, forthcoming.

UNWTO (2011), *Tourism Towards 2030/Global Overview*, Advanced edition presented at UNWTO 19th General Assembly, 10 October, World Tourism Organization, www.e-unwto.org/doi/book/10.18111/9789284414024.

World Bank (2013), "Fish to 2030: Prospects for fisheries and aquaculture", *Agriculture and Environmental Services Discussion Paper 03*, World Bank, Washington, DC, http://documents.worldbank.org/curated/en/2013/12/18882045/fish-2030-prospects-fisheries-aquaculture.

Chapter 8.

Ocean industries to 2030

Building on the OECD Ocean Economy Database *and the model described in Annex 8.A1 and in much more detail in a forthcoming OECD working paper, this chapter presents the development of the ocean economy to 2030 under a "business-as-usual" scenario, followed by two alternative scenarios.*

It should be emphasised from the outset that the scenarios are not forecasts. Rather they are projections whose purpose here is to explore how ocean-based industries might evolve in the next couple of decades on the basis of a set of underlying assumptions, e.g. on economic growth, environmental degradation and technological innovation.

The scenarios provide insights into the possible prospects for growth and employment in ocean industries, and help to identify likely upcoming issues and challenges, for example the potential impact of rapid growth of ocean industries on the ocean environment, its consequences for the use of maritime space and implications for ocean spatial management.

Global value added (GVA) in the ocean economy in 2030 (in constant 2010 USD) is estimated to grow to more than USD 3 trillion – roughly equivalent to German GDP in 2010 – thereby maintaining its 2.5% share of total world GVA (estimated at USD 120 billion GVA in 2030). Maritime and coastal tourism, including the cruise industry, is expected to take the largest share (26%), followed by offshore oil and gas exploration and production with 22% and port activities with 16%. In 2030, the ocean-based industries in the business-as-usual scenario are anticipated to employ more than 40 million (roughly the size of Germany's labour force), representing more than 1% of the global workforce of around 3.8 billion people (including part-time, self-employed and unemployed people).[1] A majority would be working in the industrial capture fisheries sector and maritime and coastal tourism industry. More than half of the ocean-based industries are projected to see their value-added rise more quickly than that of the global economy. Almost all of these industries would see employment growth outpace that in the world economy as a whole.

Business-as-usual scenario

The business-as-usual scenario, or baseline scenario, assumes a continuation of past trends, no major policy changes, no abrupt technological or environmental developments, and no major shocks or surprises. Value added and employment growth in the ocean-based industries continue to progress along the same trajectory as in the past reference period. The model designed for this project requires country- and industry-specific employment and physical capital stock to be extrapolated under the assumption that past growth rates continue until 2030. These values are then substituted into the Cobb-Douglas production function to compute employment and value added in 2030 for fisheries, fish processing, water transport, and shipbuilding and repair. It is more difficult to make such projections for those industries that are not included in the International Standard Industrial Classification of All Economic Activities (ISIC) Rev.3. For these industries, value added and employment to 2030 are computed by applying industry-specific methodologies.[2]

This approach has several important advantages. First, it allows the specifics of each industry to be taken into consideration. In particular, it permits precise and realistic projections based on expert knowledge and empirical evidence. Second, this approach allows considerable flexibility in the construction of the scenarios. Assumptions about the paths of the separate sectors lead to a rich set of possible scenarios for the ocean-based industries. Third, the approach allows the interdependencies between the different sectors to be explicitly modelled, to the extent that data permit.[3]

In addition, the last section of the chapter offers two alternative scenarios – "sustainable growth" and "unsustainable growth" – which shape the future ocean economy in two different directions, one accelerating and the other slowing the future development of the ocean-based industries by 2030.

Summary of the results

Table 8.1 summarises the results of the business-as-usual projections. It compares rates of change of value added and employment in ocean-based industries between 2010 and 2030. The compound annual growth rate for value added of the ocean-based industries combined between 2010 and 2030 is estimated at 3.45%, broadly in line with the anticipated compound annual growth rate for value added of the global economy. However, the total growth of employment (approximately 30%) in the ocean-based industries over the 20-year period is expected to outpace markedly the overall growth rate of the global workforce (approximately 20%).

Table 8.1. **Overview of estimates of industry-specific growth rates in value added and employment between 2010 and 2030**

Industry	Compound annual growth rate for GVA between 2010 and 2030	Total change in GVA between 2010 and 2030	Total change in employment between 2010 and 2030
Industrial marine aquaculture	5.69%	303%	152%
Industrial capture fisheries	4.10%	223%	94%
Industrial fish processing	6.26%	337%	206%
Maritime and coastal tourism	3.51%	199%	122%
Offshore oil and gas	1.17%	126%	126%
Offshore wind	24.52%	8 037%	1 257%
Port activities	4.58%	245%	245%
Shipbuilding and repair	2.93%	178%	124%
Maritime equipment	2.93%	178%	124%
Shipping	1.80%	143%	130%
Average of total ocean-based industries	**3.45%**	**197%**	**130%**
Global economy between 2010 and 2030	**3.64%**	**204%**	**120%**[1]

1. Based on projections of the global workforce, extrapolated with the UN medium fertility rate.

Source: Authors' calculations based on OECD STAN, UNIDO INDSTAT, UNSD; Lloyd's Register Group (2014; 2013); World Bank (2013); IEA (2014); FAO (2015).

Value added and employment in the ocean economy in 2030

Business-as-usual scenario

Global value added in the ocean economy in 2030 is estimated to grow to more than USD 3 trillion (in constant 2010 USD), maintaining its share of 2.5% of total global GVA (estimated at USD 120 billion for 2030).

Figure 8.1. **Value-added of the ocean economy in 2030 in the business-as-usual scenario**

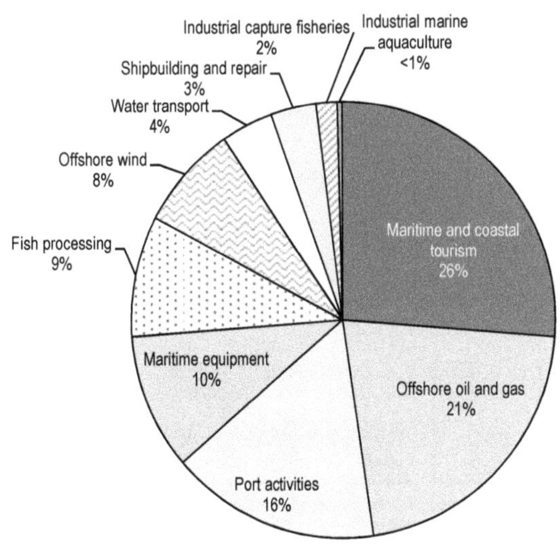

StatLink http://dx.doi.org/10.1787/888933334632

Note: Artisanal fisheries are not included in this overview.

Source: Authors' calculations based on OECD STAN, UNIDO INDSTAT, UNSD; Lloyd's Register Group (2014; 2013); World Bank (2013); IEA (2014).

Figure 8.1 shows that in a business-as-usual scenario, maritime and coastal tourism takes the largest share, accounting for more than a quarter of global value added. The second biggest share falls to offshore oil and gas exploration and production, contributing 21%, followed by port activities with 16%. Industrial fish processing and maritime equipment are estimated to account for 9% and 10% respectively. The remaining industries' shares of the market vary between 0.3% and 8%.

In 2030, the ocean-based industries in the business-as-usual scenario are anticipated to employ more than 40 million direct full-time equivalent jobs, around 1% of the global workforce (and 1.5% of the actively employed workforce, assuming a global participation rate of 63%). Figure 8.3 shows that the majority of jobs in the ocean economy are distributed among industrial capture fisheries (26%) and maritime and coastal tourism (21%).

Figure 8.2. **Overview of industry-specific value added 2010 and 2030**

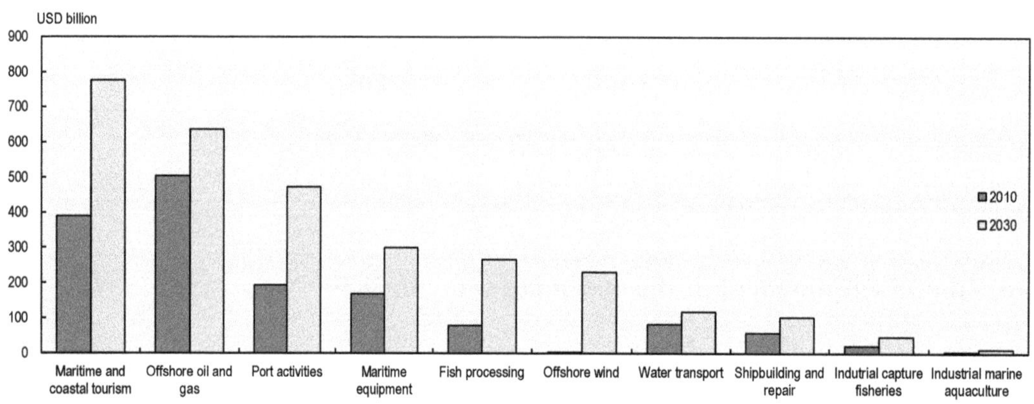

StatLink http://dx.doi.org/10.1787/888933334759

Note: Artisanal fisheries are not included in this overview.

Source: Authors' calculations based on OECD STAN, UNIDO INDSTAT, UNSD; Lloyd's Register Group (2014); Lloyd's Register Marine (2013); World Bank (2013); IEA (2014).

Figure 8.3. **Comparison of the direct employment in the ocean economy in 2010 and 2030**

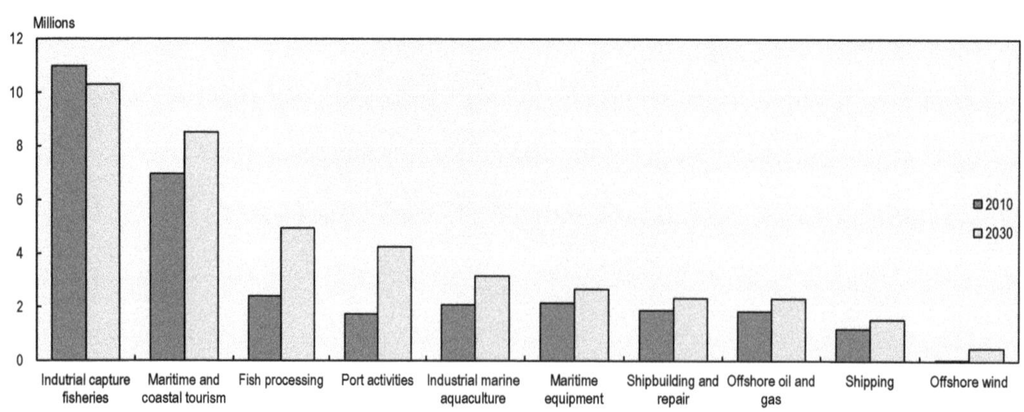

StatLink http://dx.doi.org/10.1787/888933334769

Source: Authors' calculations based on OECD STAN, UNIDO INDSTAT, UNSD; Lloyd's Register Group (2014); Lloyd's Register Marine (2013); World Bank (2013); IEA (2014); FAO (2015).

Industry-specific value added and employment in 2030

Water transport

In the business-as-usual scenario, the past growth of inter-regional trade is assumed to continue for the next 20 years. Seaborne trade will be dominated by intra-Far East trade, trade between the Far East and Oceania, the Far East and Latin America, the Far East and Europe, and the Far East and the Middle East, leading to the strongest industry growth in Asia. Value added in water transport in OECD countries and selected OECD partner economies is estimated to grow to more than USD 118 billion, with the highest share in Asia.

Officially registered full-time employment in water transport in OECD countries may reach more than 600 000 jobs in the business-as-usual scenario. Adding seafarers from emerging and developing economies more than doubles the total employment figure to around 1.5 million jobs.

Shipbuilding and repair

Based on previous OECD work on shipbuilding and data from SEA Europe and IHS Global Insights, total new building vessel requirements are expected to reach around 1 230 million gross tonnage (GT) during the next 20 years. Of that total, tankers are likely to account for around 420 million GT, bulkers could make up about 550 million GT and containers are expected to reach a total of roughly 264 million GT. Future vessel requirements are not expected to return to the 2011 peak level of completions until 2035. As a consequence, in 2030 global future vessel new building requirements are likely to be around 70 million GT, compared to 67.7 million GT vessel completions in 2008.[4] Without future capacity closures, the effects of the excess capacity situation in the shipbuilding industry, created during 2009 and 2014, are likely to continue to be felt for the next 20 years.

Conditioned by the low vessel requirements due to overcapacity in the industry, in the business-as-usual scenario the global value added for shipbuilding and repair is estimated to contribute around USD 103 billion to the global economy, assuming a continuous trend to more high-value ships. Within this scenario, OECD Asian countries are expected to continue to dominate the market, with the biggest shipbuilding capacity in the People's Republic of China (hereafter "China"), Korea and Japan. Due to the comparatively low new build vessel requirements in 2030, employment in shipbuilding will grow by only around 24 percentage points, resulting in around 2.3 million full-time equivalent jobs.

Maritime equipment

Based on data from BALance Technology Consulting (2011), the global value added for marine equipment is expected to contribute USD 300 billion to the global economy by 2030. Most of the future demand in maritime equipment is determined by the growth of shipbuilding and repair. However, it should be noted that good data were only available for Europe. Given the lack of consistent data for other parts of the world, these European data had to be applied to non-European regions. The result may therefore overestimate global value added and underestimate employment.

Employment is expected to amount to approximately 2.7 million jobs worldwide, concentrated in China, Japan, Korea and other emerging shipbuilding nations in Asia, such as the Philippines and Viet Nam.

Port activities

In order to estimate value added and employment, the model draws on projections of future port throughput to 2030 (based on GDP forecasts as one of the core indirect determinants of increasing global trade) (OECD and ITF, 2015). Using the OECD's International Transport Forum's (ITF) projections, which are based on the port throughput of the 830 largest ports in the world in terms of tonnage and almost 100% of cargo handling worldwide, the business-as-usual scenario estimates the direct value added of global port activities in 2030 to be around USD 473 billion. Further, it was estimated that the rate of global port throughput would lead to direct employment to the tune of more than 4.2 million full-time jobs in 2030.

This result involves two major assumptions. First, based on a meta-study of the value creation of ports in developed countries (OECD, 2014), an average of USD 100 is assumed for value added per tonne of port throughput. However, many ports are not located in a high-income country, and the economic impact would arguably be lower in lower income countries. It is assumed that in a middle-income country, value added per tonne of port throughput would be a third of that generated in developed countries' ports. The distribution of port volumes across the world is approximately one-third for high-income countries and two-thirds for middle- and low-income countries, whereby more than one-half of the total port-throughputs is expected to stem from Asia. Second, it is assumed that around 10% of the total value added is direct. The remaining part of total value added consists of indirect and induced effects. In addition, at bigger ports, many related industries are located in proximity of bigger ports (e.g. chemicals, refineries), where the growth of port activities leads (through forward linkages) to growth in other industries. Consequently, indirect effects in bigger ports are larger than in smaller ports (OECD, 2014).

Maritime and coastal tourism

Even though international tourism to destinations in other parts of the world is expected to increase to 2030, tourist arrivals are expected to remain concentrated in Europe. The business-as-usual scenario anticipates that Europe receives the lion's share with over 700 million international tourist arrivals, followed by Asia and the Pacific with over 500 million international tourist arrivals. Consequently, the biggest market share is expected to fall to Europe with 41%, followed by Asia and the Pacific which, combined, are expected to account for around 30% of the global tourism market. North-east Asia is likely to be the most visited sub-region in 2030, with 293 million international tourist arrivals, followed by southern and Mediterranean Europe with 264 million international tourists.

Outbound tourism by region of origin is expected to remain the highest in Europe, with 832 million international tourists going abroad. However, Asia and the Pacific are likely to be the outbound regions that will grow the strongest, from 204 million in 2010 to 541 million tourists by 2030.

In more than half the cases, the purpose of visit in 2030 is expected to be leisure; this ratio stays roughly the same as in 2010 (UNWTO, 2011).

In the business-as-usual scenario, marine and coastal tourism is estimated to contribute over USD 777 billion in value added to the global economy. Global maritime and coastal tourism is estimated to employ more than 8.5 million people in 2030.

Industrial capture fisheries

The projections of the business-as-usual scenario for capture fisheries are based on the Cobb-Douglas production function which was developed for this project. The global value added for industrial capture fisheries in 2030 is expected to be approximately USD 47 billion. Figure 8.4 shows that value added in capture fisheries is likely to be highest in the North American Free Trade Agreement (NAFTA) countries, equalling USD 12.4 billion, followed by Asia and Oceania with USD 10.7 billion, Africa and the Middle East with USD 8.6 billion, and Europe with just over USD 8 billion. Value added in these regions is higher than for the other regions since they are home to the majority of the biggest producers. Top producers are China, Indonesia, Peru, the United States, India, the Russian Federation, Myanmar, Japan, Viet Nam, the Philippines and Norway.

Figure 8.4. **Value-added of industrial capture fisheries in 2030 by region in the business-as-usual scenario**

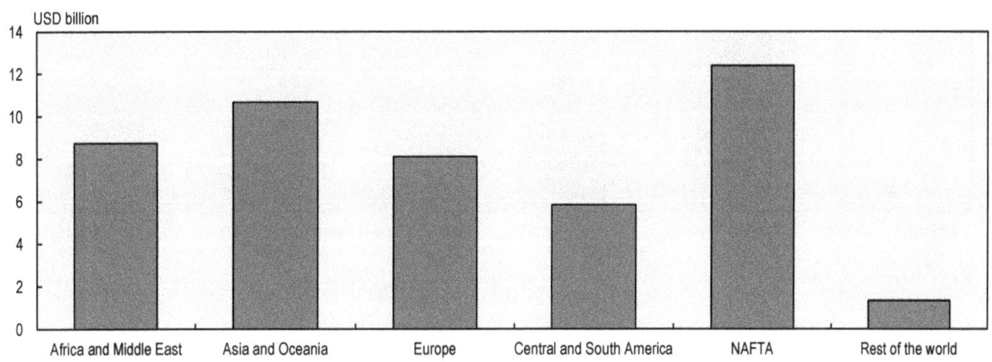

StatLink http://dx.doi.org/10.1787/888933334777

Source: Authors' calculations based on UNSTAT, OECD STAN; World Bank (2013).

Under the business-as-usual scenario, global employment in industrial capture fisheries is expected to be more than 10 million, with the highest employment in Asia at around 5 million jobs, followed by Africa with more than 3 million jobs. The high employment figure in Asia is explained by the large population in China and Indonesia. Nevertheless, it should be noted that artisanal fisheries are not included in this estimate. (See Chapter 6 for further discussion on this topic.)

Industrial marine aquaculture

Similarly, the projections of the business-as-usual scenario for industrial aquaculture are based on the Cobb-Douglas production function. Global value added in industrial marine aquaculture in the business-as-usual scenario is estimated at around USD 11 billion, the biggest share falling to Asia (Figure 8.5). Marine aquaculture is expected to be dominated by Asian countries, in particular, China, India, Indonesia, Viet Nam, Bangladesh and Thailand, with a total value added of almost USD 10 billion. In addition, some of the non-Asian countries, such as Norway, Egypt and Chile, are expected to continue to expand significantly their national production. Nevertheless, it should be noted that value added in aquaculture is most likely underestimated due to the methodology that was developed on the basis of limited data availability. The main data source used for aquaculture, "ISIC Rev.3", code "05 fisheries", reports on the combined national fish production but does not distinguish between capture fisheries and aquaculture. The ratio of production between capture fisheries and aquaculture is drawn from "Fish to 2030" (World Bank, 2013) and applied to the total production value based on ISIC Rev.5. However, this approach can underestimate the figure for employment in capture fisheries and overestimate employment in aquaculture. Whereas capture fisheries is comparatively more labour intensive, aquaculture is comparatively more capital intensive. In other words, the same amount of fish produced in aquaculture contributes to a higher value added with an input of fewer human resources. See Liebender et al. (forthcoming) for more details.

Figure 8.5. **Value-added of marine aquaculture in 2030 by region in the business-as-usual scenario**

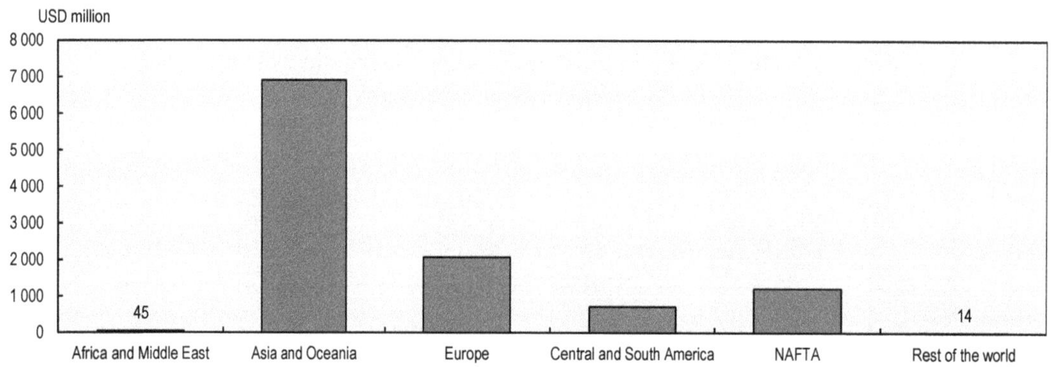

StatLink http://dx.doi.org/10.1787/888933334784

Source: Authors' calculations based on UNSTAT, OECD STAN; World Bank (2013); FAO (2015).

Under the business-as-usual scenario, industrial marine aquaculture is expected to employ approximately 3 million people. As most of the production takes place in Asia, most of the jobs are expected to be there too. Specifically, most jobs will be in China, India, Indonesia, Bangladesh, Pakistan, Viet Nam and the Philippines. These countries are expected to account for 89% of employment in industrial marine aquaculture (excluding artisanal activities).

Industrial fish processing

It is assumed that industrial fish processing is largely determined by global fish supplies, with most of the production of capture fisheries and aquaculture being concentrated in Asia (FAO, 2014). Hence, in 2030, the global value added of fish processing is estimated to be around USD 266 billion, the biggest share being retained by Asia. The region could account for almost 53% of the global market. For other regions, such as Africa, this share would be lower, at 31%. Europe, the American continent and the rest of the world are estimated to account for a total of around 16%.

Global employment in fish processing under the business-as-usual scenario is likely to account for approximately 5 million full-time jobs. More than 3 million jobs are likely to be in Asia, followed by Africa with around 1 million.[5]

Offshore oil and gas

Based on the *World Energy Outlook* (IEA, 2014), in the business-as-usual scenario, the offshore oil and gas industry contributes a global value added of around

USD 636 billion. This represents a 26% increase compared to 2010 values.[6] However, in the coming years, independently of what happens onshore, offshore oil production is expected to grow much more slowly than offshore gas, both in shallow and deep water. The IEA (2015) predicts that offshore oil and gas would grow at significantly different rates. Whereas oil is expected to grow at 0.4% per year, gas could grow more strongly at 1.5% per year. In terms of offshore production, offshore crude oil total production should thus rise from approximately 25 million barrels of oil-equivalent per day (mboe/d) in 2014 to approximately 28 mboe/d in 2040. Gas comes in addition, and could grow strongly from slightly above 17 mboe/d to 27 mboe/d. Also according to the IEA (2015), total offshore crude oil production is expected to see a significant increase in deep-water production, whereas the production of offshore oil in shallow water fields is expected to slightly decrease; for offshore gas production, strong growth is expected both in shallow and deep water. Based on the estimates of Rystad Energy and the IEA *World Energy Outlook 2012* (IEA, 2012), the shares of offshore oil and gas production would differ significantly between shallow water and deep water. Assuming the same ratio of value added per unit of production in 2010 and 2030 (which may not necessarily be the case due to higher capital and technology costs in deeper water), and based on the IEA estimates of an 88% share for shallow-water production and 12% for deep-water production in 2030, total value added of shallow-water production increases by around 19% to 2030, whereas the value added of deep-water offshore oil and gas would be expected to increase by 116% during the 20-year time period.

Global employment in offshore oil and gas could amount to more than 2 million jobs. However, as the underlying assumption cannot take technological progress into account, the actual figure in 2030 may be smaller than the current projection. Employment is expected to remain highest in Latin America, generating 24% of global offshore oil and gas jobs. Whereas Europe's employment share in the total may decrease by 1 percentage point, the share of employment in Asia and North America would increase by 2 percentage points, and the share of jobs in Africa and the Middle East may increase by 1 percentage point.

Offshore wind

Based on national targets for operational capacity in offshore wind in 2030,[7] global value added for offshore wind is estimated to reach around USD 230 billion, with the largest share falling to Europe (Figure 8.6). Europe is anticipated to make up more than half of the global market, followed by China at 23%, and subsequently the United States with a 20% share. For other offshore wind producers, such as Japan and Korea, this share is approximately 1% each. Analogous to the methodology used in current value estimation in offshore wind (Chapter 6), value added for China and the United States is likely to be somewhat overestimated.[8]

By 2020, it is anticipated that a large number of countries will have multiple gigawatts of wind power (including onshore and offshore) installed, ranging from just under 10 gigawatts (GW) in Africa to more than 600 GW in China. One decade later, offshore wind capacity is expected to be installed in the United States, Central and South America, Europe, the Pacific, China and other Asian countries. OECD partner economies are likely to produce approximately 17% of global wind energy, compared to 83% for OECD countries. Based on IEA projections, this ratio could increase by the middle of the century to 57% for OECD partner economies, and decrease to around 43% for OECD countries (IEA, 2014).

Figure 8.6. **Shares of value-added of offshore wind in 2030**

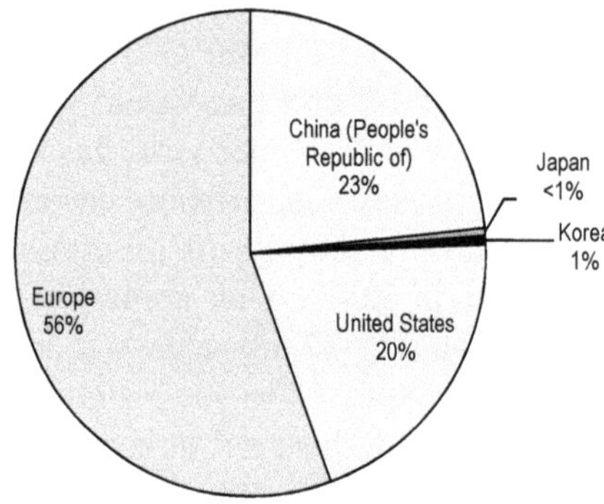

StatLink http://dx.doi.org/10.1787/888933334795

Source: Authors' calculations based on EWEA (2011); IEDC (2013); IEA (2015; 2013); IRENA (2014); BTM Consulting (2010).

Based on previous employment and capacity projections (IEA, 2014; EWEA, 2011), total employment in offshore wind under the business-as-usual scenario is estimated at around 435 000 full-time jobs.

Ocean industries to 2030 in two alternative scenarios

Two alternative scenarios are offered – sustainable growth and unsustainable growth – which shape the future ocean economy in two different directions, one accelerating and the other slowing the future development of the ocean-based industries by 2030. The main drivers shaping these alternative scenarios were defined in an internal workshop with the Project Steering Group in 2014. They include economic growth, technological development, governmental regulations and the state of the climate and ocean environment by 2030.

- The "sustainable scenario" assumes high economic growth and low environmental deterioration due to the development of resource-efficient and climate-friendly technologies combined with a supportive governmental framework that provides the right incentives to allow the ocean economy to thrive economically while meeting environmental standards.
- The "unsustainable scenario" assumes low economic growth and serious environmental deterioration. Coupled with faster than expected climate change and environmental damage and low rates of technological innovation, the ocean economy experiences a challenging outlook beyond 2030.

Existing industry-specific projections (see Liebender et al. [forthcoming] for details)[9] were adapted to serve as a framework for the development of the alternative scenarios and the project team's own projections with regard to value added and employment. See the forthcoming OECD working paper for details.

Figure 8.7 compares the value added in the ocean economy in 2010 and 2030 under different scenarios. Value added in the ocean economy in 2010 is USD 1.5 trillion. In 2030, value added in the "sustainable" scenario is more than USD 3.2 trillion, compared to USD 3 trillion in the business-as-usual scenario. Value added in 2030 in the "unsustainable" scenario is estimated to be around USD 2.8 trillion. Hence, the share of total global GVA (estimated at USD 120 billion in 2030) would be around 2.7% for the "sustainable" scenario and 2.3% for the "unsustainable" scenario. Similarly, employment in 2030 in the ocean economy is almost 43 million jobs in the "sustainable" scenario and around 7 million jobs smaller in the "unsustainable" scenario. The difference between the two alternative scenarios regarding their value added and employment would grow with time.

Figure 8.7. **Value added in the ocean economy under different scenarios**

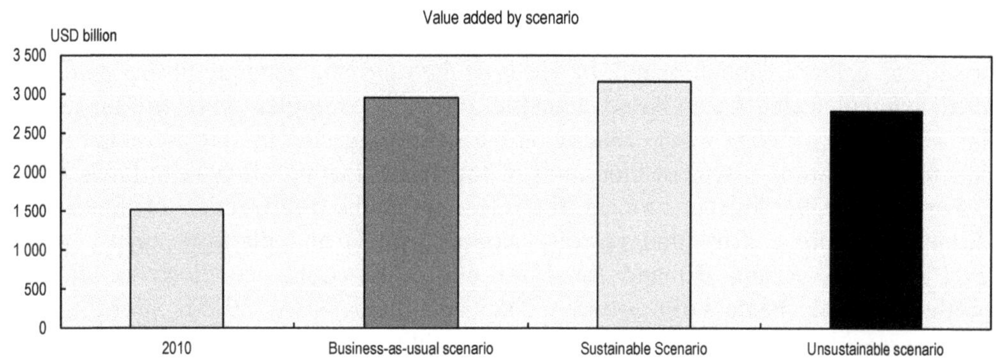

StatLink http://dx.doi.org/10.1787/888933334807

Source: Authors' calculations based on UNSTAT; OECD STAN; Lloyd's Register Group (2014); Lloyd's Register Marine (2013); World Bank (2013); IEA (2014).

The higher value added of the ocean economy in the "sustainable" scenario results from a higher production of offshore wind and higher total fish production and processing due to an intensified aquaculture production and increased fish yield that is made possible by sustainable fish stock management. The difference between the projected value added and employment in the "unsustainable" scenario compared to that in the business-as-usual scenario is quite small, for three reasons. First, activities of offshore oil and gas, water transport and ports are expected to increase in the "unsustainable" scenario at a faster rate than in the 'sustainable" scenario. Second, employment and value added in aquaculture and offshore wind are expected to decrease slightly compared to the business-as-usual scenario based on FAO assumptions; capture fisheries and fish processing are expected to decrease only slightly compared to the business-as-usual scenario. However, by the middle of this century, the differential between the total overall value added of the two alternative scenarios would be expected to widen significantly.

Concluding observations

What emerges from the above projections is that the ocean economy is an increasingly vibrant and vital part of the world economy. Over the projection period, many of the ocean-based industries are likely to outpace performance of the world economy as a whole, both in terms of economic contribution (i.e. value-added) and employment. Indeed, some sectors are likely to do so by a considerable margin. This applies in particular to offshore wind energy production, marine aquaculture, capture fisheries, fish processing, port activities and some segments of marine tourism, such as the cruise industry. Although lack of comprehensive and consistent data have prevented projections being made in this report for a range of other activities such as ocean renewable energy, marine biotechnology, and ocean monitoring and surveillance, evidence (see Chapter 7) suggests that, in the not too distant future, they too might well be added to the list of strongly performing activities.

Such dynamism in those rapidly expanding sectors combined with expectations of moderate growth in already large industries like maritime and coastal tourism, offshore oil and gas, shipbuilding and maritime equipment, points to a marked acceleration of economic activity in the ocean. As a consequence, it seems almost inevitable that pressures on the ocean's natural assets will increase in the coming years, as demands continue to grow on marine sources of food, energy, minerals, leisure pursuits and so on. Similarly, ocean space in many regions of the world risks becoming ever more crowded, as maritime trade, marine aquaculture, ocean renewable energy, and marine and coastal tourism, etc. gather momentum and, by virtue of their growth, generate further demand in related, interconnected ocean-based industries. Several examples serve to illustrate the point. Growth in offshore wind capacity on the scale suggested by this and other reports points to the addition of tens of thousands of fixed and floating offshore turbines around the world by 2030. That, in turn, is likely to require the construction of hundreds of additional offshore construction vessels, support vessels and platform supply vessels (OECD, 2015b). Rising demand for LNG and LPG could see close to 900 new specialised vessels being built between 2015 and 2035 (SEA, 2015). Strong volume growth in maritime trade will trigger significant additional port business, with the move to ever larger ships likely to raise demand for more feeder vessels. And the anticipated expansion of marine and coastal tourism is triggering demand for more cruise capacity – alone new building requirements are expected to see around 55 new cruise ships enter service by 2020 (CLIA, 2015).

Growth of ocean activity on such a scale makes it imperative that substantial progress be made towards much improved management and governance of the high seas, of exclusive economic zones and coastal areas. That is the subject of Chapter 9.

Notes

1. Based on the International Labour Organization, employment is defined as the group of persons, above a specified age (15-60 years), who during a specified brief period, were in the following categories: 1) paid employment; 2) self-employment. The global employment figure in 2010 (including self- and part-time employment) from Chapter 6 was projected with the UN medium fertility rate to 2030.
2. For more details see Annex 8.A1.
3. In particular, this approach presents two possible extensions of the models that consider two types of interdependencies: intermediate products and technological spillovers. See the Annex C of the methodology discussion paper (Liebender et al., forthcoming).
4. Hence, the projection for shipbuilding and repair industry is based on 2008 values in order to exclude the creation of oversupply of vessels between 2009 and 2014.
5. This overestimate may result from inconsistent national data within the low-income group.
6. The projection for offshore oil and gas is possibly underestimating the real value in 2030. The underlying assumption due to limited data is that the production ratio

in 2030 will be the same as in 2010. Additionally, only countries that reported their production in 2010 could be included in the analysis; consequently, the Russian Federation was not included in these estimates.

7. Countries were included given that operational capacity was published for 2010 and 2030. This was the case for China, Europe, Japan, Korea and the United States. Due to the lack of data, Mexico was excluded from this overview.

8. See the methodology paper for details (Liebender et al., forthcoming).

9. The sustainable scenario for capture fisheries was based on the simulations in the World Bank's "Fish to 2030" study, which aimed at reflecting the benefits of taking action to stop overharvesting and protect aquatic ecosystems from biological collapse. On the basis of a study from the FAO and the World Bank (2009), it was estimated that successfully restored and managed world fisheries would sustainably provide 10% more yield annually relative to the 2004 harvest level though sustainable fisheries management (e.g. restoring and improving the productivity of stressed capture fisheries will be possible in many cases if appropriate actions are taken by country governments, marine resource managers, and the fishing fleets and communities. These actions would include management improvements and proper tenure reforms to reduce fishing effort, letting the aquatic ecosystems and stocks recover, reducing the open-access nature of fisheries, and sustainably managing their productivity. See FAO [2014]). The environmental constraints of increased aquaculture on the environment are reflected in this figure.

Annex 8.A1.
Methodology of the business-as-usual scenario

ISIC Rev.3 reported on fisheries, fish processing, water transport, and shipbuilding and repair. Their industry-specific value added and employment creation are projected in the following way:

- Project the national level of $GDP_{j,2030}$, $L_{j,2030}$,$K_{j,2030}$,$h_{j,2030}$, using IMF and World Development Indicators (WDI) database and Cohen-Soto database (see Duval and de la Maisonneuve [2009]). $A_{j,2030}$ is calculated implicitly by solving the Cobb-Douglas function for multi-factor productivity. $GDP_{j,2030}$ and $K_{j,2030}$ are collected in 2010 international USD as $GDP_{j,2010}$ and $K_{j,2010}$. These values are gross domestic product and physical capital stock converted to international dollars using purchasing power parity rates.
- Calculate the growth rate of country- and industry-specific value added, employment and physical capital stock. Project the growth rates into the rates between 2029 and 2030. Acquire the compound growth rate from 2010 to 2030. Multiply the compound rate to country- and industry-specific $GVA_{i,j,2010}$, $K_{i,j,2010}$, and $L_{i,j,2010}$ to compute $GVA_{i,j,2030}$,$K_{i,j,2030}$, and $L_{i,j,2030}$. Implicitly calculate the country- and industry-specific multi-factor productivity $A_{i,j,2030}$ using analogous method as step 1. (Income-group specific weighted averages are calculated and used to compute the values for non-reporting countries. Country- and industry-specific $GVA_{i,j,2030}$ and $K_{i,j,2030}$ are collected in 2010 international USD.
- Insert $K_{i,j,2030}$, $L_{i,j,2030}$, $HC_{i,j,2030}$ and $A_{i,j,2030}$ into a Cobb-Douglas production function in order to acquire $GVA_{i,j,2030}$.

$$GVA_{i,j,2030} = A_{i,j,2030} \times K_{i,j,2030}^{\alpha} \times (HC_{i,j,2030} \times L_{i,j,2030})^{1-\alpha}$$

Industries that were not defined in ISIC Rev.3 were projected individually. Please see Liebender et al. (forthcoming) for details.

Methodology of the "sustainable and unsustainable growth" scenario

The development of alternative scenarios was based on the framework of existing industry-specific projections. For the development of the projections on value added and employment creation, one possible approach would be to borrow the projected growth rate from these studies. However, a majority of studies do not develop country- and industry-specific projections of value added and employment creation. Therefore, the projected production (Y) from those studies issued to project GVA and employment, included the following steps:

- Collect the country- and industry-specific output ,${Y^A}_{i,j,2030}$ that match the definition of green and black scenarios where A denotes the scenario, $A \in \{B, G\}$ with B for the unsustainable and G for the sustainable scenario.

- Calculate the ratio of output to the baseline scenario, $\frac{Y^{A}{}_{i,j,2030}}{Y_{i,j,2030}}$.
- Calculate the value added and employment under the alternative scenarios as $GVA^{A}{}_{i,j,2030} = \frac{Y^{A}{}_{i,j,2030}}{Y_{i,j,2030}} \times GVA_{i,j,2030}$, and $L^{A}{}_{i,j,2030} = \frac{Y^{A}{}_{i,j,2030}}{Y_{i,j,2030}} \times L_{i,j,2030}$.

References

BALance Technology Consulting (2014), "Competitive position and future opportunities of the European marine supplies industry", European Commission, available at: http://ec.europa.eu/DocsRoom/documents/4233/attachments/1/translations/en/renditions/native.

BTM Consulting (2010), *International Wind Energy Development: World Market Update 2010*, Navigant Consulting.

CLIA (2014), "Chartering a source to success", 2014 CLIA Annual Report.

Douglas-Westwood Limited (2005), "World marine markets", a report to WTSH, report number 328-05, March.

Duval, R. and C. de la Maisonneuve (2009), "Long-run GDP growth framework and scenarios for the world economy", *OECD Economics Department Working Papers*, No. 663, OECD Publishing, Paris, http://dx.doi.org/10.1787/227205684023.

EWEA (2011), "Wind in our sails: The coming of Europe's offshore wind energy industry", November, European Wind Energy Association, Brussels, available at: www.ewea.org/fileadmin/files/library/publications/reports/Offshore_Report.pdf.

FAO (2015), *Global Aquaculture Production* (database), updated to 2013, Summary information, available at: http://www.fao.org/fishery/statistics/global-aquaculture-production/query/en.

FAO (2014), *The State of World Fisheries and Aquaculture*, Food and Agriculture Organization, Rome, available at: www.fao.org/3/a-i3720e.pdf.

FAO and the World Bank (2009), *The Sunken Billions: The Economic Justification for Fisheries Reform*, The World Bank, Washington, DC, available at: http://siteresources.worldbank.org/EXTARD/Resources/336681-1224775570533/SunkenBillionsFinal.pdf.

IEA (2015), *IEA Wind: 2014 Annual Report*, IEA Wind, Paris, available at: www.ieawind.org/annual_reports_PDF/2014/2014%20AR_smallfile.pdf.

IEA (2014), *World Energy Outlook 2014*, International Energy Agency, Paris, http://dx.doi.org/10.1787/weo-2014-en.

IEA (2013), *Medium-Term Renewable Energy Market Report 2013: Market Trends and Projections to 2018*, International Energy Agency, Paris, http://dx.doi.org/10.1787/9789264191198-en.

IEA (2012), *World Energy Outlook 2012*, OECD Publishing, Paris, http://dx.doi.org/10.1787/weo-2012-en

IEDC (2013), "Creating the clean energy economy: Analysis of the offshore wind energy industry", International Economic Development Council, Washington, DC, available at: www.ourenergypolicy.org/wp-content/uploads/2016/02/IEDC_Offshore_Wind.pdf.

IRENA (2014), *REmap 2030: A Renewable Energy Roadmap*, International Renewable Energy Agency, Abu Dhabi, United Arab Emirates, www.irena.org/remap.

Liebender, A.-S. et al. (forthcoming), "Measuring the global economic contribution of ocean-based industries – Methodology paper", *OECD Science, Technology and Industry Working Papers*, OECD Publishing, Paris, forthcoming.

Lloyd's Register Group (2014), "Global marine fuel trends 2030", Lloyd's Register Global Technology Centre, London, available at: www.lr.org/en/_images/213-34172_Global_Marine_Fuel_Trends_2030.pdf.

Lloyd's Register Marine (2013), "Global marine trends 2030", Lloyd's Register Marine.

OECD (2015a), "Shipbuilding and the offshore industry", C/WP6(2015)5/FINAL, OECD, Paris, www.oecd.org/sti/ind/Shipbuilding-and-offshore-industry.pdf (accessed 1 February 2016).

OECD (2015b), "Oversupply in the shipbuilding industry", www.oecd.org/sti/ind/shipbuilding.htm.

OECD (2014), *The Competitiveness of Global Port-Cities*, OECD Publishing, Paris, http://dx.doi.org/10.1787/9789264205277-en.

OECD and ITF (2015), *ITF Transport Outlook 2015*, OECD Publishing/ITF, http://dx.doi.org/10.1787/9789282107782-en

SEA (2015), "Shipbuilding market monitoring 2014 1Q, Report", No. 35, June, Europe Ships & Maritime Equipment Association.

UNWTO (2011), *Tourism Towards 2030/Global Overview*, Advanced edition presented at UNWTO 19th General Assembly, 10 October, World Tourism Organization, available at: www.e-unwto.org/doi/book/10.18111/9789284414024.

World Bank (2013), "Fish to 2030: Prospects for fisheries and aquaculture", *Agriculture and Environmental Services Discussion Paper 03*, World Bank, Washington, DC, available at: http://documents.worldbank.org/curated/en/2013/12/18882045/fish-2030-prospects-fisheries-aquaculture.

Chapter 9.

Towards integrated ocean management

This chapter takes a longer term forward view of the challenges facing ocean management and some of the opportunities that are emerging which may help address those challenges. It begins with a brief overview of the implications of growing geopolitical multipolarity and institutional fragmentation for governing the high seas before turning its attention to the management of the ocean in exclusive economic zones (EEZs). Here, the problems present themselves differently, since it is individual governments that are generally responsible for resources and human economic activity in EEZs. Nonetheless, it is only recently that national strategic policy frameworks for managing national waters and seabed have begun to take shape, and that integrated ocean management has gathered noticeable momentum. Moreover, management of the marine EEZ is fraught with difficulties that are hampering its effective implementation. The chapter suggests three pathways to the urgent improvements required: better integration of economic analysis and economic tools; innovation in governance structures and processes; and greater use of science and technology, in particular in gathering better data.

Ocean governance is facing numerous risks and uncertainties. These include a plethora of different agencies looking after different activities, gaps in the governance framework, weak compliance and enforcement, new and emerging uses, and lack of an equity framework for exploitation of genetic resources. At the same time, the geopolitical challenges to ocean governance are growing, not least the increasing multipolarity and fragmentation of power structures and the emergence of new state and non-state players. The signs are that ocean governance is expected to continue to evolve along mainly sectoral lines rather than through comprehensive approaches. Yet, there is a clear need for more integrated ocean management to address the interconnected nature of ecosystems, growing economic activity, mounting pressures on ocean resources and increasingly crowded ocean space. Innovation in governance, greater use of economic tools and a stronger scientific knowledge base are among key strategies to be pursued.

A changing geopolitical landscape and governance of the high seas

A number of recent long-term trend studies suggest that it is highly unlikely the world will become a less complex and volatile place in the decades to come (e.g. European Commission, 2009; Shell, 2013; NIC, 2012; OECD, 2011). The trends identified in Chapter 2, including, for example, the growing importance of emerging and developing countries, and shifts in the centre of economic gravity, suggest that humankind is progressing ever further towards a distinctly multipolar world. This entails, among other things:

- the gradual disappearance of hegemony and the emergence of numerous countries and regions vying for economic power and the benefits that can be derived from projecting their growing economic power on to the geopolitical stage
- the emergence of new state players demonstrating their strength in particular crucial sectors – such as energy and other natural resources, space technologies, ICT – which allows them to assume a strategic importance and punch above their weight in the global arena
- the appearance of state-like and non-state actors from different societal, commercial or public-sector origins, which have seen their influence in the world grow as the high concentrations of knowledge, skills, financial clout and scale/network efficiencies raise their profile internationally.

Taken together, these and other challenges have focused the attention of many governments on issues that, at first glance, have little to do with the oceans per se. However, studies such as that of the Global Ocean Commission (GOC, 2014) indicate that there are profound links and ramifications that are likely to influence the way in which humankind governs the oceans in the coming decades. The GOC argues that the high seas are facing a cycle of declining ecosystem health and productivity, brought on by an increased demand in living and non-living resources; the development of new technologies; declining fish stocks; climate change, biodiversity and habitat loss; as well as weak ocean governance.

Perhaps one of the most profound impacts on the oceans stemming from the above described trend toward a more multipolar world, with its inherent complexity and volatility, is an increased fragmentation in international law and governance. While the implications of such fragmentation are not entirely clear, concern has been great enough for the United Nations to task its International Law Commission (ILC) to address this issue in some detail. The UN ILC described the fragmentation of international law as a process of diversification and expansion, whereby it has developed from "a tool dedicated to the regulation of formal diplomacy" to one that is expected to "deal with the most varied kinds of international activity, from trade to environmental protection, from human rights to scientific and technological cooperation". In its study on the subject, the ILC argued that while "fragmentation does create the danger of conflicting and incompatible rules, principles, rule-systems and institutional practices", at the same time it "reflects the expansion of international legal activity into new fields and the attendant diversification of its objects and techniques" (UN ILC, 2006). This is a trend that is very much present in international ocean governance. Ocean governance is often presented as a swinging back and forth between the comprehensive approach, as reflected in the United Nations Convention on the Law of the Sea (UNCLOS), and highly specialised agreements. The signs are that, in the coming years, ocean governance will continue to develop along highly sectoral axes, often based on different underlying legal principles. Substantial initiatives are expected to continue or newly emerge in areas as diverse as:

- the negotiation of an international legally-binding instrument under UNCLOS on the conservation and sustainable use of marine biological diversity of areas beyond national jurisdiction
- the ongoing processes related to the state applications to establish the outer limits of their juridical continental shelves beyond the 200-mile exclusive economic zone under the UN Commission on the Limits of the Continental Shelf
- first steps forward to prepare for negotiations on an exploitation regulation for deep-sea mining under the International Seabed Authority (ISA)
- continued efforts to devise and implement rules to counter overfishing and, in particular, illegal, unreported and unregulated (IUU) fishing
- increasing calls for the development of international agreements pertaining to environmental and safety standards for offshore drilling in the continental shelf, as well as for an international convention regulating compensation and liability.

As these and other initiatives develop, they will be confronted by big challenges, ranging from threats to international peace and security to activities jeopardising the ecological integrity of the seas. On the side of peace and security, some major challenges include maritime boundary disagreements in various regions around the world as well as continued fears over piracy. Concerning the marine environment, the G7 has recently pledged to tackle marine litter, which is considered by many to be an increasingly important issue with serious economic implications. Overall, the GOC (2014) recently concluded that ocean governance was facing numerous risks and uncertainties. These include:

- a plethora of different agencies looking after different activities
- gaps in the governance framework
- weak compliance
- lack of enforcement
- new and emerging uses, including high seas industries such as energy production
- lack of an equity framework for exploitation of genetic resources.

Taken together, there is a widely held view that there remains fundamental uncertainty as to where ocean governance is heading.

The implications of the risk and uncertainty associated with current developments in ocean governance will impact a variety of economic-related activities, including for example, a lack of legal clarity about economic activities in the oceans beyond national jurisdiction as well as the potential of increased competition between states for access to resources in the seas.

With respect to legal uncertainty: in areas beyond national jurisdiction some of the legal regimes are currently being developed to address the exploitation of, for example, fisheries, seafloor minerals and biological resources. Invariably, these different contexts will develop different regulations concerning security of tenure, fees, ownership of royalties, intellectual property, etc. But there will remain areas of uncertainty, for example, as related to contract law. One illustrative case raised in the academic literature is deep-sea corals, which are affected by fisheries law, constitute a mineral resource in the Area and thus constitute part of the common heritage of humankind as well as a biological resource under the Convention on Biological Diversity (see Prows, 2006). At the same time, there is no direct international agreement covering their protection and use (European Marine Board, 2015). Overall, companies and lawyers have long argued that if substantial private and public investments are to be expected in the responsible economic development of the deep sea, then there needs to exist a clear, overarching legal regime covering the relations between states as well as the role of private commercial entities.

With respect to competition for resources: despite the fragmentation of international law and the diversity of interests amongst states in addressing fundamental issues of ocean governance, there has been little or no direct conflict over marine resources over that past few decades. Although there have been tensions between states on the edges of claimed territorial waters, overall peace and order have been maintained at an inter-state level. One reason is almost certainly the lack of perceived urgency or necessity to exploit high-value marine resources, such as minerals, in the Area. Another is that states have been quite successful in establishing a process that offers the opportunity of progressively extending their sovereign rights over resources out over the continental shelves, thus removing large parts of the oceans and seafloors from international relations. Moreover, the International Tribunal for the Law of the Sea is able to adjudicate on many of the conflicting interests of states. However, at the same time, it has been argued in the scholarly literature that little effort is being placed on building into the ocean governance system incentives to develop joint inter-state activities. For example, despite all the co-operation relating to the articulating of a deep-sea mining regulation, the contract system remains on a first-come-first-served basis and single-party contracts. Thus, there is a built-in system of competition. What implications this has for the long-term remains to be seen (Fritz, 2015).

Governance in economic exclusion zones

While governance of the high seas is likely to continue to develop along sectoral lines, numerous recent initiatives might suggest that ocean management in economic exclusion zones (EEZs) is endeavouring to become more comprehensive and coherent.

As noted above, ocean activities are considered essential to meet future global challenges. However, pressures on the ocean environment – including over-fishing, pollution and habitat destruction – have continued to mount, not least as a consequence of growing ocean use. These pressures are attributed in large part to what has been historically an *ad hoc*, sector-by-sector management and regulation of ocean activities.

Much as a response to those growing pressures, recent years have seen a significant increase in the number of countries and regions putting in place strategic policy frameworks for better ocean management. Most coastal nations of the world already have a variety of sectoral policies in place to manage different uses of the ocean (such as shipping, fishing, oil and gas development). But over the last couple of decades, a good number of them have undertaken sustained efforts to develop an integrated, ecosystem-based vision for the governance of ocean areas under their jurisdiction. These visions encompass goals and procedures to harmonise existing uses and laws, to promote sustainable development of ocean areas, to protect biodiversity and vulnerable resources and ecosystems, and to co-ordinate the actions of the many government agencies that are typically involved in oceans affairs (Cicin-Sain, Vanderzwaag and Balgos, 2015).

The countries concerned range from many, if not most, OECD coastline countries (e.g. Australia, Belgium, Canada, France, Ireland, Japan, Korea, Norway, Portugal, Sweden, the United Kingdom and the United States) to the emerging economies of Brazil, the People's Republic of China (hereafter "China"), Indonesia and South Africa, as well as a number of developing countries (e.g. Malaysia, Viet Nam). Some of these countries have their strategic policy framework already in place, while others are at various stages of design and implementation. Below national level, many regions are also forging ahead in this direction. Recent examples include Quebec, Canada (Gouvernement du Québec, 2016) and the north-east regions of the United States, (Ocean Frontiers, 2016) as well as numerous European regions responding to the European Union's Marine Strategy Framework Directive (Scottish Government, 2015).

At the root of this overall policy shift is the growing recognition that management of the ocean needs to be based on an ecosystem approach. The term ecosystem governance is used to describe the process by which the long-term societal and environmental goals for a specific place are defined and the processes and structures are assembled by which to achieve them (Olsen, Olsen and Schaefer, 2011). The interrelationship among uses and processes in the coast and ocean makes it imperative that ocean governance be integrated, precautionary and anticipatory.

Currently, some 50 countries have some form or another of spatial ocean management initiatives underway. Eight countries have government-approved marine plans that cover about 8% of the world's EEZs. As more countries come on-stream (e.g. through the relevant European directives) this figure is expected to increase to around 25% by 2025 (Ehler, 2015). However, the scale and scope of each initiative differs considerably between countries.

In addition to its spatial dimension, integrated ocean management has a temporal dimension. The temporal dimension comes into play at several levels. For example, potential conflicts over ocean use may be mitigated under certain circumstances by staggering competing activities over a given period. Equally, however, effective planning and management need to be anticipatory. They require advance knowledge of likely future changes in the ocean environment and ocean economic activities, since the two are interlinked and impact on each other.

The spatial dimension is reflected in various diverse efforts to implement geographically explicit management of marine resources and the use of oceans and coasts. The last two decades have seen a rapid increase in interest and action at varying political levels to implement spatially explicit management of marine resources (McLeod and Leslie, 2009; Halpern et al., 2012) through such instruments as integrated coastal zone management (ICZM), marine or maritime spatial planning (MSP), and marine protected areas (MPAs).

Integrated coastal zone management

Extending the concept of terrestrial planning out past the low water mark, ICZM is a process of integrated planning and multiple-use zoning for coastal areas (Olsen, Tobey and Kerr, 1997). Introduced more than 30 years ago, ICZM has been attracting increased attention recently. It is a process for managing the coast using an integrated approach, regarding all aspects of the coastal zone, including geographical and political boundaries, in an attempt to achieve sustainability. In particular from the point of view of land-sea interactions, an important aim of ICZM is to ensure effective integration with river catchment and water basin management, and coastal ground water management. Authorities and stakeholders with coastal interests collaborate in addressing common issues such as nature conservation, coastal flooding and defence, and local economic development (Allmendinger, Barker and Stead, 2002).

Marine spatial planning

Marine spatial planning (also known as maritime spatial planning and coastal and marine spatial planning) extended the ICZM approach further out to sea in the 2000s. MSP is a place-based planning approach that offers an opportunity for more integrated, sustainable ocean management than has occurred to date (Lester et al., 2013). While both ICZM and MSP are largely based on terrestrial processes and planning, the two concepts differ in a number of important principles and approaches.

In its broadest sense, MSP can be defined as "Analyzing and allocating parts of three-dimensional marine spaces to specific uses or non-use, to achieve ecological, economic, and social objectives that are usually specified through a political process" (Ehler and Douvere, 2007). MSP identifies which areas of the marine environment are appropriate for different uses or activities in order to reduce conflicts and achieve ecological, economic and social objectives. Thus, MSP brings a spatial dimension to the regulation of marine activities by helping to establish geographical patterns of sea uses within a given area. In contrast, ICZM does not generally result in the allocation of space to particular activities in the way that MSP does, and relies more upon voluntary co-operation than the formal designation of areas for certain uses. ICZM also has a stronger overlap with the land, and draws in terrestrially focused agencies and bodies more strongly than MSP, which generally extends its remit no further inland than the high-water mark (Morrissey, forthcoming).

Marine protected areas

Initial experience of MSP was strongly environmentally motivated, and particularly oriented to the offshore environment (Jay et al., 2012). Indeed, MSP originally started as a nature conservation approach through the use of MPAs in the Great Barrier Reef Marine Park in Australia (Schaefer and Barale, 2011). As such, initial MSP legislation focused on MPAs. MPAs are geographically defined areas that are regulated and managed to achieve specific conservation objectives. They cover many different types of protection. Some are "no-take zones" that are essential to enable fish stocks to recover, whereas others allow multiple uses of their resources. However, while MPAs continue to be an important policy instrument for MSP, MSP has broadened to include economic and social objectives (Schaefer and Barale, 2011). This is particularly evident in Europe, where MSP is seen as a means of supporting the "Blue Economy" and an opportunity to create an optimal investment climate for maritime sectors and give operators more certainty as to what opportunities for economic development are possible.

MPAs are one of the few management tools that address the activities of multiple sectors and constitute therefore a potentially important tool in the present and future management of deep-sea ecosystems in the high seas. There are some 7 300 MPAs in place around the world today (some of them very large scale indeed), covering about 3.4% of the global marine area. The target is to cover 10% of the ocean by 2020. The vast majority of MPAs are in EEZs, with very few (well below 10%) established in areas beyond national jurisdiction (Karousakis, 2015).

The future is likely to see mounting pressure to combine these three different approaches. Indeed, there is increasing recognition that there should be stronger integration between marine and terrestrial planning systems because of the economic dependencies on both land and sea for marine industries. This is partly because of the physical interaction between land and sea; for example, much marine pollution, such as eutrophication and plastics, originates on land, whilst, conversely, the coastal environment is sensitive to maritime activities such as aquaculture and shipping. Also, maritime activities rely upon and benefit terrestrial communities; for instance, ports and associated industries require considerable land for their development and provide employment and other socio-economic benefits.

However, in light of the expected rapid future expansion of ocean industry activity around the world and the increasingly crowded ocean space, time is of the essence in extending effective integrated management to as many coastal countries as possible. However, many obstacles stand in the way of more effective integrated ocean management, which will need to be addressed in the near future. They include for example:

- lack of scientific knowledge and data on ocean environment – compounded by complexity and uncertainty of the ocean environment
- insufficient use of the scientific and technological tools to gather, process and analyse those data
- lack of relevant socio-economic data
- the challenge of balancing the perceived interests of stakeholders, the distributional implications and equity considerations
- the slow pace at which science has been catching up with policy requirements with respect both to assessing and communicating trade-offs among human uses of the ocean and to identifying strategies to mediate these trade-offs.

Pathways to more effective ocean management

Three routes in particular offer themselves as means for enhancing the effectiveness and diffusion of integrated ocean management:

- greater use of economic analysis (e.g. cost-benefit analysis – identifying and quantifying types of cost, types of benefit; valuation techniques) and economic instruments (e.g. taxes, fees, tradable permits)
- innovation in governance and stakeholder engagement (co-ordination across government agencies, and wider but more effective and cost-efficient stakeholder consultation)
- better use of innovations in science and technology (e.g. advances in satellite applications, especially in combination with other technological innovations in

such uses as drones, unmanned airborne vehicle (UAVs), sensors, mapping, imaging) and in data quality and use.

Greater use of economic analysis and economic instruments

Valuing ocean ecosystem services

Economics is about choice and the ability of every decision to be weighed among different alternatives (TEEB, 2010). However, ecosystem services are often in the nature of public goods, which means that they may be enjoyed by any number of people without affecting other peoples' enjoyment. The problem with public goods is that although people value them, no one person has an incentive to pay to maintain the good (TEEB, 2010). Thus, markets only shed light on information about the value of a small subset of ecosystem processes and components that are priced and incorporated in transactions as commodities or services. This poses structural limitations on the ability of markets to provide comprehensive pictures of the ecological values involved in decision-making processes (TEEB, 2010). Moreover, an information failure arises from the difficulty of quantifying most ecosystem services in terms that are comparable with services from human-made assets (TEEB, 2010). From this perspective, the logic behind ecosystem valuation is to unravel the complexities of socio-ecological relationships, make explicit how human decisions would affect ecosystem service values, and express these value changes in units (e.g. monetary) that allow for their incorporation in public decision-making processes (TEEB, 2010).

The concept of ecosystem services has become a major conceptual framework for discussing economy-society-environment interactions. From an economic perspective, ecosystem services are the contributions of the natural world that generate goods and services that people value. Ecosystems services, however, are dependent on one another and exhibit complex interactions that generate trade-offs in the delivery of one service relative to the delivery of others. A central challenge for natural resource management is therefore developing rigorous yet practical approaches for balancing the costs and benefits of diverse human uses of ecosystems (Lester et al., 2013).

Cost-benefit analysis

Economic theory has a long history of evaluating trade-offs in returns from different assets to identify optimal investment strategies (Gamenda and Pascual, 2013). Cost-benefit analyses can reveal inferior management options, demonstrate the benefits of comprehensive planning for multiple, interacting services over managing single services, and identify "compatible" services that provide win-win management options (Lester et al., 2013). Cost-benefit analysis has become one of the cornerstones of ecological economics and is generally considered the most appropriate framework for determining optimal economic decisions in the realm of ecosystem management (Lester et al., 2013; Pearce, Markandy and Barbier, 2006; Pearce, 1998). Within an environmental framework, economic valuation is seen as a method of communicating that many natural resources are scarce and their depreciation or degradation has associated societal costs. Economic valuation is seen as an important tool for an ecosystem system-based approach.

Traditional project appraisal methods, such as feasibility analysis, suitability analysis and environmental impact assessment, have limited capability to incorporate economic analysis within their frameworks. Integrated ocean management, on the other hand, by incorporating economic information within its framework, has the capacity to provide important comparison of the economic value of one activity relative to another, thereby facilitating what is referred to as "best use" decision making (Tyldesley, 2004).

The economic benefits can be divided into three categories (Tyldesley, 2004): lower co-ordination costs; lower transaction costs (including search costs, legal costs, administrative costs and cost of conflicts); and enhanced investment climate. A report by the European Commission (2011) indicated that MSP could lead to significant economic benefits. It found that a reduction of 1% in transaction costs could lead to positive economic effects ranging from EUR 170 million to EUR 1.3 billion in 2020. An integrated management approach would also allow for an effective and efficient co-ordination of the various authorities and agencies involved in ocean-related decision making, thereby leading to a reduction in co-ordination costs.

Significant benefits can also be expected from the establishment of marine protected areas, as attested by international overviews of MPA valuation studies (see, for example, OECD [2016]).

Use of economic instruments

Economic instruments contrast with traditional, "command-and-control" approaches to managing natural resource problems, but can also usefully supplement them. Command-and-control approaches are governments' applied regulations with which individuals or corporate entities must comply (Davis and Gartside, 2001). Economists have long argued that market-based incentives, which apply monetary values, are more efficient for environmental management than those based on "command-and-control" approaches. Yet environmental management has been dominated by the regulatory approach (Davis and Gartside, 2001), particularly in the marine environment. Economic instruments intend to address the externalities associated with the use of natural resources by, for example, applying taxes, charges or tradable rights. The main attraction of these pricing mechanisms is that they provide clear signals in the market to consumers about the cost of producing a particular product, and to producers about the relative valuations (based on willingness to pay) that consumers place on the resources (Davis and Gartside, 2001).

Table 9.1. **Economic instruments for ocean management**

Economic instrument	Implementation
Price-based instruments	These include the implementation of taxes, charges and user fees. Examples include (but are not limited to) minerals and mining taxes, sand, gravel and quarrying charges, fisheries permits, tourism charges and national parks and reserves charges, soil pollution charges, incentives for conservation and incentives for organic farming.
Individually transferable quotas	Participants are allocated a portion of total allowable catch (TAC) of a species, which is transferable among participants, e.g. fishing individual transferable quota (ITQ).
Subsidies	A benefit, usually cash based, given by the government to individuals to remove the burden of regulation, e.g. financial support for the installation of waste management systems on board of ships, free waste water service for cruise ships in ports.
Payments for ecosystem services	Individuals/communities are paid to manage their natural resources in a more environmentally-friendly way. Payments are conditional on service delivery – or a management use presumed to produce that service.
Biodiversity offsets	Based on the polluter pays principle. Includes one-off offsets, in lieu of fees and bio-banking.

Source: Karousakis (2015).

Economic instruments can have both an incentive-effect and a revenue-raising effect, with the relative importance depending on the ability of the market to respond to the "price signal". When environmental costs are fully internalised into the price of a product or an activity/service, consumers are encouraged to substitute away from these products with higher relative prices to alternative products that are relatively cheaper priced and more environmentally friendly. Economic instruments also have the potential to have strong redistributive effects. It is important before choosing/implementing an economic instrument that *ex ante* distributional analysis is considered. Economic instruments such as environmental taxes, charges and user fees can produce what is referred to as a double dividend (Hynes et al., 2009). That is, when the instruments are implemented, not only is the pollution reduced, but the revenue created from the tax can be used to reduce other distortionary taxes, such as personal income taxes. Therefore, an important question before implementing any instrument is: what will the distributional impact of the charge be?

Non-market valuation techniques

The implementation of economic instruments within an environmental context has been slow as many of the parameters necessary for determining charge rates and values of ecosystem services are not readily known. However, with the increased sophistication of non-market valuation methods, estimates of the values associated with ecosystem services are becoming more robust. Non-market valuation methods are used to estimate non-use values and some direct use values, which can be defined as unpriced benefits from coastal and marine ecosystems because they are not commonly traded in the market. In particular, the direct use values not traded in marketplaces can refer to non-consumptive recreation and ecotourism, aesthetic values and cultural values (Koundouri, Remoundou and Kountouris, 2009).

Non-market valuation techniques can be grouped in two main categories, revealed preference and stated preference approaches. Revealed preferences take into account observable market information, which can be adjusted and used for revealing the individual's preference and thus quantifying the associated welfare benefits. Revealed preference methods include the Travel Cost Method (TCM), Hedonic Price approach (HP) and Averting Behaviour Approach (ABA) (Koundouri, Remoundou and Kountouris, 2009). The common underlying feature is a functional dependency of environmental benefits on the consumption of a specific market good (weak substitutability). Stated preference approaches include the Contingent Valuation Method (CVM) and Choice Experiments (CE). These are survey-based methodologies using constructed or hypothetical markets, in which respondents are asked to state their willingness to pay to enjoy and/or protect the resource (Koundouri, Remoundou and Kountouris, 2009). The respective differences between the two methodologies relate to the way in which the economic values are elicited. In a contingent valuation questionnaire, respondents are asked about their maximum willingness to pay, while in a choice experiment questionnaire respondents are presented with a set of choices and are asked to choose their most preferred. Stated preference methods have the advantage to be able to identify and measure passive or non-use values (Koundouri, Remoundou and Kountouris, 2009).

Through non-market evaluation methods, economic instruments have the potential to become meaningful tools for better ocean management.

Innovations in the governance and management of ocean space

There are many challenges facing the process of spatial planning and management in the ocean which are of particular relevance for the next decades.

Some of these have to do with the fundamental issue of lack of knowledge. For example: there is a great deal of uncertainty as to what is actually in the ocean; very little is known of the interactive effects of different uses and users in the ocean; and the ocean is a dynamic environment undergoing significant changes because of climate change (Ásgeirsdóttir, 2015).

- ***Uncertainty*** about the location and value of resources found in the ocean is considerable. It exists for both stationary resources, such as oil and gas, and non-stationary resources such as fishing. Given the prospect of rising sea temperatures, fish stocks are very likely to change their migration patterns, making a static endeavour such as mapping difficult, but not impossible, to implement.
- The ocean and its uses are highly ***complex***, and our understanding of the interactions involved is quite poor, a knowledge deficiency that is coming increasingly to the fore as ocean management moves from a sector-by-sector basis to a more integrated mode. For example, there is lack of knowledge of predator-prey relationships, of how biological resources interact with manmade structural features such as offshore wind farms, and how existing and new ocean uses will interact with future environmental changes. In the absence of significant advances in research, governance structures will need to include explicit considerations of how to think across multiple uses and users and potential interactive effects.
- In addition to more variety of uses, the ocean is facing unprecedented environmental ***change*** in the form of, for example, warming waters and ocean acidification. Significant changes in the quality of the ocean water will likely lead to movement of the ideal locations of resource production (e.g. for fisheries and marine aquaculture), making it important for governance structures to react speedily and flexibly.

Other challenges for the future relate more directly to the governance and management of the ocean. Three stand out in particular: the issue of property and user rights; the need for institutional efficiency and flexibility; and improving the necessary co-ordination of different maritime sectors, users and stakeholders, as well as that of different responsible authorities and governance levels. Innovation is required in all three areas.

Applying user and property rights

First, in order to be able to respond effectively to the rapidly growing use of the ocean and its resources, governance structures will need to be able to assign and enforce rights, fairly and in a timely manner. They will also need to have sufficient flexibility to adjust to changing ocean environment conditions.

Unlike terrestrial planning, which is intimately connected to private property rights in developed countries, ocean planning in the EEZ is firmly in the hands of the states. These allocate use rights to certain areas, and property rights to other resources, resulting in a patchwork of rights which in turn have different time-horizons, different spatial distribution and different quantitative restrictions (Yandle, 2007). Stationary resource users have longer time horizons, fairly set spatial distribution and do not often have quantitative restrictions. Fisheries on the other hand have shorter time horizons and desire flexibility in the allocation of spaces in order to be able to catch stocks that are often subject to severe quantitative restrictions.

These different institutional structures of property rights will impact the future preferences of actors, notably when major environmental changes (ocean warming and acidification) begin to impact different types of resources in different ways. While a trawler can chase a fish stock as it changes its migration pattern, an aquaculture operation would have to seek a new area for operation. Hence, different actors would be expected to display different preferences over the spatial planning process. For example, the users of stationary resources would be expected to be concerned about their exclusive rights to an area and their ability to move, while users of mobile resources should be concerned with freedom of access to all areas to pursue fishing. As conditions change, demands to adjust established spatial plans are likely to increase. This will pose a challenge to governance structures since changes can introduce new user-to-user tensions and user-to-environment conflicts. The answer to that challenge, however, may well reside in efficient institutions.

Building flexibility into institutional arrangements

A central aspect in the process of rule-setting, and a key to institutional efficiency, is the quest for rules that can reduce uncertainty. It is a condition for minimising transaction costs, thereby making room for extensive exchange and innovation. Public policies, regulation and planning must be understood in that context. However, there is an important gap in the literature on the economic role of institutions (Ménard, 2015). Much of the attention so far has been on the role of formal and general institutions such as the political system, laws and the role of the judiciary, the general characteristics of the administrative system. However, formal institutions (and even less formal ones, such as customs and traditions) do not most of the time have a direct impact on agents, whether these agents are organisations (firms, non-profit organisations, etc.) or individuals.

Rules of the game interact with agents through intermediate institutional arrangements that: 1) translate general laws, etc. into specific standards; 2) connect agents to lawmakers and other policy makers through channels of communication and information; and 3) play an important role in implementing and enforcing rules. These are known as "meso-institutions", those institutional arrangements through which general laws and rules are translated into specific, operational ones, through which they are implemented and enforced, and through which agents usually exert "voice". Examples are public bureaus (e.g. the Department of Fisheries in a Ministry of Agriculture), agencies (such as the National Oceanic and Atmospheric Administration [NOAA] in the United States), regional councils (e.g. the regional fisheries management organisation [RFMO]) and so on.

An essential feature of sustainable governance structures in the future is likely to be efficient meso-institutions, institutional arrangements that have the flexibility needed to adapt to changing circumstances while benefiting from a large support from stakeholders, and generating comparatively low political as well as economic transaction costs. According to Ménard (2015), the specific conditions for such efficient, i.e. flexible, institutional arrangements can be summarised as follows:

- The design of "meso-institutions" should make them clearly identifiable by stakeholders, with responsibilities clearly defined. This issue is central and much more significant than the formal rules established by laws, decrees, etc. when it comes to both legitimacy and acceptability.
- Transparency in procedures along which decisions are taken is crucial to support the legitimacy of institutional arrangements and their capacity to efficiently implement the policies adopted.

- Unambiguous rules in the definition, allocation and implementation of rights of access is determinant for the acceptability of policies that necessarily impose limitations if overuse of marine resources and the exhaustion of these resources are to be faced adequately.
- Room for "voice" embedded in meso-institutions and allowing to take the norms and beliefs of stakeholders into consideration in the decision-making process is an essential condition to avoid exponential transaction costs (political as well as economic transaction costs), particularly with respect to the implementation of rules.

Improving co-ordination across government

In many important respects, the challenges facing integrated ocean management are common to many other areas of public management: in an increasingly globalised and interdependent world, policy issues are increasingly complex, dynamic and inter-connected. However, current government structures and policy toolkits have often failed to keep abreast of this growing complexity, leaving governments ill-prepared and ill-equipped to deal with the new operating environment. Moreover, the growing numbers and types of stakeholders with a vested interest in policy outcomes do not always share the same understanding of the causes of the problem or goals. It has long been recognised that the solution to such problems is to build a joined-up approach among sectors, integrating diverse insights, experience and expertise from both within and outside government (OECD, 2013a).

That, however, calls for new policy frameworks and toolkits, which build on the strategic capacity, organisational design and management structures of the public sector. Traditional top-down models for forward policy planning are no longer appropriate and need to be replaced by strategic cross-sectoral approaches. As policy environments become increasingly open and accessible, new behavioural approaches are needed, including: innovative pathways for consensus building; the sharing of diagnostics and policy options; strong co-ordination with government policy-making capability; and information sharing and communication (OECD, 2013a). The question that is relevant also to ocean management is, how to develop concrete options and strategies that can address the challenges and effectively deliver on multidimensional and complex policy outcomes.

Various governance tools are available that can help develop broad strategies to tackle complex problems. These include: first, instruments that help ensure multi-sectoral sharing of information, as well as co-ordination mechanisms, whether these involve markets, networks or more traditional top-down approaches. Second, instructive parallels can be drawn from other areas of policy making that have made great strides in recent years towards more forward-looking, joined-up governance: one such policy area is that of the management of major risks – from natural catastrophes and pandemics to financial crises and breaches of cyber security (OECD, 2011; IRGC, 2013). Third, strategic foresight has proved particularly effective in generating innovative policy initiatives (Kuosa, 2011; Fuerth and Faber, 2012). The challenge to public policy is the effective interweaving of all three strands.

Recent OECD work suggests that a powerful mechanism to bring about and sustain co-ordination across ministerial boundaries is the strengthening of strategic state capacity at the centre of government (see, for example, OECD, 2013a; 2013b). This requires strong leadership and changes to the way in which the public administration sees its role. It is an area where countries are constantly experimenting with many ongoing reform efforts. While many countries have launched initiatives to join-up government, improve horizontal co-ordination and strengthen strategic steering, data suggest that policy coherence and collaboration across sectors remains a challenge for many countries. Co-ordination mechanisms based on horizontal networks may have greater potential for managing complex issues. On the other hand, too much reliance on network co-ordination is unlikely to break down policy silos, since that requires a combination of hierarchical and network co-ordination mechanisms (Lægreid et al., 2013). Much remains to be done, therefore, to identify the enabling factors and barriers in building a whole-of-government approach.

This is no less true in the field of ocean management. Despite often deep-seated variations in institutional cultures as well as in national and geographic characteristics, it would seem to be a worthwhile exercise to identify cases in marine management which have proven successful in bringing about stronger, more effective co-ordination across the public administration, investigating the mechanisms and incentives used, and the reasons for their success.

Innovating the mechanisms of stakeholder engagement

Stakeholder engagement is an essential ingredient of modern-day ocean planning and management. It is practised widely, but in many different forms and using a wide variety of different processes and tools in a diverse range of cultural and political contexts. A common challenge to all such processes is the need to include a broad spectrum of stakeholders as effectively and efficiently as possible. Unsurprisingly, outcomes of stakeholder consultation and engagement tend to vary considerably. Many factors are at play in determining the success and timely implementation of such exercises, not least the design of the process, the scale of the consultation and the tools deployed.

In light of the growing pressures on ocean space and resources, timeliness and cost-effectiveness are of the essence, both in the establishment and diffusion of ocean management schemes and, by extension, in the process of stakeholder engagement. Innovation will need to be an integral part of future solutions – in the design and implementation of the engagement process and in the choice of instruments.

Lessons from stakeholder engagement around the world in the field of water governance (OECD, 2015), for example, point to a number of steps that can help ensure successful outcomes. These include:

- stakeholder mapping to identify early on who is responsible for what and at which level
- aligning engagement mechanisms with the intended objectives
- calibrating the mechanisms to the stakeholders concerned and to local needs
- evaluating the stakeholder engagement process, including through cost-benefit analysis
- implementing open government data to ensure greater transparency towards stakeholders.

Opportunities for innovation are also emerging in ICT-based platforms and tools. In addition to virtual meetings, web-based information systems, crowd-sourcing and knowledge-sharing through apps and social media, as well as e-voting, original ideas are being tested to stimulate stakeholder involvement in the search for appropriate solutions to local problems (e.g. 3D vision games).

Specifically in the field of spatial management, scenario development is gaining momentum; practical planning experiments such as "Beta Testing" are demonstrating their importance in providing the core ideas, impetus and energy for spreading maritime spatial planning to new areas; and new decision support tools for MPA zoning are emerging – geospatial tools combined with an application of adaptive cross-sectoral planning process and a high degree of stakeholder engagement (Merrie and Olsson, 2014).

Innovative initiatives to assemble diverse stakeholder interests, sectors and disciplines around ocean issues are also gaining ground. The Laboratoire de la Blue Society, for example, promotes initiatives to highlight the human and social dimension of ocean-related issues, working through dialogue with multiple segments of society, business and the public sector (Marine Oceans, 2016). In the domain of the deep sea, with its complex, highly interconnected ecosystems, new international endeavours are starting up which are approaching the issue of deep ocean governance as a cross-disciplinary, multi-stakeholder, multi-sectoral undertaking. For example, the Deep Ocean Stewardship Initiative (DOSI) brings together experts from across disciplines and sectors to develop new ideas for balancing sustainability and responsible use of deep-ocean resources (DOSI, 2016). A key component of its work is capacity building for developing countries in whose waters many deep-sea resources are located.

Making better use of science, technology and innovation

Data and technological infrastructure to support ocean management

An essential component of good marine spatial management is a sound information base, comprising both natural and social science information. Using the information, applied research needs to be conducted to reduce the uncertainty of management decisions related to the effects on both natural and socio-economic systems (Huang, Corbett and Jin, 2015). This is a data-intensive process and requires analytical tools for assessing real-time spatial conflicts and synergies among sectors. The last decade has seen an explosion in the amount of data generated across all aspects of life – big data. Bell, Hey and Szalay (2009) argue that scientific research is now entering a "fourth paradigm", whereby science is driven by real-time, accessible data. From an accessibility perspective, the processing costs associated with data are declining, while cloud infrastructure increases enabling open source technologies at scale. At the same time, advances in application programme interface (API), data processing algorithms and machine learning ensure that data may be turned into actionable insights. However, further value lies in the creation of user-friendly, open access applications and services.

In order to develop, assess and communicate governance frameworks, spatial planning and management processes, scientists and policy makers require data to develop and implement appropriate, effective and measurable indicators that assess performance in relation to stated goals and objectives. This applies to both scientific knowledge about the marine environment and the actual and potential impacts of human activities upon it. Considerable emphasis is therefore placed upon the need for data gathering, monitoring and evaluation to improve the knowledge of a poorly understood environment. Such data would help in:

- policy development and data requirements
- initial policy assessment
- implementing monitoring programmes

- developing programmes of measures
- implementing programmes of measures
- evaluation and adaption measures.

Data collection needs to be structured if it is to be used effectively, for example, for marine spatial planning (Shucksmith and Kelly, 2014).

However, at present, the collection of ocean data is substantially fragmented with data for governance being highly sectoral (e.g. fisheries), data for economic purposes being to a large extent proprietary (e.g. oil and gas) and most other ocean data being collected for the specific scientific purposes.

On the data management side, efforts have begun in some regions to make data more accessible. In some countries, all data collected with public funds is made public (e.g. the United States). In other cases, such as for example, the EU, efforts have started to develop data management tools that will assist MSP and other decision-making processes. These include a European Marine Observation and Data Network (EMODNET), a system to make marine data more readily available and accessible (currently under development by the European Commission's DG MARE), the European Atlas of the Seas and the Copernicus Marine Service. However, large information gaps remain (Halpern et al., 2012). For example, many national and regional statistical agencies simply do not collect data related to the ocean economy. As a result, data on, for example, marine resource is not only fragmented and difficult to locate, but it is biased towards scientifically interesting physical and ecological characteristics of the resource (Morrissey, O'Donoghue and Hynes, 2011). This is also due to the historical single-sector approach to planning in the marine environment and the previous emphasis on the biophysical rather than economic and social processes associated with the marine environment. When data are available there is a diversity of data sources and data formats through which policy makers, researchers and the public must sift (Jay and Gee, 2014). Thus, for the successful application of an ecosystem approach to ocean spatial management, the following data collection framework is required:

- regular and sustained involvement of experts in a broad range of natural and social sciences and user knowledge
- the identification of the best scale(s) for collecting and reporting data
- the compilation of available data, models and other information into a coherent framework for analysis
- the development of user-friendly, open-source, efficient and transparent tools for data visualisation, integration and sharing
- a set of clear, reliable and measurable indicators for monitoring the effectiveness of spatial planning in achieving the objectives set during the planning process.

Thus, new methods and technologies for collecting data are required that capture the uncertainty, complexity and change associated with the marine environment (see Chapter 3). At the institutional level there is a need to ensure that information services are streamlined and interconnected between local, national, regional and global levels. Cross-border co-operation on data collection, management and accessibility is therefore essential for the successful implementation of ocean planning and management. One effort to this end is a European Commission funded flagship project entitled AtlantOS

(Developing in-situ Atlantic Ocean Observations for a better management and sustainable exploitation of the maritime resources). Though European funding has kick-started this project, AtlantOS is a transatlantic effort with partners from Brazil, Canada, South Africa and the United States. A process has been established between government representatives of the participating transatlantic countries and regions to consider how AtlantOS can be established as a long-term, integrated effort to collect, manage and make available to the public and private sectors data from the Atlantic Ocean.

To create a functional, modern data commons, existing e-infrastructure requires:

- better data integration and sharing
- easier access and attractiveness in terms of content, functionalities and interfaces
- increased and consistent use of metadata in a variety of programming languages
- increased online information services
- geo-referenced data
- virtually interconnected systems (interoperable)
- e-reporting.

The tools available for data collection and ocean monitoring have increased significantly over the last decade and include ship missions, landers and observatories, vehicles, autonomous underwater vehicles (AUV) and satellites. Furthermore, many of these new methods allow for the collection of data in real-time and in a 3D format. Sensor systems have shifted from simple observation of meteorological and physical oceanography parameters to complex acoustical, optical, chemical and biological sensors. These advances are primarily driven by the need to understand how anthropogenic changes are altering ocean ecosystems and what effects these alterations will have in the long term (Omerdic et al., 2009). Thus, these tools are rapidly making visible what had previously been hidden or inaccessible information, and have the potential to revolutionise marine resource management by filling in data gaps, detecting erroneous reporting and linking real-time operational data.

However, while these tools are the current state-of-the-art in marine monitoring, the relatively high costs of these platforms limit their spatial and temporal density (Omerdic et al., 2009). Accordingly, the benefits of data obtained from space-based technology have never quite reached a "tipping point" where the value of their contribution makes them indispensable to marine monitoring (Millard, 2015). Marine scientists, technologists and planners must therefore recognise that major changes in satellite and observation technology are likely to occur outside marine-based science and technology (Omerdic et al., 2009). Inter-disciplinary research and development is key to better integration of satellite technology in marine monitoring. A recent report commissioned by the European Space Agency (ESA) looked at trends that could affect the supply of data from satellites. Some of these are of particular relevance to the marine spatial planning community. These trends are related to satellite technology advancements, but equally to changes in the data market related to advances in how we store, manage and distribute large datasets. Box 9.1 presents four potentially disruptive trends in satellite technology for ocean management.

Also "disruptive" could be the kind of ocean-scale undersea observation networks planned by the National Science Foundation's Ocean Observatories Initiative (NSF-OOI).

This will involve the construction of a network of instruments, submarine cables and instrumented moorings extending across the western hemisphere. "The OOI will be one fully integrated system and will measure physical, chemical, geological, and biological phenomena in carefully selected key coastal, regional, and global areas." (NSF, 2016). Canada and Japan have similar seafloor observatories already in use (Nature, 2013).

Box 9.1. Potentially disruptive trends in satellite technology with implications for ocean management

More data

Between now and 2020 the amount of satellite data available is set to double. First, more satellites are being launched and it is getting much cheaper to launch these satellites. Second, improvements in making and launching satellites mean that the average mission operational lifespan is almost nine years now compared to three years in the 1970s. Third, more data per instrument are being collected as a result of the increased spatial and spectral resolution of the new generation of instruments.

Better data

The spatial and spectral resolution of instruments is increasing. New approaches in deployable optics means the resolution of instruments can be increased. Advances in radar techniques are improving both the number of radar frequencies used and spatial resolution which will allow for more applications to benefit from observations not limited to clear, daylight planet. There are also emerging cross-over techniques like GNSS-R, where analysis of the signal in positioning applications gives information on sea state.

Drones and unmanned airborne vehicles

Drones and unmanned airborne vehicles (UAVs) are set to be game changers when combined with satellites. Unlike aircraft, UAVs are low cost to deploy and infinitely more taskable. UAVs have benefited from the miniaturisation that has taken place in the satellite sector, meaning more advanced payloads can be carried by UAVs.

Big data

Satellite data are big data, which means what is happening in the big data arena benefits the satellite arena. New approaches to processing large volumes of data quickly and cheaply, as well as building APIs to the data for developers to access, provides the glue that enables satellite-derived data to be part of a richer information ecosystem.

The big disruptive change will come about from processing services that will deliver precise slices of information from multiple satellite (and non-satellite) platforms to application providers. Advances in generic big data management are advancing and enabling this.

Source: Millard (2015).

Ocean management and spatial planning should be built up on the best available data and knowledge. However, there is no ideal dataset or perfect information. In some planning areas, large amounts of data are available, while other planning areas have extremely sparse data with little possibility of collecting new data quickly enough for a planning effort. Whatever the process, it needs to allow for the continual updating of data based on a strong research basis and stakeholders' involvement (Schaefer and Barale, 2011).

It is also important to note that not all datasets, even those of high quality, are useful for analytical or illustrative purposes in marine spatial planning and management. For example, the initial objectives associated with developing a MSP programme in one region will be very different to the objectives for developing MSP in a different region, limiting the transferability of datasets. Consequently, from the outset, well-articulated aims and objectives are critical for the development of marine spatial planning schemes. The establishment of a science advisory panel can help determine the types of data needed to address each objective.

Data, assessment and monitoring

Ocean planning and management is an adaptive process that needs to be based on continuous evaluation and monitoring throughout the life-course of the process. Evaluation is an assessment of the extent to which a plan is achieving its aims; monitoring provides the evidence needed to support the evaluation. The development of a flexible, integrated data commons is central to the evaluation and monitoring processes. Using the best available data, measurable objectives of the plan should be linked to distinct indicators and targets at each step of the process. The design of criteria and indicators is an iterative approach, and can be refined as more experience is gathered and better information becomes available. In turn, evaluation is essential for adaptive management, whereby adjustments can be made to a plan to allow for changing circumstances or for any shortcomings, such as insufficient representation of certain interests.

In Europe, the Strategic Environmental Assessment Directive (SEA, Directive 2001/42/EC) has important implications for marine spatial planning, as it requires environmental assessments to be undertaken for individual projects (Environmental Impact Assessment Directive) or development programmes and plans (Strategic Environmental Assessment Directive). Incorporating the SEA in MSP enables a holistic assessment of all uses of the ocean's ecosystem rather than the current sector-by-sector approach. The SEA provides a practical tool for integration of the ecosystem approach in planning, specifically by providing:

- scoping – focus, ecosystem-based objectives
- framework for a system-based holistic approach
- development and aggregation of knowledge
- assessment of alternatives/planning options in relation to good environmental status
- consultations and participation
- alternative development – scenarios, adaptive management
- integration of social economic evaluation of ecosystem services.

The SEA has been already used in Germany and Poland as part of BaltSeaPlan. The forthcoming Swedish Marine Spatial Planning will include the integration of the SEA in the planning process (Schmidtbauer Crona, 2015).

Concluding remarks

The worldwide trend to multipolarity and increasing fragmentation of power is mirrored to a large extent in the structures governing the oceans. Governance of the high seas is particularly complex, exercised as it is through a multitude of different international and regional agencies and bodies and through regulatory and legal frameworks that are neither comprehensively complied with nor consistently enforceable. Reform appears to be moving in two directions at once. On the one hand, there are clear indications that the past and current trend toward sectoral solutions is set to continue. On the other hand, meaningful steps have been taken recently towards global agreements on addressing, for example, biodiversity and climate change. The most promising path to operationally and geographically enhanced ocean management most likely lies in concentrating on efforts to leverage regional agreements around ocean and sea basins.

In EEZs, integrated management of ocean space and resources is making some progress, guided in many instances by national and regional strategic policy frameworks and operationalised by spatial planning and management tools as well as environmental assessment. However, given the acceleration expected in the use of the ocean and its resources over the coming years, it will be essential to move more quickly than at present in stepping up both the effectiveness and the geographic spread of integrated ocean management around the world. More widespread application of economic analysis and tools, innovation in ocean governance structures and processes, and making more intensive use of science and technology, all offer avenues along which efforts should be made to strengthen the ocean management of the future.

References

Allmendinger, P., A. Barker and S. Stead (2002), "Delivering ICZM through land use planning", *Planning Practice and Research*, Vol. 17, No. 2, pp. 175-196, http://dx.doi.org/10.1080/02697450220145931.

Ásgeirsdóttir, A. (2015), "Enhancing coherence in MSP through new and/or more effective governance processes and structures", Extended abstract of presentation at OECD Workshop on "The Future of Maritime Spatial Planning and Ocean Monitoring: What Potential for Economic Tools and Satellite Technology?", Lisbon, June.

Bell, G., T. Hey and A. Szalay (2009). "Computer science: Beyond the data deluge", *Science*, Vol. 323, No. 5 919, pp. 1 297-1 298, http://dx.doi.org/10.1126/science.1170411.

Cicin-Sain, B., D. Vanderzwaag and M.C. Balgos (eds.) (2015), *Routledge Handbook of National and Regional Ocean Policies*, Routledge Taylor & Francis Group.

Davis, D. and D.F. Gartside (2001), "Challenges for economic policy in sustainable management of marine natural resources", *Ecological Economics*, Vol. 36, No. 2, pp. 223-236, http://dx.doi.org/10.1016/S0921-8009(00)00251-2.

DOSI (2016), "Deep Ocean Stewardship Initiative", http://dosi-project.org/.

Ehler, C. (2015), "International progress in maritime spatial planning around the world", Extended abstract of presentation at OECD Workshop on "The Future of Maritime Spatial Planning and Ocean Monitoring: What Potential for Economic Tools and Satellite Technology?", Lisbon, June.

Ehler, C. and F. Douvere (2007), "Visions for a sea change", Report of the First International Workshop on Marine Spatial Planning, Intergovernmental Oceanographic Commission and Man and the Biosphere Programme, UNESCO, Paris.

European Commission (2011), "Study on the economic effects of maritime spatial planning", European Union, Brussels, http://ec.europa.eu/maritimeaffairs/documentation/studies/documents/economic_effects_maritime_spatial_planning_en.pdf.

European Commission (2009), *The World in 2025, Rising Asia and Socio-ecological Transition*, European Commission, Directorate-General for Research, Brussels, https://ec.europa.eu/research/social-sciences/pdf/policy_reviews/the-world-in-2025-report_en.pdf.

European Marine Board (2015), "Delving deeper", *EMB Policy Brief*, No. 2, November.

Fritz, J.-S. (2015), "Deep sea anarchy: Mining at the frontiers of international law", *The International Journal of Marine and Coastal Law*, Vol. 30, No. 3, pp. 445-476, http://dx.doi.org/10.1163/15718085-12341357.

Fuerth, L.S. and E.M.H. Faber (2012), "Anticipatory governance practical upgrades: Equipping the executive branch to cope with increasing speed and complexity of major challenges", National Defense University, Center for Technology & National Security Policy, Washington, DC, www.gwu.edu/~igis/assets/docs/working_papers/Anticipatory_Governance_Practical_Upgrades.pdf.

Gamenda, E. and U. Pascual (2013). "A justice critique of environmental valuation for ecosystem governance", in: Sikor, T. (ed.), *The Justices and Injustices of Ecosystem Services*, Routledge.

GOC (2014), "From decline to recovery, rescue package for the global ocean", Global Ocean Commission, Oxford, United Kingdom, www.globaloceancommission.org/wp-content/uploads/GOC_Report_20_6.FINAL_.spreads.pdf.

Gouvernement du Québec (2016), "Stratégie Maritime", https://strategiemaritime.gouv.qc.ca/en/.

Halpern, B.S. et al. (2012), "Near-term priorities for the science, policy and practice of coastal and marine spatial planning (CMSP)", *Marine Policy*, Vol. 36, No. 1, pp. 198-205, http://dx.doi.org/10.1016/j.marpol.2011.05.004.

Huang, W., J. Corbett and D. Jin (2015). "Regional economic and environmental analysis as a decision support for marine spatial planning in Xiamen", *Marine Policy*, Vol. 51, January, pp. 555-562, http://dx.doi.org/10.1016/j.marpol.2014.09.006.

Hynes, S. et al. (2009), "A spatial microsimulation analysis of methane emissions from Irish agriculture", *Ecological Complexity*, Vol. 6, No. 2, pp. 135-146, http://dx.doi.org/10.1016/j.ecocom.2008.10.014.

IRGC (2013), "Preparing for future catastrophes: Governance principles for slow-developing risks that may have potentially catastrophic consequences", Concept note prepared for the IRGC Expert Workshop on the Governance of Slow-Developing Catastrophic Risks, Zürich, June.

Jay, S. and K. Gee (2014), *TPEA Good Practice Guide: Lessons for Cross-border MSP from Transboundary Planning in the European Atlantic*, University of Liverpool, Liverpool, United Kingdom.

Jay, S. et al. (2012), "Coastal and marine spatial planning: International progress in marine spatial planning", *Ocean Yearbook*, Vol. 27, No. 1, pp. 171-212, http://dx.doi.org/10.1163/22116001-90000159.

Karousakis, K. (2015), "Applying economics tools to the management of MPAs", Extended abstract of presentation at OECD Workshop on "The Future of Maritime Spatial Planning and Ocean Monitoring: What Potential for Economic Tools and Satellite Technology?", Lisbon, June.

Koundouri, P., K. Remoundou and Y. Kountouris (2009), "A note on the implementation of the economics of the EU water framework directive under data limitations: A rapid appraisal approach", *DEOS Working Papers*, Athens University of Economics and Business.

Kuosa, T. (2011), "Practicing strategic foresight in government", *RSIS Monograph*, No. 19, Booksmith, S. Rajaratnam School of International Studies of Nanyang Technological University, Singapore.

Lægreid, P. et al. (2013,) "Lessons from emerging coordination arrangements in European public sectors", *COCOPS European Policy Brief*, May, www.cocops.eu/wp-content/uploads/2013/07/COCOPS_PolicyBrief_3.pdf.

Lester, S.E. et al. (2013), "Evaluating tradeoffs among ecosystem services to inform marine spatial planning", *Marine Policy*, Vol. 38, March, pp. 80-89, http://dx.doi.org/10.1016/j.marpol.2012.05.022.

Marine Oceans (2016), "La Laboratoire de la Blue Society interpelle le gouvernement Valls", www.marine-oceans.com/economie-maritime/7672-le-laboratoire-de-la-blue-society-interpelle-le-gouvernement-valls.

McLeod K.L. and H.M. Leslie (2009), *Ecosystem-based Management for the Oceans,* Island Press.

Ménard, C. (2015), "What economic tools? For what purposes? Lessons from fisheries that can be relevant for MSP", Extended abstract of presentation at OECD Workshop on "The Future of Maritime Spatial Planning and Ocean Monitoring: What Potential for Economic Tools and Satellite Technology?", Lisbon, June.

Merrie, A. and P. Olsson (2014), "An innovation and agency perspective on the emergence and spread of marine spatial planning", *Marine Policy*, Vol. 44, February, pp. 366-374, http://dx.doi.org/10.1016/j.marpol.2013.10.006.

Millard, K. (2015), "Remote sensing and satellite technology to support MSP: What's in the innovation pipeline?", Extended abstract of presentation at OECD Workshop on "The Future of Maritime Spatial Planning and Ocean Monitoring: What Potential for Economic Tools and Satellite Technology?", Lisbon, June.

Morrissey, K. (forthcoming), "The future of maritime spatial planning and ocean monitoring: What potential for economic tools and satellite technology?", *OECD Science, Technology and Industry Working Papers*, OECD Publishing, Paris, forthcoming.

Morrissey, K., C. O'Donoghue and S. Hynes (2011), "Quantifying the value of multi-sectoral marine commercial activity in Ireland", *Marine Policy*, Vol. 35, No. 5, pp. 721-727, http://dx.doi.org/10.1016/j.marpol.2011.02.013.

Nature (2013), "Marine science: Oceanography's billion-dollar baby", *Nature*, No. 501, pp. 480-482, doi: 10.1038/501480a, www.nature.com/news/marine-science-oceanography-s-billion-dollar-baby-1.13803.

NIC (2012), *Global Trends 2030: Alternative Worlds*, National Intelligence Council, Washington, DC.

NSF (National Science Foundation) (2016), "Ocean Observatories Initiative", www.interactiveoceans.washington.edu/story/NSF_Ocean_Observatories_Initiative.

Ocean Frontiers (2016), "US Ocean Plans moving ahead!", http://ocean-frontiers.org/us-ocean-plans-moving-ahead/.

OECD (2016), "The economics of marine protected areas", work in progress. www.oecd.org/environment/resources.

OECD (2015), *Stakeholder Engagement for Inclusive Water Governance*, OECD Studies on Water, OECD Publishing, Paris, http://dx.doi.org/10.1787/9789264231122-en.

OECD (2013a), "Building a government for the future: Improving policy performance and managing complex challenges", GOV/PGC(2013)14, OECD, Paris, www.oecd.org/officialdocuments/publicdisplaydocumentpdf/?cote=GOV/PGC%282013%2914&docLanguage=En.

OECD (2013b), "Strategic insights from the Public Governance Reviews: Update", GOV/PGC(2013)4, OECD, Paris, www.oecd.org/officialdocuments/publicdisplaydocumentpdf/?cote=GOV/PGC%282013%294&docLanguage=En.

OECD (2011), *Future Global Shocks: Improving Risk Governance*, OECD Publishing, Paris, http://dx.doi.org/10.1787/9789264114586-en.

Olsen, S., E. Olsen and N. Schaefer (2011), "Governance baselines as a basis for adaptive marine spatial planning", *Journal of Coastal Conservation*, Vol. 15, pp. 313-322, http://dx.doi.org/10.1007/s11852-011-0151-6.

Olsen, S., J. Tobey and M. Kerr (1997), "A common framework for learning from ICM experience", *Ocean & Coastal Management*, Vol. 37, No. 2, http://dx.doi.org/10.1016/S0964-5691(97)90105-8.

Omerdic, E. et al. (2009), *Marine Monitoring Platforms: Paradigms for Development in Ireland*, Cambridge Scholars Publishing.

Pearce, D.W. (1998), "Cost-benefit analysis and environmental policy", *Oxford Economic Review*, Vol. 14, No. 4, pp. 84-100, http://dx.doi.org/10.1093/oxrep/14.4.84.

Pearce, D.W., A. Markandy and E. Barbier (2006), *Blueprint for a Green Economy*, Earthscan, Oxford.

Prows, P. (2006), "Tough love: The dramatic birth and looming demise of UNCLOS Property Law", *Public Law Research Paper*, No. 06-19, 10 July 10, NYU Law School, http://dx.doi.org/10.2139/ssrn.918458.

Schaefer, N. and V. Barale (2011), "Maritime spatial planning: Opportunities & challenges in the framework of the EU integrated maritime policy", *Journal of Coast Conservation*, Vol. 15, pp. 237-245, http://dx.doi.org/10.1007/s11852-011-0154-3.

Schmidtbauer Crona, J. (2015), "Strategic environmental assessment in MSP – Implementing the ecosystem approach for sustainable use of marine resources", Extended abstract of presentation at OECD Workshop on "The Future of Maritime Spatial Planning and Ocean Monitoring: What Potential for Economic Tools and Satellite Technology?", Lisbon, June.

Scottish Government (2015), "Scotland's National Marine Plan", http://www.gov.scot/Publications/2015/03/6517.

Shell (2013), "New lens scenarios: A shift in perspective for a world in transition", Shell, www.shell.com/content/dam/royaldutchshell/documents/corporate/scenarios-newdoc.pdf.

Shucksmith, R.J. and C. Kelly (2014), "Data collection and mapping: Principles, processes and application in marine spatial planning", *Marine Policy*, Vol. 50, pp. 27-33, http://dx.doi.org/10.1016/j.marpol.2014.05.006.

TEEB (2010), *Mainstreaming the Economics of Nature: A Synthesis of the Approach, Conclusions and Recommendations of TEEB*, The Economics of Ecosystems & Biodiversity, www.teebweb.org/publication/mainstreaming-the-economics-of-nature-a-synthesis-of-the-approach-conclusions-and-recommendations-of-teeb.

Tyldesley, D. (2004), "Coastal and marine spatial planning framework for the Irish Sea pilot project", Defra, United Kingdom, http://jncc.defra.gov.uk/pdf/Tyldesley%20Marine%20spatial%20planning.pdf.

UN ILC (2006), "Report of the Study Group of the UN International Law Commission: Fragmentation of international law: Difficulties arising from the diversification and expansion of international law", A/CN.4/L.702 18 July, http://legal.un.org/avl/ha/fil/fil.html.

Yandle, T. (2007), "Understanding the consequences of property rights mismatches: A case study of New Zealand's marine resources", *Ecology and Society*, Vol. 12, No. 2, article 27, www.ecologyandsociety.org/vol12/iss2/art27.

Annex A
Acknowledgments

We wish to acknowledge with sincere thanks the financial and in kind support to the Future of the Oceans Project provided by the following organisations:

Contributing organisations	Representative on the Steering Group	Country
Calouste Gulbenkian Foundation	Louisa Hooper, Programme Manager, Environment	United Kingdom
Directorate General for Maritime Policy	Angela Lobo, Technical Advisor, Department of Strategy/ Conceição Santos, Head of Strategy Department	Portugal
Foundation for Science and Technology	Telmo Carvalho, Head, Gabinete Oceano da FCT	Portugal
Fundação Calouste Gulbenkian	Catarina Grilo, Colaboradora	Portugal
Government of Flanders	Gert Verreet, Flemish government, Department of Economy, Science and Innovation	Belgium
Government of Quebec	Denis Provençal, coordonnateur ministériel pour le Programme d'acquisition de connaissances du milieu marin du golfe du Saint-Laurent	Canada
Government of South Africa	Dowelani Ndiitwani, Assistant Director, Multilateral Cooperation, Department of Science and Technology	South Africa
IEA Ocean Energy Systems	Eoin Sweeney, Vice-Chair, OES	NGO
International Union for Conservation of Nature (IUCN)	Francois Simard, Advisor	NGO
KDM German Marine Research Consortium	Jan-Stefan Fritz, Head Brussels Office	Belgium
Kongsberg Gruppen ASA - Kongsberg Oil & Gas Technologies	Jon Stærkebye, Senior Vice President, Software & Services	Norway
Korea Maritime Institute	Youngil Cho, Senior Researcher	Korea
Marine Institute, Ireland	Eoin Sweeney	Ireland
Marine Scotland	Sam Anson, Head of Marine Analytical Unit	United Kingdom
MEDDE - Ministry of Ecology, Sustainable Development and Energy	Nicolas Fairise, Chef du bureau des affaires globales/ Pascal Bargiarelli, Policy Advisor for OECD, WTO, G7/G20 issues	France
Ministère des Affaires étrangères et du Développement international	Laura Recuero Virto, Head of Unit, Economic Analysis	France
Ministry of Economic Affairs, Bureau of Foreign Trade	Jason Liao	Chinese Taipei
Ministry of Marine Affairs and Fisheries	Wiwik Fitrianingsih, Assistant Deputy Director	Indonesia
Ministry of Oceans and Fisheries	Kuk Il Choi, Senior Deputy Director	Korea
SINTEF Fisheries and Aquaculture Ltd.	Karl A. Almås, CEO	Norway
The Research Council of Norway	Christina Abilgaard, Director, Department for Bioresources and Environmental Research	Norway
TOTAL S.A.	-	France

We also acknowledge with sincere thanks the participation and support from persons taking part in the Stakeholder Scoping Meeting and the meeting of the Steering Group of the Oceans Project. The persons listed below attended the meetings by virtue of being Invited Guests, invited experts, Observers, Member of the Steering Group/Partner or members of the OECD/IEA Secretariats:

Christina I.M. Abildgaard, Director, Department for Bioresources and Environmental Research, The Research Council of Norway, Norway; Gianni Aksungur, Rédacteur OCDE/ONU économique, Ministère des Affaires étrangères, France; Aldo Aldama, First Secretary, Permanent Delegation of Mexico to the OECD, Mexico; Karl Andreas Almås, Special Adviser, SINTEF Fisheries and Aquaculture, Norway; Fachtarul Amin, Deputy Director for Institutional Cooperation, Ministry of Marine Affairs and Fisheries, Indonesia; Sam Anson, Head, Marine Analytical Unit, Scottish Government, United Kingdom; Anne-Charlotte Armynot du Châtelet, Chargée de mission OCDE-OMC, Sous-direction du changement climatique et du développement durable, Ministère de l'Écologie, du Développement durable et de l'Énergie, France; Pascal Bargiarelli, Policy Advisor for OECD, WTO, G7/G20 issues, Ministère de l'Écologie, du Développement durable et de l'Énergie, France; Christian Besson, Senior Energy Analyst, International Energy Agency; Olivier Bommelaer, Counsellor, Permanent Delegation of France to the OECD, France; Petyo Bonev, Assistant Professor, Economics, Mines ParisTech, France; Antoine J. Borelli, Directeur Associé-Managing Partner, d2m Technologies, France; Sarah Box, Senior Economist/Policy Analyst, Shipbuilding, Directorate for Science, Technology and Industry, OECD; Anders Carlberg, Maritime expert, Region Västra Götaland, Sweden; Telmo Carvalho, Executive-Director, EurOcean – European Centre for Information on Marine Science and Technology, Portugal; Youngil Cho, Senior Researcher, Korea Maritime Institute, Korea; Kuk Il Choi, Senior Deputy Director, Ministry of Oceans and Fisheries, Korea; Florence Coroner, Institut Français de Recherche pour l'Exploitation de la Mer (Ifremer), France; Anthony Cox, Deputy Director, Environment Directorate, OECD; Veronica Cunningham, Research Office, Marine Institute, Ireland; Kathleen D'Hondt, Policy Analyst – Biotechnology, OECD; Laurent Daniel, Senior Economist/Policy Analyst, Directorate for Science, Technology and Innovation, OECD; Ophélie Darses, Chargée de mission forêts et océans, Ministère de l'Écologie, du Développement durable et de l'Énergie, France; Claire Delpeuch, Fisheries Policy Analyst, Directorate for Trade and Agriculture, OECD; Dimitra Dertsou, Second Secretary, Permanent Delegation of Greece to the OECD, Greece; Nicolas Fairise, Chef du bureau des affaires globales, Ministère de l'Écologie, du Développement durable et de l'Énergie, France; Arne Fredheim, Research Director, SINTEF, Norway; Jan-Stefan Fritz, Head, Brussels Office, Konsortium Deutsche Meeresforschung, Germany; Gregory Garramone, Environment, Science, Technology and Health Councellor, Permanent Delegation of the United States to the OECD, United States; Catarina Grilo, Iniciativa Oceanos/Oceans Initiative, Fundação Calouste Gulbenkian, Portugal; Mark Hannington, Professor, GEOMAR – Helmholtz Center for Ocean Research Kiel, Germany; Lae Hyung Hong, Senior Fisheries Policy Analyst, Directorate for Trade and Agriculture, OECD; Louisa Hooper, Programme Manager, Environment, Calouste Gulbenkian Foundation, United Kingdom; Pierre Ingmarsson, Project Manager, Renewable Energy, SP Technical Research Institute of Sweden, Sweden; Berit Johne, Special Adviser, JPI Oceans, Brussels; Hiroyuki Kamai, First Secretary (Science and Technology Advisor), Permanent Delegation of Japan to the OECD, Japan; Shih-Ming Kao, Assistant Professor, National Sun Yat-sen University, Chinese Taipei; Katia Karousakis, Policy Analyst – Biodiversity, Environment Directorate, OECD; Florence Kim, Policy Analyst, Ministry of Oceans and Fisheries, Korea; Denis Lacroix, Animateur de la veille stratégique prospective, Ifremer, France; Mónica Lafon, Analyst, Permanent Delegation of Mexico to the OECD, Mexico; Carlos Sánchez Lafuente, Director, Fundación INNOVAMAR, Spain; An Ho Lee, Counsellor, Permanent Delegation of Korea to the OECD, Korea; Jason Liao, Economic Secretary, Bureau de Représentation de Taipei en France, Chinese Taipei; Pedro Liberato,

Counsellor, Permanent Delegation of Portugal to the OECD, Portugal; Øystein Lie, Dean, Norwegian University of Life Sciences, Norway; Angela Lobo, Technical Advisor, Directorate General for Maritime Policy, Ministry of Agriculture and Ocean, Portugal; Bruce McCallum, Counsellor (Science and Innovation), Ministry of Business, Innovation & Employment, New Zealand Mission to the European Union, New Zealand; Rudolf Müller, Consultant, Switzerland; Lars Nerdrum, Counsellor for Education and Research, Permanent Delegation of Norway to the OECD, Norway; Jenny O'Leary, Policy, Innovation & Research Support, Marine Institute, Ireland; Alex Olsen, Group Project Manager, Sustainable Production, A. Espersen A/S, Denmark; Agus Pakpahan, Expert, Natural Resources Economics, Republic of Indonesia, Indonesia; Isabella Maria Palombini, Scientific Attaché, Permanent Delegation of Italy to the OECD, Italy; James Philp, Policy Analyst – Industrial and Environmental Biotechnology, OECD; Dirk Pilat, Deputy Director, Directorate for Science, Technology and Innovation, OECD; Agung Tri Prasetyo, Deputy Director for Bilateral Cooperation, Ministry of Marine Affairs and Fisheries, Indonesia; George Prevelakis, Ambassador, Permanent Delegation of Greece to the OECD, Greece; Denis Provençal, Coordonnateur ministériel du Programme d'acquisition de connaissances du milieu marin du golfe du Saint-Laurent, Government of Quebec, Canada; Teodoro Ramirez, Representative in Brussels, Spanish Institute of Oceanography, IEO (MINECO), Spain; Torger Reve, Professor, BI – Norwegian Business School, Norway; Widya Sadnovic, First Secretary, Embassy of the Republic of Indonesia, Indonesia; Francesca Santoro, Programme specialist, Tsunami Unit, UNESCO; Conceição Santos, Head of Strategy Department, Directorate General for Maritime Policy, Portugal; Pierre-Alain Schieb, Counsellor, Directorate for Science, Technology and Industry, OECD; Carl-Christian Schmidt, Head, Fisheries Policies Division, OECD; Filipe Silva, Consultant, Directorate for Science, Technology and Industry, OECD; François Simard, International Union for Conservation of Nature (IUCN); Rolf Skjong, Director/Chief Scientist, Det Norske Veritas AS (DNV), Norway; Björn Södahl, Program Manager, Lighthouse, Chalmers University, Sweden; Namgeun Song, First Secretary, Permanent Delegation of Korea to the OECD, Korea; Peter Sonnenhol, Counsellor for Education, Environment and Employment Labour and Social Affairs Advisor, Permanent Delegation of Germany to the OECD, Germany; Jon Starkebye, Senior Vice President, Software & Services, Kongsberg Oil & Gas Technologies, Norway; Lisa Emelia Svensson, Ambassador for Oceans, Seas and Fresh Water, Government Offices of Sweden, Sweden; Eoin Sweeney, Vice-Chair of the Ocean Energy Systems Implementing Agreement, IEA/Marine Institute, Ireland; Joseph Tay, Centre Director Europe, Singapore Economic Development Board, Singapore; Maja Svankjær Thagaard, Chief Advisor, Danish Maritime Authority, Denmark; Justine Tung, Researcher, Industrial Technology Research Institute (ITRI), Chinese Taipei; Kristof Vandenberghe, Assistant Programme Specialist, Section for Bilateral Government Funding Sources, UNESCO; Gert Verreet, Policy Officer, Flemish Government, Belgium; Laura Recuero Virto, Chef de pôle, Ministère des Affaires étrangères, France; Frederik von Dewall, Managing Director, Von Dewall Advisory & Management, Netherlands; Dries Willems, Délégué adjoint du Gouvernement Flamand, Ambassade de Belgique – Délégation Flamande, Belgium; Dongsik Woo, Project Manager, Fisheries Policies Division, Directorate for Trade and Agriculture, OECD.

All together the project has arranged ten workshops and experts meetings. We gratefully acknowledge the funding and sponsorships received:

Workshop	Co-hosts and sponsors	Representative	Role
Challenges and Opportunities related to the Development of Marine Tourism to 2030	Region Västra Götaland	Anders Carlberg	Co-host
Exploring the Prospects for Marine Renewable Energy to 2030	IEA Ocean Energy Systems	Ana Brito e Melo	Co-host
Future of Maritime Spatial Planning and Ocean Monitoring	Calouste Gulbenkian Foundation	Louisa Hooper	Co-host
	Directorate General for Maritime Policy	Conceição Santos	Co-host
	EEA Grants, National Contact Point Portugal	Madalena Callé Lucas	Sponsor
	FCT - Fundação para a Ciência e Tecnologia	Telmo Carvalho	Co-host
Maritime Safety	Korea Maritime Institute	Sung Gwi Kim	Co-host
	Ministry of Oceans and Fisheries (Korea)	Kuk Il Choi	Co-host
Offshore Oil and Gas: The New Frontiers	Kongsberg Oil & Gas Technologies	Jon Stærkebye	Co-host
	Statoil ASA	Per Gerhard Grini	Co-host
	The Research Council of Norway	Christina I.M. Abildgaard	Co-host
Offshore Wind Experts Meeting	Marine Scotland	Sam Anson	Sponsor
Prospects and Challenges of Deep-Sea Mining	GEOMAR/Federal State of Schleswig-Holstein	Peter Herzig	Sponsor
	Konsortium Deutsche Meeresforschung	Jan-Stefan Fritz	Co-host
Symposium	Ministry of Oceans and Fisheries (Korea)	Kuk Il Choi/Hong Gilsu	Co-host
	Korea Maritime Institute	Youngil Cho/Jo Jeong-hee	Co-host
The Prospects for Marine Aquaculture	Marine Harvest ASA	Kristine Gramstad	Co-host
	Ministry of Ecology, Sustainable Development and Energy (France)	Soizic Schwartz	Co-host
	The Research Council of Norway	Kjell Emil Naas	Co-host
Workshop on Marine Biotechnology: Completing the Scene for Blue Growth Challenges	AZTI Marine Research Division	Lorenzo Motos	Sponsor
	EUSKAMPUS	Jordi Campas	Sponsor
	Norwegian University of Life Sciences	Øystein Lie	Co-host
	The Research Council of Norway	Steinar Bergseth	Sponsor
	University of the Basque Country	Ionan Marigómez	Co-host

The 273 workshop participants are acknowledged in the workshop reports with sincere thanks for their participation. One hundred eighty-one of them came from 23 OECD member countries, 12 from OECD Key Partner countries, 16 from “other countries” and 64 from NGO/IGOs.

In particular for the modelling and scenario work for this report we wish to acknowledge with sincere thanks the following persons for their active involvement, their advice, data provided and their constructive review of our work:

- Sam Anson, Scottish Government
- Petyo Bonev, École des Mines
- Antoine Borelli, BORA Développement s.a.s.
- Jenny Braat, Danish Maritime
- Webb Colin, OECD
- Laurent Daniel, OECD
- Christine de la Maisonneuve, OECD
- Alexandra de Matos Nunes, OECD
- Kathleen D’Hondt, OECD
- Ceresa Fabiana, OECD

- Peter Haxton, OECD
- Lae Hyung Hong, OECD
- Luis Martinez, OECD
- Olaf Merk, OECD
- Martin von Lampe, OECD
- Jari Kauppila, OECD
- James Philp, OECD
- Karin Strodel, OECD

Annex B
Workshops

The ten workshops and experts meetings were held in the following place and date:

Workshop	Date	Place
Offshore Wind Experts Meeting	14 April 2014	Paris, France
Exploring the Prospects for Marine Renewable Energy to 2030	15 May 2014	Paris, France
Workshop on Offshore Oil and Gas: the New Frontiers	25-26 June 2014	Trondheim, Norway
Workshop on Future Prospects of Marine Aquaculture	9-10 September 2014	Bergen, Norway
Scenario Workshop	6 October 2014	Paris, France
Prospects and Challenges of Deep-Sea Mining	25-26 November 2014	Kiel, Germany
The Maritime Safety Industry and the Ocean Economy	7 May 2015	Seoul, Korea
Workshop on the Future of Maritime Spatial Planning and Ocean Monitoring: What Potential for Economic Tools and Satellite Technology	4-5 June 2015	Lisbon, Portugal
Workshop on Challenges and Opportunities related to the Development of Marine Tourism to 2030	24-25 June 2015	Gothenburg, Sweden
The long-term potential of marine biotechnology	29-30 September 2015	Plentzia, Spain

The workshops generated reports that will be made available as OECD Working Papers on the OECD Website. In addition, one methodology Working Paper was produced as a companion paper to Chapters 6 and 8.

ORGANISATION FOR ECONOMIC CO-OPERATION AND DEVELOPMENT

The OECD is a unique forum where governments work together to address the economic, social and environmental challenges of globalisation. The OECD is also at the forefront of efforts to understand and to help governments respond to new developments and concerns, such as corporate governance, the information economy and the challenges of an ageing population. The Organisation provides a setting where governments can compare policy experiences, seek answers to common problems, identify good practice and work to co-ordinate domestic and international policies.

The OECD member countries are: Australia, Austria, Belgium, Canada, Chile, the Czech Republic, Denmark, Estonia, Finland, France, Germany, Greece, Hungary, Iceland, Ireland, Israel, Italy, Japan, Korea, Luxembourg, Mexico, the Netherlands, New Zealand, Norway, Poland, Portugal, the Slovak Republic, Slovenia, Spain, Sweden, Switzerland, Turkey, the United Kingdom and the United States. The European Union takes part in the work of the OECD.

OECD Publishing disseminates widely the results of the Organisation's statistics gathering and research on economic, social and environmental issues, as well as the conventions, guidelines and standards agreed by its members.

OECD PUBLISHING, 2, rue André-Pascal, 75775 PARIS CEDEX 16
(92 2016 02 1 P) ISBN 978-92-64-25171-7 – 2016

www.ingramcontent.com/pod-product-compliance
Ingram Content Group UK Ltd.
Pitfield, Milton Keynes, MK11 3LW, UK
UKHW051459290926
15471UKWH00008B/1306

9 789264 251717